A.V. Perelmuter

CONVERSATIONS ABOUT THE STRUCTURAL MECHANICS

Short Course of Lectures

Translation from Russian by Tatyana Veryuzhkaya

SCAD Soft
ASV Construction
Stockholm, Sweden 2019

UDK 624.0.07

Recommended for publication by:
The Department of Structural Mechanics of the Tomsk State University of Architecture and Civil Engineering, head of the department, RAACS Academician, D.Sc. in engineering, prof. L.S. Lyakhovich.

The Department of Structural Mechanics of the Kiev National University of Civil Engineering and Architecture, head of the department, corresponding member of the National Academy of Education of Ukraine, D.Sc. in engineering, prof. V.A. Bazhenov.

Perelmuter A.V.
Conversations about the Structural Mechanics. Third Edition, Revised and Updated / SCAD Soft, ASV Construction, 2019. — 316 p.

ISBN 978-91-982223-6-4

The book discusses some topics of modern structural mechanics, which, as experience shows, are not sufficiently studied at the universities. It has been written to provide an in-depth presentation of the fundamentals of the methods used in the design software, with a focus on analyzing basic assumptions and explaining the physical meaning of computational operations.

This book is not intended for students who have just begun to study structural mechanics; it is aimed at structural engineers who want to further enhance their theoretical training. It can also be recommended to graduate and post-graduate students of construction universities.

UDK 624.0.07

All right resereved. This book, or any part thereof, may not be reproduced in any form without written consent from the publisher.

ISBN 978-91-982223-6-4

© SCAD Soft, 2019
© ASV Construction, 2019
© A.V. Perelmuter

Preface

Not knowing the theory does not make you a man of practice.
L.G. Khachiyan Selected Works.— M.: MTsNMO, 2009 - 520 p.

The purpose of computing is insight, not numbers.
R.W. Hamming. Numerical Methods for Scientists and Engineers — New York: Dover Publications, 1987.— 752 p.

The higher the standards of theory, the more incomprehensible the books become. There is not enough enthusiasm and inspiration to write simple books, which are intrinsic to the early stages of the ideology development...
V. Boss. Lectures in Mathematics. Volume 7.— M.: KomKniga, 2006.— 216 p.

The man in the street, or the man in the workshop, thinks he needs virtually no theoretical knowledge. The engineering don is apt to pretend that to get anywhere worthwhile without the higher mathematics is not only impossible but that it would be vaguely immoral if you could. It seems to me that ordinary mortals like you and me can get along surprisingly well with some intermediate – and I hope more interesting – state of knowledge.
J.E. Gordon. Structures: Or Why Things Don't Fall Down.— Da Capo Press, 2003.— 421 p.

Idea

At the beginning of the twentieth century, a small group would gather in St. Petersburg to listen to an outstanding engineer and professor, who taught several generations of Russian engineers, V.L. Kirpichev, talk about mechanics. These talks were later published in a book [5] that had many editions and has not yet lost its relevance. The author has decided that it is time to write a similar book on *structural mechanics (in the broad sense of the word).*

V.L. Kirpichev

The thing is that all more or less complex design calculations are now performed using computer technology. Experience shows that training courses for users of structural analysis software, such as LIRA, SCAD, ANSYS etc, usually come down to getting acquainted with the buttons. It also turns out that any software manual is useless if the user does not understand the basics of the methods applied in the software.

It is important to have *an understanding* of the basic principles, which, unfortunately, are poorly covered in modern textbooks. I have repeatedly asked novice engineers: "Is it possible to prestress a statically determinate system?" And too many times have I heard an affirmative answer. Prestressed reinforced concrete beams were used as a proof. Noone has told these students that they are actually statically indeterminate.

The relationship between knowledge and understanding is an important aspect of the problem (it is hardly necessary to prove that they are not the same thing). Understanding comes when a phenomenon has several interpretations. You can understand much more by comparing them than by analysing the most detailed description, be it a drawing, a diagram, a mathematical model or anything else.

K.S. Zavriev

K.S. Zavriev, a professor at the Tbilisi Institute of Railway Engineers, used to ask his students a brilliant question[2]:

The behavior of a bearing structure is largely determined by a level arm of internal forces. It is equal to the distance between the chords in a truss, to the distance from the apex to the tie in an arch, to approximately the distance between the top and the base ring in a dome. And what is the level arm of internal forces in a doubly curved rectangular shell?

---

[2] L.G. Dmitriev, a student of K.S. Zavriev, told me about it.

In order to answer this question, you have to understand the behavior of the structure "as a whole", which is in many ways contrary to the commonly practiced detailed analysis of the stress-strain state. This analysis focuses on studying the details (finding peak stresses, maximum deflection points etc.), and sometimes leads away from considering a holistic picture of the phenomenon. As Henri Poincare said: "*...should a naturalist who had never studied the elephant except by means of the microscope think himself sufficiently acquainted with that animal?*" [4].

I would also like to quote a passage from the foreword to the book by Ya.G. Panovko [3]: "*The Leningrad graphic artist B. Semenov... recalls how his father took him to an art gallery, when he was a boy, and said: "Understanding art is an exquisite science". I would like to add that it can be inverted: "Understanding science is an exquisite art*", and thus serve as an epigraph to this book".

Ya.G. Panovko

The content of this book was largely determined by the questions asked by SCAD users. They naively believed that software developers should fill in the gaps in their education. In such cases we really wanted to direct them to a specific textbook page instead of just giving an answer. But we had to give detailed explanations and answers to these naive questions.

Then came the idea of writing this book. The author arrogantly believes that practicing engineers will want to read it and begin to use modern computer methods for calculating complex and important building structures more consciously. However, a hope that a user will read anything other than a software Help is not very realistic. Therefore, the author has added a lot of informal comparisons and anecdotes, which just might help.

Presentation

Since this book is intended for readers who have at least formally taken a course in structural mechanics, the presentation is fragmentary and does not stick to any textbook structure. For example, the calculations of the coefficients of canonical equations of the force and displacement method are not considered here, because they are quite sufficiently studied at university, and they are embedded in the design software which are used today for almost all structural analyses.

The author did his best to present the information in the simplest way possible (as they say "without formulas"), using clear illustrations in some cases. Structural stability and dynamics problems are considered in more detail here, since they are hardly tackled in the university courses at all and some important properties of systems are often assumed to be given.

If the reader does not believe the author and begins to look for evidence (in literature or elsewhere), then the author will consider his goal accomplished, since he has aroused curiosity about the subject.

The book is written with the understanding that "*...when studying science, the examples are more useful than the rules*" (Isaac Newton). You should keep in mind that there are two types of examples: a) explaining the technique (method, algorithm) of solving the problem; b) illustrating certain properties, phenomena or effects. We prefer the second type of examples, and when borrowing some results we do not describe the way they were obtained, and only provide the refferences.

Nowadays, in the computer design era, beautiful analytical solutions of particular problems are gradually (but steadily) giving way to fairly universal numerical design methods implemented in a variety of widely used software developments. It goes without saying that this does not mean a complete abandonment of analytical solutions, especially when they carry qualitative information or are examples that illustrate certain aspects of theory.

However, the author believes that today it is more important to thoroughly study fundamental aspects of the theory allowing the engineer to use computation tools consciously and cautiously, and also to evaluate the results of such calculations at least on a qualitative level. Thus, engineers have to understand the underlying principles of the software they use.

The main difficulty was to define the boundary between a precise (and often complicated) description of the problem and a somewhat illustrative presentation of its main points. In this regard V. Boss [2] says: "*To oversimplify, even to lie a little, since the truth dosage is the keystone of explanation. Results overloaded with details simply do not get through.*"

This book imitates a conversation where the main information on each topic is presented by *lecturers*, questions are asked by *students*, and the answers are given by *experts*. Many of these characters have real prototypes, but they are represented in the book by a set of images that only vaguely resemble real people (and only for the author). These images were shamelessly taken from the Internet (we could not find anyone to ask for permission to use them).

As for the questions, many of them were actually asked by SCAD users, others were made up by the author who tried to imitate an inquisitive student, inquisitive and meticulous, although maybe the author should have remembered a famous poem by Renata Muha:

...Sometimes kids smarter than fathers are found,
But mostly it is the other way round.

Acknowledgements

The book contains (sometimes simplified) excerpts from previous publications by the author and V.I. Slivker, whose contribution to great many ideas in this book can hardly be overestimated.
Our long-lasting creative collaboration has developed a common style and form of presenting results. I think you will notice it when reading this book.

V.I. Slivker

The Conversations about the Structural Mechanics has been much inspired by an excellent textbook by A.R. Rzhanitsyn [6], a profound monograph by V.I. Slivker [7], a textbook by A.V. Aleksandrov, V.D Potapov et. al. [1], a fundamental three-volume book by A.P. Filin [9], the mentioned book by V.L. Kirpichev [5] (which has also inspired the title) and a brilliant work by V.I. Feodosiev [8]. To all these great minds, who, alas, are no longer with us, goes my grateful and everlasting memory.

While working on the manuscript, I discussed it with my colleagues and friends. Their comments and suggestions were gratefully accepted. I will mention those who had the greatest influence: RAACS Academician, prof. L.S. Lyakhovich, prof. V.N. Gordeev, prof. O.V. Kabantsev.

References

1. *Aleksandrov A.V. et al.* Structural Mechanics: In 2 books. Book 1. Statics of Elastic Systems / V.D. Potapov, A.V. Aleksandrov, S.B. Kositsyn, D.B. Dolotkazin.— M.: High School, 2007. Book. 2: Dynamics and Stability of Elastic Systems / A.V. Aleksandrov, V.D Potapov, V.B. Zylev.— M.: High School, 2008.
2. *V. Boss* Intuition and Mathematics. — M. 2003.
3. *Panovko Ya.G.* Solid Mechanics — M.: Nauka, 1985.
4. *H. Poincare.* The Value of Science. — New York: The Science Press, 1907.
5. *Kirpichev V.L.* Conversations about Mechanics/ 5-th edition — M.-L.: Gostekhteorizdat, 1951.
6. *Rzhanitsyn A.R.*, Structural Mechanics. – M.: Stroyizdat, 1982.
7. *Slivker V.I.* Structural Mechanics. Basic Variational Principles. — M.: ASV, 2005.
8. *Feodosiev V.I.*, Ten Talks on Strength of Materials.— M.: Nauka, 1969.
9. *Filin A.P.* Applied Solid Mechanics. In 3 volumes. – M.: Nauka, 1978.

Cycle 1

Fundamentals of Statics and Kinematics

"I used to pee my bed and was very ashamed of it. After seeing a psychiatrist I am still peeing my bed... But now I am proud of it."

Coluche

Conversation 1.1. A Few Words about the Design Model: Hypothesis Analysis

Modern buildings and structures are usually complex multi-element systems created in order to implement a vast variety of functions. Many operation states take place during their life cycle.

The design features of the structure affecting its load-bearing capacity analysis are of utmost importance to the analyst. However, its pure structural (bearing) function cannot always be distinguished easily.

Selecting a Load-Bearing Part
While it is fairly easy to select main structural elements in a frame building (although some problems can arise here too), a preliminary analysis of several competing hypotheses is required in the case of other types of structures.

Selecting a load-bearing part of a structure is the first step of idealization. This step is quite ambiguous due to the fact that some structural elements play different roles under different loadings: an element can be just an enclosure under certain loadings while under other conditions it can considerably affect the stress distribution.

Geometric Modeling
Once a structural part that will be considered in the analysis is selected, we proceed to the second step of idealization – *geometric modeling*.

The real three-dimensional geometry of the structure remains the same in the design model only in trivial cases. In reality, this model is assembled from such idealized elements as a line (bar axis) or a surface (midsurface of the slab or the shell). One- and two-dimensional elements are usually used in the design model instead of the three-dimensional ones. This might be the cause of interaction forces arising between elements of different dimensions which are not typical for real structures — concentrated forces at the ends of bar elements, or forces uniformly distributed along the line on the ends of plates and shells. The problems that arise in this case will be described later.

We will only note here that idealized images of structural parts (bar, plate, etc.) are used here not due to the fact that they enable to simplify the geometry of the problem, but because they are well studied, their internal properties are known, their behavior is expected, and, therefore, the problem comes down to determining the interaction of objects with known properties.

One more aspect of geometric modeling should be considered. The thing is that some parts of the structure can often be represented in a form completely different from the real one. If for some reason the detailed picture of the stress-strain state of such parts is not required, you can model only their functional role in the considered structure without modeling their real geometry. For example, a real pile can be modeled by an elastic spring.

Material Model

The next stage is the *idealization of the material* of the structure, or rather the set of its physical and mechanical properties. The most common approach is to treat the material as perfectly elastic or perfectly plastic. Values of the parameters that describe the material (elastic modulus, Poisson's ratio, yield stress etc.) are taken from a reference manual, and they are assumed to be constant within rather big parts of the structure (or throughout the whole structure). The correspondence between the real values and the assumed ones is hardly ever analyzed[3].

Let us consider the Poisson's ratio. The initial volume of the body changes under the triaxial compression by stresses $\sigma_x = \sigma_y = \sigma_z = \sigma$ of the elastic material sample with the volume V_0, elastic modulus $- E$ and Poisson's ratio $- \nu$. The new volume is reduced by the value $\Delta V = kV_0$, where the compressibility factor is $k = (1 - 2\nu)\sigma / E$. It is plain to see that at $\nu > 0{,}5$ the compressed sample increases in volume, which is physically impossible (it can be shown that if this were so, it would be possible to design a perpetual motion machine). Hence a strict limitation appeared $\nu \leq 0{,}5$, which is common to all elastic and plastic bodies, and liquids for which the incompressibility condition is often used $\nu = 0{,}5$.

However, in the codes for timber structures it is stated that the Poisson's ratio for plywood should be taken as 0,6 (and even 0,7 for some types). The thing is that the above compressibility factor refers to an isotropic material, and timber and plywood are anisotropic materials. They are characterized by different elastic moduli E_0 and E_{90} (along and across the grain), and Poisson's ratios $\nu_{0,90}$ and $\nu_{90,0}$, with a relationship $E_0 \nu_{0,90} = E_{90} \nu_{90,0}$. There are no limitations of the type $\nu_{0,90} \leq 0{,}5$ or $\nu_{90,0} \leq 0{,}5$.

One typical error is related to the Poisson's ratio. It occurs for example in the analysis of flexural plates. Having specified two opposite hinged sides and two free sides of a rectangular plate, the analyst expects to obtain cylindrical bending. However, the isolines of displacements (shown in Fig. 1.1) do not confirm this expectation, and the internal forces are not reduced to moments and shear forces in one direction, non-zero values of M_x, M_y, M_{xy}, Q_x and Q_y are obtained in the calculations. Cylindrical bending can be obtained only when the Poisson's ratio is set to zero.

---

[3] Unfortunately, such deductions are not always reasonable. For example, idealized and homogeneous properties are often assigned to the subsoil, which can be not justified and even inconsistent with the data of the geological surveys.

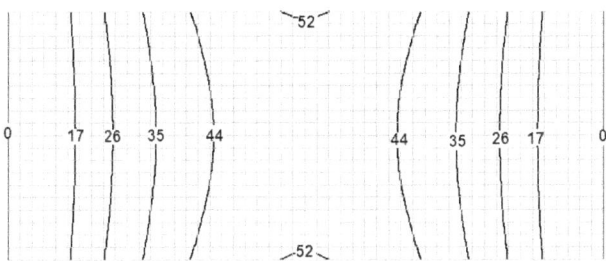

Figure 1.1

Modeling of Loads

Idealization of loads applied to the structure in different operation modes is quite a serious procedure. Loads are one of the least studied components of the system. They are highly variable in time and space, and the design models used in practice are rather coarse.

The concept of load is a convenient way to describe an interaction of a structure with the environment, but this is not the only form of such interaction. It is often necessary to describe a kinematic interaction rather than the force one, when some external (with respect to the considered system) devices restrain the displacements or rotations of individual points, or impose their own displacements. These conditions called constraints are almost always present in a design model. It is worth noting that a given displacement of a certain point is always implemented as a displacement of the respective constraint, and a conventional support constraint is a particular case of this kinematic action when the said given displacement has a zero value. Of course, an infinitely rigid constraint imposing a certain (possibly zero) displacement is an idealization: in reality the interaction with the environment is implemented with the help of some devices of possibly very large but not infinite rigidity.

Modeling of Constraints and Boundary Conditions

Idealization of constraints includes, among other things, a description of laws of interaction between individual elements of the system. Most commonly used conditions of complete equality of displacements or mutual rotations in the joints (a rigid constraint), as well as their alternative, i.e. absolutely no interaction between the considered types of displacements (hinge, slider) are obviously strong idealizations of the actual interaction behavior.

Decisions are usually made on the basis of the hypotheses of force interaction rather than kinematic junction conditions. Looking at the design of a joint of a certain truss (Figure 1.2), one can hardly make the decision that the mutual rotations of end sections of the bars coming into the node are absolutely unrestrained. At the same time, there is a hypothesis that leads to this conclusion: the hypothesis of negligible bending moments under purely nodal loads sounds quite reasonable.

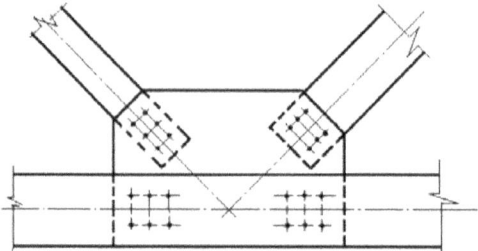

Figure 1.2.

In the conclusion of this introductory conversation it should be noted that the vast majority of design analyses are based on the linear elastic design models. In addition to the hypothesis of the validity of Hooke's law the following assumptions are used when creating these models: about the possibility of considering the equilibrium conditions in the geometry of an undeformed system, about the possibility of applying the superposition principle (independence of forces), about perfect external and internal constraints, and about the validity of the Saint-Venant's principle. Neither of these hypotheses is universal and each one requires a justification.

Question:
Constraints were treated as restraints imposed on the displacements. However, forces were suddenly considered in the example with the justification of the hinged truss model. Isn't there a contradiction?

Answer:
Due to the principle of the release from constraints the role of a constraint can be performed by its reaction which provides the same equilibrium conditions.

This implies the possibility of a dual force and kinematic description of the boundary conditions.

It comes down to one of the following formulas:

- "*a certain mutual displacement is prohibited*" ≡ "*a certain force is resisted*";
- "*a certain mutual displacement is allowed*" ≡ "*a certain force is not resisted*".

This approach greatly facilitates the analysis. In particular, arguments of this type are appropriate when considering the conditions of interaction between elements of the design model. If a reinforced concrete floor slab laid on a brick wall does not transfer the moment to the masonry (because the masonry can not take it), then it becomes necessary to provide the respective freedom of the mutual rotation of elements in the design model (install a hinge).

It is especially important to perform this analysis for thermal loadings. Even a tiny mutual slip in the joints dramatically changes the stress state caused by the thermal load. Therefore an installation of "sliders" or modeling of an elastic joint instead of a rigid one can be an important technique.

Question:
Following the previous question: constraints were treated as restraints or some other conditions imposed on the displacements, can the constraints be imposed on forces?

Answer:
Yes, there are cases when the constraints are imposed on forces/stresses in the elements of the system. A structure supported by a system of hydraulic jacks can serve as an example (this situation sometimes occurs when analyzing the erection states).

The requirement of equal fluid pressure in each of the jacks with a common hydraulic system leads to a system of equations between the reactions transmitted to the system by these jacks.

If we consider as an example a two-span continuous beam (Fig. 1.3.*a*) with different support reactions under normal conditions (Fig. 1.3.*b*), then the changes made by force constraints can be illustrated by the case when there is a requirement of two equal reactions (result in Fig. 1.3.*c*) or when these reactions are required to have different signs (result in Fig. 1.3.*d*).

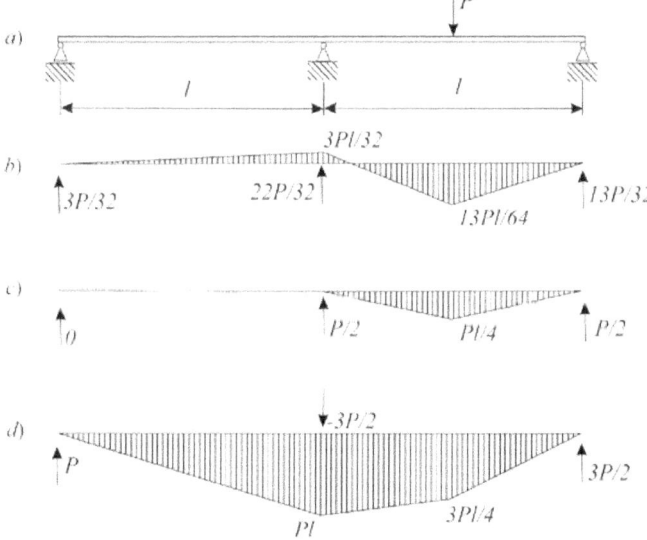

Figure 1.3.
Mechanical interpretation of the above force constraints is given in Fig. 1.4.

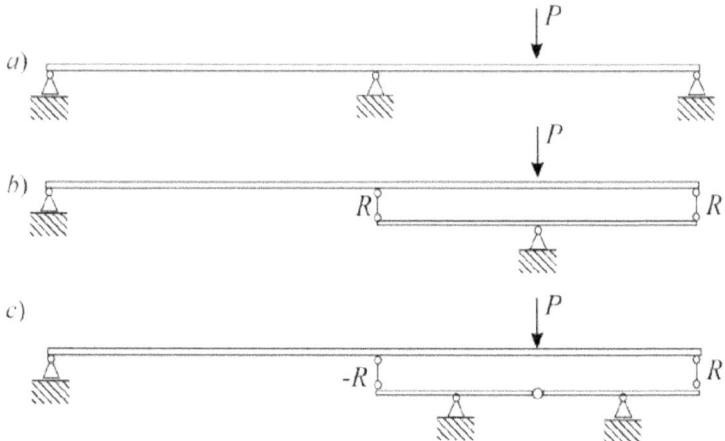

Figure 1.4

It is easy to see that the system shown in Fig. 1.4.*a* is formed from modified systems shown in Fig. 1.4.*b* or in Fig. 1.4.*c*, if we restrain rotations of the corresponding balancers.

> *Imposing a force constraint corresponds to removing a certain kinematic constraint. And vice versa, introducing a kinematic constraint is equivalent to removing a force constraint.*

Question:
Could you please elaborate on the Saint-Venant's principle? Almost nothing is said about it in the standard structural mechanics courses.

Answer:
The essence of Saint-Venant's principle is that if a system of forces is applied within a certain area of the elastic body, then the stresses and deformations at distances much greater than the dimensions of this area are virtually identical for all statically equivalent forces (for example, for a given group of forces and their resultant).

The Saint-Venant's principle allows, for example, to replace a distributed load acting on a small portion of the body surface with a concentrated force, and vice versa, the concentrated force can be replaced with a distributed load by applying it to a small portion of the surface.

As an example illustrating the Saint-Venant's principle, let us consider the change of the stress state in a steel plate 300×50×5 mm for different variants of its loading with a statically equivalent load applied to its edges. Load application patterns and isolines of normal stresses (σ_x) are shown in Fig. 1.5.

CONVERSATIONS ABOUT THE STRUCTURAL MECHANICS 17

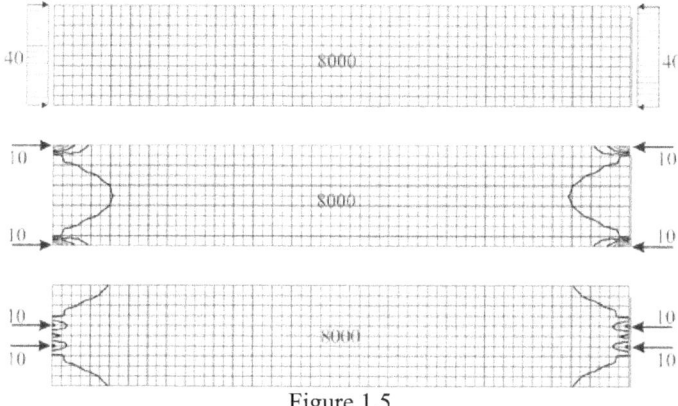

Figure 1.5

Isolines show that statically equivalent load application patterns change only in the edge areas; the stress state becomes uniform in the middle section of the plate at the distance from the edges of about 0,7 of the plate width.

You should keep in mind that the Saint-Venant's principle is not universal. It cannot be applied to thin-walled bars, where the bimoment (action statically equivalent to zero) leads to the so-called restrained warping of the entire bar (Fig. 1.6).

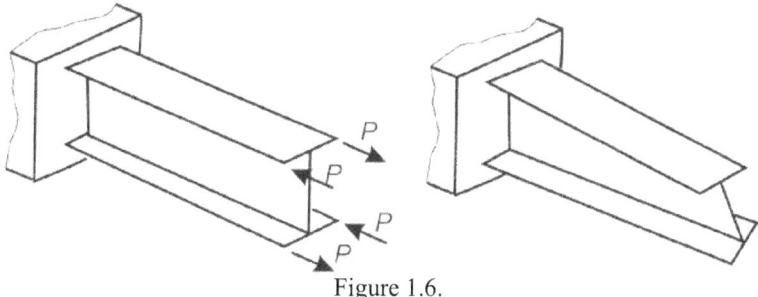

Figure 1.6.

A simple physical explanation can be given according to V.I. Feodosiev [10]. Unlike the solid section the cross-section of a thin-walled bar is also characterized by the thickness. Each flange of an I-section is loaded by a moment (a pair of forces), and if it were not for the web, the flanges would bend independently. The web of a solid section is very rigid, and the distribution of stresses from each of the four forces in a cross-section is limited by a narrow area. The thinner the web, the greater the effect of the restrained warping. Hence, the degree of damping of the edge characteristics is defined by the "damping" action of the additional constraints present in the system.

Conversation 1.2. Basic Concepts. Principle of Virtual Displacements

Let us recall some basic concepts and formulate them more clearly than in the university textbooks, which are intended for readers who are new to the subject, and therefore do not provide full information.

Structural mechanics considers design models of mechanical systems

> *A system* is a set of *elements* interconnected in a certain way and therefore working together.

Elements are usually elastically or inelastically deformable bodies of standard shape: bars, disks, plates etc. In the general case

> *an element* is a material object (or rather its idealization or abstraction), studied enough to be able to analyze its behavior in the system.

A displacement reference system is usually connected to a special immobile non-deformable element conventionally called "earth", for which the conditions of equilibrium do not have to be satisfied. The interaction of the elements of the system with the objects not included in the system is represented in the form of forces. Such idealized objects as "force" and "earth" enable to localize the system among the unlimited number of interacting objects.

When considering the equilibrium of a rigid body (this is the main subject of analytical mechanics) it is sufficient to know the forces applied to the body. You do not have to know the motion the body will get if the equilibrium is disturbed. However, when considering systems other than the non-deformable rigid body and consisting of parts interacting with each other, it is necessary to know the motion that will occur when the equilibrium is disturbed.

The equilibrium condition in such cases is closely related to its virtual displacements.

Virtual displacements are defined by the constraints, i.e. by the geometric conditions which must be satisfied during the motion. It can be a requirement that a certain point always remains on a particular surface, or that a value of a certain displacement is equal to a predefined value (including zero), or, for example, that a distance between certain points remains constant etc. You should keep in mind that we are dealing with infinitely small displacements, and that virtual displacements can be treated as finite values only in the cases of linear systems.

> *Infinitely small virtual displacements, i.e. allowed by the constraints, appear in the equilibrium conditions of the system.*

It is assumed that all constraints are perfect, do not create friction and similar resistances, and thus do not restrain virtual displacements. These constraints are mechanical devices which make the system move in a certain way due to the internal forces arising in the constraints (reactions of the constraints) and acting on the system.

Internal forces are forces arising between two parts of the body in a certain section. According to the law of action and reaction, internal forces are always pairwise equal in magnitude and opposite in direction. If the left part of the body acts on the right one with a force R, then the right part in turn acts on the left one with a force $-R$.

Internal reactions of constraints act in the same way. They can be shown in the model if we imagine that a constraint is broken (removed). One reaction component of the pair acts on the "earth" and its action has no effect. The other one acts on the structure, and its action imposes the displacements on the system.

> *This is also evidenced by the principle of release from constraints: the equilibrium of the system will not be disturbed and its configuration will not change if a constraint is replaced by its reaction.*

In theoretical mechanics, the general equation of statics of the systems with perfect bilateral constraints is formulated as the following *principle of virtual displacements*:

> *The necessary and sufficient condition of equilibrium is that the sum of works done by all the applied active forces is equal to zero for each **virtual** displacement of the system.*

A characteristic feature of the reactions developed by perfect constraints is the fact that the sum of elementary works done by these forces is equal to zero for any displacement of their application point allowed by the constraints. This follows from the above pairing property of forces arising in the constraints. Therefore, the above formulation considers only active applied forces and does not consider the reactions of constraints.

If you want to take into account friction in the joints, the friction force has to be considered as one of the external applied forces and added to other external forces. It is also necessary to add viscous, elastic and other forces if they are active.

A deformable body can be considered as a certain variable system of material points the displacements of which are restrained by the elastic forces. If the elastic forces are taken into account explicitly, the formulation of the principle of virtual displacements is transformed:

> *The necessary and sufficient condition of equilibrium is that the sum of works done by all active and reactive forces is equal to zero for **any** displacement of the system.*

It should be noted that *any* displacements of the points of the elastic system are considered instead of the *virtual* displacements, because having introduced elastic forces (internal stresses) into the equations of work we have removed the constraints restraining virtual displacements of each point of the elastic system.

The following conclusion can be also made from the principle of virtual displacements:

if the system is in equilibrium, then this equilibrium is not disturbed by the introduction of new constraints.

In particular, according to the principle of virtual displacements each equation of equilibrium is an expression of the law that the sum of the works done by the active forces for a certain displacement allowed by the constraints is equal to zero. However, the same equilibrium equations can be applied if the same displacements are considered in an elastic body as for a rigid body.

This replacement is equivalent to imposing additional constraints, which naturally can not disrupt the equilibrium of the body. This statement is known as the *solidification principle*.

Theoretical mechanics states that any system of forces applied to a rigid body can be replaced by another system statically equivalent to the first one without disturbing the equilibrium of the body. Structural mechanics, however, considers deformable bodies, and therefore a system usually can not be replaced by a statically equivalent one.

For example, a beam subjected to two forces (Fig. 1.7,*a*), and the same beam loaded by a single force which is a resultant of the above forces bend in different ways (Fig. 1.7,*b*).

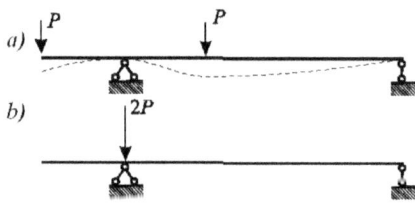

Figure 1.7

A well-known joke comes to mind: The resultant of the hydrostatic pressure acting on a dam is a force applied at a height of 1/3 of the liquid level. It is suggested to make a microscopic hole in the dam at this point (so small that the water leakage will be insignificant). The concentrated force will fly away through this hole, and the dam will not experience loads from the water pressure. Telling this tale, professor K.S. Zavriev asked his students to find pitfalls in this reasoning.

Question:
Only external active forces are considered in the formulation of the principle of virtual displacements. However, in some cases a system can be subjected to a kinematic action, e.g. thermal action. How should I proceed in these cases?

Answer:
The principle of virtual displacements forms the

equilibrium conditions using only displacements of a rigid body (a system of rigid bodies). If the constraints of the system restrain such displacements, the equations of equilibrium of a rigid body can not be applied directly to it. This is precisely the case of the thermal action, when the thermal elongations of the parts of the system contradict the assumption that the rigid body is non-deformable.

But then we can replace the constraints restraining the given displacements with forces and consider these forces (reactions) as external forces. Only then can we apply the equations of equilibrium of a rigid body to our system. Otherwise, we come to the paradoxical conclusion that the work done by the internal forces of a body subject to thermal actions is zero (there are no external forces in this case).

Question:
The principle of virtual displacements is often used in course books to prove some properties of the system. Can it be used to solve the equilibrium problems directly without writing and solving the equilibrium equations?

Answer:
In some cases the direct use of the principle of virtual displacements enables to obtain the solution of the problem in a simpler way, although it should be noted that such cases are not too frequent and, most importantly, there are no general and formalized methods.

As an example let us consider the problem from the book by A.V. Darkov and N.N. Shaposhnikov [4].

The task is to prove that the system shown in Fig. 1.8 consisting of six disks, five bars and four identical sections is dimensionally stable, and the force in the bar 1-2 is tensile and is equal to $4P$ (when the number of sections is equal to n, the force in the bar 1-2 is equal to nP).

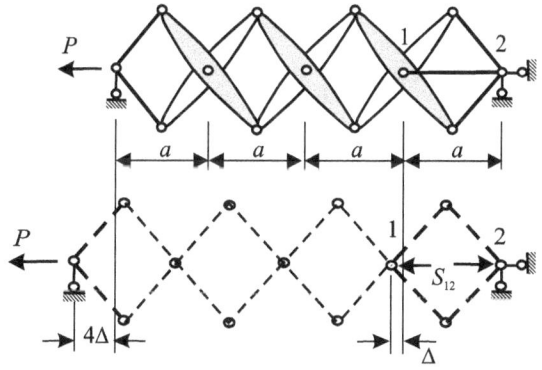

Figure 1.8

Having replaced the constraint 1-2 by the force S_{12}, and having thus released the horizontal displacement of the node 1, shift this node by Δ. In this case all cells of the system will be distorted in the same way and the leftmost node will shift by $n\Delta$. Now we can write the equation of work $(P \cdot n\Delta) - (S_{12} \cdot \Delta) = 0$ and obtain the necessary solution of the problem.

Question:
How many equations of equilibrium does the principle of virtual displacements provide?

Answer:
According to this principle the necessary and sufficient condition of equilibrium is that the sum of works done by all the active forces is equal to zero for each virtual displacement of the system. Hence, the provided number of equations is equal to the number of different virtual displacements of the system.

Displacements are considered as different if they can not replace each other. If having several different displacements we find another one which can be replaced by a linear combination of the former, it can not be considered as a new displacement. It will not provide a new equilibrium condition, and we will get only an equation which is a consequence of the other equilibrium equations derived for the former displacements.

Basically, the number of equilibrium equations is defined by the number of irreducible virtual displacements, or, in other words: the number of degrees of freedom of the system.

It should be noted that the system of infinitely rigid bodies (possibly connected by elastic springs) has a finite number of degrees of freedom, since the position of each point of such a body is uniquely defined by the displacements of a certain point and rotations about the coordinate axes. In contrast, a deformable body has an infinite number of degrees of freedom (displacements of any of its points). However, if we apply the hypothesis about a set of some known deformation modes of this body, then the number of degrees of freedom will be equal to the number of parameters defining these modes. For example, assuming that the bar can bend only sinusoidally with one or two half-waves, we see that the virtual displacements are determined only by two parameters: the amplitude values of these sinusoids.

Conversation 1.3: Static and Kinematic Equations

If we use the classic method of cutting out nodes subjected to forces of the adjacent bars S_j and the external nodal loads P_{rk} (the component of the nodal load of the r-th node directed along the k coordinate axis), then the condition of equilibrium of a spatial hinged bar system consisting of n bars and m nodes can be written as the sum of the projections of all forces acting on the node on the coordinate axes equal to zero[4]:

$$\sum_{j=1}^{n} D_{rj} C_{jk} S_j + P_{rk} = 0 \quad (r = 1,...,m;\ k = 1,2,3). \quad (1.1)$$

Here D_{ij} are incidence coefficients which are equal to one if the bar j is adjacent to the node r (is incidental to this node) and is equal to zero in the other case, and C_{jk} are cosines of the angles between the bars j and the k coordinate axis. The structure of these equations is shown in the Figure 1.9.

S_1	S_2	...	S_n	1		i
$D_{11}C_{11}$	$D_{12}C_{21}$	...	$D_{1n}C_{n1}$	P_{11}	Node 1, projection on the axis 1	1
$D_{11}C_{12}$	$D_{12}C_{22}$	...	$D_{1n}C_{n2}$	P_{12}	Node 1, projection on the axis 2	2
$D_{11}C_{13}$	$D_{12}C_{23}$	...	$D_{1n}C_{n3}$	P_{13}	Node 1, projection on the axis 3	3
$D_{21}C_{11}$	$D_{22}C_{21}$	...	$D_{2n}C_{n1}$	P_{21}	Node 2, projection on the axis 1	4
$D_{21}C_{12}$	$D_{22}C_{22}$	...	$D_{2n}C_{n2}$	P_{22}	Node 2, projection on the axis 2	5
$D_{21}C_{13}$	$D_{22}C_{23}$	...	$D_{2n}C_{n3}$	P_{23}	Node 2, projection on the axis 3	6
...	...	...	...	...	...	...
$D_{m1}C_{11}$	$D_{m2}C_{21}$	...	$D_{mn}C_{n1}$	P_{21}	Node m, projection on the axis 1	$3m-2$
$D_{m1}C_{12}$	$D_{m2}C_{22}$	...	$D_{mn}C_{n2}$	P_{22}	Node m, projection on the axis 2	$3m-1$
$D_{m1}C_{13}$	$D_{m2}C_{23}$	...	$D_{mn}C_{n3}$	P_{23}	Node m, projection on the axis 3	$3m$

Figure 1.9

---

[4] Only the displacements of nodes are considered as the degrees of freedom of the truss due to the hypothesis about straightness of the truss bars (the position of end nodes of the truss completely defines the position of all points of the bar). Hence follows the conclusion about the necessary number of equilibrium equations.

After the respective renumbering dealing with the introduction of a new index $i=r+m(k-1)$ as shown in the right column of the Figure 1.9, and the replacement of the product $D_{rj}C_{jk}$ by A_{ij}, we obtain

$$\sum_{j=1}^{n} A_{ij}S_j + P_i = 0 \quad (i=1,\ldots,3m). \tag{1.2}$$

Suppose now that the truss bars experience small elongation λ_j ($j=1,2,\ldots,n$), and the nodes experience displacements u_i ($i=1,2,\ldots,3m$) together with the elongation, and the forces S_j appear in the truss bars. We will further use the following designation $s=3m$.

According to the *principle of virtual displacements* the work done by the internal forces of the system must be equal to the work done by the external forces applied to it:

$$\sum_{j=1}^{n} S_j \lambda_j = \sum_{i=1}^{s} P_i u_i. \tag{1.3}$$

If we substitute the values of P_i from (1.2) into this equation, we obtain

$$\sum_{j=1}^{n} S_j \lambda_j = \sum_{i=1}^{s} \left(-\sum_{j=1}^{n} A_{ij} S_j \right) u_i = -\sum_{j=1}^{n} S_j \sum_{i=1}^{s} u_i A_{ij},$$

and thus derive the conditions of kinematic compatibility of elongations λ_j and nodal displacements u_i.

$$\lambda_j = -\sum_{i=1}^{s} u_i A_{ij} \quad (i=1,2,\ldots,n), \tag{1.4}$$

The matrix of the coefficients of this equation is the inverse transpose of the matrix of the coefficients of the system of equilibrium equations (1.2). This result is not random, it is common for all calculations performed for non-deformed models, and the following statement is true:

> When the calculation is performed for a non-deformed model, the system of linear equilibrium equations and the system of linear kinematic equations **form a dual pair** in the sense that:
> a) variables of one system and constant terms of the other system are corresponding generalized forces and generalized displacements;
> b) the matrix of coefficients of one system can be obtained from the other by inverse transposition.

In practice a matrix which is the easiest to obtain is created. For bar systems the equilibrium conditions are usually the easiest to formulate, and the respective matrix of coefficients can be created, and the kinematic matrix can be obtained by the transposition. In the case of continual systems it can be sometimes easier to formulate the compatibility conditions.

As an example, let us consider the truss shown in Fig. 1.10. It is necessary to find the values of elongation of its bars in the case when the node has a displacement Δ. It is very easy to write the equation of equilibrium in this case

$$1 \cdot S_1 + \frac{\sqrt{3}}{2} \cdot S_2 + \frac{1}{2} \cdot S_3 + 0 \cdot S_4 = 0.$$

Transposing the row matrix of coefficients of this equation, we obtain

$$\lambda_1 = \Delta; \quad \lambda_2 = \frac{\Delta\sqrt{3}}{2}; \quad \lambda_3 = \frac{\Delta}{2}; \quad \lambda_4 = 0.$$

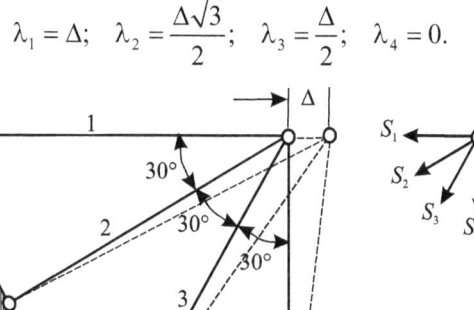

Figure 1.10.

Technically, the equilibrium conditions (1.2) should be considered in relation to the deformed state of the system (Fig. 1.11,*b*), when the cosines of angles φ* are included in the equations (Fig. 1.11,*a*). These angles take into account the displacements Δ, which are defined by the elongation of the bars Δ*l*, and therefore, in turn, depend on the forces in the elements of the system.

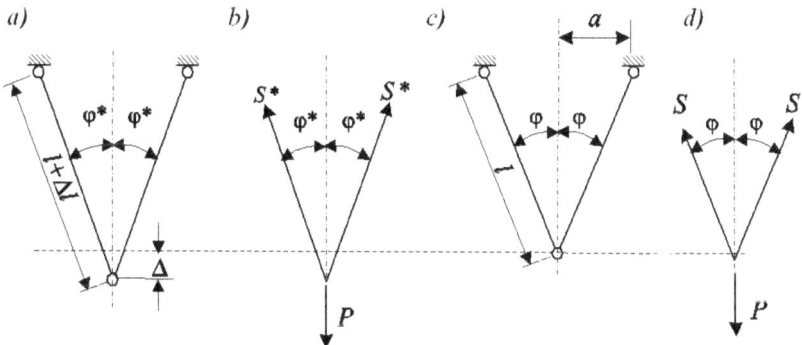

Figure 1.11.

In this case we have to conclude that

> it is impossible to find the internal forces in a system the calculation of which is performed for a deformed model using only the equilibrium equations (the system is statically indeterminate).

Indeed, in the simple example in Fig. 1.11.c the angle between the bars of the non-deformed system is 2φ, after the deformation it is $2\varphi^*$, and the difference $\varphi^* - \varphi$ depends on the elongation of the bars.

In the case of the deformed model the equilibrium equations

$$S_1^* \sin\varphi^* - S_2^* \sin\varphi^* = 0; \quad S_1^* \cos\varphi^* + S_2^* \cos\varphi^* - P = 0$$

lead to the following solution

$$S_1 = P \Big/ \big[2\cos\varphi^* \big] = P \Big/ \Big[2\sqrt{1-\sin^2\varphi^*} \Big] = P \Big/ \Big[2\sqrt{1 - a^2/(l+\Delta l)^2} \Big],$$

If, however, the increment Δl can be neglected in comparison with l, the force in the bar is determined by the formula

$$S_1 = P \Big/ \Big[2\sqrt{1 - a^2/l^2} \Big] = P \Big/ \Big[2\sqrt{1-\sin^2\varphi} \Big] = P / (2\cos\varphi),$$

which corresponds to the calculation for a non-deformed model, when the equilibrium equations have the form

$$S_1 \sin\varphi - S_2 \sin\varphi = 0; \quad S_1 \cos\varphi + S_2 \cos\varphi - P = 0.$$

Further, we will consider the equilibrium equations written for a non-deformed model without any special remarks.

Question:

Do you mean to say that in the case of the calculation for a non-deformed model it is sufficient for the expected displacement values to be small?

Answer:

This is not quite true. The thing is that the very concept of "small displacement values" is undefined until you indicate the values compared to which these displacements are considered to be small. We could rather talk about the smallness of the variation of the bar angles with respect to the design position (smallness of the deviation angles of the bars).

However, even in the cases of small displacement and deviation values it can be sometimes important to take into account the fact that external loads acting on the system can cause a considerable additional moment. The simplest example is a frame of a tall building experiencing relatively small lateral displacements and subjected to significant vertical loads from the self-weight causing additional bending moments at its base. These moments can be determined only in calculations for a deformed model. It is sometimes called the $P-\Delta$ effect.

Conversation 1.4: Properties of Solutions

When deriving the equations (1.2) and (1.4), no other limitations except for the assumption about the smallness of displacements have been introduced, so these equations are true for any number of bars n and nodes m, as well as for the plane ($k=1,2$) and spatial ($k = 1,2,3$) cases. Therefore a question of solvability of the resulting systems of linear equations arises which will be further addressed.

If we compare the number of unknown forces n with the number of equilibrium equations $s=3m$ (number of degrees of freedom), then the following cases are possible (Fig. 1.12): $n<s$, $n=s$ and $n>s$, which define the configuration of the matrix of the coefficients of equilibrium equations (**c**) and of the strain compatibility equations (**κ**). Each of these cases is considered separately, and the rank of the matrix[5] can be complete when it is equal to the smaller matrix dimension, or incomplete and the matrix is degenerate. The order-r principal minor of the coefficient matrices given next to each model is darkened in Fig. 1.12.

The number of unknown forces is less than the number of degrees of freedom ($n<s$)

In this case the structure does not have enough constraints to provide the dimensional stability and is in fact a mechanism (Fig. 1.12,*a*). However, at $r<s$ (Fig. 1.12,*b*) the mobility of this mechanism is limited only by infinitely small displacements, since in order for them to develop the lower chain of three bars has to experience considerable deformations. Such a system is called *instantly rigid.*

The number of unknown forces is equal to the number of degrees of freedom ($n=s$)

First of all, let us consider the case when the system of equilibrium equations is such that all internal forces can be unambiguously determined from it for arbitrary loads P_u. As we know from linear algebra the number of equations should be equal to the number of unknowns ($n = s$), and the determinant of the system of equations should be other than zero in this case, otherwise $r = s$ (Fig. 1.12,*c*).

Systems possessing such properties are *statically determinate.* If there are not enough equations of equilibrium to determine all internal forces, such systems are *statically indeterminate.*

---

[5] The rank of a matrix is the maximal number of linearly independent rows (columns). This is the same as the size of the largest possible non-vanishing determinant (principal minor), which can be made up of the elements of the considered matrix.

> These properties do not depend on whether the elements of the system are made from the linearly elastic (obeying Hooke's law) or from the physically non-linear material.

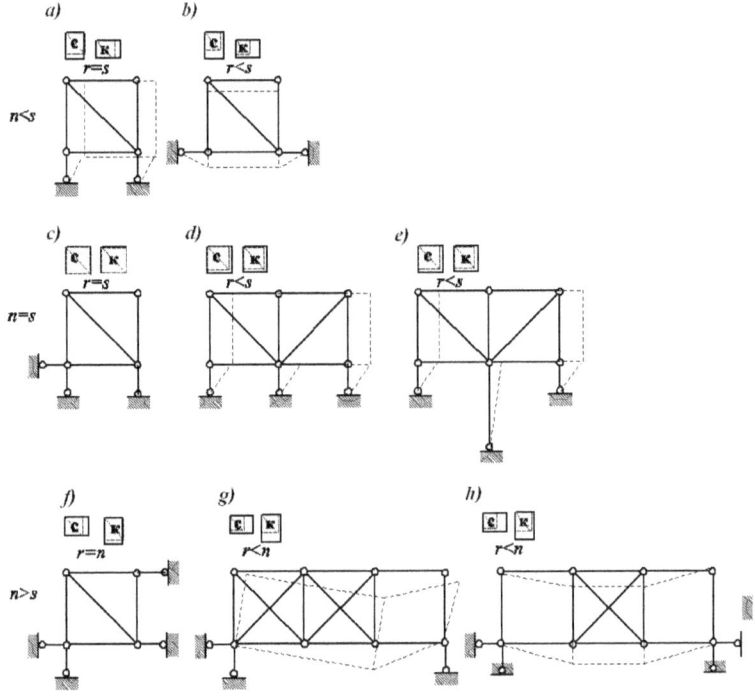

Figure 1.12

In both cases statically determinate systems have the following wonderful properties:

a) ability to represent all internal forces as linear combinations of external loads;

b) validity of the principle of independence of force actions.

The first follows directly from the assumption that the system of linear equations is solvable. Indeed, if the system is solvable, there is an inverse matrix

$$\left[\alpha_{ij}\right] = \left[A_{ij}\right]^{-1},$$

and all the unknown internal forces are expressed in terms of its elements:

$$S_j = \sum_{i=1}^{3m} \alpha_{ij} P_i \quad (j = 1,...,n) \qquad (1.5)$$

As for the second property of statically determinate systems, its validity also follows from the expression (1.5). It should be noted that *in the general case of systems with non-linear elastic elements, the linear expressions (1.5) refer only to statically determinate systems*, and they can not be applied to the statically indeterminate systems.

Remaining within the framework of the assumption that $n = s$, it is still necessary to consider the case when the system of equilibrium equations has a zero determinant, i.e. its rank $r < s$ and the solution (1.5) can not be obtained. In such cases the mechanical system is *unstable* (Fig. 1.12.*d*) or *instantly unstable* (Fig. 1.12.*e*).

Like in the case of an instantly rigid system the mobility of an instantly unstable system is limited only by infinitely small displacements. In particular, the rotation angle of the central support column which lags with respect to the rotation angles of the edge columns prevents the development of the displacements of the system shown in Fig. 1.12.*e*.

The number of unknown forces is greater than the number of degrees of freedom (n>s).

The system has an excessive number of constraints and another two possibilities can be considered here:

a) the rank r of the matrix $\left[A_{ij} \right]$ is equal to the number of equations ($r=n$);

b) the matrix $\left[A_{ij} \right]$ has an incomplete rank ($r < n$).

As we know from linear algebra, in the case $r=n$ (Fig. 1.12.*f*) the homogeneous system of linear equations

$$-\sum_{i=1}^{s} A_{ij} u_i = 0 \quad (i=1,2,...,n) \tag{1.6}$$

can only have a zero solution

$$u_i \equiv 0 \quad (i=1,...,s). \tag{1.7}$$

The system is statically indeterminate, because the number of unknown forces exceeds the number of degrees of freedom.

If $r < n$, then the system (1.6) has nonzero solutions in addition to the trivial one (1.7), i.e. the considered bar system allows nonzero nodal displacements u_i without elongation of its elements (all deformations $\lambda_j = 0$). The system is either dimensionally unstable due to the irregular structure (redundant constraints in one part of the system and the absence of necessary ones in the other part as in the Figure 1.12.*g*), or instantly unstable (Fig. 1.12.*h*).

> *In conclusion, it should be noted that the limited mobility of the instantly unstable and instantly rigid systems (they are called **special** systems) can be studied only on the basis of the geometrically nonlinear analysis.*

Solutions of the System of Equilibrium Equations

In addition to the question of the compatibility of the system of equilibrium equations, the question of the form the solution of the system (1.2) takes has to be considered as well. Linear algebra proves that if the rank of the matrix of the coefficients of the system of s equations with n unknowns ($s \leq n$) is equal to r, it is enough to solve only those r equations which contain the principal determinant relative to those r unknowns whose coefficients are included in the principal determinant. This solution gives an expression for r unknowns in the form of linear functions of the other (n-r) unknowns whose values remain independent and completely arbitrary, i.e. linear relations of the following type can be obtained:

$$S_j = \sum_{\alpha=1}^{r} a_{\alpha j} P_\alpha + \sum_{\beta=r+1}^{n} b_{j\beta} S_\beta \quad (j=1,...,r). \tag{1.8}$$

It is assumed that the principal determinant is in the first r columns of the matrix of the coefficients of the equilibrium equation system, and this means that the equilibrium equations can be written in the following form

$$\sum_{j=1}^{r} A_{ij}^{(1)} S_j + \sum_{j=r+1}^{n} A_{ij}^{(2)} S_j + P_i = 0 \quad (i=1,...,s) \tag{1.9}$$

and the matrix $\left[A_{ij}^{(1)} \right]$ has an inverse $\left[a_{ij} \right] = \left[A_{ij}^{(1)} \right]^{-1}$. This inverse matrix enables to determine the first r forces, i.e. the condition (1.8) is obtained where

$$b_{j\beta} = \sum_{\alpha=1}^{r} a_{j\alpha} A_{\alpha\beta}^{(2)}.$$

> It follows from the formula (1.8) that there can be (n-r) **independent self-stressed states**, i.e. such sets of internal forces $S_1^0, S_2^0, ..., S_r^0$, that would satisfy the equilibrium equations at zero external load.

Self-stressed states obviously can not be created in the statically determinate systems. It follows from the fact that the rank of the matrix of a statically determinate system r=n and therefore the number of self-stressed states n–r = 0.

It should be noted that there can be bars in a statically indeterminate system with the coefficients in the expression (1.8) $b_{j\beta} = 0$ $(j = r+1,...,n)$, i.e. there are no self-stress forces in these bars. Then instead of (1.8) we will have, for example

$$S_j = \sum_{\alpha=1}^{r} a_{\alpha j} P_\alpha + \sum_{\beta=r+1}^{n} b_{j\beta} S_\beta \quad (j=1,...,t)$$

$$S_j = \sum_{\alpha=1}^{r} a_{\alpha j} P_\alpha \quad (j=t+1,...,n)$$

Forces in bars with numbers $j = t+1,..., r$ can be determined only from the equations of equilibrium, i.e. these bars form a statically determinate part of a statically indeterminate system (Fig. 1.13.a).

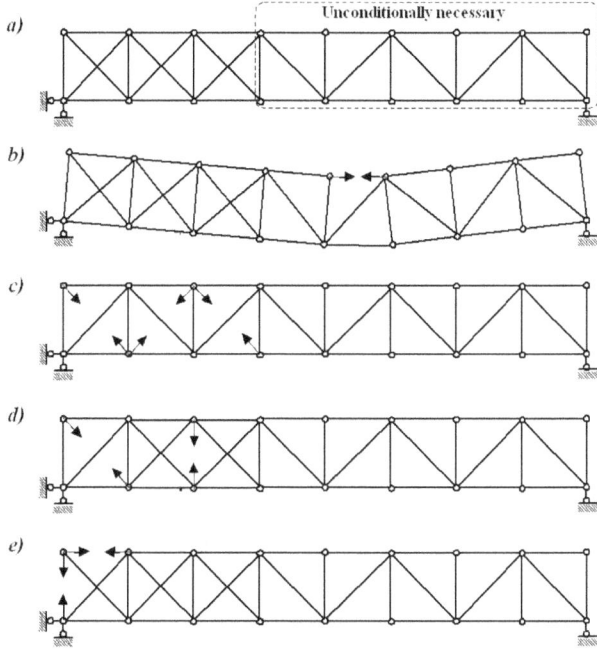

Figure 1.13.

Like any statically determinate system, where the exclusion a bar turns it into a mechanism (Fig. 1.13.*b*), the given group of bars has the same property. Therefore, they are called *unconditionally necessary*, unlike the bars with numbers $\beta = r+1, \ldots, n$, which can be removed from the system without disturbing its dimensional stability (Fig. 1.13,*c,d*). Those are the so-called *redundant bars*. This "redundancy" obviously refers only to the function of providing the stability of the system. It does not mean that any combination of $n-r$ (degree of static indeterminacy) redundant bars can be removed without disturbing the stability (Fig. 1.13.*e*).

Question:
According to standard textbooks on structural mechanics unstable systems can not be used as structures. Does it mean that they are set into motion by any load?

Answer:

No, not by any. A dimensionally unstable system will maintain its equilibrium under certain loads. It is possible to select a certain class of *equilibrium loads* from a myriad of possible loads which when applied to a dimensionally unstable system help to maintain its equilibrium.

For example, two equal and oppositely directed forces applied along the axis of a bar are balanced within this bar.

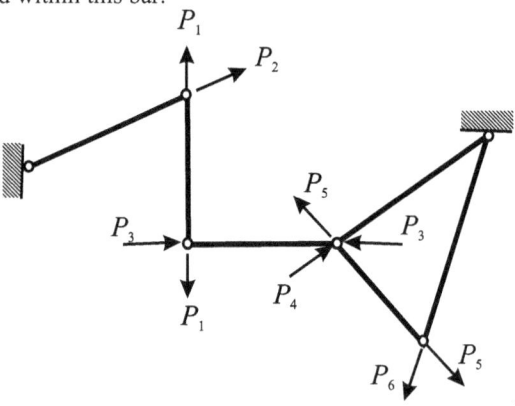

Figure 1.14.

Therefore, it is always possible to apply loads as shown in Fig. 1.14, and for any linear combination of such pairwise equal forces the resulting load will be classified as equilibrium.

Question:

When unconditionally necessary bars were considered, it was noted that forces in them can be determined only from the equations of statics. What if some forces in the bar can not be determined from the equations of statics, will this bar be considered as unconditionally necessary?

Answer:

It should be noted that the concept of static determinacy is relative in the general case. In the most narrow sense, it applies to any one internal force. If any internal force can be determined only from the equilibrium conditions, then this force can be called statically determinate.

For example, in the case of a beam shown in Fig. 1.15 the equations of statics enable to determine the bending moments but not the longitudinal forces. Conditions of compatibility of deformations are required to determine the latter.

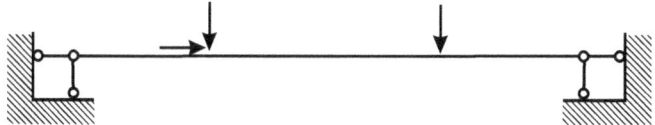

Figure 1.15.

Thus static determinacy can be considered with respect to a certain group of forces. So if the reactions of the constraints connecting the system to the ground can be determined from the equilibrium conditions, then this system is *externally statically determinate* (it would be more correct to consider static determinacy with respect to the reactions).

Question:

Can the degree of static indeterminacy of a continual system be considered?

Answer:

The problems of the analysis of continual systems (plates, shells, three-dimensional bodies) are statically indeterminate and, as a rule, the degree of their static indeterminacy is infinite. Their finite-dimensional description (for example, using the finite element method) is approximate. We will talk about it in the following conversations.

However, there are exceptions to this rule, we will demonstrate one of them. Let us consider a fabric shell (Fig 1.16) formed by two families of threads which lie in the planes parallel to the coordinate planes X0Z and Y0Z, and the shell surface is described by the following equation

$$z = \frac{4f_1 x^2}{a^2} - \frac{4f_2 y^2}{b^2}.$$

Let us find out whether the shell can have this shape without an external load, and if so, let us determine the allowable prestress. Consider homogeneous equilibrium equations

$$\frac{\partial \sigma_x}{\partial x} = 0; \quad \frac{\partial \sigma_y}{\partial y} = 0; \quad \frac{8f_1 x}{a^2}\sigma_x - \frac{8f_1 y}{b^2}\sigma_y = 0.$$

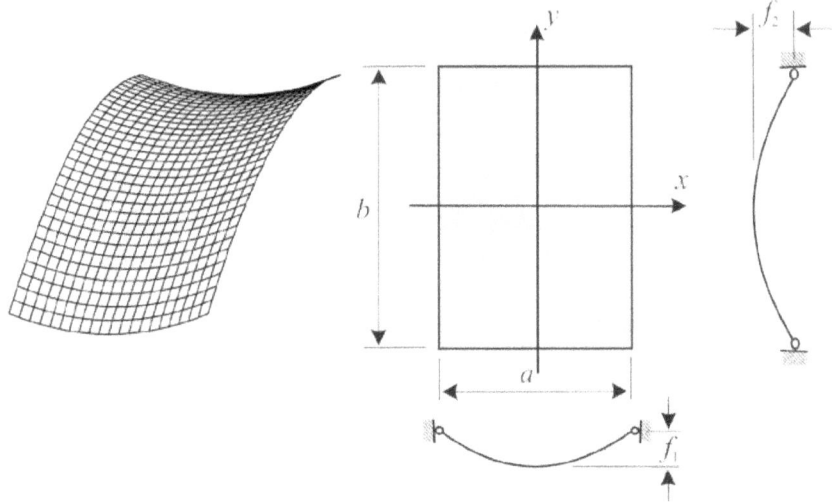

Figure 1.16.

It follows from the first two equations that

$$\sigma_x = \sigma_x(y); \quad \sigma_y = \sigma_y(x),$$

and this means that the third equation can be satisfied only under the following condition

$$\frac{f_1}{a^2}\sigma_x = \frac{f_1}{b^2}\sigma_y = C,$$

hence

$$\sigma_x = \frac{Ca^2}{f_1}; \quad \sigma_y = \frac{Cb^2}{f_1}.$$

Thus, a shell with the given geometric shape can exist assuming the found prestress field which is determined up to an arbitrary constant C. The fact that the solution of homogeneous equilibrium equations contains one arbitrary constant indicates a single static indeterminacy of the considered system. This absolutely nontrivial result was obtained by V.N. Gordeev [3].

Question:
Stability or instability is given in the form of black and white "yes-no" logic. Are there any intermediate characteristics of the system? Can the systems be almost unstable?

Answer:

Yes, of course. When we talked about the solvability of the equilibrium equations or the compatibility of deformations and determined the properties of their solutions, we used the concept of degeneracy (when the determinant of the system is equal to zero). However, a non-zero determinant can turn out to be very small, and the system will behave as "almost unstable".

For example, let us consider a simple statically determinate system shown in Fig. 1.11. If the angle φ is close to 90°, the system behaves as almost unstable. The vertical displacement of the node Δ is related to the elongation of the bar λ by the following condition $\Delta = \lambda / \cos\varphi$ and tends to infinity even at small elongation of the bars (we are obviously dealing with the analysis of a linearized system).

It should be noted that the classic definition of instability as a property of the system to have nodal displacements which do not cause deformations of its elements (displacement as a rigid mechanism) was generalized by Yu.B. Shulkin [12] and replaced by the following:

> *A system is considered to be unstable if it allows small non-zero displacements causing deformations of the elements which are either zero or have the values of higher order of smallness.*

Thus, the logic of the kinematic classification ceased to be black and white and was enriched by a mechanism of comparing the orders of smallness of displacements and deformations.

Conversation 1.5. Comparison of Properties of Statically Determinate and Indeterminate Systems

The students are introduced to the concept of static determinacy or static indeterminacy at the very beginning of the structural mechanics course, and then quickly proceed to the methods of their solution focusing mainly on the calculation technique.

However, some general issues are left aside which should be considered in more detail. The question about the possibility of prestressing a statically determinate system mentioned in the preface is one of such "left out problems".

We will not describe here the details concerning the procedure of writing classic equations of the force or displacement method, believing that this material has been sufficiently hammered into the reader's head by the "training system" typical of modern engineering education.

The analysis of very simple hinged bar systems taken from the textbook by A.P. Filin [11] is considered here. However, all conclusions can be applied to arbitrary bar systems, as well as to continual systems if they are considered in the finite element approximation.

Distribution of forces. Let us consider a simple model shown in Fig. 1.17, assuming that the cross-sectional areas of bars $A_1=A_2$, A_3 and the elastic moduli $E_1=E_2$, E_3.

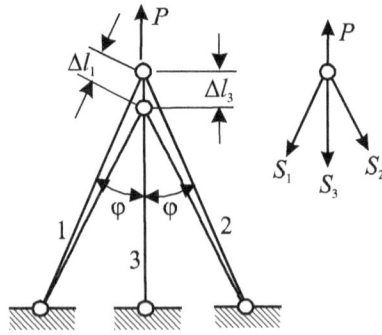

Figure 1.17

The equilibrium equations are:

$$-S_1 \sin\alpha + S_2 \sin\alpha = 0; \quad -S_1 \cos\alpha - S_3 - S_2 \cos\alpha + P = 0.$$

The kinematic consistency condition is written as
$$\Delta l_1 = \Delta l_3 \cos\alpha.$$
Let us write the physical equations defining the relationship between the elongations of the bars and the forces in them
$$\Delta l_1 = S_1 l_1/(E_1 A_1); \quad \Delta l_3 = S_3 l_3/(E_3 A_3),$$
and express the condition of compatibility of deformations in terms of forces:
$$S_1 l_1/(E_1 A_1) = S_3 l_3 \cos\alpha/(E_3 A_3).$$
Taking into account the fact that $l_3 = l_1 \cos\alpha$, we have
$$S_1 = \left[E_1 A_1/(E_3 A_3) \right] S_3 \cos^2\alpha,$$
which makes it possible to obtain the values of all forces:
$$S_1 = S_2 = P \cdot \frac{E_1 A_1 \cos^2\alpha/(E_3 A_3)}{1 + 2 E_1 A_1 \cos^2\alpha/(E_3 A_3)},$$
$$S_3 = P \cdot \frac{1}{1 + 2 E_1 A_1 \cos^2\alpha/(E_3 A_3)}.$$

As we can see the forces in a statically indeterminate system depend on the *ratios of rigidities* of the elements of the system.

> *The higher the relative stiffness of the element of a statically indeterminate system, the greater the part of the external load it takes.*

The role of increasing rigidity. It is useful to consider how the change in the cross-sectional area of a conditionally necessary truss bar affects the forces (the change in the cross-section of an unconditionally necessary bar does not affect the distribution of forces in any way).

In order to perform such an analysis, let us imagine that the considered bar with the length l and the cross-sectional area A is cut, and its effect on the system is replaced by forces X (Fig. 1.18).

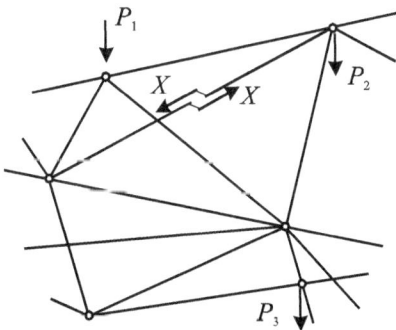

Figure 1.18.

The force method equation can be used to determine the force X. As we know the meaning of this equation lies in the fact that in reality the change in the distance between the edges of our imaginary cut is equal to zero:

$$\delta_{11}X + \delta_{1P} = 0,$$

where the displacements in the direction of the considered bar δ_{11} (from the force $X=1$) and δ_{1P} (from the load) are calculated in the system with one removed bar and this system could still be statically indeterminate. Hence, we find

$$X = -\frac{\delta_{1P}}{\delta_{11}}.$$

It should be noted that the displacement δ_{11} can be given as a sum of two values: approach of the bar ends Δ and elongation (shortening) of the bar itself, i.e.

$$X = -\frac{\delta_{1P}}{\Delta + l/EA}.$$

Two important conclusions can be made based on the analysis of this formula:

a) with a gradual increase in the cross-sectional area (up to infinity), the force in the considered bar asymptotically tends to a finite limit $X_a = -\delta_{1P}/\Delta$;

b) no change in the cross-sectional area of the bar can lead to a change in the sign of the force in it.

Erection forces. If a certain element of a statically determinate system is made inaccurately, its configuration will be distorted during the erection, but no forces will appear in the elements. The respective illustration is given in the figure, where a design system is shown in Fig. 1.19,*a*, and the actual system (dashed line) after the erection provided that the length of the right bar is less than the design one by δ is shown in Fig. 1.19,*b*.

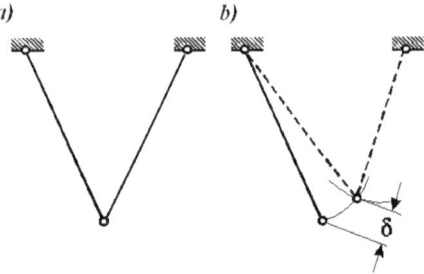

Figure 1.19.

If the system is statically indeterminate, the so-called *erection forces* appear in this case, which are *self-balanced*, i.e. existing in the absence of an external load.

Fig. 1.20,*a* shows a model of the system in which the length of the bar 2 turned out to be smaller than the design value. Fig. 1.20,*b* shows a system after connecting the elements in the lower node (dashed line), and Fig. 1.20,*c* shows a node and self-balanced forces appearing in the truss elements in the result of the erection.

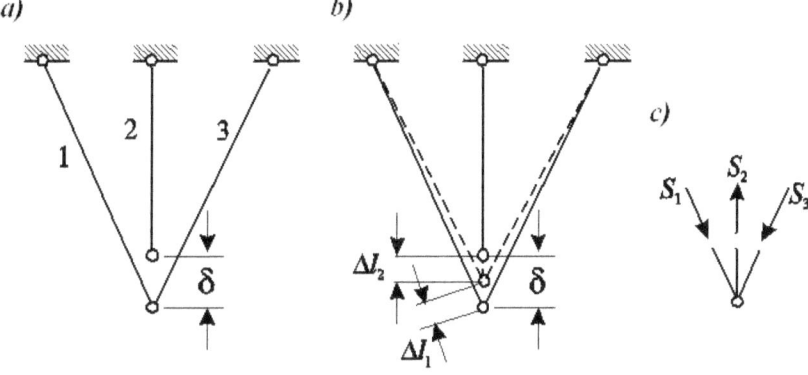

Figure 1.20.

The values of these forces are determined with the help of the equilibrium equations

$$S_1 = S_3; \quad 2S_1 \cos\varphi = S_2$$
$$\delta = \Delta l_2 + \Delta l_1 / \cos\alpha$$

and the equation of compatibility of deformations $\delta = \Delta l_2 + \Delta l_1 / \cos\alpha$. Taking into account that

$$\Delta l_1 = S_1 l_1 / EA_1; \quad \Delta l_2 = S_2 l_2 / EA_2,$$

we obtain the equation of compatibility of deformations expressed in terms of the forces:

$$\delta = S_2 l_2 / EA_2 + S_1 l_1 / (EA_1 \cos\alpha).$$

Solving this equation together with the equilibrium equations we obtain the values of the erection forces

$$S_1 = \frac{\delta}{\left[l_2 \cos\alpha / (E_1 A_1)\right]\left[1/\cos^3\alpha + 2E \cdot A_1 / (E_3 A_3)\right]};$$

$$S_2 = \frac{2\delta}{\left[l_2 / (E_1 A_1)\right]\left[1/\cos^3\alpha + 2E \cdot A_1 / (E_3 A_3)\right]}.$$

It should be noted that according to Fig. 1.20, S_1 and S_3 are compressive forces, and S_2 is a tensile force.

Thermal forces. If a *non-uniform temperature increment field* appears in a statically determinate system with respect to the temperature field at which the *system was erected* (*restraint temperature*), the configuration of the system will change, but no forces will appear in its elements (Fig. 1.21,a). If the system is statically indeterminate, the so-called *thermal forces* appear in this case, which are self-balanced (Fig. 1.21,*b*).

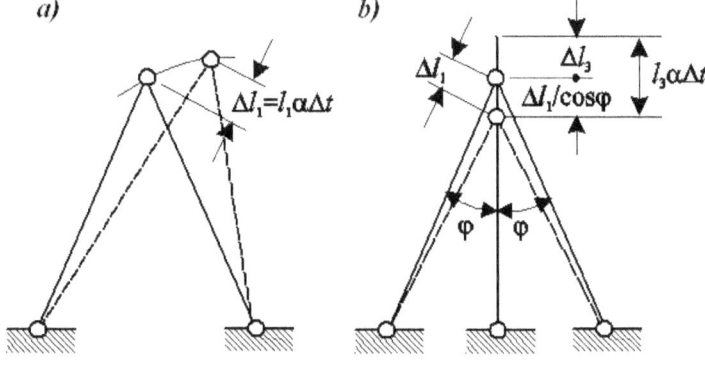

Figure 1.21.

The equilibrium and physical equations have the same form as when determining erection forces, and the compatibility of deformations is expressed by the following equation:

$$l_3 \alpha \Delta t = \Delta l_3 + \Delta l_1 / \cos \varphi.$$

Then the equation of compatibility of deformations expressed in terms of forces is written as follows:

$$l_3 \alpha \Delta t = S_3 l_3 / (E_3 A_3) + S_1 l_1 / (E_1 A_1 \cos \varphi).$$

Solving static, kinematic and physical equations, we obtain thermal forces

$$S_1 = S_2 = \alpha \Delta t \cdot \frac{E_3 A_3 \cos^2 \varphi}{2 \cos^2 \varphi + E_3 A_3 / (E_1 A_1)},$$

$$S_3 = \alpha \Delta t \cdot \frac{E_3 A_3 \cos^3 \varphi}{2 \cos^2 \varphi + E_3 A_3 / (E_1 A_1)}.$$

> As we can see thermal forces depend on the degree of non-uniformity of the temperature increment field.

Indeed, if at $A_1 = A_2 = A_3 = A$, $E_1 = E_2 = E_3 = E$ all three truss bars were heated by the same number of degrees, no forces in bars would appear — the change in the length of the middle bar would not be constrained by the edge bars.

Forces from the displacement of supports. In the case of a relative displacement of supports in a statically determinate system, the configuration of the system changes, but no forces appear in its elements. A system shown in Fig. 1.22,*a* can serve as an example. If the system is statically indeterminate (Fig. 1.22,*b*) self-balanced forces appear in the elements in a similar situation (for example, when a node of the middle bar is lowered by Δ).

The equilibrium and physical equations have the same form as when determining erection forces, and the compatibility of deformations (Fig. 1.22) is expressed by the following equation:

$$\Delta l_x = (\Delta - \Delta l_3) \cos \alpha.$$

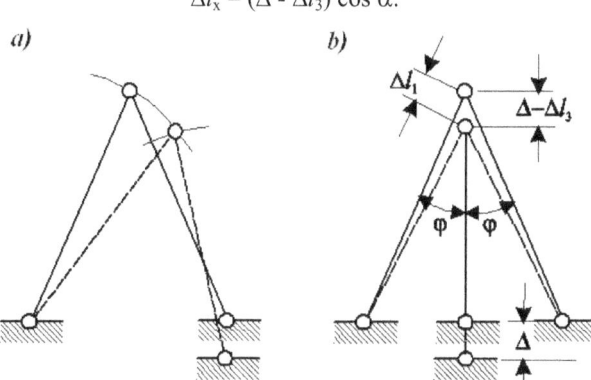

Figure 1.22

Solving equilibrium equations, physical equations and the condition of compatibility of deformations, we obtain the values of internal forces

$$S_1 = S_2 = \frac{\Delta}{l_1} \cdot \frac{EA\cos\varphi}{(1+2\cos^2\varphi)}; \quad S_3 = \frac{\Delta}{l_1} \cdot \frac{EA\cos^2\varphi}{(1+2\cos^2\varphi)}.$$

In this and in previous cases we are dealing with a system of self-balanced forces characteristic only for statically indeterminate systems. Such forces do not appear in statically determinate systems.

Conversation 1.6. Force and Displacement Methods

In this lecture we consider classic methods of structural mechanics using standard vector-matrix notation. The author apologizes in advance to those readers who may have to get reacquainted with the simplest mathematical concepts to understand the lecture.

They can skip this section of course and blindly trust that the conclusions are reasonable without any critical analysis.

We will consider a fairly general system. For the time being, we will assume that it contains a certain number of nodes with the adjacent elastic elements.

Elements of the system are considered to be attached only to the nodes of the design model, *they are not directly connected to each other*. This peculiarity of creating a design model is not always visible when the traditional representation of the design model is used, and then an obscure issue of the "multiplicity of hinges" appears in the analysis of the kinematic properties.

For example, a traditional representation of the design model shown in Fig. 1.23,*a* may suggest that the elements are directly connected to each other, while a more detailed representation shown in Fig. 1.23,*b* helps us to avoid this conclusion. It should be noted that other peculiarities of creating the design model are visible in the detailed representation, in particular, the possibility of performing the same kinematic conditions using different sets of constraints (compare different methods of describing the support nodes in Fig. 1.23).

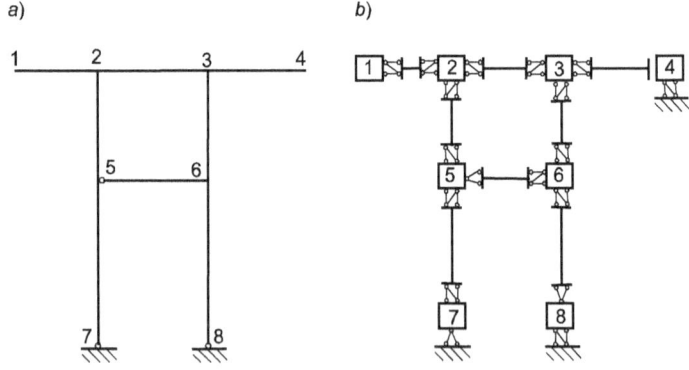

Figure 1.23.

If we do not go into details, then every element of the system can be characterized by a certain set of *internal displacements* (*deformations*) $\mathbf{u}_e$ and the corresponding *internal forces* (*forces*) s_e. Hereinafter, subscript e indicates that the value corresponds to a certain finite element.

Vectors u_e and s_e of the considered linear elastic system are related to each other by the law of state (physical law) expressed by the equality

$$s_e = F_e u_e \qquad (1.10)$$

with a symmetric positive definite (hence nondegenerate) matrix F_e. The latter assumes that any vector of internal displacements u_e, other than zero, causes deformation of the finite element (change in its shape and/or dimensions), accompanied by the accumulation of strictly positive internal energy in the element. This means, in particular, that the vector u_e does not contain rigid body deformation modes of the finite element. Therefore, it is terminologically acceptable to identify internal displacements with deformations of the finite element.

The displacements u_e of end points of the element are related with the nodal displacements u by the conditions of compatibility of deformations

$$u_e = Q_e^T u + d_e,$$

where d_e— vectors of kinematic actions specified for the elements of the system (for example, thermal elongations), and the forces s_e satisfy equilibrium conditions

$$Q_e s_e = p.$$

A complete set of equations defining the behavior of the system as a whole:

$$\left. \begin{array}{l} \text{equilibrium equations} \ldots\ldots\ldots\ldots Qs = p, \\ \text{geometric equations} \ldots\ldots\ldots \Delta = Q^T u + d \\ \text{physical equations} \ldots\ldots\ldots\ldots s = F\Delta \end{array} \right\} \qquad (1.11)$$

with respect to the unknowns s, Δ and u.

The transition from the unknowns u_e and s_e deals with renumbering, it is implemented by the so-called *assembling procedure* and is quite formal.

The dimensions of the "reduced" vectors s, Δ, d are the same and are equal to the total number m — number of unknown *internal* forces. The dimensions of the vectors u and p are also the same and are equal to the total number of unknown nodal displacements n. The matrix of the equilibrium equations Q has a dimension $n \times m$. A square symmetric matrix F of order m has a block-diagonal structure, the number of its blocks is equal to the number of elements, the size of each block is equal to the number of internal unknowns of the respective element. In particular, in the case of trusses the matrix F will be diagonal.

Displacement method

If according to the *displacement method* the nodal displacements u are taken as the main unknowns, then the vectors s and Δ should be excluded from (1.11). Their values from the second and third equations (1.1) are substituted into the first equation, and we obtain

$$QFQ^Tu = p - QFd.$$

The number of unknown components n of the displacement vector **u** is called *the degree of kinematic indeterminacy of the system*, and the square matrix

$$K = QFQ^T$$

is called *the stiffness matrix of the system*. The governing equations can be written as follows

$$Ku = p - QFd. \quad (1.12)$$

We obtain from (1.12)

$$u = K^{-1}(p - QFd). \quad (1.13)$$

The forces in the elements are calculated according to the following formula

$$s = F(Q^Tu + d) = FQ^TK^{-1}p + (I - FQ^TK^{-1}Q)Fd, \quad (1.14)$$

and it completes the determination of the parameters of the stress-strain state of the system.

Let us consider the simplest system, the model of which is shown in Fig. 1.24.

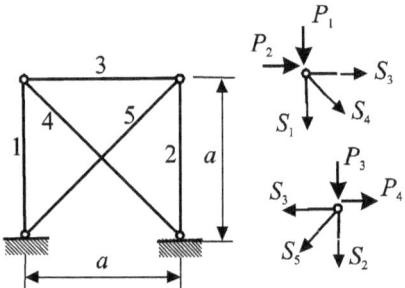

Figure 1.24.

The matrix **Q** of the equilibrium equations for this structure

$$Q = \begin{bmatrix} -1 & 0 & 0 & 0{,}7071 & 0 \\ 0 & 0 & 1 & 0{,}7071 & 0 \\ 0 & 1 & 0 & 0 & 0{,}7071 \\ 0 & 0 & 1 & 0 & 0{,}7071 \end{bmatrix}$$

If the stiffness values of all elements EF_i ($i = 1, \ldots, 5$) are assumed to be the same, then

$$\mathbf{F} = (EF/a) \begin{bmatrix} 1 & 0 & 0 & 0 & 0 \\ 0 & 1 & 0 & 0 & 0 \\ 0 & 0 & 1 & 0 & 0 \\ 0 & 0 & 0 & 0{,}7071 & 0 \\ 0 & 0 & 0 & 0 & 0{,}7071 \end{bmatrix}$$

The stiffness matrix calculated as $\mathbf{K} = \mathbf{QFQ}^T$ will be equal to

$$\mathbf{K} = (EF/a) \begin{bmatrix} 1{,}3536 & 0{,}3536 & 0 & 0 \\ 0{,}3536 & 1{,}3536 & 0 & 1 \\ 0 & 0 & 1{,}3536 & 0{,}3536 \\ 0 & 1 & 0{,}3536 & 1{,}3536 \end{bmatrix}$$

After inverting this matrix and using (1.13), we obtain the following vector of nodal displacements

$$\begin{bmatrix} u_1 \\ u_2 \\ u_3 \\ u_4 \end{bmatrix} = (a/EF) \begin{bmatrix} 0{,}8845 & 0{,}5578 & 0{,}1155 & 0{,}4422 \\ 0{,}5578 & 2{,}1356 & 0{,}4422 & 1{,}6933 \\ 0{,}1155 & 0{,}4422 & 0{,}8845 & 0{,}5578 \\ 0{,}4422 & 1{,}6933 & 0{,}5578 & 2{,}1356 \end{bmatrix} \bullet \begin{bmatrix} p_1 \\ p_2 \\ p_3 \\ p_4 \end{bmatrix}$$

The vector of internal forces is obtained from (1.14) as follows

$$\begin{bmatrix} s_1 \\ s_2 \\ s_3 \\ s_4 \\ s_5 \end{bmatrix} = (EF/a) \begin{bmatrix} 0{,}8845 & 0{,}5578 & 0{,}1155 & 0{,}4422 \\ 0{,}1155 & 0{,}4422 & 0{,}8845 & 0{,}5578 \\ 0{,}1155 & 0{,}4422 & 0{,}1155 & 0{,}4422 \\ 0{,}1633 & 0{,}7887 & 0{,}1633 & 0{,}6253 \\ 0{,}1633 & 0{,}6253 & 0{,}1633 & 0{,}7887 \end{bmatrix} \bullet \begin{bmatrix} p_1 \\ p_2 \\ p_3 \\ p_4 \end{bmatrix}$$

Force method

The second possible solution is based on the *force method*. An important role is played by such characteristics as the already mentioned rank r of the equilibrium matrix $\mathbf{Q}$ and the degree of static indeterminacy of the system k, related by the following relation $r = \text{rank } \mathbf{Q}$, $k = m - r$.

According to (1.8) the general solution of the equilibrium equations $\mathbf{Qs} = \mathbf{p}$ is as follows[6]

---

[6] Compare with (1.8)

$$s = Ax + Bp. \quad (1.15)$$

At the mathematical level, the first term on the right-hand side of (1.15) is the general solution of the respective homogeneous equilibrium equations, and the second term is a particular solution of the inhomogeneous equations. All columns of the matrix A are linearly independent, forming the so-called *fundamental system of solutions* of homogeneous equations with the matrix Q; thus rank A is equal to k — the degree of static indeterminacy of the system.

It should be noted that the solution (1.8) assumes the possibility of specifying forces, S_β in some bars with numbers $\beta = r+1,...,n$. Internal forces S_β can be specified only when the bars with these numbers are cut, because only external forces can be specified, but not the internal ones. Therefore, the equations (1.8) can be related to a system with a certain number (equal to its degree of static indeterminacy) of cut bars. Such a system is called *the primary system of the force method*.

Thus, the matrix A with dimensions $m \times k$ is a matrix of forces in the primary system of the force method from the action of the unit values of the unknowns x, the number of which is equal to k, and the matrix B with dimensions $m \times n$ is a matrix of forces in the primary system from the unit values of the nodal loads. These two matrices are such that

$$QA = 0, \quad QB = I. \quad (1.16)$$

where 0 is a rectangular zero matrix with dimensions $n \times k$, I is a unit matrix of order n.

If we consider the example of a once statically indeterminate system shown in Fig. 1.24 again, we can assume

$$A = \begin{bmatrix} 1 \\ 1 \\ 1 \\ -1,4142 \\ -1,4142 \end{bmatrix}, \quad B = \begin{bmatrix} -1 & 1 & 0 & 0 \\ 0 & 0 & -1 & -1 \\ 0 & 0 & 0 & 0 \\ 0 & -1,4142 & 0 & 0 \\ 0 & 0 & 0 & 1,4142 \end{bmatrix}.$$

The conditions (1.16) are satisfied for these matrices, which confirms their correctness.

After excluding the deformations Δ from the geometric equations of the group (1.11) with the help of the physical equations, we obtain the following relationship between the vector of internal forces s and the vector of external displacements u

$$F^{-1}s - Q^T u = d,$$

and after substituting (1.15) we obtain

$$F^{-1}Ax - Q^T u = d - F^{-1}Bp.$$

Multiplying this equation on the left by $\mathbf{A}^T$, we obtain

$$\mathbf{A}^T\mathbf{F}^{-1}\mathbf{A}\mathbf{x} - \mathbf{A}^T\mathbf{Q}^T\mathbf{u} = \mathbf{A}^T\mathbf{d} - \mathbf{A}^T\mathbf{F}^{-1}\mathbf{B}\mathbf{p}. \qquad (1.17)$$

The second term in the left part of (1.17) is annihilated due to the first condition (1.16). After introducing the compliance matrix

$$\mathbf{D} = \mathbf{A}^T\mathbf{F}^{-1}\mathbf{A}$$

we obtain a governing equation

$$\mathbf{D}\mathbf{x} = \mathbf{A}^T\mathbf{d} - \mathbf{A}^T\mathbf{F}^{-1}\mathbf{B}\mathbf{p}. \qquad (1.18)$$

It follows from this equation that

$$\mathbf{x} = \mathbf{D}^{-1}(\mathbf{A}^T\mathbf{d} - \mathbf{A}^T\mathbf{F}^{-1}\mathbf{B}\mathbf{p}). \qquad (1.19)$$

The internal forces are calculated after substituting (1.19) into (1.15), which gives

$$\mathbf{s} = \mathbf{A}\mathbf{D}^{-1}\mathbf{A}\mathbf{T}\mathbf{d} + (\mathbf{I} - \mathbf{A}\mathbf{D}^{-1}\mathbf{A}\mathbf{T}\mathbf{F}^{-1})\mathbf{B}\mathbf{p}.$$

This is the end of the force method calculation.

Question:
We were taught quite differently at the university. We obtained the canonical equations of the force method from the conditions of the absence of displacements in the cuts introduced at the transition from the considered model to its primary system. How does it all make sense?

Answer:
The physical meaning of the governing matrix equations (1.12) and (1.18) can be seen if we carefully examine the chain of the above transformations.

When deriving the equations of the displacement method, the force values from the third equation (1.11) and the nodal displacements from the second equation (1.11) were substituted into the first equation, which was the equilibrium condition.

Consequently, the displacement method operates with equilibrium conditions, and its governing equations express this condition.

Let us now consider, for example, the i-th equation of the system (1.12), assuming for simplicity that there are only force actions, and the vector $\mathbf{d}$ is equal to zero.

$$K_{i1}u_1 + K_{i2}u_2 + \ldots + K_{ij}u_j \ldots + K_{in}u_{n2} - p_i = 0. \qquad (1.20)$$

Each term of this equation of type $K_{ij}u_j$ is a force caused by an unknown displacement u_j, and a certain nodal displacement can be created in the system only when the respective constraint is imposed on the system, i.e., as in the classic explanation, we are dealing with a system with imposed additional constraints — *the primary system of the displacement method*. The very condition (1.20) says that the total force in the i–th additional constraint is equal to zero because there is no such constraint in the real structure.

In the case of the force method equation, the internal forces obtained from the equilibrium equations in the form (1.15) were substituted into the geometric equations of the group (1.11) after excluding the nodal displacements (with the help of the physical equations), and consequently the final governing system expresses the condition of compatibility of deformations.

Each equation in (1.18) indicates the absence of displacements in the cuts made in the "redundant" bars when creating the primary system of the force method.

It should be noted that unlike the theory of elasticity, the general equations (1.11) are not explicitly used in the canonical methods of the calculation of statically indeterminate systems.

For example, the *equilibrium equations* in the force method were not written explicitly, although they were used implicitly when generating the diagrams in the primary system of the force method. They were indirectly satisfied for the whole system by generating the diagrams in the primary system of the force method. A similar situation arises in the case of the displacement method. Here, the equations of *compatibility of deformations* are indirectly satisfied when determining the unit reactions in the primary system of the displacement method. These disadvantages can be avoided if the canonical equations are written on the basis of the transformation of the general system (1.11).

Finally, it should be noted that the main methods of structural mechanics are dual and mutually complementary. For example, the following statement is true for the force method:

of all the statically possible solutions of the considered problem, the one that satisfies the conditions of the compatibility of deformations, i.e. the canonical equations of the force method, will be the real one.

In the displacement method the following dual statement corresponds to the above one:

of all the kinematically possible solutions of the considered problem, the one that satisfies the equilibrium equations, i.e. the canonical equations of the displacement method, will be the real one.

We can give another interpretation of the canonical systems of equations based on these formulations.

In the case of the force method we analyze the reaction of the primary system with removed redundant constraints to all possible changes of the stress state and take the variant corresponding to the conditions of the compatibility of deformations as a true one. Indeed, the equilibrium stress state is unambiguously defined by the forces in the primary system from an external load, and its changes are defined by the forces from the unknowns of the force method.

In the case of the displacement method we analyze the reaction of the primary system to all possible changes of the displacements of the additional constraints and take the variant corresponding to the equilibrium conditions as a true one.

Question:
Inverse matrices were used when deriving the formulas. How do we know that the stiffness matrix **K** or the compliance matrix **D** can be inverted?

Answer:
These matrices are determined by the following products

$$\mathbf{K} = \mathbf{Q}\mathbf{F}\mathbf{Q}^T, \quad \mathbf{D} = \mathbf{A}^T\mathbf{F}^{-1}\mathbf{A},$$

where the middle term is related to the nondegenerate stress-strain matrix. Since a matrix rank is determined by the rank of its factors, we have to consider the matrices **Q** and **A**.

In the case of the force method, the compliance matrix **D** is not degenerate if the rank of the matrix **A** is equal to the number of its columns k. It was noted above that all its columns are linearly independent, which is a condition of dimensional stability of the system.

Similarly, in the case of the displacement method, the stiffness matrix **K** is not degenerate if the rank r of the matrix **Q** is equal to the number of its rows, which corresponds to the case of the dimensional stability of the system.

Thus, the stiffness matrix and the compliance matrix of a dimensionally stable system are not degenerate.

Question:
You considered the dimensional stability as a condition of solvability of the equations of the force method or the displacement method. What happens in the case of an "almost unstable" system?

Answer:
The generally accepted characteristic of the quality of a system of linear algebraic equations is the so-called *conditioning* of the matrix of coefficients. A poorly conditioned matrix has the property that even a very small change in the values of its components can lead to a noticeable change in the solution of the respective system of equations.

The following system can be used as an example of a poorly conditioned system of linear equations:

$$\begin{bmatrix} 5 & 7 & 6 & 5 \\ 7 & 10 & 8 & 7 \\ 6 & 8 & 10 & 9 \\ 5 & 7 & 9 & 10 \end{bmatrix} \cdot \begin{bmatrix} X_1 \\ X_2 \\ X_3 \\ X_4 \end{bmatrix} = \begin{bmatrix} 23 \\ 32 \\ 33 \\ 31 \end{bmatrix}.$$

Its solution is $X_1=X_2=X_3=X_4=1$, but if we change the value of the first coefficient in the first equation from 5 to 4,99, we will obtain the following solution:

$X_1=6$, $X_2=-2,17$, $X_3=0,28$ and $X_4=1.32$.

Linear algebra proves that a poorly conditioned matrix has a large value of the *conditioning number*, which is equal to the ratio of the largest eigenvalue to the smallest one.

When solving the problems of the calculation of "almost unstable" structures, we have to deal with the poor conditioning of the governing equations. For example, it is generally known that poorly conditioned stiffness matrices appear often when elements of drastically different rigidities join in a single node of a design model. Let us demonstrate by a simple example how this situation can be interpreted in terms of mechanics [7].

Fig. 1.25 shows a technically stable system with two degrees of freedom and the following stiffness matrix

$$\mathbf{K} = k \begin{bmatrix} 1+\alpha & -1 \\ -1 & 1+\alpha \end{bmatrix}.$$

The eigenvalues of this matrix are $\lambda_1 = \alpha$; $\lambda_2 = 2 + \alpha$, and the conditioning number is

$H = \lambda_2/\lambda_1 = 1 + 2/\alpha$.

If the stiffness of the middle spring is big comparing to the stiffness of the end springs, then parameter α is small, and number H is great, which shows the poor conditioning and possible loss of accuracy during the solution of the system of equations with such a matrix.

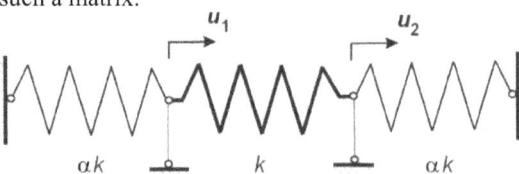

Figure 1.25.

It is easy to notice that the mechanical behavior of the considered structure approaches the behavior of an unstable system. Indeed, the displacement of the middle spring as a rigid body may occur if the resistance of the end springs is negligibly small. The reactions of the latter, due to the given ratio of rigidities, cause insignificant resistance to this deformation and the components of the stress-strain state can be calculated inaccurately when solving the equations due to the rounding errors.

However, if we change the ratio of the rigidities to the opposite (the end springs are stiff and the middle one is compliant), then the stiffness matrix will have the conditioning number $H \approx 1$. Elements of drastically different rigidities meet in the same node again, but the stiffness matrix is well-conditioned and corresponds to an elastic structure (the middle spring) attached to the ground by nearly non-deformable constraints.

> *In those cases when elements of drastically different rigidities join in a single node of a design model, a considerable loss of accuracy of the calculations might occur.*

Conversation 1.7. Prestressing

We have already considered possible self-stressed states of a statically indeterminate system. The concept of self-stress, i.e. *self-balanced stress state of the system existing without the external load*, occurred as a consequence of solving the equilibrium equations [see Formula (1.8)].

However, the real process of creating the self-stressed state was considered in the problems with thermal loading, as well as the problems with erection forces or forces from the displacement of supports. The last two variants of the occurrence of self-balanced forces of the self-stress can be used deliberately in order to *artificially regulate the forces*.

The idea of an active intervention in the performance of a s tructure by prestressing it dates back to distant times. Its use can be seen in structures made of wood, iron, stone, concrete, and more recently in plastic materials. The prestressing was often applied unconsciously, and even now there are a lot of prestressed objects, the preliminary tension of which we do not notice. Take for example wooden barrels tightened with hoops, or umbrellas made of flexible silk material stretched over the spring-loaded ribs.

Nowadays, prestressing has become one of the engineer's tools and it is no longer sufficient to rely solely on empiricism, and a more detailed analysis of prestresses is required.

First of all, you should remember that the number of different linearly independent variants of the self-stressed state of the system is equal to the degree of its static indeterminacy.

Does it mean that the number of methods of creating the prestressing is equal to this number as well? Of course not. For example, the diagram of the self-balanced moments of a two-span once statically indeterminate beam (Fig. 1.26,*a*) can have only one shape (Fig. 1.26,*b*). It can be achieved by lifting the middle support (Fig. 1.26,*c*), lowering any of the edge supports (Fig. 1.26,*d*), setting the bending moments with a jack that acts on the structures, until the middle hinge is embedded (Fig. 1.26,*e*), etc.

Taking into account that the self-stressed states we are interested in can be created by the thermal action, and the latter is equivalent to certain set elongations of the bars, we can imagine that some of the bars are equipped with length regulators which enable to create the prestressing of the system. This technique is also used in practice.

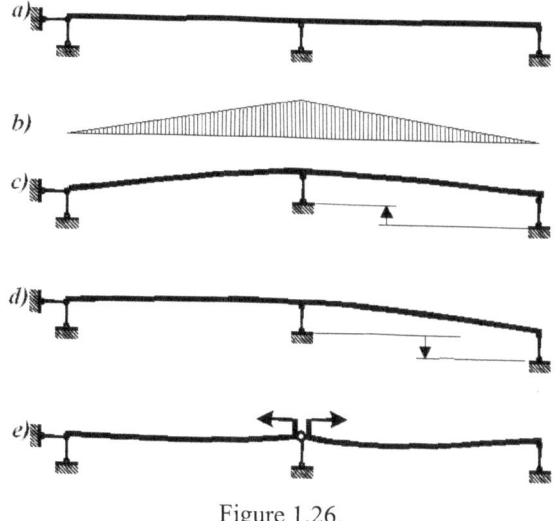

Figure 1.26.

The distribution of the self-stress forces in the above example is unique. If the system is multiple statically indeterminate, this state can be diversified, but without going beyond certain limits. These limits are defined by a certain base set of m linearly independent self-stressed states (m is the degree of static indeterminacy)

$$S^0_{1k}, S^0_{2k}, \ldots, S^0_{rk} \quad (k = 1,\ldots,m). \tag{1.21}$$

All other possible self-stressed states are their linear combinations, i.e. algebraic sums of the base values taken with the numerical coefficients:

$$S^0_j = \sum_{k=1}^{m} c_k S^0_{1k} \quad (j = 1,\ldots,r). \tag{1.22}$$

Selecting the coefficients c_k, we can only obtain different force distributions S^0_j. And if, for example, a certain bar with the number α has the value $S^0_{\alpha k} = 0$ $(k = 1,\ldots,m)$ in all elements of the set (1.21), it is completely impossible to create non-zero prestressing in this bar. All unconditionally necessary bars will be like that.

The easiest way to obtain the set (1.21) is as follows. Redundant constraints are removed from the system as it is done when creating a statically determinate primary system of the force method. Unknown forces are introduced in each removed constraint (in the cut of the element), and the calculation for each of them gives one of the sets of self-balanced forces from the set (1.21).

The removal of redundant constraints transforming a statically indeterminate system into a statically determinate one can be performed in different ways, however, the number of removed constraints will always be the same and equal to the degree of static indeterminacy m.

As an example, let us consider the system shown in Fig. 1.27.

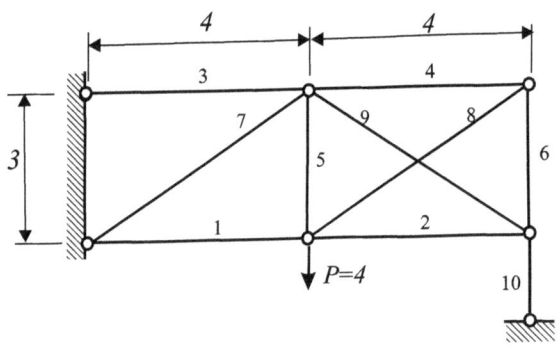

Figure 1.27

The system is twice statically indeterminate and the Table. 1.1 shows two variants of self-stress forces obtained by the above method

Table 1.1

	P	X_1	X_2	P	X_1	X_2
S_1 =	0,000	1,333	0,000	2,667	−0,500	0,000
S_2 =	0,000	0,000	−0,800	2,667	−0,500	−0,800
S_3 =	5,333	−2,667	0,000	0,000	1,000	0,000
S_4 =	0,000	−1,333	−0,800	0,000	0,000	−0,800
S_5 =	4,000	−1,000	−0,600	4,000	0,000	−0,600
S_6 =	0,000	−1,000	−0,600	0,000	0,000	−0,600
S_7 =	−6,667	1,667	1,000	−3,333	−0,633	0,000
S_8 =	0,000	1,667	0,000	0,000	0,000	1,000
S_9 =	0,000	1,000	0,000	−3,333	0,633	1,000
S_{10} =	0,000	0,000	0,000	−2,000	0,310	0,000

In the general case we can imagine different ways of removing redundant constraints when transforming a statically indeterminate system into a statically determinate one. Different self-stress states arise in this case, but all of them can be obtained from each other by linear transformations. For example, a pair of self-stress states (Fig. 1.28,*b,c*) can be easily obtained for a twice statically indeterminate system shown in Fig. 1.28,*a*, and the self-stress state shown in Fig. 1.28,*d*, is obtained as the difference between the self-stress states shown in Fig. 1.28,*b,c*.

CONVERSATIONS ABOUT THE STRUCTURAL MECHANICS 55

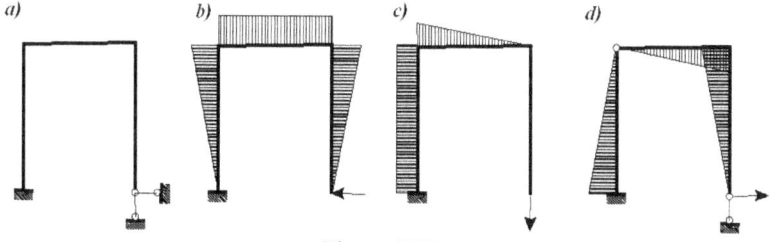

Figure 1.28.

Forces in a statically indeterminate system subjected to a thermal action are only a linear combination of possible self-stressed states. Independent thermal deformations of individual elements of the system are supplemented to the state where the kinematic consistency conditions take place with the help of the deformations caused by the self-stress forces.

If we consider the standard description of the force method when the closure conditions of the cuts introduced in the structure when creating the primary system are satisfied by selecting the values of forces in the "redundant" constraints (values of the self-stress parameters), it becomes clear that the self-stress forces play the main role in providing the kinematic consistency conditions of the system.

Question:

In all the considered examples, the self-stress forces appeared "independently and automatically" due to the loads and other actions applied to the system. Is it possible to create these forces artificially so that they are different from those obtained automatically?

Answer:

There are ways to artificially regulate the stress state of the system, but it can turn out to be only a linear combination of the possible self-stress forces.

The prestressing process itself often deals with the sequence of operations performed when creating the system (a certain order of installing and deleting elements, changing some constraints etc.).

Such operations with the design model reflect the construction process and lead to a new stress-strain state of the system, which can significantly affect the performance of the whole structure [7].

The main idea of the structural prestress is to use this possibility consciously. It was done even in those times when people could rely only on their own intuition (wooden barrels tightened with hoops, a wheel with a heated rim etc.).

A force or kinematic action can be used to create the prestress:
- when the force action is used (jacks, ballast weights, etc.), you can adjust and control the force values, but you can not control the deformation;

- when the kinematic action is used (the displacement of supports, thermal action, etc.), you can adjust and control the displacement values, but you can not control the forces.

The parameters which are not regulated can be calculated or measured, but they can not be changed within the used (force or kinematic) method.

> *You should keep in mind that the force method can be implemented only in the system with a structure different from the final one, when there is freedom of the displacements in the direction of which you want to apply the prestress forces (Fig. 1.29). In particular such forces can be applied at the erection stages when the system is still statically determinate.*
>
> *And vice versa, the kinematic method is implemented in a partially or fully assembled system, when the system is already statically indeterminate.*

Construction stage

There is no constraint - the freedom of the mutual approach of the end nodes is provided

Operating state

Constraint is closed

Figure 1.29

The following main methods of creating the prestress in the system are usually used in practice:

a) Using temporary ballast weights at some erection stages.
b) Displacement of supports by using pads or other similar items.
c) Using special tensioning devices (jack, turnbuckle, etc.).

In the latter case, it is necessary to distinguish between two options of setting the operating conditions of the tensioning device:

1) the value Δ of shortening (elongation) of the device is set (the stroke of a piston in a jack or of a turnbuckle is controlled);

2) the force N which has to appear in the tensioning device is set (the force set by the jack is controlled).

Question:
The prestressed structures are usually used in literature to describe the technology of using the tensioning devices. Can you give real examples of other approaches?

Answer:
The use of the ballast weight can be considered as an elegant technique, when the reinforced concrete roadway slabs of the constructed cantilever bridge were stacked on the cantilevers (Fig. 1.30, *a*) and the unstressed struts were installed in this state (Fig. 1.30,*b*). The ballast slabs were then transferred to the span of the bridge, and the prestress forces appeared in the struts (Fig. 1.30,*c*).

This technique was used in the construction of several city bridges, for example, the Green Bridge in Vilnius (Fig. 1.31).

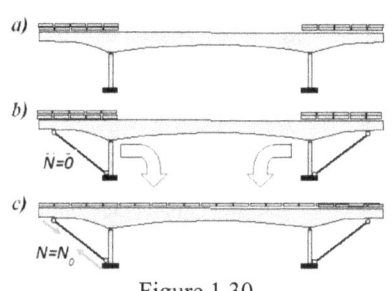

Figure 1.30   Figure 1.31

The technique of the support displacement was used in the construction of two-span crane beams. They were prestressed by lowering the end supports and tightening the bolts in the joint A, and this tightening was performed until the gap of 25 mm was closed (Fig. 1.32).

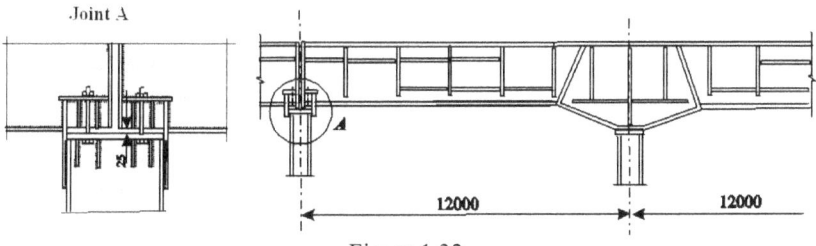

Figure 1.32

Question:
When designing tensile end-plate joints, highly pre-tightened bolts experience tensile forces, but this fact is neglected in all the design instructions. It is proposed to calculate bolts only for a tensile force, and not for a sum of a tightening force and external tension. Is it correct?

Answer:
Yes, it is correct, and in order to illustrate it, let us first consider a tube bar tightened with a bolt (Fig. 1.33,*a*). When there is no load, the tensile force in the bolt N_1^0 is equal to the compressive force in the tube – N_2^0.

If an external tensile force P is applied to the ends of the bolt, then the internal forces in the bolt and the tube are determined from the equilibrium condition of the internal and external forces
$$N_1+N_2=P$$
and the condition of compatibility of the tube and bolt deformations
$$N_1/(E_1A_1) - N_2/(E_2A_2) = \lambda_0.$$
The latter condition expresses the fact that the difference between the absolute elongations of the bolt and the bar is equal to the pre-elongation value of the bolt λ_0. Having solved these equations with respect to N_1 and N_2, we obtain

$$N_1 = \frac{P/(E_2A_2)+\lambda_0 L}{1/(E_1A_1)+1/(E_2A_2)}; \quad N_2 = \frac{P/(E_1A_1)+\lambda_0 L}{1/(E_1A_1)+1/(E_2A_2)}.$$

Here E_1 and A_1 are the elastic modulus and the cross-sectional area of the bolt, and E_2 and A_2 are the elastic modulus and the cross-sectional area of the bar.

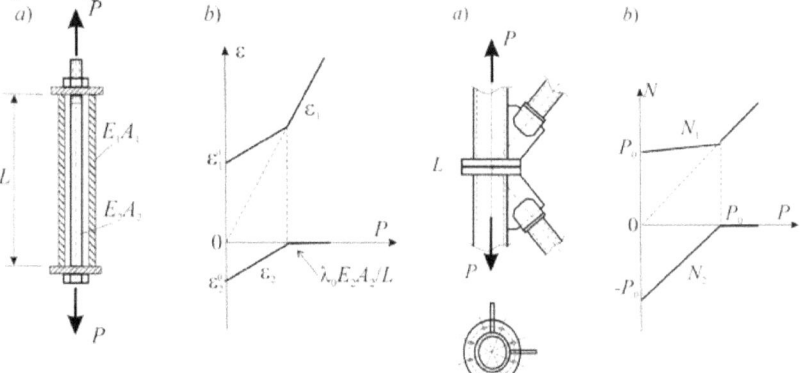

Figure 1.33   Figure 1.34

Fig. 1.33,*b* shows the graphs of the bolt strain $\varepsilon_1 = N_1/(E_1A_1)$, bar strain $\varepsilon_2 = N_2/(E_2A_2)$ vs. the external force value P relationship. These relationships are linear until the internal force in the bar becomes zero.

If the force P keeps increasing, the bar can no longer take the forces which have to be tensile, and the entire force will be transferred to the bolt. Therefore, there are break points in the $\varepsilon_1(P)$ and $\varepsilon_2(P)$ graphs when $P = P_0 = \lambda_0 E_2 A_2 / L$, and when $P > \lambda_0 E_2 A_2 / L$, it is assumed that the force P is taken only by the bolt.

Thus, if the force P is small and does not compensate the prestress, bolt elongations grow slower, and the bar precompression is exhausted (the bar begins to work in tension).

The same situation occurs in prestressed reinforced concrete structures with non-tensile concrete instead of a tube, and reinforcement instead of a bolt, and in end-plate joints (Fig. 1.34,*a*) with end-plates instead of a bar.

In the latter case, the stiffness of the end-plate is considerably greater than that of the bolts, and the total force in the bolts can be determined assuming that (E_2A_2) tends to infinity. It can be seen from the above formulas that the force N_1 is approximately equal to the bolt tightening force P_0 as long as the end-plates are in contact with each other, and afterwards it is equal to P (Fig. 1.34,*b*). In other words, the bolt strength check has to be performed not for the sum $P + P_0$, but for the larger of these two values.

Conversation 1.8. Variational Principles

The foundations of mechanics laid down by Newton are based on consideration of forces. This branch of mechanics, which can be called "vector", bases its analysis on the determination of all forces acting on each element of the system. However, at the same time Leibniz developed mechanics using the "work of a force" concept (force function, potential energy), which refers to the system as a whole. Considering a problem in terms of potential energy helps you get a bird's-eye view of it, when we lose some details, but gain a broad vision.

Newton's approach has the advantage of clarity, while the approach of Leibniz is general and compact. This compactness, though, is achieved by avoiding the consideration of systems not isolated from the environment in terms of the energy exchange (for example, inelastic systems or the case of non-conservative external actions).

The previous sections considered the vector approach, and in this section we will show some elements of an alternative approach to the problems of structural mechanics.

* * *

The concept of elementary virtual work of the points of the system has been introduced above. The elementary actual work is determined in a similar way:

$$dW = \sum_{i=1}^{m} P_i \, du_i \qquad (1.23)$$

Using this value determine the work of forces P_i during a finite displacement of the points of the system as an integral

$$W = \int_{(1)}^{(2)} dW = \int_{(1)}^{(2)} \sum_{i=1}^{m} P_i \, du_i$$

whose limits are given by the coordinates of the points of the system in the initial (1) and final (2) positions.

Let us consider the case of forces that depend only on the positions of the points (nodes) of the system. These forces are called potential if there is a single-valued function

$$\Pi = \Pi\left(x_1, y_1, z_1, \ldots, x_m, y_m, z_m\right)$$

such that the projections on the coordinate axes of the force acting on the point $M_i(x_i, y_i, z_i)$ are equal to the negative partial derivatives of Π with respect to the coordinates of this point:

$$P_{i,x} = -\frac{\partial \Pi}{\partial x_i}, \quad P_{i,y} = -\frac{\partial \Pi}{\partial y_i}, \quad P_{i,z} = -\frac{\partial \Pi}{\partial z_i}. \quad (1.24)$$

It is assumed that the function Π depends only on the coordinates of the points and the time is not included explicitly in its expression; then it follows from (1.24) that it is defined up to an additive constant. This function is called the potential energy.

According to (1.23) and (1.24) the elementary actual work of the potential forces is equal to

$$dW = -\sum_{i=1}^{m} \left(\frac{\partial \Pi}{\partial x_i} dx_i + \frac{\partial \Pi}{\partial y_i} dy_i + \frac{\partial \Pi}{\partial z_i} dz_i \right) = -d\Pi, \quad (1.25)$$

where $d\Pi$ is the total differential of the potential energy.

According to (1.24) and (1.25) the work of the potential forces during a finite displacement is equal to

$$W_{(1)\to(2)} = \int_{(1)}^{(2)} dW = -\int_{(1)}^{(2)} d\Pi = \Pi_{(1)} - \Pi_{(2)}$$

> It follows from this expression that the potential energy is equal to the work that would be done by potential forces on the final path from the considered position of the system to a position where it can be conventionally taken as zero.

If the configuration of the system is defined not by the coordinates of its nodes, but by certain generalized coordinates

$$u_i(x_1, y_1, z_1, \ldots, x_m, y_m, z_m) \quad (i = 1, 2, \ldots, 3m = n),$$

then after the respective transformations the potential energy becomes a function of only the generalized coordinates

$$\Pi = \Pi(u_1, u_2, \ldots, u_n).$$

According to (1.25) the elementary virtual work of the potential forces is equal to

$$dW = -d\Pi = \sum_{i=1}^{n} \frac{\partial \Pi}{\partial u_i} du_i. \quad (1.26)$$

On the other hand, this work must be expressed in terms of generalized forces Q_i, corresponding to generalized displacements du_i, as

$$dW = -\sum_{i=1}^{n} Q_i \, du_i. \quad (1.27)$$

Comparing (1.26) with (1.27), we obtain the expression of generalized forces in terms of the potential energy

$$Q_i = -\frac{\partial \Pi}{\partial u_i} \quad (i = 1, 2, \ldots, n).$$

Let us assume that the generalized forces $Q_1, \ldots, Q_n$ are defined, and they turned out to depend only on the generalized coordinates $u_1, \ldots, u_n$. It follows from the last equations that the forces are potential if the following conditions are satisfied:

$$\frac{\partial Q_i}{\partial u_j} = \frac{-\partial \Pi}{\partial u_i \partial u_j} = \frac{-\partial \Pi}{\partial u_j \partial u_i} = \frac{\partial Q_j}{\partial u_i} \quad (i, j = 1, 2, ..., n).$$

Potential forces have the following important property: their work depends only on the initial and final position of the application point and is in no way related to the path followed to attain the final state. The assertion that the so-called "follower" force has no potential is based on the verification of this property [13].

Figure 1.35 shows three different ways in which the cantilever beam can reach a state defined by a transverse deflection f and an angle of rotation φ of the end section. In case (a) (rotation through an angle φ with a subsequent displacement), the work done by the force P is obviously negative; in case (b) (displacement with a subsequent rotation), it is zero; in case (c) (rotation through an angle − φ, a displacement, and a final rotation through an angle 2φ), the work done is positive.

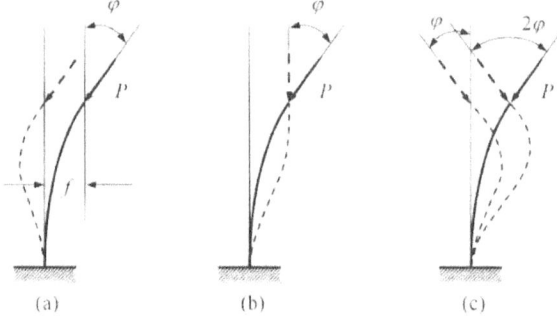

Figure 1.35. Bar with a follower force

The simplest example of potential forces are forces of constant magnitude and direction (for example, the gravity force near the surface of the Earth). The potential energy of the system in the gravity field is defined by the following expression

$$\Pi = \sum_{i=1}^{m} (gm_i) z_i,$$

where z_i is the coordinate of the center of gravity measured along the upward vertical from the Earth's surface. Indeed, the energy Π is equal to the work that would be done by the weight forces at the transition of the points of the system from their considered position to the Earth's surface.

Let us now consider the elastic forces. We will deal here only with the discrete systems with a finite number of degrees of freedom, assuming that a certain number of nodal points are connected to each other and, possibly, to the ground by elastic constraints.

The defining property of a perfectly elastic system is the fact that the elastic reactions occurring during its deformation depend only on the values defining the position of the nodes of the system, but not on their velocities, preceding deformation history, etc. Therefore, it is assumed that the generalized forces of elastic reactions are functions of only generalized coordinates of the system

$$R_i = R_i(u_1,...,u_n). \qquad (1.28)$$

Elastic forces are potential. This statement is based on the property of an elastic body to accumulate potential energy under constant loading and to return it without any loss, when the body under gradual unloading returns to its original natural state, in which its size and shape are restored.

Thus, it is assumed that the functions of the coordinates (1.28) can be given as follows

$$R_i = -\frac{\partial E}{\partial u_i} \quad (i=1,...,n), \qquad (1.29)$$

where E is the potential energy of elastic bodies included in the system.

The relations given above can be derived from (1.29)

$$\frac{\partial R_i}{\partial u_j} = \frac{\partial R_j}{\partial u_i}, \qquad (1.30)$$

and they must be satisfied by potential forces.

It is further assumed that the generalized coordinates are measured from the configuration of the system with non-stressed elastic elements. In other words, elastic reactions disappear when the generalized coordinates become zero:

$$R_i(0,...,0) = 0.$$

The main physical law is Hooke's law which expresses the presence of linear relations between the values defining the stress state in the elastic body, and the values characterizing its deformation (relative elongations and shear).

Although the fulfillment of Hooke's law does not predetermine the linear relationship between the displacements of the nodes of the elastic system and the forces applied to it (between the generalized forces of elastic reactions and generalized coordinates), we will proceed from this hypothesis assuming the fulfillment of linear relations between the forces applied to the elastic system and displacements of its nodes. This gives grounds to assume the dependencies between the elastic forces and the coordinates in the form of linear relations

$$R_i = -\sum_{j=1}^{n} c_{ij} u_j \quad (i=1,...,n), \qquad (1.31)$$

where c_{ij} are constant coefficients the set of which forms a stiffness matrix

$$\begin{Vmatrix} c_{11} & c_{12} & ... & c_{1n} \\ c_{21} & c_{22} & ... & c_{2n} \\ ... & ... & ... & ... \\ c_{n1} & c_{n1} & ... & c_{nn} \end{Vmatrix}.$$

This matrix is symmetric due to the fact that the elastic forces are potential. Indeed, the following relations can be obtained from (1.30) and (1.31)

$$c_{ij} = c_{ji} \quad (i,j=1,...,n).$$

The equations (1.31) are applicable only if the values of the generalized coordinates are sufficiently small. This corresponds to the assumptions that the deformations in the Hooke's law are small and that the elastic system does not allow large changes in size and shape.

Let us now consider the concept which is of great importance in solid mechanics, the function of the *total potential energy* of the deformed body and the load acting on it. The total energy U consists of the potential strain energy of the body (potential of internal forces) E and the energy of external forces (potential of external forces) W=-Π:

$$U = E + \Pi.$$

External forces applied statically to the elastic body and causing a change in the geometry of the body do the work Π during the respective displacements. At the same time, the potential strain energy is accumulated in the elastic body E. Thus, the elastic body is an energy accumulator. This property of the elastic body is widely used in engineering, for example, in the driving springs of a clock, in shock-absorbing springs, etc.

We will assume that an isolated system is considered.

> *It follows from the assumption about the isolation of the system (no energy exchange with the environment) that when the elastic system is under static loading, its total potential energy remains constant and only transforms from potential energy of external forces to potential energy of internal forces.*

Partial derivatives of the expression for the total potential energy of the system are the total forces acting on the nodes of the system (elastic and external), therefore, the equilibrium condition is

$$\frac{\partial U}{\partial u_i} = \frac{\partial E}{\partial u_i} - \frac{\partial \Pi}{\partial u_i} = R_i + P_i = 0 \quad (i = 1, 2, \ldots, n). \quad (1.32)$$

On the other hand, the conditions

$$\frac{\partial U}{\partial u_i} = 0 \quad (i = 1, 2, \ldots, n) \quad (1.33)$$

define the stationary point of the function of the total potential energy U. Stationarity is a necessary but insufficient condition of the function extremum.

The relation (1.33) is the content of the Lagrange variational theorem:

> *If the system is under the action of potential forces, then its position, in which the potential energy reaches an extremum, is the equilibrium position.*

The converse conclusion is incorrect: if there is a balance of forces, then conditions (1.33) are satisfied, but they are insufficient for an extremum.

References

1. *Aleksandrov A.V., Potapov V.D. et al.* Structural Mechanics: In 2 books. Book 1. Statics of Elastic Systems / V.D. Potapov, A.V. Aleksandrov, S.B. Kositsyn, D.B. Dolotkazin.— M.: High School, 2007. Book. 2: Dynamics and Stability of Elastic Systems / A.V. Aleksandrov, V.D Potapov, V.B. Zylev.— M.: High School, 2008.

2. *Bezukhov N.I., Luzhin O.V., Kolkunov N.V.* Stability and Dynamics of Structures: Examples and Problems. — M.: High School, 1987.
3. *Gordeev V.N.* Behavior of Loaded Fabric Shells // Theory of Shells and Plates.— Yerevan, AN ArmSSR, 1964.— p. 391-398.
4. *Darkov A.V., Shaposhnikov N.N.* Structural Mechanics. — M.: High School, 1986.
5. *Kiselev V.A.* Structural Mechanics. - M.: Stroyizdat, 1986.
6. *Kiselev V.A.* Structural Mechanics. Special Course. - M.: Stroyizdat,1980.
7. *Perelmuter A.V., Slivker V.I.* Design Models of Structures and a Possibility of Their Analysis: 4-th ed., revised and enlarged — M.: SCAD SOFT + ASV + DMK Press, 2011.
8. *Rabinovich I.M.* Structural Mechanics. In 2 volumes.
Volume 1. Statically Determinate Systems. - M.: Stroyizdat,1950; Structural Mechanics. Volume 2. Statically Indeterminate Systems. - M.: Stroyizdat, 1954.
9. *Rzhanitsyn A.R.*, Structural Mechanics. - M.: Stroyizdat, 1982.
10. *Feodosiev V.I.*, Ten Talks on Strength of Materials.— M.: Nauka, 1975.— 174 p.
11. *Filin A.P.* Applied Solid Mechanics. In 3 volumes. - M.: Nauka, 1978.
12. *Shulkin Yu.B.* Theory of Elastic Bar Structures. - M.: Nauka, 1984.
13. *Bolotin, V.V.* Nonconservative Problems in the Theory of Elastic Stability - M.: Fizmatgiz, 1961.

Cycle 2

Finite Element Method

CONVERSATIONS ABOUT THE STRUCTURAL MECHANICS 67

This simple idea to divide a body and consider separate areas proved to be extremely fruitful, it surpassed in efficiency many deep and subtle ideas, simply canceled a number of previously recognized methods and made some theoretical beautiful constructs of analysts inapplicable in practice.
M. Reitman, Strength Guarantee.— M. Stroyizdat, 1973 (p. 32)

Conversation 2.1. Idea of the Finite Element Method

Finite element method (FEM) is the main method of modern structural mechanics, which underlies the vast majority of modern software systems. It is designed to perform computer structural analyses and enables to almost completely automate the calculation of bar systems, although, as a rule, requires a much larger number of computational operations than classic methods of structural mechanics.

However, nowadays a large amount of computation is not a serious problem, and therefore FEM became extremely widespread with the introduction of computers in engineering practice. It enables to extend the principles of calculating bar systems to the case of continuous bodies and complex structures, and this is another attractive feature of the FEM.

Many problems of structural mechanics or applied theory of elasticity require solving partial differential equations.

For example, the problem of bending a plate with a thickness h and loaded with a transverse load $p(x,y)$ requires the solution of the Sophie Germain-Lagrange differential equation

$$\frac{\partial^4 w}{\partial x^4} + 2\frac{\partial^4 w}{\partial x^2 \partial y^2} + \frac{\partial^4 w}{\partial y^4} = \frac{p(x,y)}{D},$$

where the deflection function $w(x,y)$ is unknown, and D denotes cylindrical rigidity $D = Eh^2 / \left[12(1-v^2)\right]$.

As a rule, the exact mathematical solution of such problems is not known and we can consider only a certain variant of the search for an approximate solution. The solution is usually determined in a certain form, which predefines the answer in the form of a function specified *up to a relatively small number of parameters*. For example, in the case of a rectangular plate with the sides a and b it is assumed in advance that the deflections are represented as a sinusoidal product

$$w = f \sin\frac{\pi x}{a} \sin\frac{\pi y}{b}$$

and the characteristic height f has to be determined (one unknown parameter).

However, guessing the form of an unknown function is a very difficult task, especially if we take into account that such a function has to be suitable for all points in the area occupied by the calculated structure and, in addition, satisfy certain conditions on the boundary of the area (take, for example, zero values and have a zero derivative). It is much easier to guess the type of such a function for a small part of the area. Moreover, it is due to the smallness of such a part that we can afford a certain freedom of choice. For example, it is difficult to guess the shape of a certain curve a very flexible steel tape will take, but it is almost obvious that by replacing its true shape with a broken line with small segments, we can hope to find an approximate representation of the shape of this curve.

We have come very close to the idea of the finite element method, in particular, to one of the basic principles of this method:

dividing the solution search area into small sections (finite elements), we can preset the form of the unknown function inside this section without risking to make a big mistake for solving the problem as a whole.

So the idea of the finite element method can be represented as follows. Suppose that a certain considered elastic body occupies an area Ω (Fig. 2.1,*a*). The considered unknown value (for example, displacements of body points, or stresses, or something else) varies continuously throughout the body. When solving a problem by the finite element method, this value is approximately represented by its values in the finite number of the selected body points (nodes). It is these unknown values that have to be determined. Then the area Ω is divided into a finite number of parts (finite elements), so that the boundaries of the finite elements pass through the nodes, and the entire area is covered by finite elements. It is believed that the finite elements interact with each other only at the nodes and the considered unknown value is common for the points contacting with the node of all elements that are connected to this node (for *the star of elements of this node*).

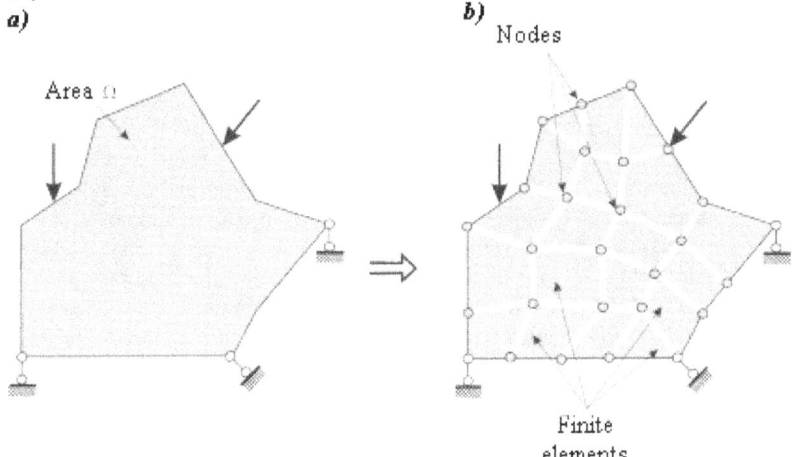

Figure 2.1.

Let us consider an arbitrarily loaded body. Divide it into separate parts using a mesh of secant surfaces. An example of such meshing for a two-dimensional body is shown in Fig. 2.1,*b*. The resulting subareas have small but finite (not infinitesimal) dimensions, therefore they are called "finite elements".

Thus, a continuous body is represented as a set of finite elements. Their properties are then considered independently. Certain points (nodes) are selected on the boundaries between the finite elements, the displacements of which are taken as the main unknowns[7].

There is an apparent analogy with the displacement method for bar systems, where the nodal displacements are also taken as the main unknowns. However, in the case of continuous bodies, a number of difficulties arise, which can be overcome only by introducing a number of additional hypotheses.

a) First of all, the question arises of how to find the displacements (hence deformations and stresses) inside each finite element, knowing the displacements of its nodes. It should be noted that in the case of bar systems, the calculation is based on the use of the technical theory of tension, bending and torsion of the beam, which allows to express the displacements and stresses in any beam section in terms of nodal displacements. This problem can be solved only approximately for a two-dimensional (plate) or three-dimensional (array) continuous body, for example, using certain assumptions about the nature of the displacement field in the element.

It is necessary to select a certain set of approximating functions that allow obtaining an approximate representation of the displacement field inside the finite element by known nodal displacements. Usually, when generating a finite-element solution, the set of local functions defining the displacement field within the finite element is specified so that one of the nodal displacements or rotations is related to each local function. Then the displacement field will be accurately defined if all the displacements in all the nodes adjacent to the element are given.

It is especially convenient to select such approximating functions that take a unit value in a certain node and a zero value in all other nodes of the element. They are commonly referred to as *shape functions* in the finite element method. When selecting the shape functions, the assumption of smallness of the finite element is of considerable help, since in this case we can hope[8] that the error from the approximate description of the displacement field is small and that with a decrease in the size of the finite elements, the approximation error will decrease as well. If, for example, the finite elements are triangular and the unknown displacements are determined in its vertices (Fig. 2.2, *a*), then we can imagine that the displacement field (the sum of these planes) within the finite element is also a plane (Fig. 2.2, *b*), and, therefore, the unknown distribution of displacements in the whole body is approximated by a certain polyhedron that is close to the desired distribution of displacements.

---

[7] Here we consider the solution in displacements. There is a kind of finite element method, where the forces of interaction between elements are taken as the main unknowns; a mixed formulation is also possible

[8] This hope can fail

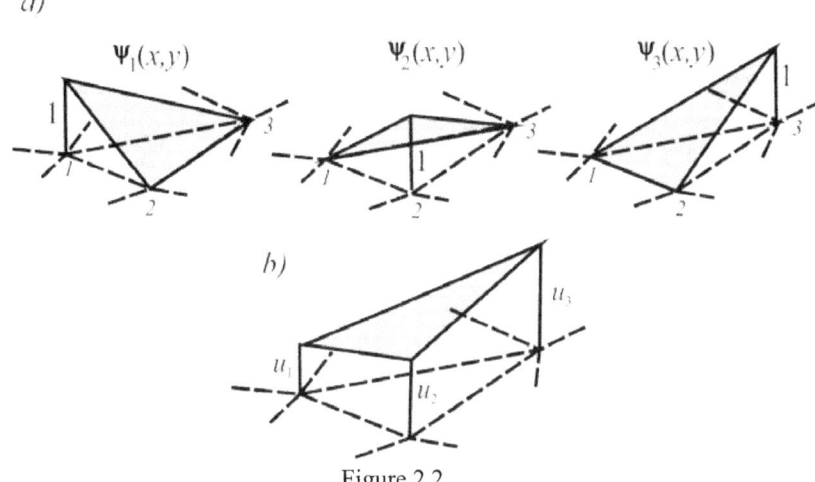

Figure 2.2.

The selection of the shape functions is one of the most important steps in the finite element method, this choice largely determines the accuracy of the solution.

> *Therefore, a finite element is not just a small area of the body, but an area of the body together with the approximating functions given in it.*

b) The second problem arises when formulating the conditions for combining finite elements into a single system. In the calculation of bar systems, it was done by writing equilibrium equations for nodal points, where the elements are connected to each other. In a continuous body the number of connection points between elements is infinitely large. Assuming the distribution of displacements within each element, we thus define the stress distribution at all points of the interelement boundary. Stresses determined independently for each element do not coincide at the interfaces of the adjacent elements in the general case. Therefore, it is impossible to provide the precise fulfillment of the equilibrium conditions on the entire interface.

> *Therefore, in the finite element method, the stresses acting along the boundary of each element can be conditionally replaced by certain equivalent forces reduced to the nodes; and the equilibrium equations are written for the nodes to which the equivalent forces are applied.*

The equivalent nodal forces are determined from the condition that the work done by them for nodal displacements is equal to the work of the actual stresses for the displacements of the points of the element boundary surface.

c) Another problem arises when considering the loading of the elastic body by distributed surface and body forces. These forces can also be taken into account by replacing them with energetically equivalent external nodal forces.

After introducing these simplifications, the body can be considered as a discrete system, i.e. as a set of elements interconnected in nodal points. A structure can be divided into subareas and approximating functions can be selected for each of them in different ways. The geometry of the body should be taken into account and a good approximation of displacements, as well as deformations and stresses expressed in terms of displacements should be provided for the whole body.

Question:

Could you please tell us more about the shape functions and give a simple example?

Answer:

As an example, let us consider the solution of the plane problem of the theory of elasticity using quadrangular finite elements. Each finite element is defined by a set of its four nodes.

In the case of a plane problem the solution is two displacement fields $u(x, y)$ and $v(x, y)$, therefore, there are two displacement components U_i and V_i in each node of the finite element model which are the unknown degrees of freedom.

We will use the linear interpolation of displacements U and V given in four nodes:

$$u(x,y) = \sum_{i=1}^{4} f_i(x,y) U_i, \quad v(x,y) = \sum_{i=1}^{4} f_i(x,y) V_i,$$

where $f_i(x, y)$ are interpolating functions, or the shape functions of the element.

These functions have a number of special properties. One of the main properties is locality, which means that these functions are specified only within this element.

Let us introduce a natural local coordinate system for an element corresponding to the geometry of the given element type. The natural coordinate system of the plane quadrangular element is the coordinate system (ξ, η) shown in Fig. 2.3.a.

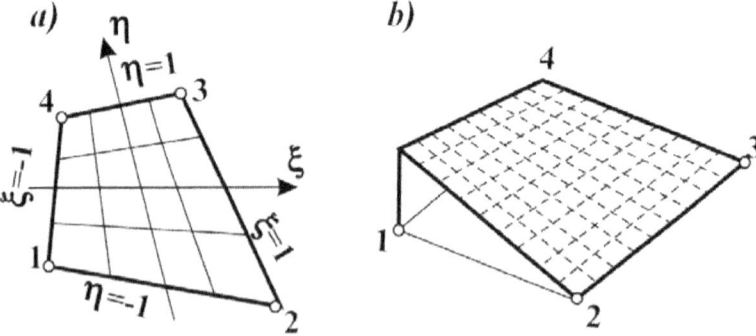

Figure 2.3

The shape functions of the element are expressed by the following relations in terms of local natural coordinates:

$$f_1(\xi,\eta) = 0,25(1-\xi)(1-\eta), \quad f_2(\xi,\eta) = 0,25(1+\xi)(1-\eta),$$
$$f_3(\xi,\eta) = 0,25(1+\xi)(1+\eta), \quad f_4(\xi,\eta) = 0,25(1-\xi)(1+\eta).$$

These functions vary linearly along the coordinate lines ξ = const, η = const. The function $f_i(\xi,\eta)$ is equal to one in the node i and to zero in all other nodes. However, they are not linear polynomials and they are called bilinear. One of the shape functions is shown in the graphical form in the Fig. 2.3.b.

Question:
As I understand it, the solution of the problem by the finite element method is obtained in displacements. However, in the previous cycle this approach was associated with the stiffness matrix. How is the transition from the shape functions to the stiffness matrix performed?

Answer:
The easiest way to show this is by starting from the equilibrium conditions (1.33), i.e. based on the expression for the total energy of the system. Without delving into the general theory, let us consider an example of generating a stiffness matrix of the simplest bar element, while considering the plane case (Fig. 2.4,a).

If only bending deformations are taken into account, the total potential energy of the system consisting of only one bar will be represented as

$$U = E + \Pi = \frac{1}{2}\int_0^L EI\vartheta^2 dx - \sum_{i=1}^{4} P_i u_i,$$

where ϑ is the curvature of the deformed bar axis.

The equation describing the curved bar axis is expressed in terms of the end displacements with the help of the shape functions $\psi_i(x)$, which are essentially the displacements of the points of the bar axis at $u_i=1$, $u_j=0$ ($i \neq j$). Then the axis equation is given as a sum

$$u(x) = \sum_{i=1}^{4} \psi_i(x) \cdot u_i,$$

and the curvature as

$$\vartheta(x) = u''(x) = \sum_{i=1}^{4} \psi_i''(x) u_i.$$

The stationarity condition for the total potential energy:

$$\frac{\partial U}{\partial u_i} = \frac{1}{2}\int_0^L EI\vartheta \frac{\partial \vartheta}{\partial u_i} dx - P_i = 0 \quad (i = 1,...,4).$$

If we substitute the expression for the curvature, we obtain

$$\frac{\partial U}{\partial u_i} = \frac{1}{2}\int_0^L EI\left(\sum_{j=1}^{4}\psi_j''(x)\,u_j\right)\psi_i''\cdot dx - P_i =$$

$$= \frac{1}{2}\sum_{j=1}^{4}\left(\int_0^L EI\cdot \psi_i''(x)\cdot\psi_j''(x)\cdot dx\right)u_j - P_i = 0 \quad (i=1,\ldots,4).$$

The solution of these equations defines the shape of the curved bar axis, and, therefore, the set of internal forces: bending moments and shear forces.

Let us give the shape functions in the form of Hermite polynomials (Fig. 2.4.*b*):

$$\psi_1(x) = 1 - 3\left(\frac{x}{L}\right)^2 + 2\left(\frac{x}{L}\right)^3; \quad \psi_3(x) = x\left(1-\frac{x}{L}\right)^2;$$

$$\psi_2(x) = 3\left(\frac{x}{L}\right)^2 - 2\left(\frac{x}{L}\right)^3; \quad \psi_4(x) = \frac{x^2}{L}\left(\frac{x}{L}-1\right).$$

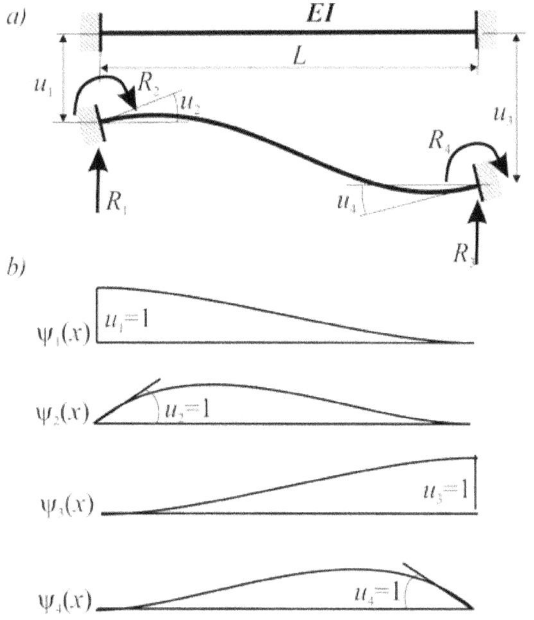

Figure 2.4

The elements of the stiffness matrix of the bar element are determined as

$$r_{ij} = \frac{\partial^2 U}{\partial u_i\,\partial u_j} = \int_0^L EI(x)\psi_i''(x)\psi_j''(x)dx.$$

Then, after the substitutions and integration, we obtain

$$\left[\left[r_{ij}\right]\right] = \frac{2EI}{L^3}\begin{bmatrix} 6 & 3L & -6 & 3L \\ 3L & 2L^2 & -3L & L^2 \\ -6 & -3L & 6 & -3L \\ 3L & L^2 & -3L & 2L^2 \end{bmatrix}.$$

The stiffness matrices for the finite elements of the other type are determined in a similar way. The shape functions are obviously selected by the software developers, and the practicing engineers only use the results. However, in order to perform a conscious analysis of these results, engineers should know which shape functions are used by the program, and if there are competing options in the finite element library, they should choose the most suitable one for a certain problem.

Question:

Is it possible to obtain the exact solution of the problem with the help of the FEM?

Answer:

Yes, if the functions determining the exact (corresponding to the equations of the theory of elasticity or the strength of materials) distribution of displacements within a finite element on the basis of the known nodal displacements are used as the shape functions. It can be done only for bar finite elements, but not always.

In particular, the commonly used cubic relationships (*Hermite polynomials*) are the exact solutions for the bar, but only in static problems and without the consideration of the elastic subgrade. Only an approximate representation of the natural modes can be obtained with the help of these polynomials, and in the case of two-dimensional and three-dimensional problems we simply do not know any exact solutions that could play the role of shape functions.

The principle of superimposing a grid of nodes on the space of the considered structure can be illustrated by a comparison with a raster image, when its quality is defined by the number of pixels per unit length or area. If a rough image is satisfactory (the considered result of the analysis), the number of pixels (nodes) can be taken as minimal. In the case of a detailed study of the result of the static analysis (detailed examination of the image), the number of nodes (pixels of the image) should be increased to the required level.

An image with a small number of pixels (one pixel in an absolute minimum) can barely be called satisfactory. This image can correspond to any original.

However, in the case of the finite elements with a precise description of the approximating functions (for example, a spatial bar) the application of one finite element for the approximation of one structural element is entirely possible, provided that there is no interaction of this structural element with other structures at the intermediate points.

It should be noted that in the structural mechanics of bar systems, an exact solution for a bar enables to take displacements and rotation angles only in the frame nodes as the unknowns of the displacement method, and this provides the basis for a more than dubious concept of the degree of kinematic indeterminacy of a system. In reality, nothing prevents us from creating additional nodes in other parts of the frame, i.e. there can be any degree of kinematic indeterminacy (unlike the degree of static indeterminacy). It depends only on what we consider to be a studied element of the primary system of the displacement method.

Question:
What is the relationship between the displacement and stress fields obtained by the finite element method?

Answer:
In the classic FEM based on the solution in displacements the stress field is obtained from the deformation field, which in turn is determined by differentiating the displacement field.

This differentiation makes the solution of the problem less accurate with respect to stresses, which can be demonstrated as follows. Suppose, for example, the finite elements are triangular, and the linear functions are used as the shape functions. Then the unknown displacement function will appear in the form of a polyhedron with planar faces and vertices (meshing nodes) located near the desired displacement function (Fig. 2.5.a).

Note that the nodal displacements belong simultaneously to all triangular finite elements coming into one node, i.e. the compatibility of displacements in the nodes of the finite element mesh is provided. But since the shape functions are linear, the compatibility in the pair of nodes means that the displacements coincide in all points of the inter-element boundary, which is a straight line segment between the considered pair of nodes.

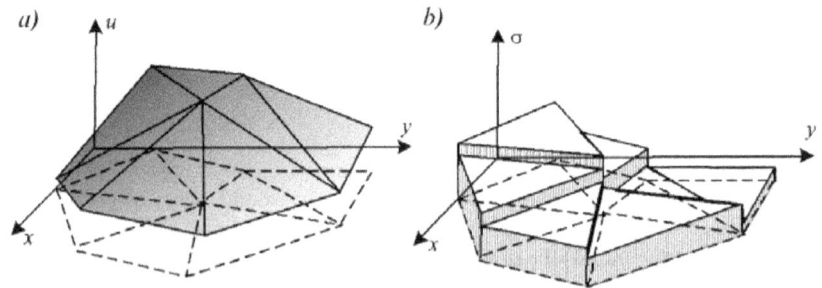

Figure 2.5

However, deformations (and, consequently, stresses) are defined by the first derivatives of displacements, and in the considered case of linear shape functions they, as derivatives of displacements, will be equal to the constants inside the element, and these constants do not have to coincide for the adjacent elements. Therefore, stresses will have discontinuities along the line between the adjacent finite elements, and the spatial stress diagram will be stepped (Fig. 2.5.b).

Conversation 2.2: Boundary Conditions

Constraints are important characteristics of the FEM design model. Obviously not all the unknown displacements of the nodes of the system are independent; some of them are predefined by boundary conditions or, say, symmetry conditions. There can also be other, more complex, relationships between the components of the vector of unknown displacements describing the features of the structural behavior dealing with the limitations caused by the constraints.

The constraint equations in linear systems are mathematically written in the form of linear homogeneous equations

$$\sum_{j=1}^{n} c_{ij} \Delta_j = 0 \quad (i = 1,...,p),$$

where Δ_j are the displacements of the nodes of the system, c_{ij} are the coefficients, p is the number of constraints. The above equation indicates the relationship between individual displacements and usually refers to *internal constraints*. For example, if the constraint prohibits the mutual change in the distance between the nodes 1 and 13 along the X axis, then we will have the following condition $\Delta_{1,x} - \Delta_{13,x} = 0$, and if the displacement of the 16th node at an angle of 45° to the X and Y axes is prohibited, then the respective expression will be as follows $(\sqrt{2}/2)\Delta_{16,x} + (\sqrt{2}/2)\Delta_{16,y} = 0$.

The simplest variant of such equations is the prohibition of certain displacements

$$\Delta_j = 0,$$

where the index j takes a set of values. This variant of constraints describes the connection of the system to the "ground", i.e. refers to the *external constraints* of the structure and describes its boundary conditions.

In the considered case of an external constraint we are dealing with fixed constraints, which is why the right-hand side of the equation is zero. If the external actions applied to the system cause a certain forced displacement of the constraint (the case of the specified displacement), then the right-hand side should include the value of this forced displacement.

It should be emphasized that the specified displacement is implemented only as a displacement of a constraint, the displacements of the free nodes obey the game of forces in the system and do not have to be equal to the externally specified value.

The considered limitations imposed by the constraints on the displacements of the system Δ_j are provided by certain material bodies or devices which are actually present in the system, and the fact of their existence depends neither on the wish of the designer, nor on the variant of the load acting on the structure. Therefore, the following phrase from [3, p.106] can seem extremely confusing "If you have to perform a calculation for the given displacement in one loading, and the respective nodal displacement is present in other loadings (i.e. there is no constraint in this direction), it is necessary to use two different matrices K (we are talking about stiffness matrices — *A.P.*)»

The fixed internal constraint can be considered as a rigid body included in the structure. From a certain point of view, it can be treated as a specific type of a finite element. Its relationship to finite elements can be noticed at least from the fact that the rigid body unites nodes attached to it. Roughly, a rigid body can be considered as a limiting case of a finite element as the rigidity properties of this element approach the infinity.

The effect of an infinitely rigid body is often described with the help of merged displacements of different nodes of the model, i.e. forcing the displacements of one node to be equal to those of the other. This method is usually used to neglect some deformations of the system. For example, if you merge horizontal displacements of nodes at the beam-to-column joints of a single-storey frame, this action will be equivalent to using the hypothesis of a girder rigid with respect to tension/compression.

However, not all properties of a rigid body can be described by merged displacements. The compliance of floor slabs in a multi-storey frame can be often neglected, treating them as rigid disks. If all horizontal displacement components of all nodes of each floor are merged in such a model, the torsion of the floor slabs causing different displacements at different points of the slab will become impossible.

In conclusion, it should be noted that the considered structure is always a part of a more general system, and by taking a structure from its environment we either idealize its effect in the form of an absolute prohibition of certain types of displacements (connection of the system to the "ground"), or describe this effect in the form of an external load on the system. This load can be specified explicitly or it can be given as a reaction of some elastic devices (springs) connecting the structure to the ground. In the latter case, it is said that elastic constraints are imposed on nodal displacements (constraints of finite rigidity). It refers to the elements of the system lying on the elastic subgrade the stiffness of which is characterized by the subsoil parameters.

Constraints of finite rigidity are elastic elements of the system the same as other elastic elements (bars, plates etc.). Using the concept of a constraint of finite rigidity we avoid a detailed description of the elastic devices creating these constraints. In other words, ***it is not the geometric image that is modeled, but the function of such a device.***

Question:

How small can a finite element be? In structural mechanics a bar was defined as an object with the length much greater than its cross-sectional dimensions. The same applied to plates and shells.

Answer:
Indeed, it might seem that there is an evident violation of the accepted definitions of a bar, plate or shell. In fact, there is no violation here, and the assumption of sufficient bar length or small shell thickness was necessary only to justify the form of the respective differential equation.

By the way, an infinitesimal element was considered when deriving this differential equation, and this fact for some reason does not bother the designer. As for the method of solving the resulting differential equation, when a sufficiently fine division of the bar is used (i.e., the integration interval) into sections, this does not affect the form of the equation in any way.

You should keep in mind that the representation of a design model of a structure in the form of an ensemble of finite elements does not correspond to "real modeling" when a structure is assembled from a set of small plates, bars, etc. The finite element is not an actual plate or bar, but a certain image of a plate or bar describing its geometric shape and having a set of functions approximating the deformed state within an element by the displacements of its nodes. The analyzed structure should have the properties of a bar, plate or shell, but not the finite elements it is divided into.

Question:

When a model is divided into small finite elements some programs give a solution with an error greater than in the case of a coarser meshing. Isn't there a violation of the assumption of small thickness?

Answer:
The problem is not in the mentioned violation of the assumption of small thickness, but in the obtained poor conditioning. A cantilever beam loaded with a force at its free end can serve as a good example for explaining this effect.

The beam bends along a smooth curve resembling the first natural bending mode, while the stiffness characteristic of the beam is proportional to the value $G = EJ/L^3$. Errors in the calculated deflections can give the bending line an oscillatory character close to the highest natural bending mode, while the stiffness parameter is proportional to $K = EJ/(L/n)^3$, where n is the number of half-waves or the number of finite elements along the length of the beam.

The conditioning number of the stiffness matrix χ, which is equal to the ratio of the extreme eigenvalues, roughly corresponds to the ratio G/K and has the order $\chi \sim 1/n^3$, which gives $\chi \sim 10^5$ for the number of elements $n = 50$.

The nature of the accumulated error is evidenced by the results of the following numerical experiment: let us consider a 10-meter-long cantilever loaded by the force of 1 ton at its free end. A moment in the clamped end should be equal to 10 tm. If you divide a bar into 2000 elements, you will obtain a moment of 10,001 tm, and if you divide a bar into 8000 elements, you will obtain a moment of 9,619 tm. To make sure that the problem is not in the short element, let us consider an 8000-meter-long cantilever divided into 8000 elements, and we will obtain a moment of 7187,6 tm instead of 8000 tm.

It should be noted that the change in the used units of measurement can lead to the change in the conditioning number of the system of governing equations and to the loss of accuracy in the case when this change increases the conditioning number. It would seem that the scaling that occurs when replacing meters by millimeters, should not affect the calculation. However, the thing is that in the case of such replacement the dimensions of the rotation angles (radians) remain unchanged, therefore, for example, the components of the stiffness matrix EA/L of the bar elements corresponding to the linear displacements, and $6EJ/L^2$, corresponding to the rotation angles, vary to different extents, which leads to other relationships between the maximum and minimum eigenvalues of the matrix, i.e., to a change in the conditioning number.

Conversation 2.3: Meshing Parameters. FEM Convergence

The most important stages of the finite element analysis are the division into elements and the selection of functions approximating the displacement field. A certain adjustment of the displacement fields of individual elements is required, which is achieved by selecting the respective shape functions.

The simplest and most widespread method of such adjustment is the use of the so-called *conformal elements*. The shape functions of conformal elements are such that at equal nodal displacements of adjacent elements all displacements coincide at their interelement boundary, as well as those derivatives of displacements in spatial coordinates which are included in the expression for potential energy.

One of the most important properties of a finite element model is the maximum diameter of the elements

$$h = \max_{e} \left(\sup_{x,y \in \Omega_e} |x-y| \right),$$

depending on which the errors of the method are often estimated. In other words, h is a minimum diameter of a sphere which can be described around any finite element of the design model (Fig. 2.6). Moreover, it is usually assumed that in the case of an infinite reduction in diameter, i.e. when $h \to 0$, the following regularity conditions are met — a sphere with a radius $\rho \leq Ch$ can be embedded into every finite element, where the constant C does not depend on h. This prevents the use of the so-called "*needle*" elements (too elongated rectangles, triangles with very small angles, etc.).

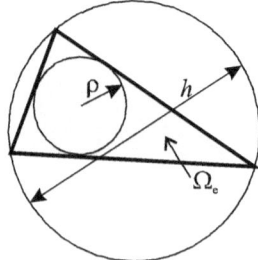

Figure 2.6

Such "irregular" elements can greatly distort the results of the finite element analysis. Even a small error in the displacements calculated for such elements leads to large errors in the angles and curvature (and they are proportional to the bending moments), which is illustrated by Fig. 2.7, where a small error in the deflection ε even changed the sign of the curvature.

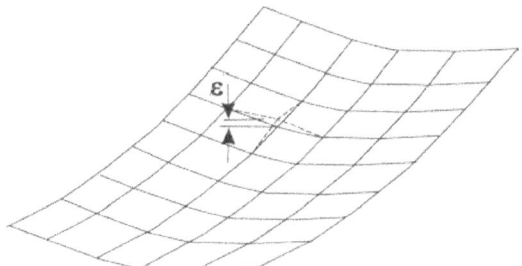

Figure 2.7

The approximating functions in FEM are usually polynomial or piecewise polynomial (subdomain method), although there are also elements with fractional-rational (so-called isoparametric elements), trigonometric, logarithmic and other approximations of the displacement field. The selection of the degrees of freedom of the element and the corresponding approximating functions completely defines the rate of convergence and the FEM error estimate.

If we fix all parameters of a finite element design model, except for the size of the finite elements h, we can imagine that by changing this size, we will obtain a sequence of the approximate solutions of the problem $\mathbf{u}_h$. When talking about the convergence of FEM, we mean that this sequence tends to an exact solution of the problem $\mathbf{u}^*$, when $h \to 0$.

Intuitively, it seems obvious that the denser the finite element mesh, the higher the accuracy of the resulting solution. In fact, this convergence of the approximate solution to the exact one takes place only when finite elements that satisfy certain requirements are used, which are considered in more serious books (see, for example, [6], [7]).

> *Every elastic body has an infinitely large number of degrees of freedom. The limitation of the number of degrees of freedom by a set of nodal displacements reduces the deformation freedom, which is equivalent to the introduction of additional constraints, and this results in a stiffness value exceeding the true one. The displacements obtained by the finite element method in its considered form will, on average, be less than their exact values.*

The finer the mesh the greater the number of nodal displacements (i.e. the number of degrees of freedom of the body). It is important to establish the conditions accompanied by an improvement in the solution, i.e. its convergence to the exact one.

It is proved that the convergence is provided if each displacement component can be represented within a finite element by a polynomial *not lower than the first degree*. This requirement is sometimes called the *completeness condition of a finite element*.

> *The completeness condition can be formulated as follows. An element is assumed to be complete if, firstly, its **displacements as a rigid body** are included in the approximating functions, and, secondly, if a **uniform** (i.e. not depending on the coordinates) strain state with arbitrary deformation components can exist in the element.*

Let us explain these conditions in more detail. Suppose that the nodes of the finite element have displacements corresponding to its displacement in space as a rigid body. If in this case the deformations found by the elasticity theory formulas turn out to be zero, this means that the rigid displacements are accurately represented in the used approximating functions.

The second requirement is based on the following considerations. With a decrease in the size of the finite elements, the changes in the deformations within each of them will become less and less significant in comparison with the deformations themselves, i.e., the strain state will approach the uniform one. In order to obtain a convergent solution, the approximating functions should allow to produce such a limit state.

Let us now consider the inconsistent elements. The convergence of the solution to the exact one takes place in this case as well if the terms creating the inconsistency disappear in the approximating functions in the limit (i.e., at the mesh refinement). Consequently, convergence will be provided if inconsistent finite elements are able to produce the linear displacement field and turn out to be consistent in the limit.

> *A stricter requirement is usually used, according to which the continuity of the body must be ensured under the conditions of a linear displacement field for any dimensions of the element, and not only in the limit.*

The following consideration should be taken into account. If the elements are inconsistent, certain displacements which do not exist in the continual design model may occur along their borders (for example, mutual rotation angles of plates), which correspond to the absence of certain constraints.

As the number of the finite elements increases while their size decreases, the total number of the degrees of freedom of the structure increases, and, hence, the effect of the imposed nodal constraints decreases. This process, provided that certain conditions are met, ensures the convergence of the method for the consistent finite elements. On the other hand, this process leads to the reduction of the mutual displacements at the boundaries between inconsistent elements, and this fact can be treated as the re-imposition of the previously removed constraints. Consequently, the convergence of inconsistent elements can take place only in cases when a positive tendency of overcoming imposed constraints prevails over a negative tendency of imposing constraints on the boundaries between elements.

It should be noted, that the absence (removal) of constraints at the interelement boundaries of the inconsistent elements does not allow to claim that the convergence of the solution at the mesh refinement has a monotonous character and the above statement, that the displacements obtained by the finite element method will be on average less than their exact values, loses its validity. While in the case of consistent elements, the displacements only increased at the mesh refinement, monotonously approaching the exact solution from below, in the case of the inconsistent elements there can be solutions either with a lack or with an excess, i.e., an approach to an exact solution from both sides.

Question:
It is clear that the lack of convergence casts doubt on the results of the finite element analysis. Does it mean that if the convergence is proved, the results of the calculation are reliable?

Answer:
It should be taken into account that the known theoretical estimates of the convergence rate are oriented at the determination of the asymptotic properties of the solution, while a practical designer is interested in the accuracy of an approximate solution obtained on a particular finite element mesh.

Of course, in most cases the asymptotic convergence is accompanied by an appropriate "practical convergence". The latter term will mean the possibility of obtaining an acceptable accuracy with a comparatively rough meshing. However, this rule has its exceptions too.

> *You should also keep in mind, that the theoretical estimates of the convergence rate are based on certain worst assumptions about the form of the displacement field which are not necessarily true for the specific problem.*
>
> *Moreover, a chain of increasing inequalities is usually used when proving the convergence theorem, and, finally, the estimates of the convergence rate contain an unknown constant. Therefore, the analysis of a sequence of solutions on refined finite element meshes is often used in practice, and the decision on the acceptability of the adopted mesh is made based on the results of this comparison.*

An example of this analysis is given in Fig. 2.8 showing four variants of the finite element meshing of a square plate clamped along the contour. The plate is loaded with a uniformly distributed load $q = 50$ kN/m^2, the elastic modulus of the plate material is $E=880$ kN/cm^2, the Poisson's ratio is assumed to be zero.

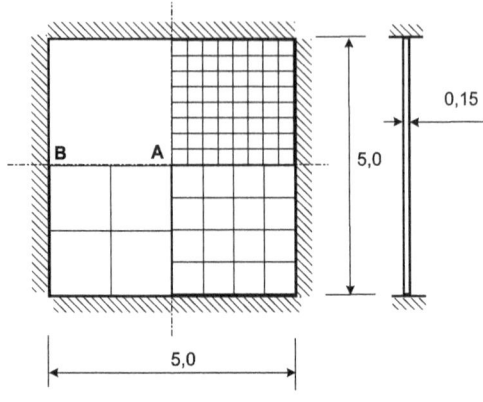

Figure 2.8

The change in the calculation results for meshes of different density is given in the Table 2.1. It can be seen that different results stabilize at different rate, and if an 8×8 mesh is sufficient for deflections, a denser mesh is required for the components of internal forces.

Table 2.1

Result	Mesh 4×4	Mesh 8×8	Mesh 16×16	Exact solution
Deflection at the point A, [mm]	17,25	16,34	16,07	16,00
Moment at the point A, [tm/m]	26,46	23,41	22,69	22,01
Moment at the point B, [tm/m]	59,20	63,72	64,95	64,43
Shear force at the point B, [t/m]	66,63	88,60	100,12	111,61

Certainly, it is hardly reasonable to solve a whole big problem on gradually refined meshes, but this analysis obviously makes sense for characteristic fragments of a design model. The empirical fact of the solution stability at the mesh refinement is a rather convincing argument "pro" this approach.

Question:
If the convergence is proved and confirmed, can all the results be trusted with the same degree of certainty?

Answer:
A satisfactory practical convergence of displacements does not necessarily imply a good convergence of internal forces or stresses the designer is interested in. Those are determined by the differentiation of the displacements, and the differentiation is an incorrect operation in the sense that a slight variation of a function value may cause a substantial variation of the function derivative.

Indeed, suppose a certain function $y=f(x)$ is determined with an error δ. We assume that this error is small, i.e. that the value $y_1=f(x_1)$ at a point x_1 is approximately equal to $y_1 \pm \delta$. If we determine the derivative numerically, taking

$$f'(x_1) \cong [f(y_2) - f(y_1)] / (x_2 - x_1) = \Delta y / \Delta x,$$

then it is not difficult to see that $f'(x_1) = \Delta y / \Delta x \pm 2\delta / \Delta x$.

If the difference Δy is small, the relative error of the derivative $\varepsilon = 2\delta/\Delta y$ can turn out to be quite considerable. And this happens with each differentiation, for example, three times when determining shear forces (see Table 2.1 again). The refinement of the finite element mesh might not help the solution of the problem, because not only does the value of the initial error δ decrease, but the nodal values of the function converge (Δy decreases) and, therefore, the relative error can increase. The data on asymptotic convergence are important for the assessment of the possible appearance of the effects of this kind.

Question:
What is the practical significance of the convergence of a finite-element solution to an exact result?

Answer:
The data on the values of the convergence parameter enable to assign an approximate density of the finite element mesh on the basis of the following peculiar considerations [2, p.55]:

"...let us just note that the convergence takes place assuming some natural limitations of initial data and the meshing of the area are satisfied, and the error of the determination of stresses/strains is of the order $C(h/L)$, where C denotes a constant depending on the shape of the area; h is the mesh spacing; L is a characteristic size of the area. This estimate should guide the definition of the mesh spacing, depending on the desired accuracy (average). For example, if you want the accuracy of the approximate solution to be 5%, choose the spacing of the mesh of around 1/20 of its characteristic size...", i.e. a characteristic two-dimensional spot would include about 400 nodes, and in the case of a three-dimensional problem there would be about 8,000 nodes.

You should keep in mind that the above consideration is true only in average, and the accuracy depends much not only on the finite element type but also on the position of the finite elements and their orientation with respect to the flows of principal stresses. The latter fact can be seen from a characteristic example taken from the paper [4] and shown in Fig. 2.9.

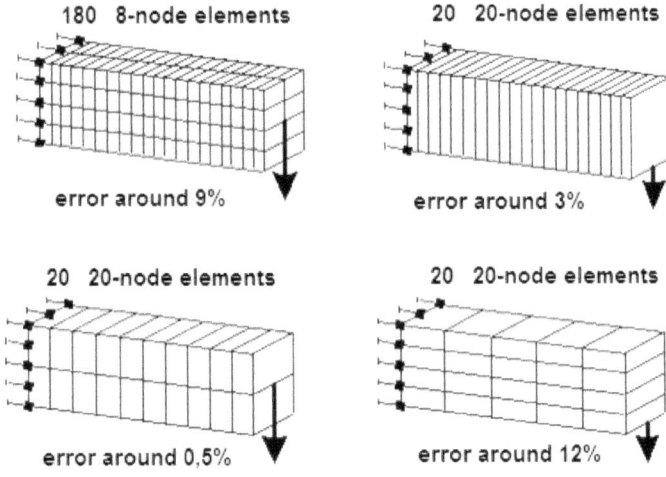

Figure 2.9.

Of course, in most cases the asymptotic convergence is accompanied by an appropriate "practical convergence". The latter term will mean the possibility of obtaining an acceptable accuracy with a comparatively rough meshing. However, this rule has its exceptions too. In this regard, we would like to cite from a great mathematician and physicist A. Poincare (quoted from [1, p.52]):

"...of two series where their general terms are 1000n/n! and n!/1000n, mathematicians would name the first one to be convergent... because the millionth term is much less than the 999,999th, whilst the second term would be treated as divergent for its general term may grow unlimitedly. Astronomers, on the contrary, would take the first series for a divergent one because its first 1,000 terms go increasing; and the second series would be called by them convergent because its first 1,000 terms go decreasing and this decrease is quick enough at the beginning." And then follows a breathtaking conclusion: "Both views are valid: the first one in theoretical investigations, and the second one in computational applications".

Apparently, when solving any responsible problem, an analysis of the solution quality must be performed. The solution can be checked by solving the problem repeatedly with a different finite element mesh. Certainly, it is hardly reasonable to solve a whole big problem on gradually refined meshes, but this analysis obviously makes sense for characteristic fragments of a design model. The empirical fact of the solution stability at the mesh refinement is a rather convincing argument "pro" this approach.

Conversation 2.4. Finite Elements are Different

Finite elements of the same shape can have different properties if they are created on the basis of different shape functions. In particular, there are so-called hybrid models of the finite element method, where the displacement field is defined only at the boundaries of the elements, and all other characteristics are based on the assumed stress distribution.

In many numerical experiments hybrid finite elements do indeed show excellent results, especially on medium meshes. However, it would be incorrect to say that hybrid elements are always better than classic finite elements generated on the basis of the approximations of the displacement fields.

We will consider here another classification of the differences between finite elements. It is related to the fact that an element might not react to certain components of nodal displacements and not take the respective components of the nodal load. For example, the reactions of the same shaped finite elements of a flexural plate, of the plane problem of the theory of elasticity, or of a shell differ as shown in the Table 2.2.

This property of the elements should be taken into account, and in order to avoid the dimensional instability, nodal constraints should be introduced in some cases in those directions where the used elements can not provide the necessary immobility.

Table 2.2

Elements	Displacements						Loads					
	X	Y	Z	φ_x	φ_y	φ_z	P_x	P_y	P_z	M_x	M_y	M_z
of a flexural plate			+	+	+				+	+	+	
of the plane problem	+	+					+	+				
of a shell	+	+	+	+	+		+	+	+	+	+	

Moreover, certain problems also arise when connecting elements with different nodal force reactions to the displacement of the node.

For example, the absence of a reaction to the rotation angle in the elements of a plane problem (when the nodal rotation does not cause an elastic moment resisting this rotation) causes the effect of a hinged connection if a bar is attached to the wall modeled by such elements (Fig. 2.10).

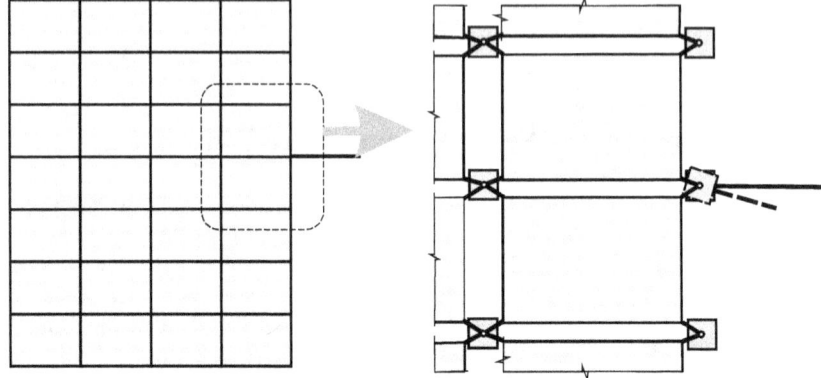

Figure 2.10

In the general case, if a certain (for example, i-th) finite element does not have all the degrees of freedom provided in a node of the design model, then:
- in some cases a constraint has to be imposed on an "unrestrained" degree of freedom in order to obtain a correct solution of the problem;
- other finite elements adjacent to this node (included in *the star of elements* of this node) will not interact with the i-th element.

The requirement of consistency of the properties used in the finite element analysis is very significant. There have been cases when serious errors were missed due to the violation of these requirements.

In general, the possibility of performing complex practical structural calculations is largely defined by the set of available finite elements. Elements or groups of elements included in the *finite element library* are usually used. This is not just a collection of formulas and programs implementing them, but to an extent a structured system united by the accepted rules for describing the unknowns, generating stiffness matrices, calculating stresses and, in particular, matching the boundary conditions of elements.

The finite element libraries of the modern software usually contain the elements of bars, membranes, plates, shells, solids (Fig. 2.11) etc.

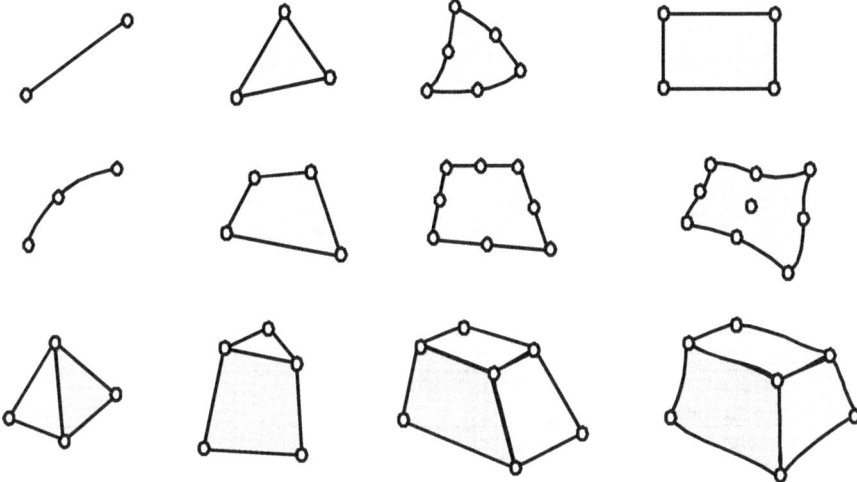

Figure 2.11

Each finite element included in the library is characterized by the following properties:
- a dimensionality of the used space (one-dimensional, two-dimensional, three-dimensional);
- a geometric shape, which is usually one of the simplest geometrical figures (line segment, triangle, rectangle, quadrangle, tetrahedron, etc.);
- a set of nodes placed (as a rule, though not always) on lines (surfaces) that divide the elements and are common for the adjacent ones;
- a set of the used degrees of freedom usually related to the nodes (though not necessarily to the nodes) — displacements, rotations, etc.;
- a system of approximating functions which are defined within the area Ω_e and which enable to approximately express the components of the displacements in any point of the element in terms of its degrees of freedom;
- a physical law that defines a stress-strain relationship;
- a class of problems to which this finite element type can be applied (plane stress state plate FE, Kirchhoff–Love plate FE, FE of the Reissner plate resting on the bi-parametric elastic subgrade, Timoshenko bar for a spatial problem, etc.).

Table 2.3.

Element name	Exponent in the estimates of the convergence rate of:			
	u	σ	M	Q
Rectangular plate element	2	—	1	—
Triangular plate element	2	—	1	0
Quadrangular (from 4 to 8 nodes) plate element	2	—	1	0
Rectangular element of the plane problem of the theory of elasticity	2	1	—	—
Triangular element of the plane problem of the theory of elasticity	2	1	—	—
Quadrangular (from 4 to 8 nodes) element of the plane problem of the theory of elasticity	2	1	—	—
Quadrangular (from 4 to 12 nodes) element of the plane problem of the theory of elasticity	2	1	—	—
Parallelepiped	2	1	—	—
Tetrahedron	2	1	—	—
Triangular prism	2	1	—	—
Spatial isoparametric six-node element	2	1	—	—
Spatial isoparametric eight-node element	2	1	—	—
Spatial isoparametric twenty-node element	2	1	—	—
Rectangular shell element	2	1	1	0
Triangular shell element	2	1	1	0
Quadrangular shell element	2	1	1	0
Quadrangular (from 4 to 8 nodes) shell finite element	2	1	1	0

One of the most important characteristics of a set of finite elements is a set of degrees of freedom related to their nodes. This characteristic enables to distinguish the class of finite elements where all degrees of freedom are linear displacements and/or rotations of the nodes.

Finite elements given in the library of a certain software are usually checked for convergence of the solution to an exact one at the mesh refinement. As an example, Table 2.3 provides information on the convergence of the elements of the SCAD library for displacements (u), stresses (σ), moments (M) and shear forces (Q).

It should be noted that convergence is an asymptotic property and its presence does not mean that we do not need to perform the check of the solution on the refined meshes. The asymptotic estimate of convergence operates with error estimates of type h^m, where h is the maximum of the characteristic dimensions of the finite element, and the exponent m characterizes the error reduction rate when h tends to zero.

It can be seen from this table, for example, that the error in displacements decreases with a quadratic velocity at the mesh refinement, while the reduction of the error in stresses is usually linear.

A coarse error in moments and even a coarser error in shear forces are caused by the fact that a transition to them involves the numerical differentiation of deflections. Even an insignificant error in the deflection, when the value $u_i+\varepsilon$ is used instead of the exact one u_i, results in the value of the first derivative $(u_i + \varepsilon - u_{i+1})/h = u' + \varepsilon/h$, where the error ε/h can be quite considerable at a small step h.

Conversation 2.5. Division into Finite Elements

Let us consider how a finite element mesh is created on a plane or on a curved surface. The simplest method is the direct specification of the coordinates of the nodes, which are then used to create finite elements (by selecting the nodes in a certain sequence to create the contour of a finite element).

This method is used mainly in simple models or in those cases when it is necessary to expand an existing finite element model. However, the main method of creating the finite element model is the automatic generation. A modern personal computer enables to solve problems with thousands or even tens of thousands of nodes. Nowadays, the "manual" compilation of a finite element mesh seems absurd, and most modern software have some kind of automatic mesh generators.

The simplest variant of generation is the case of creating *a rectangular mesh of elements* on a rectangular area of the plane. A mesh with either a variable or a constant step will be created, for example, in the XOY plane. The following mesh parameters have to be specified: the values of the steps and their number in each direction.

Thus, for example, if we specify the following meshing parameters:

Step along the X axis	Number of steps	Step along the Y axis	Number of steps
0.5	6	0.25	8
0.25	8	0.5	6
1	5		

we will obtain a model shown in Fig. 2.12.

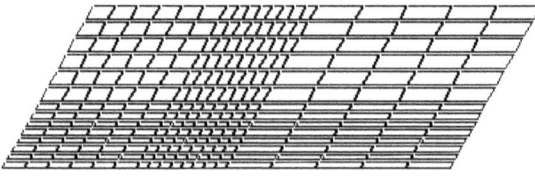

Figure 2.12.

Triangular meshing (triangulation) of an arbitrary closed area is one of the most versatile tools. This operation can be automatically performed in almost any modern software.

The convenience of using triangles as elementary areas occupied by individual finite elements is defined by the fact that the boundaries of bodies of a rather complex shape can be easily described with their help. Moreover, triangular meshes are very useful for performing refinement in the parts of the design area where high gradients of the stress state of the structure are expected, for example, in stress concentration areas near holes, re-entrant corners, etc. Triangles are very suitable for the automatic finite element mesh generation. Most of the known mesh generators included in the modern software are based on the area triangulation. It is these advantages of triangular finite elements that make them so widely used in modern software.

The area triangulation is usually performed with the help of the method based on the construction of the Voronoi diagram (Fig. 2.13,*a*), which enables to divide a plane into regions of attraction of a given set of nodes. Each edge of this diagram is a straight line segment perpendicular to the segment connecting a pair of closest points, and divides this segment in half. If we now join by segments each pair of points having a common edge in the Voronoi diagram (Fig. 2.13,*b*), we obtain a system of triangles covering the considered set of nodes (*Delaunay triangulation*).

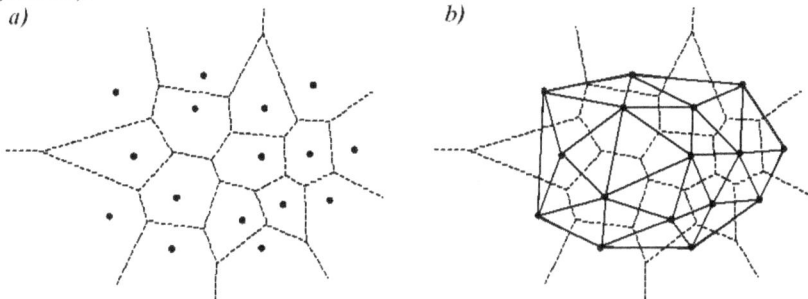

Figure 2.13.

An important property of the finite element mesh is its smoothness (gradual change in the dimensions of the elements), since a rapid change in the characteristic dimensions of the element significantly affects the resulting stress-strain state. It is especially noticeable when considering stresses given by level lines. Good mesh generators enable to control the refinement (to a point, to a line, to the center, or to the perimeter of the area, etc.), providing thus the predefined degree of smoothness of the mesh. And the mesh refinement mechanism makes it possible to study in greater detail the stress concentration areas, edge effect zones in shells etc.

The meshing density in automatic generators is controlled by such parameters as the specified maximum distance between nodes and the allowed minimum angle of the triangle.

In terms of the finite element analysis one can safely say that it is best to use equilateral finite elements (in the shape of an equilateral triangle, a square, an equilateral tetrahedron, a cube). In practice, this requirement is very rarely achieved, and the resulting meshing is not optimal. Therefore, the problem of estimating the quality of the obtained meshing arises and different measures are used (see Table 2.4).

Table 2.4

Parameter	Triangles		Quadrangles	
	Optimal	Recommended	Optimal	Recommended
Aspect ratio		1 ... 1,3		1 ... 4
Minimum angle, degrees	60	30 ... 60	90	45 ... 90
Maximum angle, degrees	60	60 ... 90	90	90 ... 135
Maximum to minimum angle ratio	1		1	
Maximum to minimum side length ratio	1	1 ... 4	1	1 ... 4
Ratio of area to perimeter squared	$2/\sqrt{3}$	0,5 ... 2	0,0625	0,04 ... 0,1
Elongation	—	—	1	0,25 ... 1

Aspect ratio is one of such measures. It is calculated as follows. For each side of the element L_i an area of an equilateral element with the same side length is determined ($0{,}433(L_i)^2$ for an equilateral triangle, $(L_i)^2$ – for a square), and then these areas are averaged.

The ratio of this averaged "idealized" area to the real area of the element is taken as a quality measure.

In order to prevent the occurrence of "needle" quadrangular elements, the elongation measure is used. The recommended and optimal values of these and other quality measures are given in the Table 2.4.

Conversation 2.6. FEM Design Models

One of the main advantages of the finite element method is its ability to solve problems where elements of different types (bar, shell, plate, etc.) interact in the design model.

> However, you should keep in mind that the finite element method is a method of approximate solution of certain differential equations describing the exact formulation of the problem. Therefore, it is necessary to know the properties of these differential equations and to understand what results can be obtained by solving them.

Thus, coupling finite elements of different dimensions (aimed at solving different differential equations) can lead to unexpected problems. We have already mentioned one of them when considering the connection between a flexural bar and a deep beam modeled by the elements of the plane problem of the theory of elasticity (see Fig. 2.10). The problem there was caused by the different dimensions of the corresponding differential equations (and hence, the number of degrees of freedom in a node). A node of a bar must have three degrees of freedom, and a node of an element of the plane problem of the theory of elasticity — two.

However, the problems can also be caused by different properties of solutions corresponding to different differential equations. Thus, for some two-dimensional problems of the theory of elasticity, concentrated actions give infinite solutions at the point of application of such an action. Let us see what this can lead to by considering an example of the connection between a flexural plate and a bar element.

Let us consider a discrete design model combining plate finite elements and bars rigidly attached to a slab. A finite element mesh is formed in such a way that the bars of the structure's frame hit the nodes of the meshed slab. This design model will provide the consistency of both vertical displacements of the slab and the frame (in the direction perpendicular to the plate) and the respective rotation angles in the nodes where the plate and bar elements join one another. However, bending moments in cross-sections of the columns adjoining the slab, calculated with this model, have nothing to do with the real distribution of internal forces. This being the case, the distribution of the internal forces in other elements of the structure's frame will be affected too.

Indeed, suppose we have a refined slab mesh, and the user believing in the convergence of the used plate finite element expects to obtain an exceedingly high accuracy of the results of the calculation. However, starting from a certain density of the mesh, the further division of the mesh results in the decrease of absolute values of the bending moments in the bars in places of their attachment to the slab. When passing to a limit, as the maximum size of the mesh cell tends to zero, these bending moments should tend to zero too. This means that this design model provides a hinged rather than rigid attachment of the frame elements to the slab.

> *The fact that the user obtains some formal nonzero numerical values of the bending moments on a specific mesh shows only a discretization error of the finite element method, but there is no reason at all to take the discretization error for a credible numerical result!*

As can be seen, the bending moment in a bar of this model, independent of the mesh step, is transferred to the slab as a moment concentrated in a node of the mesh. On the other hand, the slab under the concentrated bending moment acquires an infinite rotation angle in the moment plane at the point of its application, or, to be exact, a logarithmic singularity appears in the expression for the rotation angle. Thus the slab does not resist the concentrated rotation and does not restrain the frame elements.

We will consider the results of a calculation of a clamped square slab with a single column fixed in the center of the slab.

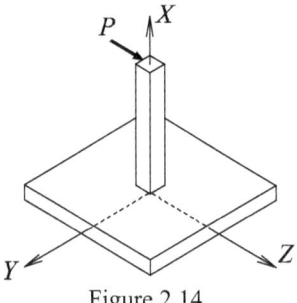

Figure 2.14.

An external concentrated force P directed along the global Z axis is applied to the free upper end of the column (Fig. 2.14). In this case, the bending moment in the lower section of the column will be a constant value, independent of the finite element mesh step, since the system is statically determinate with respect to the column.

However, the same effect can be observed in the horizontal displacement of the top of the column, which increases unlimitedly at the mesh refinement due to the growth of the rotation angle in the central node of the plate.

The second line of the Table 2.5 shows the results of the calculation of the displacements w_n of the column free end in the direction of the Z axis depending on the finite element mesh ($n \times n$) used for the quarter of the slab plan.

Table 2.5.

$n \times n$	2×2	4×4	8×8	16×16	32×32	64×64
$w_n \times 10^4$	11,826	11,996	12,162	12,326	12,492	12,659
$\underline{w_n} \times 10^4$	–	11,209	11,194	11,180	11,172	11,169

The following initial data are assumed:
- slab thickness $h = 0{,}5$ m;
- overall dimensions of the slab in plan $10{,}0 \times 10{,}0$ m;
- cross-sectional dimensions of the column $0{,}5 \times 0{,}5$ m;
- characteristics of the slab and column material $E = 3 \cdot 10^7$ t/.m², $\nu = 0{,}25$.

It is easy to see that with each doubling of the mesh the deflection w_n increases by almost the same value $\Delta \cong 0{,}167 \cdot 10^{-4}$, in other words, the deflection of the column grows linearly with the increase of $\log_2 n$, or more precisely

$$w_n = w_2 + \Delta \cdot \log_2(n-1),$$

and therefore, as expected, the rotation angle of the root section of the column increases unlimitedly with the finite element mesh refinement.

This leads to an important practical conclusion: when creating a design model, the actual boundary conditions of the slab-to-column joint should be taken into account. The following method is often used for this purpose: nodes are provided along the bottom contour of the column, through which forces are transferred from the column to the slab (Fig. 2.15,*a*). An alternative technique is to transfer the load from the column as a load distributed over the contact area (Fig. 2.15,*b*).

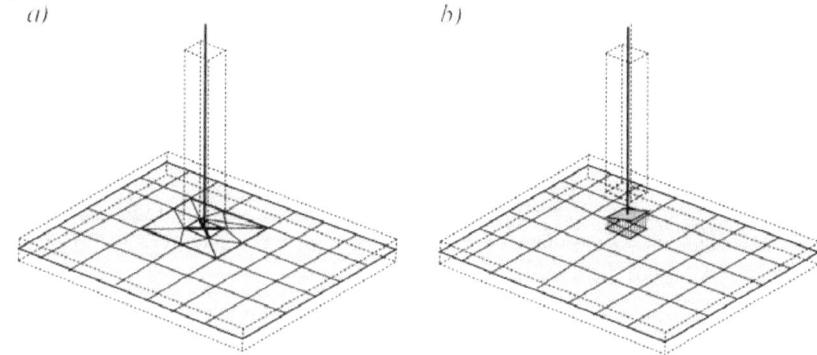

Figure 2.15.

Let us now consider the longitudinal and transverse forces in the bar elements adjacent to the disk. We can show that when a concentrated force is applied in the plane problem of the theory of elasticity, the displacement of the application point of this force in the direction of the action of the force has a singularity

Repeating the above considerations for the bending moment, we come to a conclusion that in the case of an accurate solution of a problem with a point coupling (i.e. coupling in one node) of a bar and in the case of a plane problem of the theory of elasticity, the force transferred to the bar should be equal to zero. And once again, nonzero values of transverse and longitudinal forces technically obtained in the bars in the result of a discrete model analysis are caused solely by the discretization error. The analysis of the design model (not to be confused with its discrete analog!), however, results in both zero moments and zero forces in the bars.

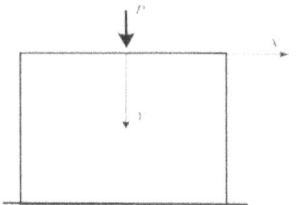

The same conclusion can also be reached from the numerical experiments, if we carefully analyze the results of the calculations of a plate with a refined mesh subjected to a concentrated force. For this purpose, let us consider the problem shown in Fig. 2.16.

Figure 2.16

Suppose the problem has the following initial data:
- plate thickness $h = 1,0$;
- overall dimensions of the plate in the (X,Y) plane $16,0 \times 16,0$;
- characteristics of the material $E = 3 \cdot 10^5$, $\nu = 0,25$;
- load $P = 1000$.

Table 2.6 shows the results of solving this problem, where v_n is the displacement of the application point of the force P in the direction of the Y axis, and it is clear that as expected the considered displacement increases unlimitedly at the mesh refinement.

Thus, the general conclusion is as follows: the point coupling of bar elements and elements of the plane problem of the theory of elasticity leads to an incorrect formulation of the problem.

Table 2.6.

$n \times n$	2×2	4×4	8×8	16×16	32×32	64×64
$v_n \times 10^4$	55,278	68,282	82,665	97,296	111,989	126,695

In the vicinity of singular points — where a strong stress concentration occurs — the use of finite elements (as well as other discretization techniques) is usually encumbered, especially in the representation of the stress field. The finite element mesh has to be refined dramatically, thus considerably increasing the dimension of the analysis.

However, the mesh refinement may not lead to a proper result, and this fact makes us perform a deeper analysis of the situation. One of the most popular judgments is the following: a concentrated force is an abstraction that does not exist in reality. If it had been actually implemented, then it would pass through a structure of any strength and run away to infinity without being resisted. So it turns out that this idealization creates an artificial difficulty which may be fought heroically only to find that this heroism is of very little practical sense.

> *It should be remembered how the force represented as a concentrated one in the model is implemented in the actual structure, then all issues of how to provide the convergence of the finite-element solution to an exact one might be resolved.*

Question:
What corrections should be made to the finite element model in order to avoid these problems?

Answer:
First of all, it is necessary to consider the design of a joint between a bar and a diaphragm in sufficient detail. For example, let a steel I-beam be embedded partly in a brick wall as shown in Fig. 2.17,*a*.

Then it suffices to add a one-dimensional bar element that penetrates into the plane stressed wall by an appropriate part of its length, to the respective design model and to its discrete counterpart, as shown in Fig. 2.17,*b*.

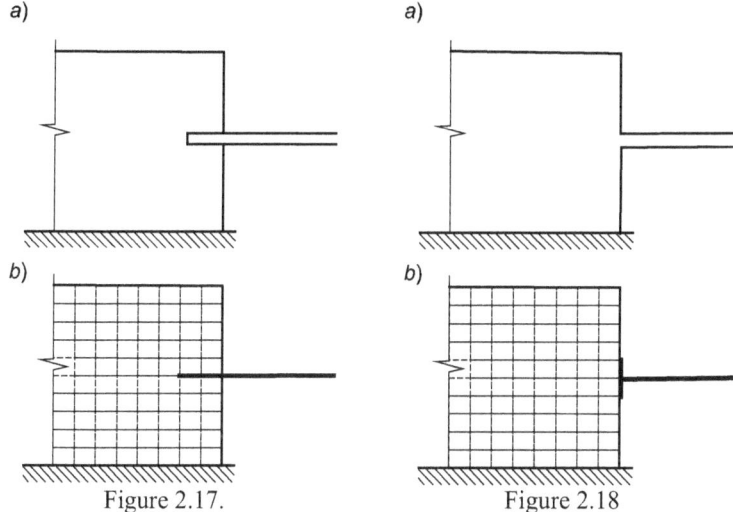

Figure 2.17.   Figure 2.18

Another design can be suggested for a monolithic joint between a reinforced concrete wall panel and a girder of the building frame — see Fig. 2.18,*a*. The actual dimensions of the cross-section can be taken into account here: the height of the girder, with a rigid body placed along the wall border as shown in Fig. 2.18,*b*. This rigid body complies with the plane section assumption for the girder itself. The assumption states that the girder section remains flat and does not change its size after its deformation.

Certainly the two ways of creating design models given here by no means comprise the wide scope of possible situations. In every particular case the designer should take into account the structural peculiarities of the problem rather than simply using some fancied and questionable general-case models.

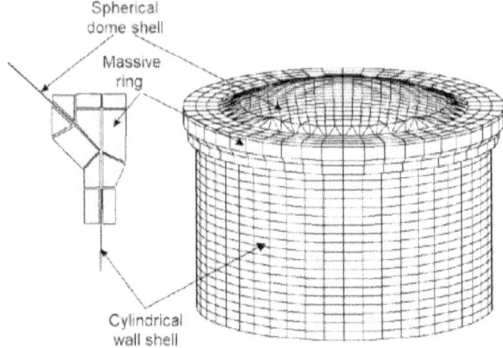

Figure 2.19.

It should be noted that the "joint area extension" technique as in Fig. 2.18 can be used to connect other types of elements of different dimensions.

Fig. 2.19 shows such an example wherein a cylindrical shell of a wall and a spherical shell of a co ver of a n uclear reactor containment are matched with a massive ring.

Conversation 2.7. Analysis of the Calculation Results

Creating a design model precedes the solution of the problem, and some of the assumptions used in modeling are based on the expected properties of the solution. For example, the assumption that the displacements are small and, in particular, the rotation angles, serves as the basis for solving the problem in a geometrically linear formulation, and the assumption that there are no strong stress concentrators underlies the application of an approximately uniform finite element mesh.

Therefore, a posteriori analysis of the obtained solution is required, and, if necessary, the design model has to be corrected in accordance with the results of this analysis.

The analysis of the calculation results is greatly facilitated by the use of simple models for which extensive experience has been gained, and the expected results are easily predicted.

> *However, you should always keep in mind that the design model is just an abstraction created for certain purposes, and therefore, it should not be treated as something divine.*

A sense of humour towards a design model distinguishes experienced and competent designers. These designers usually use (sometimes implicitly) not one, but several, in some ways similar design models, and if the obtained results of their analysis are close, the confidence in their accuracy increases dramatically.

Rather complex and excessively detailed design models are becoming increasingly popular for designing modern important structures. It is assumed that it guarantees the detection of the most stressed areas of the structure. However, it should be taken into account that this result can still be missed due to the difficulty of analyzing and understanding redundant information. The thing is that, starting from a certain level of complexity of the system, a person's ability to formulate meaningful and accurate statements about the behavior of the system begins to drop rapidly. A certain analogue of the Heisenberg uncertainty principle with respect to the level of detail and informativeness of the calculation results, which act as alternating parameters, takes place here.

When dealing with problems of large dimension, the designer is unlikely to be able to reflect all of its features in one design model so as not to simply obtain a certain set of results, but to make it accessible for understanding and qualitative analysis. The most comprehensive representation of the structure can be obviously obtained when a whole series of models is used to describe each particular feature of the structure.

For example, a television tower shown in Fig. 2.20 was analyzed:
- as a cantilever bar of variable rigidity to evaluate its dynamic characteristics,
- as a spatial truss with continuous chords to determine unfavorable combinations of forces and design values of forces in bars,
- as a shell system (fragmentarily) to determine the stress-strain state of the nodal connections,
- together with subgrade to determine long-term settlements and tilts etc.

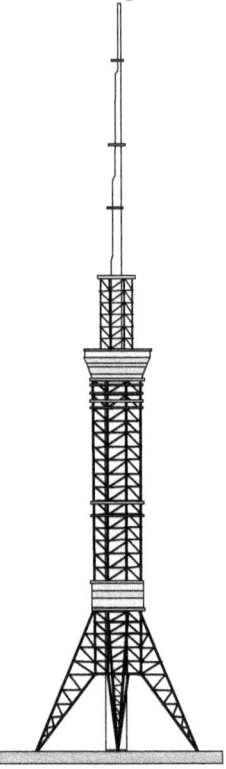

Figure 2.20.

Thus, a more convincing analysis can be performed if several design models are used which to some extent are mutually complementary and describe different properties of the system.

Moreover, it enables to easily detect and correct possible errors, since the need to explain the discrepancy between the calculation results for different models localizes the reasons for such discrepancies rather quickly.

The design experience of the last decades shows that the development of engineering CAD has a major (alas, both positive and negative) impact on the quality of design justifications. The level of detail and accuracy of calculations, which only yesterday was unattainable even for the most qualified organizations and specialists, has now become widely available. However, this availability of modern powerful design software creates a whole new set of problems.

It is sometimes advised to perform calculations by two programs, but this technique can be harmful.

We are talking about possible harm only in the sense that performing a calculation of the same design model by two programs makes you think that you have performed a double control and the obtained results of the engineering calculations have a double reliability. However, if there is an error in the design model itself, all this control will be useless.

Question:
If a double calculation was performed, how should the measure of the discrepancy between the results be evaluated? How to make a decision whether the result of the comparison is satisfactory (not satisfactory)?

Answer:
In order to perform the comparison more accurately, the discrepancy normalization should be applied. For example, if the discrepancies between longitudinal forces are calculated as the ratio

$$\Delta_N = \frac{|N_1 - N_2|}{N_1} \times 100 \ (\%),$$

for small force values, we obtain a distorted picture (all such estimates are large around zero).

It is more logical to compare the normalized values, for example, to compare the error in the stresses $\sigma_0 = |N_1 - N_2|/A$ caused by the module of the difference of the compared values (A – cross-sectional area), relating it to the design strength of the material R_y

$$\Delta_{0,N} = \frac{\sigma_{0,N}}{R_y} = \frac{|N_1 - N_2|}{AR_y}.$$

A similar procedure has to be performed for the bending moments (W – section modulus)

$$\Delta_{0,M} = \frac{|M_1 - M_2|}{WR_y}.$$

Then the discrepancies become physically meaningful, and not formal, which is easy to see from the following table taken from the analysis of a complex object.

Element	N_1	N_2	Δ_N, %	Δ_{0N}, %
1	-220,0	-222,4	1,073	0,166
2	-14,9	-12,1	18,403	0,262

| 3 | -460,9 | -462,2 | 0,281 | 0,168 |
| 4 | 61,7 | 58,7 | 4,891 | 0,181 |

We see that the seemingly large discrepancy of forces in the second element is in fact not so significant.

Question:
What if the calculations on refined finite element meshes indicate the lack of convergence of the results? Can we trust such calculations?

Answer:
Let me remind you that when it comes to the finite element method, it makes no sense to talk about "the convergence in general", because the convergence may not apply to all results, which is clearly shown in the Table 2.3.

This thesis can be easily illustrated by a simple school example.

You can divide a right triangle into elementary rectangles with side lengths $\Delta x = a/n$ and $\Delta y = b/m$ (Fig. 2.21), and calculate its approximate area as the sum of elementary areas. The greater the numbers n and m, the more accurate the result will be. But no matter how many rectangles you have, the length of the hypotenuse will still be equal to $a+b$.

> *Does this mean that a result that does not converge cannot be used in any way? No, it just does not refer to the initial design model, but to its modification in the style of the finite element method. And, as in any other case, this new design model may require verification.*

Its "similarity" to the initial design model can to some extent illustrate the behavior of other components of the result. For example, you can analyze the smoothness of stress fields. In order to do this, you have to consider the stress values not only in the nodes, but also in the adjacent finite element vertices (this function is available in SCAD, for example) and evaluate the jumps (see Fig. 2.5).

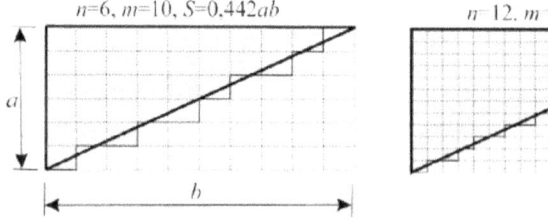

Figure 2.21

The most typical example of questionable results caused by the lack of convergence is the unrealistically large value of shear forces in shear elements. In this case local refinement of the finite element mesh can be used as a verification method. The area of peak shear forces will become less as the mesh is refined. The designer has to decide whether this stress concentration can be neglected.

A more correct method is to consider a local area as a fragment divided into finite elements of a different type (for example, 3D solid elements). Then you will be able to obtain a refined solution and decide whether to use the divergent solutions.

It should be noted that the use of divergent series is a common technique in applied mathematics [1].

References

1. *Blekhman I.I., Myshkis A.D., Panovko Ya.G.* Mechanics and Applied Mathematics: Logic and Peculiarities of Mathematical Applications. — M.: Nauka, 1983.
2. *Vovkushevsky A.V., Shoikhet B.A.* Analysis of Massive Hydraulic Structures Taking into Account Seam Opening. — M.: "Energiya", 1981.
3. *Gorodetsky A.S., Evzerov I.D.* Computer Models of Structures. — K.: "FACT", 2005.
4. *Kaplun A.B., Morozov E.M., Olferyeva M.A.,* ANSYS in the Engineer's Hands. — M.: URSS, 2003.
5. *Perelmuter A.V., Slivker V.I.* Design Models of Structures and Possibilities of Their Analysis: 4-th ed., revised and updated — M., SCAD SOFT, ASV, DMK-Press, 2011.
6. *Rosin L.A.* Problems of the Theory of Elasticity and Numerical Methods. — St. Petersburg, State Technical University, 1998.
7. *Slivker V.I.* Structural Mechanics. Basic Variational Principles. — M.: ASV, 2005.

Cycle 3
Nonlinear Static Problems

...a designer, who has entered the field of nonlinear analysis, has to get over the "stumbling blocks" which are scattered there quite generously.
M. Reitman

If you want to change the floor, you must fix the roof first.
Taken from the Internet

Conversation 3.1. Preliminaries about Nonlinear Problems

Linear structural mechanics, which was considered in the conversations of the first two cycles, is the most common, but it is not omnipotent. The problems of the analysis of load-bearing structures focused on the refined prediction of the peculiarities of the behavior of the system at all stages of its operation including the stages prior to the failure can not be usually solved by the methods of the linear structural mechanics.

Educational literature and the majority of researchers consider the following "set of nonlinearities": deviation from Hooke's law (*physical nonlinearity*), failure to consider the equilibrium conditions in geometrical terms of the non-deformed state (*geometric nonlinearity*), accounting for the possible changes in the design model during the deformation process (*structural nonlinearity*).

However, this set is not complete. It does not include the consideration of the effects caused by rheological processes in the material (for example, creep) and nonlinear effects of resistance to movements of the dry friction type or of other nature, and it does not take into account nonlinearity related to the accumulation of stress and strain during the changes of the structure as it is created (*genetic nonlinearity*). The latter type of nonlinearity can of course be considered as a type of structural nonlinearity, because systems with a varying design model are considered, but here the changes occur not as a result of the load, but according to the designer's plan, which gives grounds for its separate consideration and name.

Table 3.1, which should be carefully analyzed, provides a comparison between the linear and nonlinear problems of structural mechanics. It is not difficult to see that when switching to the nonlinear analysis many usual approaches become unsuitable, and many issues which were not a concern have to be considered now.

Without going into details, let us formulate some general warnings on the issue of the nonlinear analysis. In particular, here is a list of questions from [4], which have to be considered by the designer before trying to solve a nonlinear problem.

CONVERSATIONS ABOUT THE STRUCTURAL MECHANICS 111

Table 3.1.

Peculiarity	Linear problems	Nonlinear problems
Relationship between displacement and load	Displacements are linearly dependent on the applied load	The relationship between displacement and load is nonlinear
Relationship between stress and strain	A relationship between stress and strain is assumed	In the problems where the physical nonlinearity is considered the "stress-strain" relationship can be a nonlinear function of stress or strain
Value of displacement	The change in geometry due to the displacement is assumed to be small, and is ignored when checking the equilibrium	Displacements can be not small, it is necessary to use the deformed state to check the equilibrium
Reversibility	All deformations are completely reversible and disappear when the system is unloaded	After the load is removed, the state of the system can differ from the initial one
Boundary conditions	Boundary conditions remain unchanged during the calculation	Boundary conditions can change, for example, the contact areas change
Sequence of load application	The sequence of load application is not important, the final state does not depend on it	The state of the structure can depend on the sequence of load application
Use of the results	The results of the calculation for different loads can be added or multiplied by certain coefficients in order to combine the design states	The decomposition of the problem into components with the subsequent combination of the results is impossible
Initial stress-strain state	The initial stress-strain state is insignificant	It is usually required to specify the initial stress-strain state, especially in the case of the nonlinearity related to the behavior of the material

These issues arise due to a number of peculiarities of nonlinear problems many of which are unusual for specialists who were taught to solve only linear problems.
- How well are the properties of the materials studied?
- Is the result affected by the initial stress-strain state, for example, the residual stresses in the system? If so, how can it be determined?
- Is there a possibility of solution ambiguity, for example, different methods of solving buckling problems, or more than one supercritical state? If

so, it might be necessary to create some artificial initial imperfections in order to obtain only one solution the user is interested in.
- Does the loading history affect the structural behavior?
- Will the behavior of the material be the same in the case of loading and unloading?
- In the case of large displacements or large rotations will the direction of the load action remain constant or will it follow the shape distortion?
- Should a larger factor of safety be used to compensate for a possible error or uncertainty about the adequacy of the solution?
- How will the solutions be checked?

It should be noted that whatever the origin of the nonlinearity, a problem of solving the respective system of nonlinear equilibrium equations arises in the practical solution of the problem

$$f_i(x_1, x_2, \ldots, x_n) = 0 \quad (i = 1, 2, \ldots, n). \quad (3.1)$$

There are many methods for solving them, but perhaps the most popular is the incremental procedure, which has become an integral part of nonlinear finite element analysis [1].

General descriptions of the incremental procedure are well known, and are related to the solution of linearized equations with a gradual increase of a certain time-like parameter t (for example, the load value). First of all, it should be noted that the transition from a system of nonlinear equilibrium equations to equations with a parameter

$$F_i(x_1, x_2, \ldots, x_n, t) = 0 \quad (i = 1, 2, \ldots, n) \quad (3.2)$$

and further to a chain of linearized equations of the incremental method depends on the method of introducing a parameter t into the system, the increments of which implement the transition from step to step.

If such a parameter is selected so that the solution of the system (3.2) is known for a certain value $t = t_0$, and when $t = t^*$ the system (3.2) is identical to (3.1), differentiation with respect to t leads to a system of linear differential equations with variable coefficients

$$\sum_{j=1}^{n} \frac{\partial F_i}{\partial x_j} \cdot \frac{dx_j}{dt} + \frac{\partial F_i}{\partial t} = 0 \quad (i = 1, 2, \ldots, n), \quad (3.3)$$

with the known initial conditions at $t = t_0$. Solving the Cauchy problem for the system of equations (3.3), we obtain the integral curve

$$x_1 = x_1(t), \quad x_2 = x_2(t), \ldots, x_n = x_n(t), \quad (3.4)$$

which leads to the solution of the original problem (3.1) at $t = t^*$.

There are several variants of the incremental procedure which, in fact, differ only in the methods of introducing the parameter t and/or the methods used to obtain a numerical solution of the above Cauchy problem, in particular, it is possible to use the following modifications of the incremental method:

- simple incremental method;
- incremental method accounting for the residual;
- incremental-iterative method.

When the simple incremental method is used, a linearized problem is solved in each step ΔP, and assuming that this solution is sufficiently accurate, a transition to the next step of the nonlinear loading occurs. In practice, this procedure corresponds to the simplest method of solving a system of differential equations based on plotting an Euler polygon (Fig. 3.1) instead of an integral curve (3.4). The solution error of a nonlinear problem, i.e. the deviation of the Euler polygon in the solution process is not controlled — it is assumed that the error is small due to the selected small step of numerical integration. The stiffness of the linearized system (slope φ) is taken without accounting for the force residual.

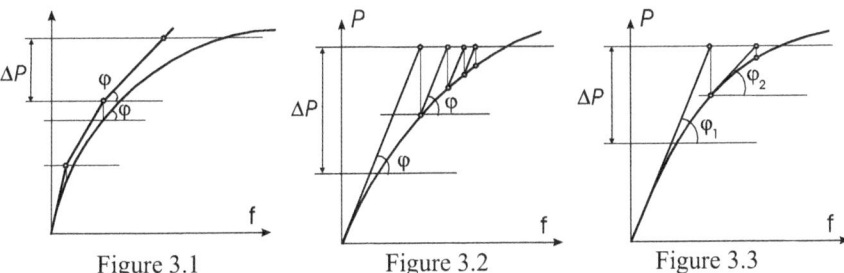

Figure 3.1   Figure 3.2   Figure 3.3

The incremental method accounting for the residual provides the iterative refinement of the nonlinear load at the subsequent step by taking into account the residual in the equations of equilibrium. Iterations are performed with a constant value of the linearized stiffness matrix (Fig. 3.2), which was calculated at the beginning of the subsequent step (angle φ remains unchanged in the step).

Finally, when the incremental-iterative method is used (Fig. 3.3), the iterative refinement is performed at each step ΔP with the adjustment of the linearized stiffness matrix at each iteration (angle φ changes within the step).

The described variants of the incremental procedure become unsuitable when the tangent slope approaches zero. In these cases a loading parameter is often changed, switching from increasing the load value to increasing the displacement, but the best effect can be achieved by the arc length method. The method is based on the idea of going through a set of possible solutions (along the equilibrium state curve) taking into account at every step the information on solutions obtained at previous steps.

It should be noted, that by varying the method of specifying the parameter t, we can obtain meaningful information about the behavior of the system under load. If we assume that such a parameter is present as a factor for all terms of equations (3.1), which directly describe external actions, then a proportional increase in the loads corresponds to its monotonic increase from $t_0 = 0$ to $t^* = 1$, and the integral curve (3.4) describes the behavior of generalized coordinates in the process of such loading. There are of course other more complex and more realistic ways of applying and alternating loads. Varying them, you can perform a series of «mathematical experiments» on the analysis of structural behavior under various loading modes.

An important feature of the incremental procedure and its attractive difference from other methods for solving nonlinear equations is that the system linearized in the vicinity of a certain loading can be analyzed by the usual methods of linear structural mechanics. The estimates of the stability factors of safety (naturally, they characterize the possibility of an increase of the load value from the level already reached) make sense or those of the natural frequencies and modes of such a linearized system. These features of the incremental procedure characterize it not only as a way of obtaining a solution of a problem, but also as a tool for analyzing the structural properties.

Question:
You have named a great number of features of nonlinear problems of structural mechanics. But what is the main difference between linear and nonlinear problems which makes us reconsider the calculation procedure?

Answer:
I believe it is a violation of the superposition principle, which in linear problems enables to perform a number of independent design calculations, thus analyzing a number of characteristic design situations, and then combining the obtained results, considering, for example, the combined action of individual loads.

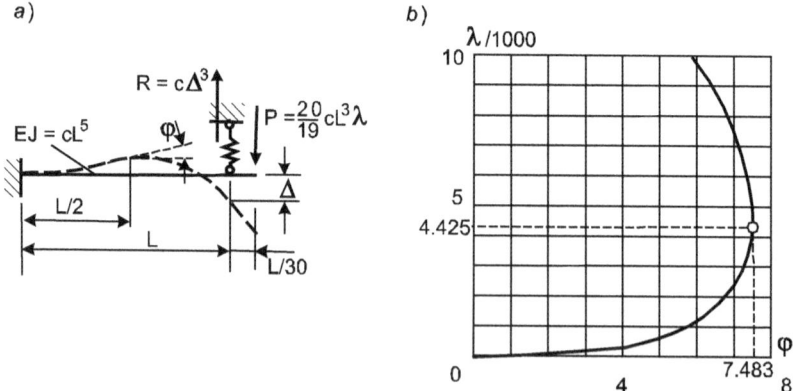

Figure 3.4

Moreover, in linear problems an unfavorable combination of temporary loads either includes the full value of such a load, or (if its effect is unloading) excludes it completely. In nonlinear problems such a "black-and-white logic" of the effect of temporary loads can turn out to be incorrect, there are examples when a combination including a part of the load, rather than its full value, is an unfavorable one. Such an example is shown in Fig. 3.4. A bar with a nonlinear elastic support is considered. The reaction of this support is proportional to the cube of the displacement. The relationship between the rotation angle φ and the force parameter λ is such that the rotation angle increases only when $0 \leq \lambda \leq 0{,}004425$, and when the load values λ are large it starts to decrease.

Conversation 3.2. Physically Nonlinear Problems

First of all, you should be careful when using the concept of "physical nonlinearity". The thing is that many programs consider a problem that differs from a linear one only in that a functional linear relationship between stresses and strains is replaced by a nonlinear function.

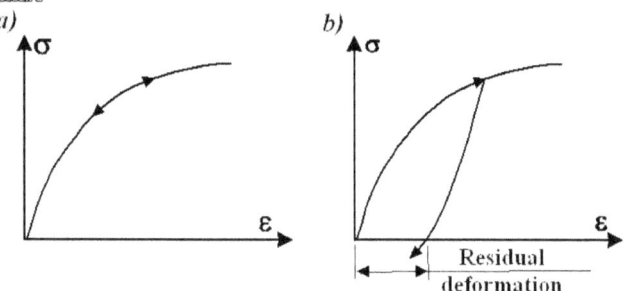

Figure 3.5.

This function is assumed to be unambiguous and identical for loading and unloading. However, such *nonlinear elastic* materials (Fig. 3.5.*a*) almost never occur in nature, and the deviation from Hooke's law for most structural materials is related to the *plasticity phenomena*. And plastic materials usually have residual deformations after unloading. The phenomenon known as the plastic flow actually lies in the formation of the residual (plastic) deformation (Fig. 3.5.*b*).

The above remark is often countered by a reference to the fact that only such structural behavior histories are considered, when all the loads only increase. The increase of loads, however, does not guarantee the increase of stresses at all points of the body, therefore, this restriction does not insure us against errors.

> *We should clearly understand that the elastic-plastic behavior of a material differs from that of a nonlinear elastic material, and it is not known in advance, that replacing one problem with another one is a conservative solution.*

Secondly, we should keep in mind that having set foot on the path of nonlinear analysis, we have deprived ourselves of the possibility to use the superposition principle, which is a basis for all methods of finding an unfavorable combination of loads. Even the very concept of a combined action of loads has to be refined, since not only the composition of the combination can play an important role, but also the sequence of the action of its components.

Let us illustrate this statement with a simple example of calculating a system (Fig. 3.6), consisting of four deformable bars connected to a rigid beam. The bars have the same cross-sectional areas and are made of ideal elastic-plastic material. The external action includes independently varying forces P_1 and P_2. The equilibrium conditions of the beam are reduced to two equations

$$\left.\begin{array}{l}(\sigma_1+\sigma_2+\sigma_3+\sigma_4)A = P_1+P_2 \\ (\sigma_2+2\sigma_3+3\sigma_4)A = 3P_2 \end{array}\right\}, \quad (3.5)$$

where A is the cross-sectional area of the bar.

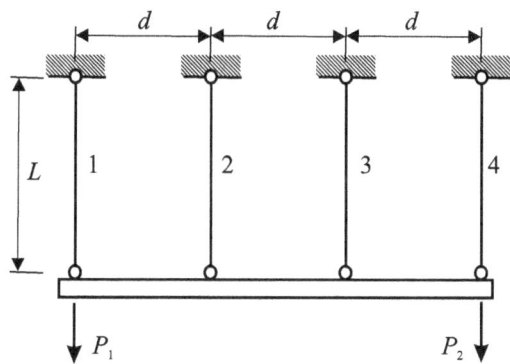

Figure 3.6.

Since the beam is rigid, the displacements of the lower ends of the bars are related as follows

$$\left.\begin{array}{l}3\Delta_2 = 2\Delta_1 + \Delta_4 \\ 3\Delta_3 = \Delta_1 + 2\Delta_4\end{array}\right\}. \quad (3.6)$$

Relative elongations of the bars are proportional to the displacements

$$\varepsilon_i = \Delta_i/L \quad (i=1,2,3,4). \quad (3.7)$$

Physical relationships are as follows

$$\varepsilon_i = \sigma_i/E + \varepsilon_{i,pl} \quad (i=1,2,3,4), \quad (3.8)$$

where E is the elastic modulus of the material, and $\varepsilon_{i,pl}$ is the plastic strain part.

If we solve a system of equations (3.5)…(3.8) with respect to stresses, we will obtain the following relationships

$$\begin{bmatrix}\sigma_1\\ \sigma_2\\ \sigma_3\\ \sigma_4\end{bmatrix} = \frac{1}{A}\begin{bmatrix}0{,}7 & -0{,}2\\ 0{,}4 & 0{,}1\\ 0{,}1 & 0{,}4\\ -0{,}2 & 0{,}7\end{bmatrix}\begin{bmatrix}P_1\\ P_2\end{bmatrix} + E\begin{bmatrix}-0{,}3 & 0{,}4 & 0{,}1 & -0{,}2\\ 0{,}4 & -0{,}7 & 0{,}2 & 0{,}1\\ 0{,}1 & 0{,}2 & -0{,}7 & 0{,}4\\ -0{,}2 & 0{,}1 & 0{,}4 & -0{,}3\end{bmatrix}\begin{bmatrix}\varepsilon_{1,pl}\\ \varepsilon_{2,pl}\\ \varepsilon_{3,pl}\\ \varepsilon_{4,pl}\end{bmatrix}. \quad (3.9)$$

It should be also noted that the relationships (3.5) are true not only for σ, P and ε_{pl}, but for the increments $\Delta\sigma$, ΔP and $\Delta\varepsilon_{pl}$ as well.

Using the equations (3.3)…(3.5) we derive the relationships between the displacements of the beam ends and forces and plastic deformations

$$\begin{bmatrix} \Delta_1 \\ \Delta_4 \end{bmatrix} = \frac{L}{EA} \begin{bmatrix} 0,7 & -0,2 \\ -0,2 & 0,7 \end{bmatrix} \begin{bmatrix} P_1 \\ P_2 \end{bmatrix} + \begin{bmatrix} 0,7 & 0,4 & 0,1 & -0,2 \\ -0,2 & 0,1 & 0,4 & 0,7 \end{bmatrix} \begin{bmatrix} \varepsilon_{1,pl} \\ \varepsilon_{2,pl} \\ \varepsilon_{3,pl} \\ \varepsilon_{4,pl} \end{bmatrix}. \quad (3.10)$$

The relationships (3.9)…(3.10) enable to trace the variation process of the plastic deformations in bars and beam displacements for the specified loading program.

The case of successive application and removal of independent loads varying in the range $0 \leq \alpha_1 = P_1/(A\sigma_T) \leq 1,62$ and $0 \leq \alpha_2 = P_1/(A\sigma_T) \leq 1,62$ is considered.

Suppose that first only P_1 grows, and $P_2 = 0$. Bar 1 will be the first one to yield and it will start when $0,7\alpha_1 = 1$, i.e. when $\alpha_1 = 1,429$. Plastic deformations in the first bar at the loading parameter $\alpha_1 = 1,62$, when other bars do not yield, which can be easily checked, can be derived from the first equation (3.9), assuming that $\sigma_1 = \sigma_T$ and that there are no plastic deformations in the bars 2, 3 and 4:

$$\sigma_T = 0,7 \cdot 1,62 \cdot \sigma_T - 0,3 E\varepsilon_{1,pl} = 1,134\sigma_T - 0,3 E\varepsilon_{1,pl}$$

or $\varepsilon_{1,pl} = 0,447(\sigma_T/E)$.

If we substitute this equation into (3.5), we obtain

$$\begin{bmatrix} \sigma_1 \\ \sigma_2 \\ \sigma_3 \\ \sigma_4 \end{bmatrix} = \sigma_T \begin{bmatrix} 1,000 \\ 0,648 \\ 0,162 \\ -0,413 \end{bmatrix}$$

It can be seen that all bars except for the first one have an elastic behavior. If we now unload the structure, and substitute a zero load value and $\varepsilon_{1,pl} = 0,447(\sigma_T/E)$ into (3.5), we will obtain the values of the residual stresses

$$\begin{bmatrix} \sigma_1^0 \\ \sigma_2^0 \\ \sigma_3^0 \\ \sigma_4^0 \end{bmatrix} = \sigma_T \begin{bmatrix} -0,134 \\ 0,178 \\ 0,045 \\ -0,089 \end{bmatrix}.$$

If we now additionally load the system with a full value of the second load $P_2 = 1,62 A\sigma_T$, then assuming that the system will have an elastic behavior under this load, using (3.9) we will obtain

$$\begin{bmatrix} \sigma_1 \\ \sigma_2 \\ \sigma_3 \\ \sigma_4 \end{bmatrix} = \sigma_T \begin{bmatrix} 1,000 \\ 0,648 \\ 0,162 \\ -0,413 \end{bmatrix} + \sigma_T \begin{bmatrix} 1,62 \cdot -0,2 \\ 1,62 \cdot 0,1 \\ 1,62 \cdot 0,4 \\ 1,62 \cdot 0,7 \end{bmatrix} = \begin{bmatrix} -0,134 \\ 0,810 \\ 0,810 \\ 0,721 \end{bmatrix}.$$

Our assumption about the elastic behavior of the structure under additional load was confirmed, and the above solution can be assumed to be correct.

However, it is necessary to pay attention to the following feature of the obtained solution:

> Having a perfectly symmetrical structure and identical actions P_1 and P_2 we have obtained an asymmetric response due to the fact that the loading sequence of the structure was asymmetric — first P_1 and only then P_2.

It is easy to see that if we reverse the loading sequence (first P_2 and then P_1), the solution will be

$$\begin{bmatrix} \sigma_1 \\ \sigma_2 \\ \sigma_3 \\ \sigma_4 \end{bmatrix} = \sigma_T \begin{bmatrix} 0,721 \\ 0,810 \\ 0,810 \\ -0,134 \end{bmatrix}.$$

It should be noted that when a nonlinear-elastic (reversible) material model is used instead of the plastic material, which has different behavior under loading and unloading, the loading sequence effect disappears.

Question:
The idea of deformation analysis has been recently promoted, when certain strain values are limited instead of stresses (for example, not higher than the yield stress or some other value of design strength). How can the results of elastic-plastic analysis be interpreted?

Answer:
Strain limitation has hardly any relation to the physics of elastic-plastic behavior. The theory of plasticity operates with a concept of allowable stress range and does not introduce any strain limitations. Force loading of a structure is considered in this case.

If, however, an action in the form of a forced deformation is considered (kinematic or deformation loading), it can make sense to introduce the respective limitations.

The difference between force and deformation loadings becomes evident when we consider a question of whether a stress factor of safety is a sufficient characteristic of reliability. The answer is negative. It is useful to consider two methods of creating stresses in a bar — by applying a certain load P, causing the stress σ in a bar section, and forced deformation ε, corresponding to the same stress σ (Fig. 3.7). In the first case the increase in stress by 1,5 times will lead to a rupture of the bar, and in the second case (the same increase in deformations) will only increase the residual deformations.

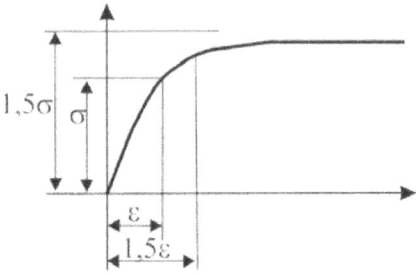

Figure 3.7

Question:
Some design codes for reinforced concrete structures provide a material behavior diagram with a descending branch of the "stress-strain" curve. Can this diagram be used to determine the ultimate load?

Answer:
When considering the stress-strain relationship given in Eurocode-2 for concrete

$$\frac{\sigma}{f_{cm}} = \frac{k\eta - \eta^2}{1+(k-2)\eta}, \qquad (3.11)$$

where $\eta = \varepsilon / \varepsilon_{c1}$; ε_{c1} – is the strain corresponding to the maximum stress f_{cm} .(ε_{c1} and f_{cm} are specified for each concrete grade); $k = 1,05 E \left|\varepsilon_{c1}\right|/f_{cm}$, you should keep in mind that the descending branch of this curve (Fig. 3.8,a) can take place only in the case of forced deformation, and it can not be detected in the case of force loading.

Therefore, the same codes recommend the following relationship for the verification calculations

$$\left. \begin{array}{l} \sigma = f_{cd}\left[1-\left(1-\dfrac{\varepsilon}{\varepsilon_{c2}}\right)^{n}\right] \quad \text{for } 0 \le \varepsilon \le \varepsilon_{c2} \\ \sigma = f_{cd} \quad \text{for } \varepsilon_{c2} \le \varepsilon \le \varepsilon_{c2} \end{array} \right\}, \qquad (3.12)$$

which does not have a descending branch (Fig. 3.8.b).

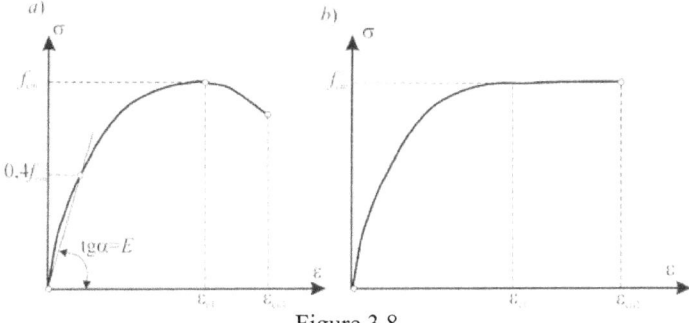

Figure 3.8

The fact that there is no such remark in our national codes is an omission of their authors.

Conversation 3.3. Behavior of Elastic-Plastic System under Increasing Load

Let us consider again a simple structure consisting of a rigid beam and four deformable bars but loaded with a force P, located under the second bar (Fig. 3.9). The distances c and cross-sectional areas of the bars A are the same; the material is perfectly elastic-plastic. Let us examine the stress variations in bars and the displacement of the left end of the beam during the increase of the force P up to its ultimate value.

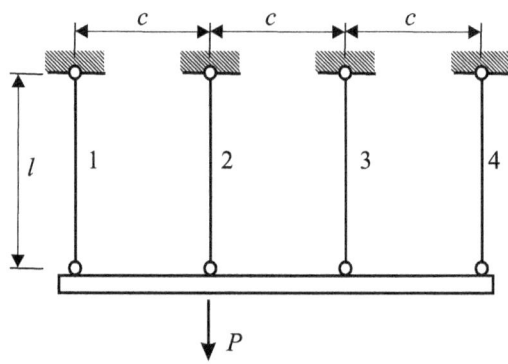

Figure 3.9

Equilibrium equations expressed in terms of forces in bars:

$$N_1 + N_2 + N_3 + N_4 = P;$$
$$N_2 c + 2N_3 c + 2N_4 c = Pc.$$

After reducing by c and dividing by A we obtain the following expressions for stresses:

$$\sigma_1 + \sigma_2 + \sigma_3 + \sigma_4 = P/A; \quad \sigma_2 + 2\sigma_3 + 2\sigma_4 = P/A. \quad (3.13)$$

The conditions of compatibility of deformations can be written as follows:

$$\Delta l_2 = 2\Delta l_1/3 + \Delta l_4/3, \quad \Delta l_3 = \Delta l_1/3 + 2\Delta l_4/3.$$

After dividing by $l/3$ we have:

$$3\varepsilon_2 = 2\varepsilon_1 + \varepsilon_4, \quad 3\varepsilon_3 = \varepsilon_1 + 2\varepsilon_4. \quad (3.14)$$

It should be noted that the equations (3.13) and (3.14) do not depend on the presence and degree of development of the plastic deformations.

Elastic stage. At the beginning of loading all bars have an elastic behavior, Hooke's law is valid:

$$\varepsilon_1 = \sigma_1/E, \quad \varepsilon_2 = \sigma_2/E, \quad \varepsilon_3 = \sigma_3/E, \quad \varepsilon_4 = \sigma_4/E.$$

It follows from this equation and the relationships (3.10) that: $3\sigma_2 = 2\sigma_1 + \sigma_4$; $3\sigma_3 = \sigma_1 + 2\sigma_4$. Adding these expressions to the equations (3.7) and solving the system, we obtain:
$\sigma_1 = 0,4P/A$, $\sigma_2 = 0,3P/A$, $\sigma_3 = 0,2P/A$, $\sigma_4 = 0,1P/A$. Displacement of the left end of the beam
$$\Delta l_1 = \varepsilon_1 l = 0,4Pl/(EA).$$

It can be seen from the above solution that the greatest stresses occur in the first bar. It reaches the yield point first. As soon as it happens, the structure will be in the *elastic-plastic* stage. The ultimate elastic load P_{el} can be determined from the following condition: $\sigma_1 = \sigma_T$, hence $P_{el} = 2,5\sigma_T/A$.

Elastic-plastic stage – the first bar is in the yield state. When the increasing force P exceeds the ultimate elastic value, the first bar will yield, the stresses in it will be constant $\sigma_1 = \sigma_T$. The second, third and fourth bars will still have an elastic behavior. Then the equilibrium equations (3.11) will take the form:
$$\sigma_T + \sigma_2 + \sigma_3 + \sigma_4 = P/A; \quad \sigma_2 + 2\sigma_3 + 2\sigma_4 = P/A. \quad (3.15)$$

It follows from the last expression that $\Delta l_1 = (4P - 7\sigma_T A)l/(3EA)$.

Comparing the stress values (3.13), we see that the second bar will reach the yield point before the third or the fourth one. Let us denote the force corresponding to the yield point of the second bar as P_{e2}, and find its value: $\sigma_T = \sigma_2 = (5P_{e2} - 8\sigma_T A)/(6A) \Rightarrow P_{e2} = 2,8\sigma_T/A$.

Elastic-plastic stage – the first and second bars are in the yield state.
In order to reflect the behavior of the structure at this stage, we introduce the equalities $\sigma_1 = \sigma_2 = \sigma_T$. into the equilibrium equations (3.9). As a result, we obtain
$$\sigma_3 = (2P - 5\sigma_T A)/A, \quad \sigma_4 = (3\sigma_T A - P)/A \quad (3.16)$$

Deformations of bars 3 and 4 can be determined from Hooke's law:
$$\varepsilon_3 = (2P - 5\sigma_T A)/(EA), \quad \varepsilon_4 = (3\sigma_T A - P)/(EA)$$

Substituting this result into the second expression (3.10), we obtain $\varepsilon_1 = (8P - 21\sigma_T A)/(EA)$, hence $\Delta l_1 = (8P - 21\sigma_T A)l/(EA)$.

If a bar 3 or 4 passes the yield point, the structure will become dimensionally unstable and will collapse. Let us find the ultimate load P_u. The third bar will yield when $\sigma_3 = (2P - 5\sigma_T A)/A = \sigma_T$ i.e. when $P_u = 3\sigma_T A$, and the fourth one – when $\sigma_4 = (3\sigma_T A - P)/A = \sigma_T$, hence $P_u = 4\sigma_T A$. A smaller solution is the true one: $P_u = 3\sigma_T A$.

Despite the simplicity of the considered bar system, its behavior has shown features (Fig. 3.10) typical of more complex structures.

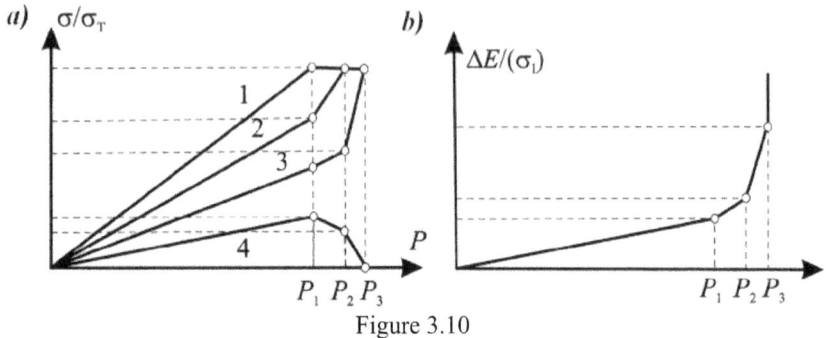
Figure 3.10

The first feature (Fig. 3.10,*a*) is that *the ultimate elastic load P_e corresponding to the ultimate elastic stress in the dangerous point is less than the ultimate load P_u.* This means that the calculation methods taking into account the plastic properties of materials make fuller use of the strength reserves of structures.

The second feature is *the redistribution of stresses in the elastic-plastic stage.* Indeed, in the case of the elastic behavior the characteristics of the stress-strain state increased proportionally to the load increase. Their ratios remained constant. However, they change when the plastic deformations appear. Thus after reaching the yield point the stress σ_1 has stopped growing, but growth rates of the stresses σ_2 and σ_3 have increased.

The third one is that despite a monotonic force increase, *local unloading can take place* (see the stress decrease in the fourth bar, Fig. 3.10,*a*).

Question:
Which of the above features of the behavior of an elastic-plastic structure can not be found using a nonlinear elastic material model?

Answer:
First of all, it is the absence of residual deformations.
However, the property of local unloading of the system in the case of monotonic load growth, which has been found in the given example, is equally important.

The load increase is often used as an argument for applying the nonlinear-elastic approach, but it can be justified only in the case of a monotonic increase in the internal forces, and there is no way it can be guaranteed.

Conversation 3.4. Extreme Properties of the Yield Limit State

Let us consider the problem of determining the ultimate load acting on an elastic-plastic statically indeterminate system of a material with a behavior diagram close to the Prandtl diagram. The load is assumed to be specified in the direction and based on the ratios between individual external forces that make it up.
Only the numerical proportionality factor characterizing the value of the ultimate load has to be determined.

Let us introduce several definitions. We will call a stress state of a system *statically allowable* if it satisfies the equilibrium conditions. A stress state of a system when the yield point is not exceeded in none of its elements will be called *safe*.

Let S_j be a certain distribution of internal forces satisfying the equilibrium equations, and let $\dot{u}_i$ be a certain velocity field satisfying the conditions imposed on the nodal displacements by the external constraints. The deformation rates $\dot{\lambda}_j$ of the elements of the system correspond to this velocity field. The introduced fields of velocities $\dot{u}_i$ and internal forces S_j are otherwise arbitrary and are not interrelated in any way. It is only important for the velocity field to correspond to the strain continuity conditions (kinematically allowable), and for the field of internal forces to correspond to the equilibrium equations (statically allowable).

If the system is in the plastic strain state and the elastic deformations are negligibly small in comparison with the plastic ones, then the following energy balance condition is true

$$\sum_{j=1}^{n} S_j \dot{\lambda}_j = \sum_{i=1}^{s} P_i \dot{u}_i , \qquad (3.17)$$

where the left-hand side is the energy dissipation rate, and the right-hand side is the power of external loads, i.e. work of these loads performed per unit time, which is necessary for plastic deformation.

> Both these expressions are nonnegative, i.e.
> $$\sum_{j=1}^{n} S_j \dot{\lambda}_j \geq 0, \quad \sum_{i=1}^{s} P_i \dot{u}_i \geq 0, \qquad (3.18)$$
> which follows from the energy considerations, and the equation (3.17) plays the same role in the plastic flow theory as the equation (1.3) of the principle of virtual displacements in statics.

Two theorems given below enable to obtain a lower and upper estimate for the loading parameter. These theorems were first formulated and proved by A.A.Gvozdev in 1936; then they were rediscovered many times by different authors.

Theorem about the lower estimate of the load-bearing capacity (static). Let S_j $(j=1,...,n)$ and $\dot{u}_i$ $(i=1,...,s)$ be an unknown true solution of the problem of a limit state of a system subjected to the action of loads P_i $(i=1,...,s)$, and S_j^* $(j=1,...,n)$ be a certain allowable distribution of forces corresponding to these loads on the system. We assume that the equilibrium equations and the condition of not exceeding limit values defined by the limit point $S_j^* \leq S_{j,\lim}$ $(j=1,...,n)$ are satisfied for the allowable distribution of forces.

Let us write the equilibrium equations in the form of the principle of virtual displacements both for the actual and for the allowable state taking the virtual velocity field as the actual velocity field (not known in advance)

$$\sum_{j=1}^{n} S_j \dot{\lambda}_j = \sum_{i=1}^{s} P_i \dot{u}_i, \qquad (3.19)$$

$$\sum_{j=1}^{n} S_j^* \dot{\lambda}_j = \sum_{i=1}^{s} P_i^* \dot{u}_i. \qquad (3.20)$$

Here P_i are actual loads corresponding to the limit state of the system, P_i^* are loads corresponding to the allowable state S_j^*.

Subtracting (3.20) from (3.19), we obtain

$$\sum_{i=1}^{s} P_i \dot{u}_i - \sum_{i=1}^{s} P_i^* \dot{u}_i = \sum_{j=1}^{n} \left(S_j - S_j^* \right) \dot{\lambda}_j. \qquad (3.21)$$

However, due to (3.18) the right-hand side is nonnegative, therefore

$$\sum_{i=1}^{s} P_i \dot{u}_i \geq \sum_{i=1}^{s} P_i^* \dot{u}_i. \qquad (3.22)$$

> Consequently, the power of external forces in the actual limit state is not less than the power of the static virtual external forces.

Inequality (3.22) serves for the lower estimate of the load-bearing capacity. If the loads are specified in the form μP_i $(i=1,...,s)$ and the statically allowable state corresponds to the equilibrium conditions with the loads $\mu^* P_i$ $(i=1,...,s)$, then the following inequality can be easily obtained from (3.20)

$$\mu \geq \mu^*. \qquad (3.23)$$

Thus, a static extreme property of an ultimate load is formulated for a statically indeterminate system of an ideal elastic-plastic material:

> *The value of the loads balanced by the internal forces not exceeding their limit values is less than in the actual limit state.*

Theorem about the upper estimate of the load-bearing capacity (kinematic).
Let $\dot{u}_i^{**}, \dot{\lambda}_j^{**}$ be an arbitrary kinematically allowable velocity and deformation rate field, i. e. a field that satisfies the boundary conditions. Internal forces S_j^{**}, which, generally speaking, do not satisfy the equilibrium equations, are determined based on the deformation rates $\dot{\lambda}_j^{**}$.

Let us write out the equations (3.19), taking the virtual velocity field as $\dot{u}_i^{**}$

$$\sum_{j=1}^{n} S_j \dot{\lambda}_j^{**} = \sum_{i=1}^{s} P_i \dot{u}_i^{**}. \qquad (3.24)$$

Add and subtract the value of power of the plastic deformation corresponding to the kinematically allowable field $\dot{u}_i^{**}$ in the right-hand side of this equation. We will obtain

$$\sum_{j=1}^{n} S_j \dot{\lambda}_j^{**} = \sum_{i=1}^{s} P_i \dot{u}_i^{**} - \sum_{j=1}^{n} \dot{\lambda}_j^{**} \left(S_j^{**} - S_j \right). \qquad (3.25)$$

However, the second term in the right-hand side is nonnegative, therefore

$$\sum_{i=1}^{s} P_i \dot{u}_i^{**} \leq \sum_{j=1}^{n} \dot{\lambda}_j^{**} S_j^{**}. \qquad (3.26)$$

> *Consequently, the power of external forces in the actual limit state for the kinematic virtual displacement rates is less than the power of forces corresponding to the given virtual velocities at these rates.*

If the external load is still given with an accuracy up to one factor, i.e. $\mu P_i \ (i = 1,...,s)$, then it follows from (3.26) that

$$\mu \leq \frac{\sum_{j=1}^{n} \dot{\lambda}_j^{**} S_j^{**}}{\sum_{i=1}^{s} P_i \dot{u}_i^{**}}. \qquad (3.27)$$

The right-hand side of this inequality is known, when the kinematic virtual velocity field is given.

If we take into account that $S_j^{**} = \mu^{**} S_j$, then considering (3.24) we obtain

$$\mu \leq \mu^{**}. \qquad (3.28)$$

Thus, a kinematic extreme property of an ultimate load is formulated for a statically indeterminate system of an ideal elastic-plastic material:

> *The value of the loads calculated according to any of the kinematic virtual plastic collapse models is greater than in the actual limit state.*

Applying the estimates (3.21) and (3.25), we can obtain an interval including an actual value of the ultimate load. If the upper and lower estimates coincide, we obtain an exact solution of the bearing capacity problem.

Example. Let us calculate according to the kinematic and static methods the system shown in Fig. 3.9, the detailed analysis of which has been performed above.

A. *Kinematic method.*

We will assume that the suspensions have the same behavior in tension and in compression. Moreover, we will assume the elastic strains to be so small, that they can be neglected in comparison with the yield strains.

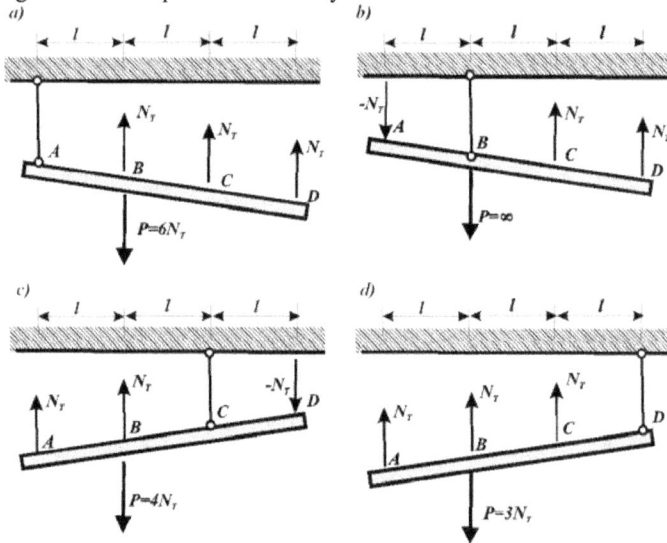

Figure 3.11

Then we can assume four kinematic virtual collapse modes of the system, i.e.: small rotations about the attachment point of each suspension (Fig. 3.11). The balancing load will be:

- in the case of the rotation about the point A (Fig. 3.11,*a*)
  $P=N_T\,(l+2l+3l)/l=6N_T$;
- in the case of the rotation about the point B (Fig. 3.11,*b*), since the arm of the force is equal to zero with respect to the pivot point
  $P=\infty$;
- in the case of the rotation about the point C (Fig. 3.11,*c*)
  $P=N_T\,(2l+l+l)/l=4N_T$;
- in the case of the rotation about the point D (Fig. 3.11, *d*)
  $P=N_T\,(3l+2l+l)/2l=3N_T$.

We see that the minimum force $P=P_u$ equal to $3N^T$, is obtained in the case of the rotation of the beam about the point D, i. e. when the first, second and third suspensions are in the yield state. This result coincides with the full calculation performed above.

B. *Static method.*
Since the system is twice statically indeterminate, we will assume such stress states when three elements are in the yield state, and the force in the fourth element has to be less than the limit one.
The following combinations are possible:
 a) $N_1 = N_2 = N_3 = N_T$;
 b) $N_1 = N_2 = N_4 = N_T$;
 c) $N_1 = N_3 = N_4 = N_T$;
 d) $N_1 = N_3 = N_4 = N_T$.

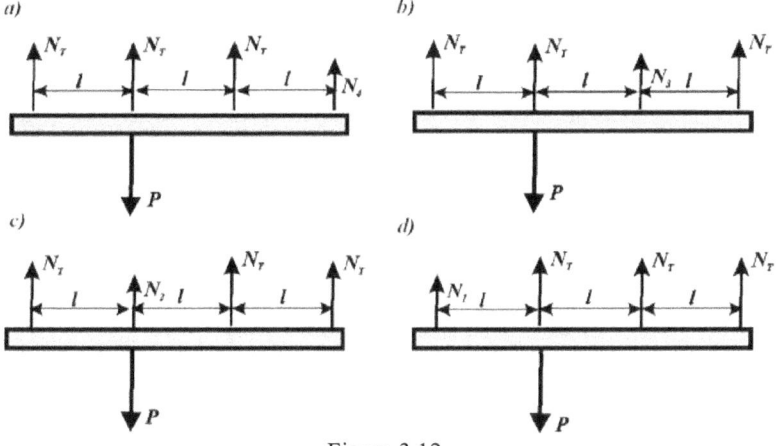

Figure 3.12

These states are shown in Fig. 3.12. The force in the remaining element which has not reached the yield point has to be determined from the condition that the moment of all forces with respect to the application point of the external force is equal to zero. We obtain:
 for the case *a*: $N_4 = 0$;
 for the case *b*: $N_3 = -N_T$;
 for the case *c*: $N_2 = \infty$;
 for the case *d*: $N_1 = 3N_T$.
We see that the third and fourth cases are eliminated, since the forces in them are greater than N_T; the second case is possible, if we assume that the third element has the same behavior in tension and in compression.
The obtained ultimate load for the first case is $P_u = 3N_T$, and for the second case is $P_u = 3N_T - N_T = 2N_T$.
The true state of ultimate equilibrium is when the load reaches its maximum value. Therefore the ultimate equilibrium state in the considered system will occur in accordance with the first case of distribution of limit forces. This result coin-

cides with that obtained by the kinematic method and by the full calculation of the system.

Question:
How does the initial stress state of the system affect the value of the ultimate load?

Answer:
It should be noted that the considered system is dimensionally unstable (mechanism) in the ultimate equilibrium state, therefore the initial stresses which could exist in the system (e.g., welding) do not affect the value of the ultimate load.

This load is determined from equilibrium equations which do not include self-stressed states, but the initial stresses corresponding to a zero external load are related to them.

Conversation 3.5. Geometric Nonlinearity

When it comes to geometrically nonlinear problems, first of all, it is necessary to clearly define the level of geometric nonlinearity. To do this, we will use the classification of geometrically nonlinear problem formulations presented in the classic work of V.Novozhilov [3].

Based on this classification, we shall distinguish the following 4 groups of geometrically nonlinear problem formulations for finite-dimensional systems.

The first group will contain the problems where all geometrically nonlinear effects can be completely neglected. In other words, it refers to geometrically linear problem formulations.

Before proceeding any further, it should be noted that geometric nonlinearity can creep into the governing equations in two ways: through the equations relating displacements and deformations, and through the equilibrium equations. We will reserve the first group for those problems where the geometric nonlinearity can creep only through the equilibrium equations.

Thus the *first group* of geometric nonlinearity considers the weakest version of the geometrically nonlinear theory. We assume that the equilibrium equations should be written for the deformed shape of the system, and the relationships between deformations and displacements are required to be linear. The structural mechanics has the concept of *a deformed-shape-based analysis*, or *a second-order theory* for the problems of the first group of geometric nonlinearity.

This group comprises a wide range of structural designs, and, first of all, bar structures, where bending moments in the elements are calculated taking into account the effect of longitudinal forces.

Let us now consider *the second group*, which differs from the first one in that the geometric nonlinearity can now also creep through the geometric equations relating the displacements and deformations. The essential thing here in comparison with the first group is that the orders of smallness of deformations and rotations are distinguished. It is assumed that the squares of the rotation angles of the elements of the considered design model are of the same order of smallness as the strain components, which in turn are negligible compared to one. The rotations are small compared to one as well. A characteristic example of problems of this group is the theory of flexible plates based on von Karman equations.

A *third group* of geometric nonlinearity features problems where the deformations are small compared to one, whereas such assumptions cannot be applied to the rotations. Structures with flexible ropes serve as an excellent example of this type of geometrically nonlinear problems.

Finally, this hierarchy is topped by the most complex problems — problems of the *fourth group* of geometric nonlinearity, when even relative deformations cannot be treated as small values compared to one. The need to perform calculations of structures made of rubber and rubber-like materials forces the designers to tackle these problems.

In the case of discrete design models the geometric nonlinearity has no effect on topological information about the design model, and the topology of the system itself is insensitive to relations between orders of geometric nonlinearity at the level of an individual finite element. Using this possibility, let us consider the simplest example of a finite element in order to illustrate the four groups of geometric nonlinearity described above — a truss bar. Let us consider a plane problem for the sake of simplicity.

Let the bar occupy the position MN in its initial state, with its beginning in the node M and its end in the node N. The *initial* state here refers to a state of the bar acquired by it after pre-tension (dislocation) by a value d. In the result of subsequent deformation, the bar will remain rectilinear and will occupy the position M^*N^*, as shown in Fig. 3.13.

We will use the following designations:
L_x, L_y are projections of the bar on the respective axes in the initial state;
L and L^* is the length of the bar in its initial and final state, respectively;
u_M, u_N, v_M, v_N are displacements of nodes M and N in the directions of the x and y axes, respectively;
e_x, e_y are elongations of the projections of the bar in its initial state on the coordinate axes;
Δ is the total elongation of the bar;
N is the longitudinal force in the bar, positive when in tension.

Let us consider a set of vectors **s** (forces), Δ (elongations), **u** (nodal displacements), **p** (nodal loads), related to a particular element (bar). The subscript "e", we used earlier to indicate that an element is considered[9], is now omitted for the sake of shortness.

We have

$$\mathbf{s} = \|[N]\|,\ \Delta = \|[\Delta]\|,\ \mathbf{u}^T = \|[u_M\ v_M\ u_N\ v_N]\|,\ \mathbf{p}^T = \|[P_{Mx} P_{My} P_{Nx} P_{Ny}]\|. \qquad (3.29)$$

---

[9] See conversation 5 from the cycle 1

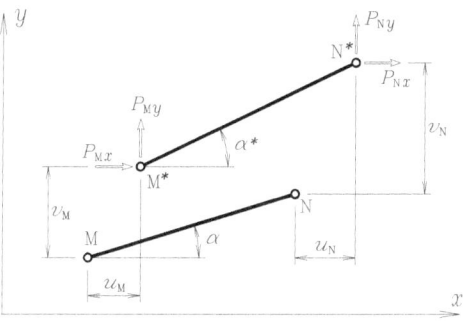

Figure 3.13

It follows from the geometric considerations (Fig. 3.13) that

$$e_x = u_N - u_M, \quad e_y = v_N - v_M, \quad \Delta = (L^* - L), \quad (3.30)$$

$$L^2 = L_x^2 + L_y^2, \quad L^{*2} = (L_x + e_x)^2 + (L_y + e_y)^2. \quad (3.31)$$

Let $\lambda_x, \lambda_y, \lambda_x^*, \lambda_y^*$ be the direction cosines of the segments MN and M^*N^* with respect to the fixed system of axes (x, y) (see Fig. 3.13), i.e.

$$\lambda_x = \cos\alpha = L_x/L, \qquad \lambda_y = \sin\alpha = L_y/L, \quad (3.32)$$

$$\lambda_x^* = \cos\alpha^* = (L_x + e_x)/L^*, \qquad \lambda_y^* = \sin\alpha^* = (L_y + e_y)/L^*. \quad (3.33)$$

Let us introduce the following important geometric parameters, which we will need later:

$$e = \lambda_x e_x + \lambda_y e_y, \quad \omega = (\lambda_x e_y - \lambda_y e_x)/L, \quad \varepsilon = e + 0{,}5(e^2 + \omega^2 L^2)/L. \quad (3.34)$$

The geometric meaning of the parameter e is obvious: it is a projection of the difference of displacements of the bar ends on the direction of the axis of the bar in its undeformed state. As for the parameter ω, it is actually the rotation angle of the bar provided that it is small compared to one, and that the relative parameter e/L is small compared to one.

The parameter e can be written in the matrix form as

$$e = \mathbf{Q}^T \mathbf{u}, \qquad \mathbf{Q}^T = |[-\lambda_x \; -\lambda_y \; \lambda_x \; \lambda_y]|, \quad (3.35)$$

where $\mathbf{Q}$ is the matrix of the equilibrium equations in the geometrically linear formulation.

It should be noted, that if we introduce the rotation matrix $\mathbf{\Omega}$ into consideration,

$$\mathbf{\Omega} = \begin{Vmatrix} 0 & 0 & 0 & 1 \\ 1 & 0 & 0 & 0 \\ 0 & 1 & 0 & 0 \\ 0 & 0 & 1 & 0 \end{Vmatrix}, \qquad (3.36)$$

we obtain $(\mathbf{\Omega Q})^T = \|[\lambda_y\ -\lambda_x\ -\lambda_y\ \lambda_x]\|$, so that the rotation parameter ω can be written in the matrix form as well

$$\omega L = \mathbf{Q}^T \mathbf{\Omega}^T \mathbf{u}, \qquad (3.37)$$

which will be convenient for us in the future.

The following formula relating the deformation of the bar Δ and the displacements of its ends expressed in terms of the introduced geometric parameters can be derived from the defining relations (3.30), (3.31) and (3.34), i.e.

$$\Delta \left[1 + \frac{\Delta}{2L} \right] = \varepsilon. \qquad (3.38)$$

Its correctness can be easily proved by direct substitution. Indeed, the left-hand side of (3.38) can be transformed to

$$(L^* - L)\left[1 + \frac{\Delta}{2L}\right] = \frac{L^{*2} - L^2}{2L} =$$

$$= \frac{(L_x + e_x)^2 + (L_y + e_y)^2 - L_x^2 - L_y^2}{2L} = \lambda_x e_x + \lambda_y e_y + \frac{e_x^2 + e_y^2}{2L},$$

and the expression for ε from (3.22) can be given in this form as well, if we take into account that $\lambda_x^2 + \lambda_y^2 = 1$.

The following expression for the deformation of the bar follows directly from the formula (3.38)

$$\Delta = L\left(\sqrt{1 + 2\varepsilon/L} - 1\right). \qquad (3.39)$$

It should be noted that when deriving the formula (3.39) we did not use any simplifying assumptions regarding the comparison of the orders of smallness of the values included in this formula. Therefore, the formula (3.39) is actually a nonlinear geometric equation relating the deformation Δ and the components of the displacement vector $\mathbf{u}$, which is included in the fourth group of geometric nonlinearity.

Equations relating the deformation Δ and the components of the displacement vector can be obtained for other groups of geometric nonlinearity by introducing different simplifying assumptions which allow neglectшлті certain components. The respective results are given in the Table 3.2.

Table 3.2

STOREY	Small values	Geometric equations
IV	—	$\Delta = L\left(\sqrt{1+2e/L} - 1\right)$
III	$\dfrac{\Delta-d}{L} \ll 1$	$\Delta = e + 0,5(e^2 + w^2 L^2)/L$ $\Delta = \mathbf{Q}^T\mathbf{u} + \dfrac{1}{2L}\mathbf{u}^T\mathbf{G}\mathbf{u}$
II	$e/L \ll 1$ $\omega^2 \approx e/L$	$\Delta = e + 0,5w^2 L$ $\Delta = \mathbf{Q}^T\mathbf{u} + \mathbf{u}^T\mathbf{\Omega}\mathbf{Q}\mathbf{Q}^T\mathbf{\Omega}^T\mathbf{u}$
I	$\omega^2 \ll e/L$	$\Delta = e$ $\Delta = \mathbf{Q}^T\mathbf{u}$
0	$\omega \ll 1$	$\Delta = e$ $\Delta = \mathbf{Q}^T\mathbf{u}$

Let us now consider the equilibrium equations used for different groups of geometric nonlinearity. In the general case, writing these equations for the deformed state of the bar, we obtain

$$\mathbf{Q}^*\mathbf{s} = \mathbf{p}, \qquad \mathbf{Q}^{*T} = \|[-\lambda^*_x\ -\lambda^*_y\ \lambda^*_x\ \lambda^*_y]\|, \qquad (3.40)$$

and it remains for us to find expressions for the direction cosines of the axis of the bar in its deformed state.

Using the formulas (3.32) and the fact that the rotation angle β of the bar can be given as $\beta = \alpha^* - \alpha$ (see Fig. 3.13), we obtain

$$\lambda^*_x = \cos(\alpha+\beta) = \lambda_x \cos\beta - \lambda_y \sin\beta,$$
$$\lambda^*_y = \sin(\alpha+\beta) = \lambda_y \cos\beta + \lambda_x \sin\beta. \qquad (3.41)$$

Taking into account that
$$\operatorname{tg}\alpha^* = \left(\lambda_y L + e_y\right)\left(\lambda_x L + e_x\right), \quad \operatorname{tg}\alpha = \lambda_y/\lambda_x, \qquad (3.42)$$

and using the formula for the tangent of the difference of two angles, as well as the relation $\lambda_x^2 + \lambda_y^2 = 1$, we obtain the following expression after simple transformations

$$\operatorname{tg}\beta = \left(\operatorname{tg}\alpha^* - \operatorname{tg}\alpha\right)\left(1 - \operatorname{tg}\alpha^* \cdot \operatorname{tg}\alpha\right) = \omega L(L+e). \qquad (3.43)$$

The sine and cosine of the rotation angle of the bar β included in the formulas (3.41) can be expressed in terms of the tangent of this angle

$$\cos\beta = 1/\sqrt{1+\text{tg}^2\beta} = 1/\sqrt{1+\omega^2 L^2/(L+e)^2},$$

$$\sin\beta = \text{tg}\beta/\sqrt{1+\text{tg}^2\beta} = \left[1/\sqrt{1+\omega^2 L^2/(L+e)^2}\right]\omega L/(L+e), \qquad (3.44)$$

so that
$$\lambda^*_x = [\lambda_x - \lambda_y \omega L/(L+e)]/\sqrt{1+\omega^2 L^2/(L+e)^2},$$

$$\lambda^*_y = [\lambda_y + \lambda_x \omega L/(L+e)]/\sqrt{1+\omega^2 L^2/(L+e)^2}. \qquad (3.45)$$

Formulas (3.33) for the direction cosines of the axis of the bar in the deformed state are exact, since no assumptions regarding the smallness of the strain parameters (fourth group) were used when deriving them. The results for other groups are given in the Table 3.3.

Table 3.3.

STOREY	Small values	Parameters of equilibrium equations
IV	—	$\lambda^*_x = \left[\lambda_x - \lambda_y \omega L(L+e)\right]\Big/\sqrt{1+\omega^2 L^2 (L+e)^2}$ $\lambda^*_y = \left[\lambda_y - \lambda_x \omega L(L+e)\right]\Big/\sqrt{1+\omega^2 L^2 (L+e)^2}$
III	$\dfrac{\Delta-d}{L} \ll 1$	$\lambda^*_x = \left[\lambda_x - \lambda_y \omega L(L+e)\right]\Big/\sqrt{1+\omega^2 L^2 (L+e)^2}$ $\lambda^*_y = \left[\lambda_y - \lambda_x \omega L(L+e)\right]\Big/\sqrt{1+\omega^2 L^2 (L+e)^2}$
II	$e/L \ll 1$ $\omega^2 \approx e/L$	$\lambda^*_x = \lambda_x - \lambda_y \omega, \quad \lambda^*_y = \lambda_y - \lambda_x \omega$ $\mathbf{Q}^* = \mathbf{Q} + \dfrac{1}{2L}\mathbf{\Omega Q Q}^T\mathbf{\Omega}^T\mathbf{u}$
I	$\omega^2 \ll e/L$	$\lambda^*_x = \lambda_x - \lambda_y \omega, \quad \lambda^*_y = \lambda_y - \lambda_x \omega$ $\mathbf{Q}^* = \mathbf{Q} + \dfrac{1}{2L}\mathbf{\Omega Q Q}^T\mathbf{\Omega}^T\mathbf{u}$
0	$\omega \ll 1$	$\lambda^*_x = \lambda_x, \quad \lambda^*_y = \lambda_y$ $\mathbf{Q}^* = \mathbf{Q}$

We could of course write governing nonlinear equations based on the relations given in the Table 3.3, and then try to find a method to solve them. However, with subsequent stepwise procedures for non-linear problems in mind, we will write the necessary equations in increments at once. More precisely, we will determine the structure of geometrically nonlinear equations in increments which turns out to be common for all discrete systems without specifying the type of the finite element.

Let a certain (initial) configuration of the system characterized by nodal displacements $\mathbf{u}_0$ be known. These displacements can be zero if this reference point is convenient. The following equilibrium conditions between the initial nodal loads $\mathbf{p}_0$ and initial forces $\mathbf{s}_0$ are satisfied in this configuration

$$\mathbf{Q}(\mathbf{u}_0)\mathbf{s}_0 = \mathbf{p}_0 \qquad (3.46)$$

Let now the load acquire an increment $\delta\mathbf{p}$, which should have the corresponding increments of forces $\delta\mathbf{s}$ and displacements $\delta\mathbf{u}$. The equilibrium equations for the perturbed state are written as follows

$$[\mathbf{Q}(\mathbf{u}_0) + \delta\mathbf{Q}](\mathbf{s}_0 + \delta\mathbf{s}) = \mathbf{p}_0 + \delta\mathbf{p}, \qquad (3.47)$$

and after removing the brackets and taking into account (3.46) they take the following form

$$\delta\mathbf{Q}\mathbf{s}_0 + \mathbf{Q}(\mathbf{u}_0)\delta\mathbf{s} + \delta\mathbf{Q}\delta\mathbf{s} = \delta\mathbf{p}. \qquad (3.48)$$

If components of the vector of additional displacements $\delta\mathbf{u}$ are relatively small (but nevertheless require the geometrically nonlinear analysis), then in order to obtain the equations in variations it is enough to consider only the second group of geometric nonlinearity. In this case the product $\delta\mathbf{Q}\mathbf{s}_0$ can be given as a linear function of the displacement increment, which leads to the equations

$$\mathbf{Q}(\mathbf{u}_0)\delta\mathbf{s} + \mathbf{T}(\mathbf{s}_0)\delta\mathbf{u} + \delta\mathbf{Q}\delta\mathbf{s} = \delta\mathbf{p}. \qquad (3.49)$$

For example, considering a truss bar in a plane problem, we assume the following based on the Table 3.3

$$\mathbf{Q}^T(\mathbf{u}_0) = \|[-\lambda_x\ -\lambda_y\ \lambda_x\ \lambda_y]\|,$$

$$\mathbf{T}(\mathbf{s}_0)\,\delta\mathbf{u} = \|[\lambda_y\ -\lambda_x\ -\lambda_y\ \lambda_x]\|^T \delta\omega\ N_0 = \frac{N_0}{L}\mathbf{\Omega}\mathbf{Q}\mathbf{Q}^T\mathbf{\Omega}^T\delta\mathbf{u}, \qquad (3.50)$$

where λ_x and λ_y are the direction cosines of the bar in the initial configuration of the system, and N_0 is the initial force in the bar.

The dependence between the element deformation increments $\delta\Lambda$ and the increments of the nodal displacements will be defined as follows

$$\delta\Lambda = \mathbf{Q}^T(\mathbf{u}_0)\,\delta\mathbf{u} + \delta\mathbf{Q}^T\delta\mathbf{u}. \qquad (3.51)$$

The relations (3.51) are actually varied geometric equations of the second group of geometric nonlinearity. For example, in the case of a truss bar, we have

$$\delta\Lambda = \delta e + \omega L\,\delta\omega = \mathbf{Q}^T(\mathbf{u}_0)\,\delta\mathbf{u} + \mathbf{u}_0^T\mathbf{\Omega}\mathbf{Q}\mathbf{Q}^T\mathbf{\Omega}^T/L\,\delta\mathbf{u}, \qquad (3.52)$$

so in this case

$$\delta\mathbf{Q}^T = \mathbf{u}_0^T\mathbf{\Omega}\mathbf{Q}\mathbf{Q}^T\mathbf{\Omega}^T/L. \qquad (3.53)$$

Substituting (3.51) into the physical equations relating forces and deformations which can be written as follows for the increments

$$\delta\mathbf{s} = \mathbf{F}\delta\Lambda, \qquad (3.54)$$

and then introducing the derived expressions for δs into (3.49) we obtain

$$[\mathbf{QFQ}^T + \mathbf{T(s_0)} + \mathbf{QF\delta Q}^T + \delta\mathbf{QFQ}^T + \delta\mathbf{QF\delta Q}^T]\delta\mathbf{u} = \delta\mathbf{p}. \quad (3.55)$$

These equations can be written as follows with other designations

$$[\mathbf{K}_0 + \mathbf{K}_1(\mathbf{s}_0) + \mathbf{K}_2(\mathbf{u}_0)]\delta\mathbf{u} = (\mathbf{K}_0 + \mathbf{K}_G)\delta\mathbf{u} = \delta\mathbf{p}. \quad (3.56)$$

Here, a conventional stiffness matrix $\mathbf{K}_0 = \mathbf{QFQ}^T$ acquires an increment in the form of the matrix of initial stresses $\mathbf{K}_1(\mathbf{s}_0) = \mathbf{T}(\mathbf{s}_0)$, linearly dependent on forces in the system before the load is incremented, plus the matrix of initial rotations

$$\mathbf{K}_2(\mathbf{u}_0) = \mathbf{QF\delta Q}^T + \delta\mathbf{QFQ}^T + \delta\mathbf{QF\delta Q}^T,$$

that includes not more than the second order of the displacements. The matrix

$$\mathbf{K}_G = \mathbf{K}_1(\mathbf{s}_0) + \mathbf{K}_2(\mathbf{u}_0)$$

is called a *geometric stiffness matrix*.

As an example let us consider the expressions taken from [1] for the above stiffness matrices of a simple finite element in the form of a bar of the plane design model of the hinged bar system (Fig. 3.14).

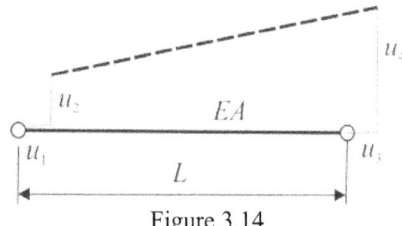

Figure 3.14

$$\mathbf{K}_0 = \frac{EA}{L}\begin{bmatrix} 1 & 0 & -1 & 0 \\ 0 & 0 & 0 & 0 \\ -1 & 0 & 1 & 0 \\ 0 & 0 & 0 & 0 \end{bmatrix}, \quad \mathbf{K}_1(\mathbf{s}_0) = \frac{S}{L}\begin{bmatrix} 0 & 0 & 0 & 0 \\ 0 & 1 & 0 & -1 \\ 0 & 0 & 0 & 0 \\ 0 & -1 & 0 & 1 \end{bmatrix},$$

$$\mathbf{K}_2(\mathbf{u}_0) = \frac{EA(u_1 - u_3)}{4L^3}\begin{bmatrix} 3(u_1-u_3) & 2(u_2-u_4) & -3(u_1-u_3) & -(u_2-u_4) \\ 2(u_2-u_4) & (u_1-u_3) & -2(u_2-u_4) & -(u_1-u_3) \\ -3(u_1-u_3) & -2(u_2-u_4) & -3(u_1-u_3) & 2(u_2-u_4) \\ -(u_2-u_4) & -(u_1-u_3) & 2(u_2-u_4) & (u_1-u_3) \end{bmatrix}.$$

If the tilts $(u_2 - u_4)/L$ and relative elongations of the bar $(u_1 - u_3)/L$ are small, the matrix $\mathbf{K}_2(\mathbf{u}_0)$ is small compared to others, and its effect can be neglected.

> In those cases when it is enough to consider only the first group of geometric nonlinearity, the matrix $\mathbf{K}_2(\mathbf{u}_0)$ can be neglected in the calculations.

It is also easy to see that in the case of a bar in tension, when $N>0$, the resistance to the bar tilt appears due to a restoring moment $M = N(u_2 - u_4)/L$, and the greater the tension, the stronger the resistance to tilt.

This effect provides the performance of many cable-stayed structures, which are classified as instantly rigid systems within the kinematic analysis framework.

Question:
Are there any problems where it is quite clear that the calculation should be performed taking into account the geometric nonlinearity of the system?

Answer:
Of course, there are. For instance, the problem of assessing the behavior of the systems which were defined as dimensionally unstable in the linear analysis. Some of these unstable systems can take external loads in a modified geometric configuration, which they acquire under the same load.

As an example let us consider a simple system of three truss bars of length $L=5000$ mm lying on one straight line (Fig. 3.15). This structure is obviously two-dimensionally unstable, and it follows from the linear analysis that it cannot bear the transverse load (kN)

$$P_1 = 0,029; \quad P_2 = 16,072; \quad P_3 = -0,029; \quad P_4 = 16,072.$$

Figure 3.15

Let us perform a geometrically nonlinear analysis assuming that the stiffness of all bars is $EA = 1000$ kN and the structure in its initial state is prestressed by a force 25,4 kN. As a result we obtain that the nodal displacements are equal to:

$$u_1 = 1500; \quad u_2 = 75; \quad u_3 = 1500; \quad u_4 = -75,$$

and the forces in bars (kN):

$$N_1 = 53,573; \quad N_2 = 53.603; \quad N_3 = 53,573.$$

It can be easily verified by a simple substitution into exact equations for the geometric consistency and equilibrium of nodes which will be written for a deformed model as:

$$\left.\begin{aligned}
(L-u_1)^2 + u_2^2 &= (L + N_1 L/(EA))^2 \\
(L+u_1-u_2)^2 + (u_3-u_4)^2 &= (L + N_2 L/(EA))^2 \\
(L+u_3)^2 + u_4^2 &= (L + N_3 L/(EA))^2 \\
N_1 \cos\alpha_1 - N_2 \cos\alpha_2 + P_1 &= 0 \\
N_1 \sin\alpha_1 - N_2 \sin\alpha_2 - P_2 &= 0 \\
N_2 \cos\alpha_2 - N_3 \cos\alpha_3 + P_3 &= 0 \\
N_2 \sin\alpha_2 - N_3 \sin\alpha_3 - P_4 &= 0
\end{aligned}\right\}.$$

It should be taken into account that

$$\sin\alpha_1 = u_1/(L-u_1);$$
$$\sin\alpha_2 = (u_3-u_4)/(L+u_1-u_2);$$
$$\sin\alpha_3 = u_3/(L+u_3).$$

Conversation 3.6. Structural Nonlinearity

Systems where restrictions of displacements are defined by the inequality-conditions (unilateral constraints) are more common than is usually thought. The simplest examples are a structure simply supported on a certain surface which prohibits the displacement towards this surface and does not prevent the displacement in the opposite direction, flexible ropes, which allow the approach of its end points and not allow them to be removed by more than the length of the rope.

Other typical examples are dry masonry, connection between the foundation of the structure and the underlying soil. Loose soils or absolutely flexible membranes can serve as examples of more complex systems with unilateral constraints.

The parameters of the initial state of a unilateral constraint are its distinctive feature. For example, the gap Δ_0 in a unilateral constraint or the prestressing which can be interpreted as the negative gap, i.e. $\Delta_0 < 0$, can be taken into account for the simplest model of the bar which can take tension and is disabled when compression appears (Fig. 3.16,a).

If you want to enable a constraint when working in the system, it is necessary to select the gap first, or if you want to disable it, it is necessary to overcome the prestress.

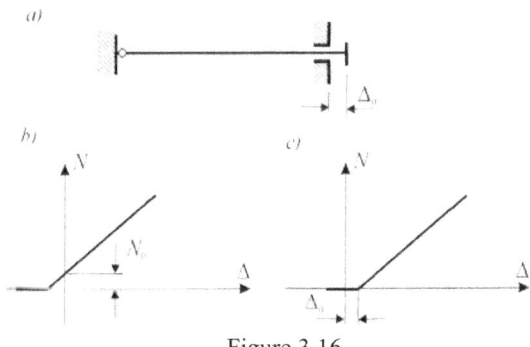

Figure 3.16

Two variants of the diagram of the behavior of the element as the relationship between the longitudinal force H and the increase of the distance between the end points Δ are given in Fig. 3.16,b and 3.16,c, where a variant with prestressing (equal to N_0) corresponds to the case a, and a variant of the system with a gap Δ_0 corresponds to the case b.

The slope of the diagram is equal to EA/L (EA — tensile stiffness of the bar, L — length of the bar).

It is useful to point out some peculiarities related to the description of the potential energy of the system with unilateral constraints, which is not a smooth function of generalized coordinates in the considered case.

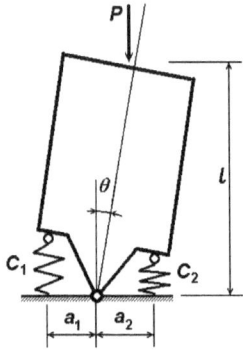

Figure 3.17.

For example, the expression for the potential energy of a single degree of freedom system consisting of a rigid disk the position of which is defined by the rotation angle θ, and two compressive elastic elements with the stiffness values C_1 and C_2 (Fig. 3.17) is as follows

$$U = \begin{cases} \dfrac{C_1}{2} a_1^2 \sin^2\theta - Pl\sin\theta & \text{for } \theta \geq 0 \\ \dfrac{C_2}{2} a_2^2 \sin^2\theta - Pl\sin\theta & \text{for } \theta < 0. \end{cases} \quad (3.57)$$

It can be seen that when $C_1 a_1 \neq C_2 a_2$ the function $U(\theta)$ has a discontinuity of the second derivative at the origin caused by an instantaneous change in stiffness at the moment of switching the unilateral constraints.

Next, we will consider the case of small displacements in order to simplify the presentation as much as possible. In this case, instead of (3.57), we have

$$U = \begin{cases} \dfrac{C_1}{2} a_1^2 \theta^2 - Pl\sin\theta & \text{for } \theta \geq 0 \\ \dfrac{C_2}{2} a_2^2 \theta^2 - Pl\sin\theta & \text{for } \theta < 0. \end{cases} \quad (3.57, a)$$

The second characteristic feature of the elastic systems with unilateral constraints is that if the system has rigid unilateral constraints, its potential energy becomes a function defined not for all possible values of generalized coordinates. Structural mechanics of elastic systems usually defines the potential energy as a function of generalized coordinates, which can take arbitrary values, and a certain open set serves as a domain of the potential energy function.

For inequality conditions that appear when unilateral constraints are taken into account, this property is no longer observed, and the potential energy can turn out to be a function defined on a closed set of values of generalized coordinates.

A typical example is shown in Fig. 3.18,*a*, where a single degree of freedom system can have only displacements $x \geq -\Delta$. Its potential energy (see Fig.3.18,*b*) is

$$U = \begin{cases} \dfrac{C}{2}x^2 - Px & \text{for } x \geq -\Delta \\ \text{not defined} & \text{for } x < -\Delta \end{cases}. \tag{3.58}$$

a)

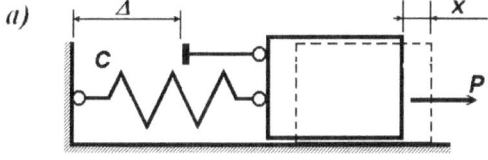

b)

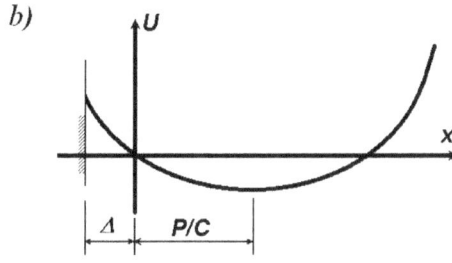

Figure 3.18.

Finally, a simple system with two degrees of freedom which has both these peculiarities is shown in Fig. 3.19, *a*.

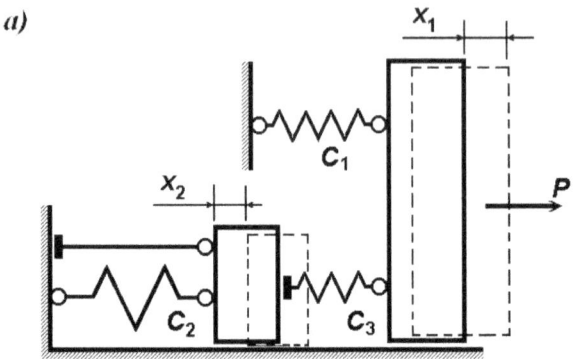

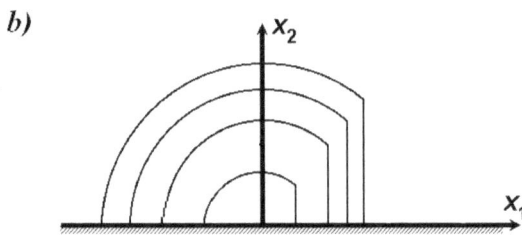

Figure 3.19.

The potential energy of this system is described as

$$U = \begin{cases} \dfrac{1}{2}c_1 x_1^2 - Px_1 & \text{for } x_1 \geq x_2; x_2 \geq 0 \\ \dfrac{1}{2}c_1 x_1^2 + \dfrac{1}{2}(c_1+c_2)(x_1-x_2)^2 + \\ \quad + \dfrac{1}{2}c_2 x_2^2 - Px_1 & \text{for } x_1 < x_2; x_2 \geq 0 \\ \text{not defined} & \text{for } x_2 < 0 \end{cases} \qquad (3.59)$$

The surface $U = U(x_1, x_2)$ is shown by level lines in Fig. 3.19,b. The function (3.59) is defined on a closed set (half-plane $x_2 \geq 0$) and has a discontinuity in the derivative along the line $x_1 = x_2$, caused by the switching of a unilateral constraint. It should be noted that in general nonsmoothness of the function U can be overcome by introducing additional unknowns (redundant coordinates). Thus, in addition to the displacement θ, two more unknown displacements x_1 and x_2 of the support points of the springs can be introduced for the system shown in Fig. 3.17, and then

$$U(\theta, x_1, x_2) = \frac{c_1}{2}(a_1\theta - x_1)^2 + \frac{c_2}{2}(a_2\theta - x_2)^2 - Pl\theta, \qquad (3.60)$$

but the following restrictions have to be satisfied

$$x_1 \geq 0, \quad x_2 \geq 0, \qquad (3.61)$$

i.e. the smooth function (3.60) is now defined on a closed set. This method is widely used below in discussions related to the construction of the so-called auxiliary systems.

Let us now consider a certain elastic system with s unilateral constraints indexed by Greek letters. We select such a sign convention for reactions R in these constraints, so that the force allowed by the nature of the constraint (compression for a retaining constraint or tension for a constraint in the form of a flexible rope) can be considered positive. Displacements u not restrained by a unilateral constraint will be considered positive as well (for example, the approach of the ends of a flexible rope). Since a unilateral constraint can only be in one of the following states: operating (the constraint is enabled), when $R > 0$ and $u = 0$ or non-operating (the constraint is disabled), when $R = 0$ and $u > 0$, the following inequalities and equalities should be satisfied for all unilateral constraints of the system:

$$R_\alpha \geq 0 \;;\quad u_\alpha \geq 0 \;;\quad R_\alpha u_\alpha = 0 \quad (\alpha = 1, \ldots, s)\,. \tag{3.62}$$

These conditions are written for rigid unilateral constraints, such as, for example, a unilateral retaining constraint. In the case of elastic unilateral constraints (for example, tensile springs of finite rigidity) and the selected sign convention the following should be written instead of (3.62)

$$R_\alpha = \tfrac{1}{2} k_\alpha (|u_\alpha| - u_\alpha) \quad (\alpha = 1, \ldots, s)\,, \tag{3.63}$$

where k_α is the rigidity of the elastic unilateral constraint.

Indeed, in the case of a positive displacement u_α not restrained by a unilateral constraint, we obtain $R_\alpha = 0$ from (3.62), while in the case of a negative displacement, the linear relationship $R_\alpha = - k_\alpha u_\alpha$ with a positive force (taken by a unilateral constraint) follows from (3.63). We will further assume that all unilateral constraints in the considered system are rigid. In fact, as will be shown at the end of this section, this circumstance is not a restriction on the class of unilateral constraints, since any elastic unilateral element can be modeled by placing a rigid unilateral constraint on its end, as shown in Fig. 3.16.

The main problem of calculating a system with unilateral constraints is that it is required to find out which of the constraints get involved under the action of a given load, i.e. to establish a *working system*. It should be noted that if you decide to simply go through all the variants, you will have to analyze 2^s different models, which in most cases is almost impossible (if $s = 10$, it means that there are 1024 different variants to analyze!).

If the working system is established, then replacing the active unilateral constraints by bilateral ones and removing the inactive constraints, we obtain a conventional system which can be analyzed by any method known in structural mechanics. It goes without saying that the result of calculating the working system should be such so that the forces in the replaced constraints and the displacements in the direction of the removed constraints correspond to the performance of unilateral constraints that actually exist in the system and are only mentally modified at the transition to the working system.

It is useful to study the behavior of the system under the load variation. The simplest case of the variable loading is a single-parametric one when the relations between all loads on the system are given, and only the value of the load components changes.

First of all, let us consider some qualitative considerations based on physically obvious assumptions and ideas about the behavior of the system under load.

If a certain working system corresponds to a certain value of the external load parameter (loading level), it can be assumed that the same working system corresponds to other loading levels close in value, i.e. the working system does not change within a certain range of loads (possibly even in the range of zero length), and the given system with unilateral constraints behaves like an ordinary linearly deformed structure.

In the case when unilateral constraints are installed without gaps and there is no prestress, simply increasing the load value (multiplying all forces by a positive number $\lambda > 0$) can not lead to a change in the working system. However, if there are gaps in the unilateral constraints, the system might be affected at a certain value of λ, i.e. a gap will be selected and the working system will be modified. The same can happen when the prestress of a certain unilateral constraint gets exhausted with the load increase and the system will not be affected anymore.

If we represent the relationship between a certain force S_k in the k-th element of the system and the load parameter P in the form of a graph, then a certain range of variation of P, at which the working system does not change, will have a corresponding line segment. The angle of this segment depends on the stiffness properties of the system and the state of its unilateral constraints.

If the working system changes, then the angle of the line segment may change as well, since the state of unilateral constraints changes in the new working system corresponding to the new range of the load variation (Fig. 3.20). It follows from the physical considerations that if the relationships between forces in different elements of the system S_k and the load value P are plotted on the graph, then all breakpoints will lie on the same verticals (as shown in Figure 3.20), although for some values of S_k, the angles of two adjacent sections of the graph might coincide.

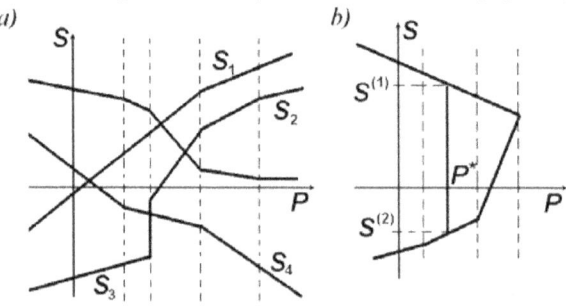

Figure 3.20

Let us now prove that the graph $S_k = S_k(P)$ of the type shown in Fig. 3.20,*b* is impossible. It follows from the fact that the forces $S_k^{(1)}$ and $S_k^{(2)}$ belong to the same working system, and since it is usually an elastic system, then the uniqueness theorem should be satisfied for it.

Unfortunately, it does not mean that the relationship between the force (displacement) and the parameter P is monotonic since there can be curves $S_k = S_k(P)$ with the same values of forces or displacements corresponding to different values of the load parameter. The simplest example is given in Fig. 3.21 showing a system with two unilateral constraints and a force in the first unilateral constraint vs. P graph.

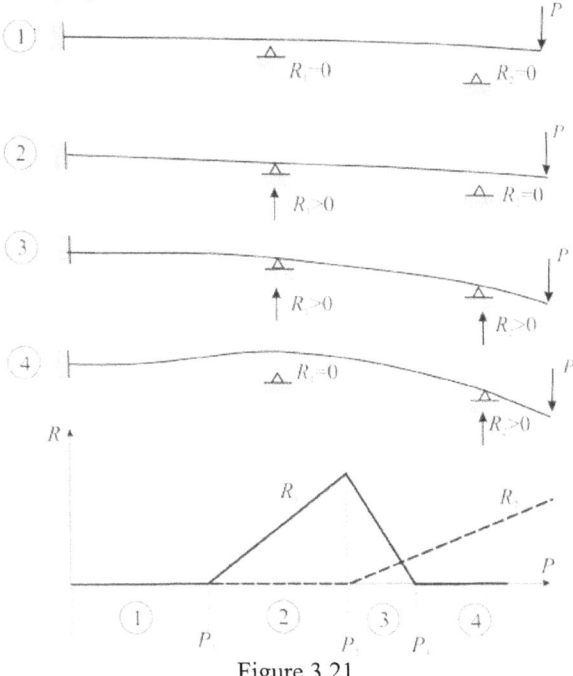

Figure 3.21

As long as $P < P_1$ the bar does not touch any of the constraints and we have $R_1 = 0$, then when $P = P_1$ the first unilateral constraint is enabled and the force in it grows until $P = P_2$ and the second constraint is enabled. With a further increase in P the force in the first constraint begins to decrease, and when $P = P_3$ a separation occurs and the constraint is disabled.

We have the effect which was discussed earlier (see Fig. 3.4), namely, one of the parameters of the stress-strain state reaches its maximum value not at the limit load values.

It should be noted that in spite of the fact that the curve $S_k = S_k(P)$, shown in Fig. 3.20 has two segments coinciding with the axis they correspond to different working systems.

Conversation 3.7. Genetic Nonlinearity

The process of creating a complex structure is, generally, a multi-phase procedure involving a certain sequence of structural assembling operations. The latter may include successive works on installation or removal of some members of the structure, installation/removal of ballast weights, regulation of the length of certain elements, modification of constraints etc.

Most actions performed during the erection modify the design model and/or the stress-strain state of the system.

All calculations related to the erection and prestressing process are commonly performed with the usual assumptions of linear structural mechanics for each erection stage. However, the changes the design model experiences during the transition from stage to stage make this problem nonlinear. Such nonlinearity caused by the erection history is called *genetic*.

At each step of the erection, any classic structural analysis method can be involved. Seeing the specific nature of the multi-step analysis, we think it is useful to represent these methods in such form as to reflect the variability of the system. For example, the governing equations of the slope deflection method will be

$$K_r \Delta u_r = \Delta q_r, \qquad (3.64)$$

where K_r is the system's stiffness matrix at the rth step, Δu_r and Δq_r are respective vectors of incremental displacements and incremental nodal loads related to the rth step. Knowing Δu_r, we can determine the force increments ΔN_r and obtain values of the displacements u_r and forces s_r accumulated at all r steps

$$u_r = u_{r-1} + \Delta u_r, \qquad (3.65)$$
$$Ns_r = N_{r-1} + \Delta N_r. \qquad (3.66)$$

The relevant entitlement for the relations (3.65) and (3.66) could be *laws of inheritance of erection states* of a structure. The genetic nonlinearity of the problem is caused by the requirement that the linear relations (3.62) and the laws of inheritance (3.65) — (3.66) must hold simultaneously.

The transition to the next stage of the calculation changes the stiffness matrix K_r, which receives an increment ΔK_{r+1}, positive – when elements are added at the stage $r+1$, and negative – when they are removed at the stage $r+1$:

$$Kr+1 = Kr + \Delta Kr+1. \qquad (3.67)$$

More extensively:

$$\begin{bmatrix} K_{11}^{(r+1)} & K_{12}^{(r+1)} & 0 & 0 \\ K_{21}^{(r+1)} & K_{22}^{(r+1)} & K_{23}^{(r+1)} & 0 \\ 0 & K_{32}^{(r+1)} & K_{33}^{(r+1)} & 0 \\ 0 & 0 & 0 & 0 \end{bmatrix} = \begin{bmatrix} K_{11}^{(r)} & K_{12}^{(r)} & 0 & 0 \\ K_{21}^{(r)} & K_{22}^{(r)} & 0 & 0 \\ 0 & 0 & 0 & 0 \\ 0 & 0 & 0 & 0 \end{bmatrix} + \begin{bmatrix} 0 & 0 & 0 & 0 \\ 0 & \Delta K_{22}^{(r)} & \Delta K_{23}^{(r)} & 0 \\ 0 & \Delta K_{32}^{(r)} & \Delta K_{33}^{(r)} & 0 \\ 0 & 0 & 0 & 0 \end{bmatrix},$$

and the system of governing equations of the $(r+1)^{th}$ stage is as follows:

$$\begin{bmatrix} K_{11}^{(r+1)} & K_{12}^{(r+1)} & 0 & 0 \\ K_{21}^{(r+1)} & K_{22}^{(r+1)} & K_{23}^{(r+1)} & 0 \\ 0 & K_{32}^{(r+1)} & K_{33}^{(r+1)} & 0 \\ 0 & 0 & 0 & 0 \end{bmatrix} \cdot \begin{bmatrix} \Delta u_1^{(r+1)} \\ \Delta u_2^{(r+1)} \\ \Delta u_3^{(r+1)} \\ 0 \end{bmatrix} = \begin{bmatrix} 0 \\ \Delta u_2^{(r+1)} \\ \Delta u_3^{(r+1)} \\ 0 \end{bmatrix}.$$

Here $\Delta u_1^{(r+1)}$ is a displacement increment in the previously mounted and the unchanged part of the structure, respectively, $\Delta u_2^{(r+1)}$ is a displacement increment in the nodes with new adjacent elements, $\Delta u_3^{(r+1)}$ are displacements along the new nodes. The right zero column and the bottom zero row of the stiffness matrix refer to the part of the structure which is not yet included in the calculation.

It is obvious that influences related to different steps of the same erection phase are described by conventional linear mechanical laws, and the design model of a structure changes only from one erection phase to another.

It should be noted that in certain cases some loads work only at the rth step of the erection and are removed at the steps that follow. For example, this situation is typical for a cantilever erection of a structure where the weight of the crane equipment is taken into account when forming the vector Δq_r the cranes being arranged exactly as this step of erection requires. As the new $(r+1)^{th}$ erection step begins, the nodal load vector is formed for a new arrangement of the crane equipment, and one should remember to apply also negative loads at the step $(r+1)$ to cancel the crane load upon the system applied at the previous step. If one does not do it, the inheritance laws (3.65) and (3.66) will fail to hold.

The results of calculations that take into account the erection process can significantly differ from the usual ones, when it is supposed that a complete system is created at once, and only then the external loads are applied to it.

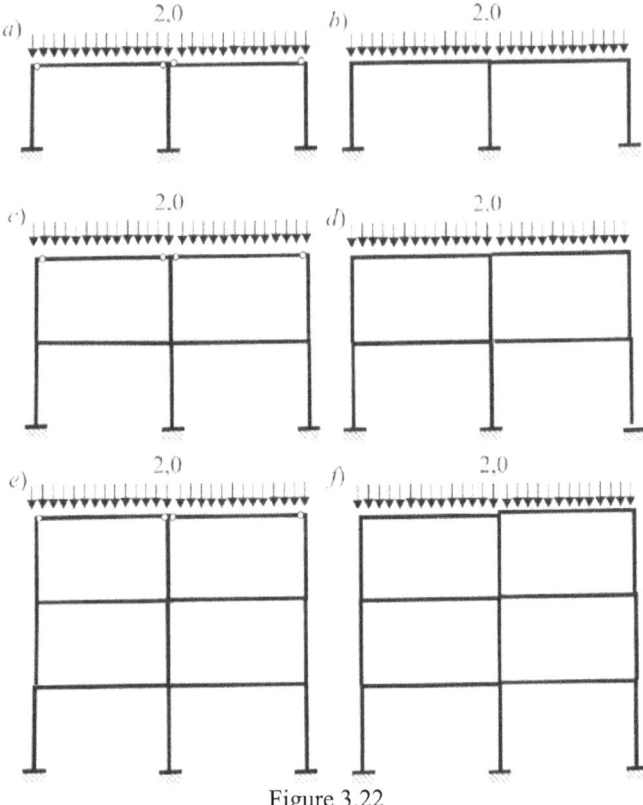

Figure 3.22

The fact that it is necessary to take into account the erection sequence can be illustrated by a simple example of calculating a two-span three-storey frame. A girder is simply supported on columns and carries the load of 2,0 t/m at the erection of each floor. The beam-to-column joints are then grouted, and the weight of the floor slabs creating an additional load of 2,0 t/m is then transferred to the girders. All floors are erected in this way (Fig. 3.22).

The left part of Fig. 3.23 shows a bending moment diagram obtained in the result of a sequential structural analysis performed for the erection stages a) ... f) and the summation of the obtained results. It can be compared to a bending moment diagram shown on the right, which is obtained for the case when a load of 4,0 t/m is applied to the girders of a complete design model.

The process of creating a complex structure is, generally, a multi-phase procedure involving a certain sequence of structural assembling operations. The latter may include successive works on installation or removal of some members of the structure, installation/removal of ballast weights, regulation of the length of certain elements, modification of constraints etc.

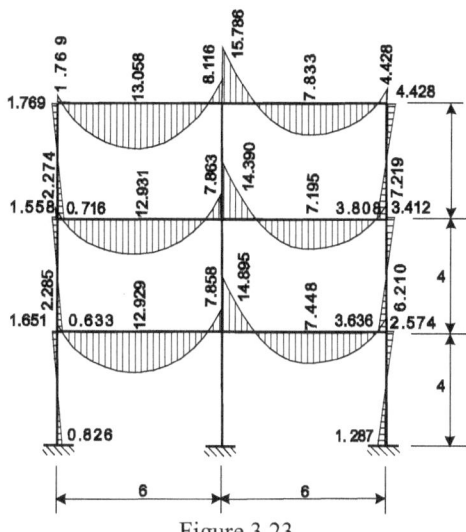

Figure 3.23

Many modern software provide means for modeling this process. LIRA and SCAD have a special ERECTION mode. It is called "birth and death of elements" in ANSYS.

All these operations create a certain preliminary stress-strain state in the design model, which can significantly affect the behavior of the structure. If a certain structural part is added to (or removed from) a system, certain elements in your design model may become "existent" (or "nonexistent"). This feature can be useful in analyzing excavation (as in mining and tunneling), staged construction (as in shored bridge erection), sequential assembly (as in fabrication of layered computer chips), and many other applications.

Two methods of removal and inclusion of elements into the system ("birth" and "death") can be considered. These variants are illustrated in Fig. 3.24.

In the first case the mounted element M is installed in such a way so that one of its ends is adjacent to the assembled part of the structure, and the other is adjacent to the node in the design position. In the second case to achieve the "element death" effect, the program does not actually *remove* "killed" elements. Instead, it *deactivates* them by multiplying their stiffness by a severe reduction factor, for example, 10^{-6}. Then the mounted element M, which did not affect the behavior of the structure due to near zero stiffness, acquires its real stiffness and begins to affect the behavior of the structure.

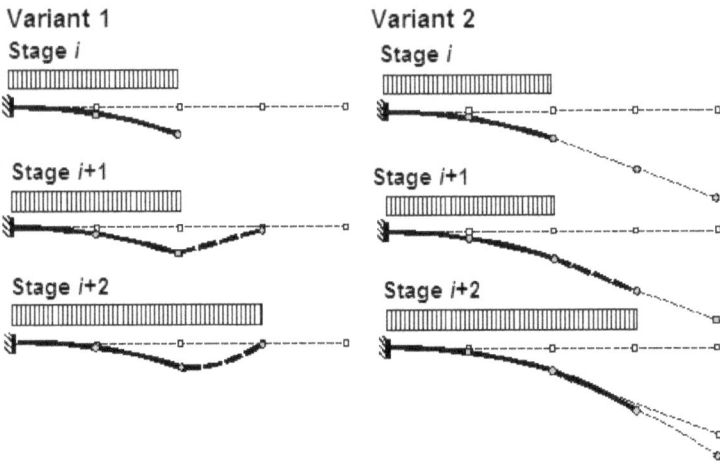

Figure 3.24

In the case of a geometrically linear calculation, when the geometry of the deformed model is identified with the original geometry, there is no practical difference between these cases. However, it is not true for a geometrically nonlinear calculation, which is clearly demonstrated in Figure 3.24 showing the cantilever erection process. In the second variant nodes belonging to the unmounted part of the system deviate from the design position under the load and the system does not acquire any unforeseen breaks that arise in the first variant of the calculation.

Calculation according to the first method is particularly relevant for the design of multi-storey buildings with a reinforced concrete frame when during the construction of each floor the formwork is set in such a way that the top surface of the concreted slab is horizontal. Essentially, it is the design column length increased by the subsidence value of the part of the building that has already been erected that is corrected. This technology is graphically illustrated by Figure 3.25, where 1 – the constructed part of the building, 2 – the formwork, 3 – design elevations, 4 – additional column section.

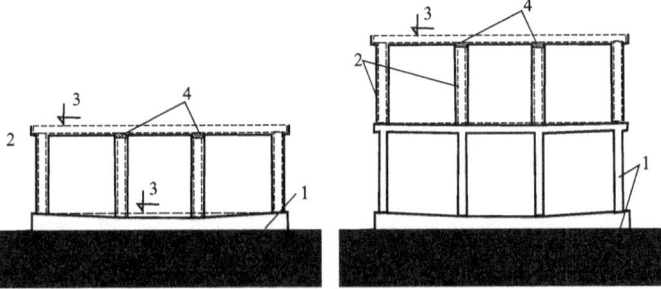

Figure 3.25

The experience of performing a series of erection state calculations shows that it is often impossible to ignore the stress-strain state defined by the erection history.

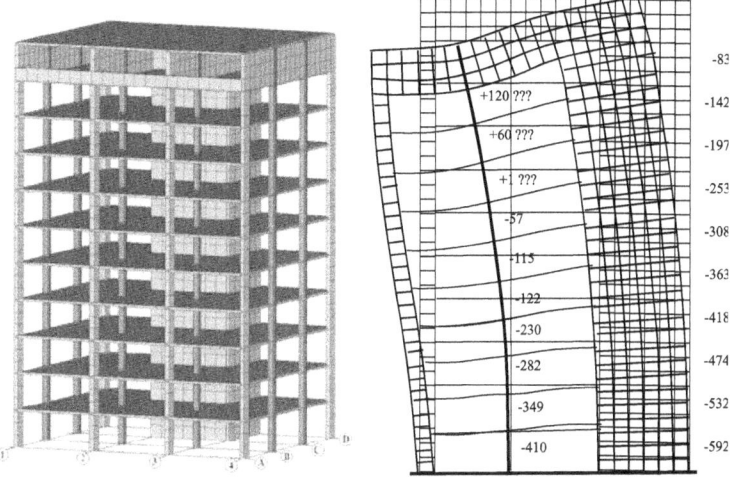

Figure 3.26

In some cases, we are not even talking about quantitative, but about qualitative differences. The example (Fig. 3.26) shows the consequences of ignoring the erection process. The column of the considered structure turns out to be "suspended" from the rigid wall of the top floor, which results in a tensile force of 120 tons in the column.

However, if the calculation is performed taking into account the erection and load application sequence, no tension appears and the compressive force in the column changes from 83 tons (top floor) to 592 tons (first floor), which completely corresponds to the expected distribution of forces.

It should be noted that the study of genetic nonlinearity began much later than other types of nonlinear analysis, and it started with the pioneering work of E.I. Rashba [8], which considered a problem of static analysis of a structure (dam) built up within the action of the gravity field. Moreover, this was the first work that pointed out explicitly the impossibility to use the deformation compatibility conditions in the analysis of the stress state of the built up body.

E.I. Rashba[10] writes in his memoirs [9]:

"I realized, that the traditional approach corresponds to the non-physical mode, when the elastic body is formed in the absence of gravity and becomes the object of gravity only after the completion of all installation operations, and that the

---

[10] Emmanuel I. Rashba wrote his paper [8] as a novice researcher temporarily forced to simply perform calculations in the Institute of Hydromechanics of the Academy of Sciences of the Ukrainian SSR. Subsequently, he became one of the leading experts in solid-state physics and the semiconductor theory. His works in this field were awarded the Lenin Prize and received world recognition.

discrepancy in the results for such an unphysical model and the reality is huge, especially in the case of flat dams. The conclusion was that the gravitational stresses depend mainly on the dam construction sequence, since the weight of the lower layers should not affect the stresses in the upper layers."

Question:
How does the stress-strain state of a loaded system change after adding or removing a constraint?

Answer:
You should keep in mind that imposing a constraint means prohibiting a displacement, which is actually a physical intrusion in the design. Therefore, it is important to know at which point in the structural life it occurred.

If a bolted or welded joint, additional support or any other similar constraint appears in the system, it does not change the existing stress-strain state and remains unstressed itself until the load acting on the system changes.

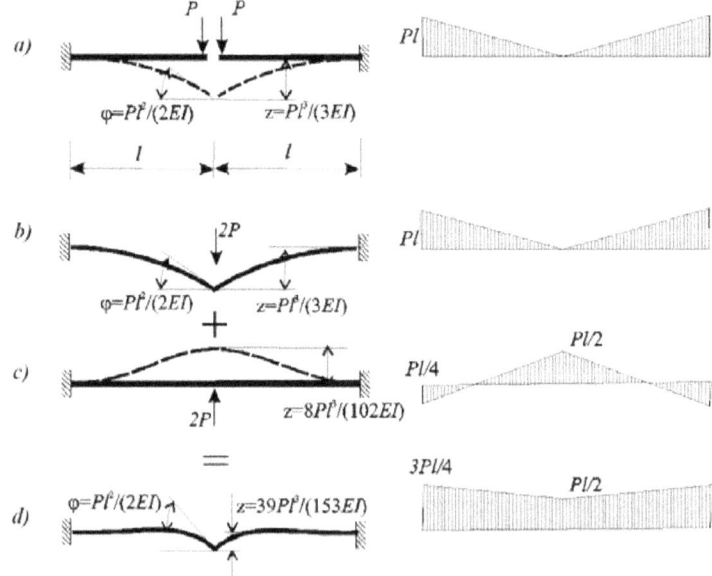

Figure 3.27

Let us, for example, consider a loaded structure consisting of two cantilever beams (Fig. 3.27.a). If you connect these cantilevers, the stress state will not change (Fig. 3.27.b).

If you now remove the previously existing load (apply it with an opposite sign as shown in Fig. 3.27.c), a certain prestress will remain in the modified system (Fig. 3.27.d), which is partially taken by the new joint.

> *If an additional constraint is introduced in a stressed system (an element is added, the stiffness of the existing element is increased), then this constraint is unstressed, and the stress state of the system changes only with the load acting on it.*

The situation is completely different if you have to remove a constraint. The thing is that in a static problem the constraint has to be unstressed first before it is removed. Thus, removing a constraint in a stressed bow without first making the reaction equal to zero (gradual release of a string) leads to a dynamic effect due to the released potential energy.

> *The removed constraint (the removed element, the reduced stiffness) immediately changes the existing stress-strain state of the system.*

References

1. *Agapov V.P.* Finite Element Method in Statics, Dynamics, and Stability of Thin-Walled Structures. — M.: ASV, 2000.
2. *Grigolyuk E.I., Shalashilin V.I.* Problems of Nonlinear Deformation. — M.: Nauka, 1988.
3. *Novozhilov V.V.* The Theory of Elasticity.— L.: Sudpromgiz, 1958.
4. *Perelmuter A.V.* Fundamentals of the Analysis of Cable and Bar Systems.— M.: Stroyizdat, 1969.
5. *Perelmuter A.V., Slivker V.I.* Design Models of Structures and a Possibility of Their Analysis.— M.:DMK Press, 2007
6. *Perelmuter A.V., Kabantsev O.V.* Structural Analysis with a Varying Design Model.— M.: SCAD Soft, ASV Publishing House, 2015.
7. *Rabinovich I.M.* Theoretical Problems of Static Design of Structures with Unilateral Constraints.— M.: Stroyizdat, 1975.
8. *Rashba E.I.* Determination of Stresses in Structures from the Action of the Self Weight, Taking into Account the Order of Their Construction // Proceedings of the Institute of Structural Mechanics, Academy of Sciences of the Ukrainian SSR. 1953. № 18. – p. 23-27.
9. *Rashba E.I.* About Myself and My Teachers, Colleagues, Friends. // http://scientists-academia-ussr.blogspot.com/
10. *Shulkin Yu.B.* Kinematic Analysis of Beam Structures // Calculation of Spatial Structures.— Issue 17.— M.: Stroyizdat, 1977.— p. 4–31.

Cycle 4

Stability of Equilibrium

 *The concept of stability is of fundamental importance. Both in nature and in human activities only stable phenomena and processes can be used for a long time.*
V.V. Bolotin

Conversation 4.1. Basic Concepts of Stability Theory

All people irrespective of their education come across the concept of the stability of equilibrium on a daily basis. To illustrate this point, let us consider two mechanical systems in equilibrium shown in Fig. 4.1.

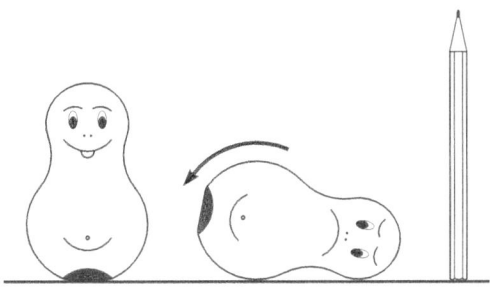

Figure 4.1.

You might remember a roly-poly toy from your childhood. However hard you push the wooden doll to the ground, as soon as you let it go, it returns to the vertical position at once. There is a lead weight on the bottom of the toy that creates a restoring moment and keeps making the stubborn figure stand upright like a soldier. Ask any person regardless of his interest in engineering whether this upright position is stable. The obvious answer is correctly suggested by the intuitive understanding of the concept of stability as the ability of a system to ignore disturbances.

On the other hand, an ordinary pencil can be balanced on its end, but our intuition tells us that this equilibrium is unstable. Why? The reason is that even a slightest perturbation (a flick, a puff, a vibration of the base, etc.) can break this equilibrium and leave no hope for the pencil to return to its vertical balanced position by itself.

In the field of engineering, though, the intuitive perception of stability is of little help and must give way to a strict mathematical definition of the concept. The methods of the equilibrium quality analysis are based on this definition.

> *The definition of the equilibrium stability concept is based on considering the motion of the system after it is displaced from the equilibrium position by giving its points small initial deviations from the equilibrium and small initial velocities. If, after disturbing the equilibrium, the system in its subsequent motion deviates very little from the considered equilibrium position, then this equilibrium position is called stable.*

A very simple example giving an idea of the stability and instability of an equilibrium state is a mechanical system in the form of a heavy ball that moves without friction over a certain surface (Fig. 4.2). If the ball has a unit weight, then the potential energy of this system is equal to the ordinate U of the point of the surface where the ball is located:

$$U = U(x),$$

where the abscissa x is the parameter of displacements of the ball.

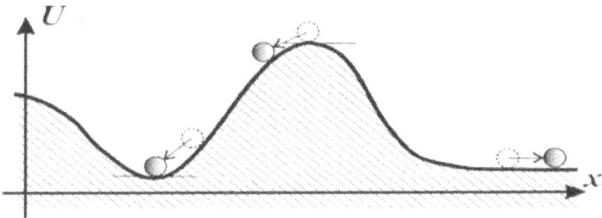

Figure 4.2

The ball is in equilibrium when

$$dU/dx = 0,$$

and this equilibrium is stable if the ball is in the center of a pit.

Then, for any small deviation of the ball from the initial state, it will return to this state as soon as the cause of the deviation is eliminated. Thus, the equilibrium position at the bottom of the pit is stable. It is obvious that the potential energy of the initial equilibrium state is less than the potential energy of any deflected state. Thus, the minimum potential energy corresponds to the stable equilibrium state of the considered system. The analytical condition for the minimum of the function U is expressed as

$$dU/dx = 0; \quad d^2U/dx^2 > 0.$$

In the case of a maximum U, for any small deviation of the ball from the initial position, it will not return to this position independently after eliminating the perturbation and will continue to move to a new equilibrium state. Hence, the equilibrium position at the top is not stable, and the maximum potential energy corresponds to this position of the system, when

$$dU/dx = 0; \quad d^2U/dx^2 < 0.$$

The third case illustrates the so-called indifferent equilibrium, when, after eliminating the perturbation, the ball does not deviate further, but does not return to its original state as well. The potential energy does not change in this case:

$$dU/dx = 0; \quad d^2U/dx^2 = 0.$$

The course of theoretical mechanics contains a proof of the following Lagrange-Dirichlet theorem:

> *Assuming the total energy to be continuous, the equilibrium of a system containing only conservative and dissipative forces is stable if the potential energy of the system has a strict minimum.*

It should be noted that the requirement of a strict minimum of the potential energy in the considered equilibrium state of the system is essential for the Lagrange-Dirichlet theorem to be true. Indeed, imagine a material particle in the bottom of a cylindrical ravine. The potential energy of the particle in the gravity field is minimal, but this minimum is not strict, because the particle is capable of moving along the bottom of the ravine while keeping its potential energy.

If the particle receives an infinitesimal initial velocity, it will move with this velocity along the ravine bottom and will deviate from its initial state of equilibrium by a specified distance after some time. The conclusion is that the equilibrium of this system is not stable.

It should be noted that the Lagrange-Dirichlet theorem gives only sufficient conditions of the stability of the equilibrium state. This important fact is not always emphasized. Moreover, it is often unreasonably stated that the equilibrium is unstable if the potential energy does not reach its strict minimum.

Question:
You always talk about the stability of the equilibrium state, and not about the stability of the system (structure). Is this true, and what is the difference between these concepts?

Answer:
The loss of stability of the equilibrium state is a change in the quality of equilibrium (loss of stability, transformation into an indifferent or unstable equilibrium).

The problem of stability of static equilibrium is extremely important in practical terms, since the vast majority of structures experiencing mechanical actions in the form of forces must, in accordance with their purpose, be in states of stable equilibrium. The loss of equilibrium stability of a static system is in most cases equivalent to its failure. On the other hand, any structural failure can be interpreted as a phenomenon of general or local loss of stability. It is especially evident in the case of a failure of a tensile steel bar.

If an external action on the bar is applied in the form of its forced deformation (rather than loading) and the deformations are small, the bar retains the original cylindrical shape of its surface, and then necking will occur within a small portion of the bar length, i.e. the cylindrical shape is lost, and a loss of stability occurs in the deformation process.

We can also consider the loss of stability in the case of a pulsating load. Let a bar with simply supported ends, one of which can move along the bar axis, be loaded with an external longitudinal harmonic force. We assume that the system is far from the longitudinal vibration resonance. Nevertheless, there are situations when the longitudinal oscillation mode of the system is dynamically unstable, i.e. any initial deviation excites transverse oscillations (parametric resonance), the amplitude of which quickly increases to a very large value – the loss of stability is observed.

In the general case the structural stability is the ability of a structure to maintain its shape excluding the possibility of such residual deformations that make the structure unserviceable and lead to its failure. As you can see it is a much broader concept than that of the stability of equilibrium.

On the other hand, you should keep in mind that the real mechanical system is idealized in the analysis of the stability of equilibrium, and ultimately we are dealing not with a mechanical object, but with a system of equations only approximately reflecting the real properties of the object. Problems of equilibrium stability are solved as a mathematical problem, i.e. the properties of equations are studied. Transferring the results of this study to a real object, i.e. the prediction of a mechanical effect should be performed with caution, because not all properties of solutions of equilibrium equations are properties of the mechanical system.

However, in practical structural analysis "the loss of stability" concept is conventionally applied to the system itself, although theoretically it is incorrect.

Question:
Structural mechanics textbooks define the stability of equilibrium in a completely different way without considering the concept of motion at all. The equilibrium of a mechanical system is considered to be stable if after being removed from the equilibrium state by a small perturbation of the generalized coordinates the system returns to the initial equilibrium state.

Answer:
This definition of the stability of equilibrium belongs to L.Euler. According to him, the equilibrium of a mechanical system is considered to be stable if after being removed from the equilibrium state by a small perturbation the system returns to the initial equilibrium state.

In this case the value of the external load increases, and it is assumed that one more equilibrium state similar to the considered one, but with an infinitesimal perturbation in the values of the generalized coordinates of the system, can appear in this process. In other words, the considered equilibrium state of the system becomes ambiguous.

The value of the load parameter $\lambda = \lambda_e$, wherein the mechanical system allows such ambiguity is called critical (according to Euler). It is also considered that when the load values are less than the Eulerian critical value, the equilibrium state is stable, and when the load values are greater than the Eulerian critical value λ_e, the equilibrium state is unstable.

The Eulerian formulation of the stability problem does not contain a hint of the above definition of the stability of equilibrium and of the Lagrange-Dirichlet theorem, which requires that the total potential energy of the system is minimal in its stable equilibrium state. Nevertheless, not only does the traditional engineering school teach the Euler approach, but it also teaches to use it when studying the stability of equilibrium of elastic systems, considering a more consistent Lagrange-Dirichlet analysis only in the early theoretical mechanics course, and not applying it to the structural mechanics problems.

Both these approaches will, of course, lead to the same results under certain conditions. The justification of their equivalence is given, for example, in the book [10], which also indicates the class of problems where the Euler approach is not applicable.

Conversation 4.2. Stability of a Single Degree of Freedom System

The essence of the stability problem can be completely revealed only by considering finite strains and nonlinear equilibrium equations. This phenomenon is usually illustrated by the buckling problem of an axially compressed thin bar solved more than 200 years ago by L.Euler.

This problem, however, describes a phenomenon which is rather complicated for an initial explanation of the concept of stability, and it is more reasonable to first consider simpler systems with a finite number of degrees of freedom and, in particular, single degree of freedom systems.

Let us consider a simple single degree of freedom system – a rigid bar with an elastically restrained end (Fig. 4.3). Displacements of this system are characterized by the deflection angle φ from the initial vertical position. A reactive moment $C\varphi$ appears in the elastic restraint, where C is the restraint stiffness ratio.

The system is subjected to a vertical force P, which does not change its direction when its application point is moved. It is easy to see that the force P creates an overturning moment in the deflected state, and if this force P is significant, the system will not be able to keep its initial undeflected position at any small perturbation, i.e. it will become unstable.

Let us consider the potential energy U of this system. When the system deviates from the vertical, the force P does work equal to the product of P by the vertical displacement of the bar end $\Delta = l(1-\cos\varphi)$. The potential energy is reduced by the value of the work $P\Delta$.

On the other hand, the potential energy of internal forces equal to $0,5C\varphi^2$ is accumulated in the elastic restraint.

Thus, the total potential energy of the system is expressed as:
$$U = 0,5C\varphi^2 - Pl(1-\cos\varphi), \quad (4.1)$$
and the equilibrium condition here is
$$dU/d\varphi = C\varphi - Pl\sin\varphi = 0. \quad (4.2)$$

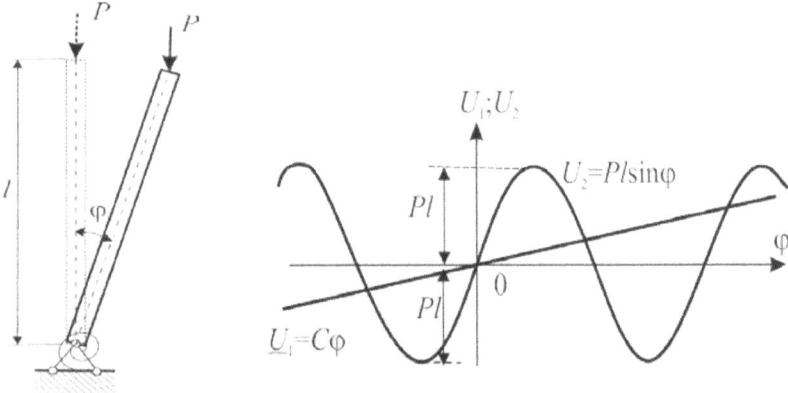

Figure 4.3   Figure 4.4

We can determine all the equilibrium positions of the system from (4.2). The roots of this equation correspond to the intersection points of the straight line $U_1 = C\varphi$ and the sinusoid $U_2 = Pl\sin\varphi$ (Fig. 4.4). The number of equilibrium positions depends on the value of P, since when the amplitude of the sinusoid Pl changes, the number of intersection points of the latter with the straight line $U_1 = C\varphi$ will change as well.

It is clear that not all equilibrium states will be stable. The equilibrium will be stable when the potential function takes the minimum value, and the maximum values correspond to the unstable equilibrium states.

Analytically, the condition of stability of the equilibrium state is expressed by the following inequality

$$d^2 U / d\varphi^2 > 0,$$

and φ here must satisfy the condition of equilibrium.

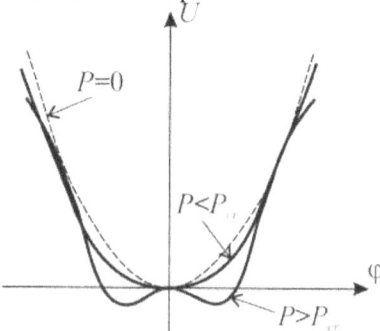

Figure 4.5

When the force P increases, the curve U changes, and the points corresponding to the equilibrium positions shift. And the equilibrium state of the points that remain in place (in our case point $\varphi = 0$) can change from stable to unstable (Fig. 4.5).

It is obvious that when the force has a certain value P, there should be an intermediate state of equilibrium, when not only the first derivative vanishes, but the second derivative $\partial^2 U/\partial\varphi^2$ passes through zero. This equilibrium position, intermediate between stable and unstable, is called a *critical equilibrium state*. Thus, analytically, the critical state of the system is determined by two equations: For this system, these equations give (4.2), and

$$d^2 U/d\varphi^2 = \varphi - Pl\cos\varphi = 0. \tag{4.5}$$

When it comes to the initial position of equilibrium $\varphi = 0$, when the condition (4.2) is satisfied for any P, then (4.5) gives:

$$C - Pl = 0. \tag{4.6}$$

Hence, we find the critical force value P for the equilibrium position $\varphi = 0$:

$$P_{cr} = C/l. \tag{4.7}$$

In the considered example, the potential energy U is a function of the deformation φ and the external force P. Therefore, it is more correct to write the equilibrium condition (4.2) as follows

$$\partial U(P,\varphi)/\partial\varphi = U_0(P,\varphi) = 0. \tag{4.8}$$

The relationship between P and φ implicitly given by this equation defines a certain curve called the *equilibrium state curve* in the coordinates φ, P.

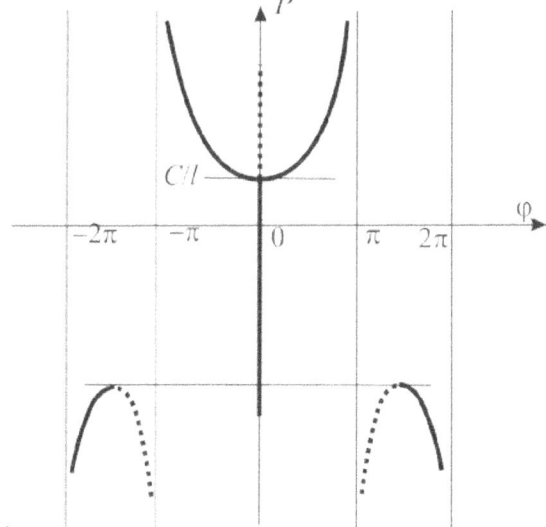

Figure 4.6

In our case it is a relationship

$$P = C\varphi/(l\sin\varphi), \tag{4.9}$$

obtained from (4.2) and shown in Fig. 4.6. In this figure the solid lines indicate the stable equilibrium states, and the dashed lines indicate the unstable ones. Let us show that the extreme points of the equilibrium state curve (4.9), for which the following equation is satisfied

$$\partial P/\partial \varphi = 0,\qquad(4.10)$$

correspond to critical equilibrium states (*limit points*). Indeed

$$\frac{dP}{d\varphi}=\frac{\partial U_0(P,\varphi)/\partial \varphi}{\partial U_0(P,\varphi)/\partial P}=-\frac{\partial^2 U/\partial \varphi^2}{\partial^2 U/(\partial \varphi \partial P)},\qquad(4.11)$$

and, therefore, the equality (4.11) is satisfied when $\partial^2 U/\partial \varphi^2 = 0$.

We have obtained the second condition of the critical equilibrium state, where an ordinary derivative is replaced by a partial one, since P is no longer considered as a constant value here.

It was noted above that, when the derivative $\partial^2 U/\partial \varphi^2$ changes its sign, there is a transition from stable states of the system to unstable ones or vice versa. However, the expression (4.11) shows that a change in sign is accompanied by a change in the sign of the derivative $\partial P/\partial \varphi$, i.e., a change in the direction of the slope of the equilibrium state curve. It follows that if the rise of the equilibrium state curve corresponds to the stable positions of the system, then after going through a maximum (4.9), we have unstable positions in the descending branch of the curve.

The equilibrium state curve (see Fig. 4.6) also has a vertical branch coinciding with the axis φ = 0 and corresponding to the non-deflected position of the system and an arbitrary value of the force P.

Close deflected stable states appear in the point B (φ = 0, $P = C/l$), and stable states (at $P < C/l = P_{cr}$) change to unstable ones (at $P > P_{cr}$) on the vertical branch. This point is called a *bifurcation point* (from the Latin *bis – twice, furca – pitchfork, bifurcatio – branching*). Both second derivatives $\partial^2 U/\partial \varphi^2$ and $\partial^2 U/(\partial \varphi \partial P)$ vanish in it. It means that this point is a special point of the equilibrium state curve, i.e. an intersection point of its two branches.

> *There can be two forms of equilibrium in the case of bifurcation – an original and a qualitatively new one, different from the original form in that some kind of deformation appears in it, which was absent in subcritical states of the system.*

Let us return again to the system shown in Fig. 4.3. Almost all the equilibrium states that can be obtained from the equation (4.2), except for the initial state $\varphi = 0$, correspond to large, and under normal conditions, practically impossible rotation angles of the bar. Therefore, it can be enough to consider the strain states that deviate little from the zero equilibrium position, and to simplify the problem, neglecting the terms with small strains φ in higher orders. By expanding the exact expression (4.1) in a series in powers φ and neglecting the orders φ higher than the second, we obtain:

$$\begin{aligned}U &= (C/2)\varphi^2 - Pl\left(1-1+\varphi^2/2!-\varphi^4/4!+...\right) \approx \\ &\approx (C/2)\varphi^2 - (Pl/2)\varphi^2.\end{aligned}\qquad(4.12)$$

The approximate expression of the function U can be graphically represented as a parabola, the graph of which can be interpreted as a somewhat distorted image of the neighborhood of a point $\varphi = 0$ on an exact curve (Fig. 4.5). Unlike the exact curve, the curve (4.9) always gives only one equilibrium position, which can be stable, unstable and critical depending on the value of the force P.

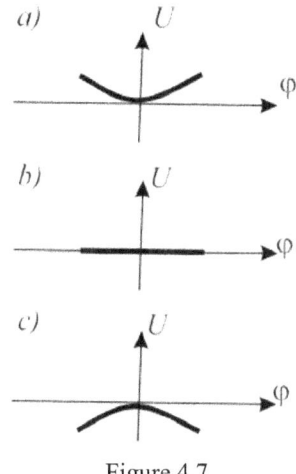

Figure 4.7

The equilibrium is stable when the parabola (4.9) is facing up, i.e. when there is a minimum U at $\varphi = 0$ (Fig. 4.7,*a*). The unstable equilibrium corresponds to a parabola facing down (Fig. 4.7,*c*). Finally, an intermediate critical equilibrium state occurs when the parabola (4.9) degenerates into a straight line that coincides with the abscissa axis (Fig. 4.7,*b*). The latter takes place when $P = C/l = P_{cr}$, which completely coincides with the critical load value determined from the exact expression for the potential energy.

Thus, when small deformations of the system are considered, the critical load is determined as one at which the equilibrium state of the system becomes indifferent, the deformation of the system can have any value, and the equilibrium conditions are not violated. As for the condition (4.5) of a vanishing second derivative of the potential function, it is observed in this case as well:

$$\partial^2 U/\partial \varphi^2 = C - Pl = 0, \qquad (4.13)$$

However, it is not governed by any specific deformation value, as in the case of the exact solution.

Thus, the linear equation has allowed us to find a critical force and a configuration of a system that has lost the stability of the original form of equilibrium, with an accuracy up to some unknown small parameter (factor).

When a linearized equation is used, it is impossible to make any judgments concerning the postbuckling behavior of the system; this loss is the cost of the achieved simplification lying in the linearization of the problem.

Question:
The determination of the equilibrium stability is based on the property of the system to resist small perturbations. Could you please tell us how this property changes with the load increase?

Answer:
Let us consider the single degree of freedom system shown in Fig. 4.3 again. If we assume that small perturbations cause small deviations in the position of the system, then in the first approximation we can take $\sin\varphi = \varphi$. Then the equilibrium equation (4.2) can be written as

$$(C - Pl)\varphi = 0 \text{ or } C(1 - P/P_{cr})\varphi = 0.$$

The value $C(1 - P/P_{cr})$ is called the *effective stiffness of the system* and describes the ability of the system to resist deviation from the vertical position. As the force P increases from zero to P_{cr}, the effective stiffness of the system decreases and becomes zero at $P = P_{cr}$.

The character of the decrease of the effective stiffness, shown in this example, is the same in other cases as well.

Question:
A small (trial) perturbation used to check the stability of the system can be given as a transverse load applied at the upper end of the considered cantilever bar. What if this load is actually applied to the real structure, does it mean that it is not necessary to check the stability?

Answer:
In this case, the initial, undeformed state of the system is not the equilibrium position. Thus, a column shown in Fig. 4.3, can be loaded by a lateral force Q in addition to the longitudinal one P as shown in Fig. 4.8. We will assume that neither the values, nor the directions of the forces P and Q change in the deformation process of the system.

The equilibrium equation of this system is

$$C\varphi - Pl\sin\varphi - Ql\cos\varphi = 0, \quad (4.14)$$

and if we assume that the displacement φ (rotation angle of the column) is small, then

$$C\varphi - Pl\varphi = Ql. \quad (4.15)$$

Equations (4.14) and (4.15) are inhomogeneous in the sense that the zero value of the variable φ is not a root of these equations.

If only small displacements are considered, then an approximate expression of the potential energy of the column shown in Fig. 4.8, in a position deflected at a small angle φ from the initial position is:

$$U = 0,5C\varphi^2 - 0,5Pl\varphi^2 - Ql\varphi.$$

This expression contains the terms depending on the load and containing variable φ in the first and second order. The part of the load that does the work in displacements proportional to the square of φ and included in the expression for the potential energy of the system of the second order (in our case, the force *P*), is called the *parametric load*. The other part of the load that does the work in displacements proportional to the first order of the displacement parameter (in our case, the force *Q*) is the *active load*.

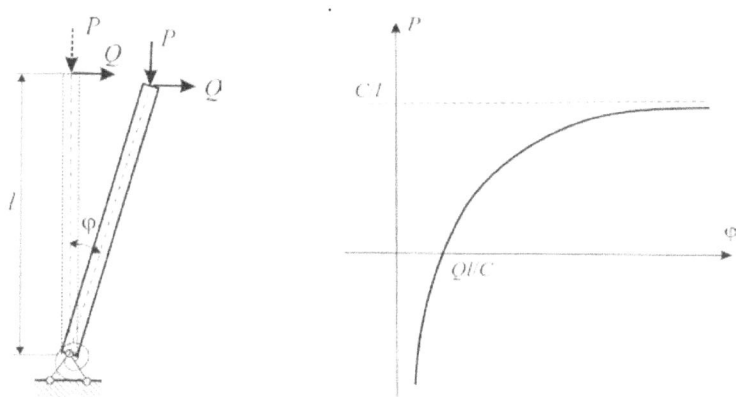

Figure 4.8   Figure 4.9

The active load is included in the free term of the equilibrium equation (4.2), which does not depend on displacements, and the parametric one is included in the term containing the displacement value of the first order.

Having solved the equation (4.2) with respect to φ, we find the displacement corresponding to the given load:

$$\varphi = Ql/(C-Pl) = \frac{Ql/C}{1-P/P_{cr}} \qquad (4.16)$$

The displacement φ is proportional to the active load and non-linearly dependent on the parametric load. At a certain value of the parametric load the displacement becomes infinite for any finite active force with the value *P* = *C/l*, coinciding with the critical load value in the homogeneous problem, i.e. in the column without the active force *Q*.

The relationship between *P* and φ at a constant force *Q* has the form of a hyperbola

$$P = -(-Ql + C\varphi)/(l\varphi), \qquad (4.17)$$

tending asymptotically to the horizontal line *P* = *C/l* (Fig. 4.9).

Conversation 4.3. On the Role of Initial Imperfections

Numerous studies have shown that in many cases, the solution obtained using the ideal linearized design model can deviate far enough from the experimental data. It was noted that the experimental results for shells are very sensitive to the imperfections of the real structure, i.e., to deviations of the real structures from their idealized design models.

Therefore, a question arises of estimating the sensitivity of a theoretical solution of the stability problem to imperfections of the system, explaining the mechanism of hypersensitivity occurrence and predicting cases when such behavior is possible.

Since it is difficult to provide an adequate description of the character of imperfections, it was proposed to use qualitative criteria. This idea expressed by V. Koiter back in 1945 [14] relates the effect of inevitable imperfections of real structures with the postbuckling behavior of an ideal structure of the respective shape. This analysis uses components of the total potential energy function of an order higher than quadratic.

Koiter's approach allows, first of all, to clarify the understanding of the system behavior near the bifurcation point, i.e. when the applied loads differ little from the critical value.

> *The strength of this approach is that the qualitative assessment of the postbuckling behavior of the system is predicted on the basis of its study at the critical point alone.*

The main idea can be easily demonstrated with an example of a single degree of freedom system. Let us denote the load parameter by λ and the parameter of the selected generalized displacement (for example, maximum deflection) by v. Let the expression for the total potential energy U contain the orders q up to the fourth inclusive, so that this expression has the form

$$U = C_2 (\lambda_{cr} - \lambda) v^2 + C_3 v^3 + C_4 v^4, \tag{4.18}$$

where λ_{cr} is the critical load parameter, C_i are some constants. We assume here that the displacements v are measured from the studied equilibrium state. Hence, it follows that the term linear in displacements is absent in the expansion (4.18), since the following condition must be satisfied in the equilibrium state, i.e. when $v = 0$

$$\frac{dU}{dv}(0) = 0.$$

We will consider the critical state first, i.e. assume $\lambda = \lambda_{cr}$. The fact that the quadratic term in (4.18) disappears under these conditions is also understandable, since, by the very definition, the following condition is satisfied in the critical state of the system

$$\frac{d^2U}{dv^2}(0) = 0.$$

Assume first that $C_3 \neq 0$, then the term containing C_4, can be dropped, so that we will have $U = C_3 v^3$ in the vicinity of the critical point. When $C_3 > 0$ and $v < 0$ or when $C_3 < 0$ and $v > 0$ the transition to the adjacent state will be accompanied by a drop in the total energy, so here the equilibrium state, corresponding to λ_{cr}, will turn out to be unstable. If $C_3 = 0$, it is necessary to examine the expression $U = C_4 v^4$. When $C_3 = 0$ and $C_4 > 0$ the deviation of the system from the main state will be related to an increase in the energy level, and the critical state will turn out to be stable. On the contrary, when $C_3 = 0$ and $C_4 < 0$ it will be unstable.

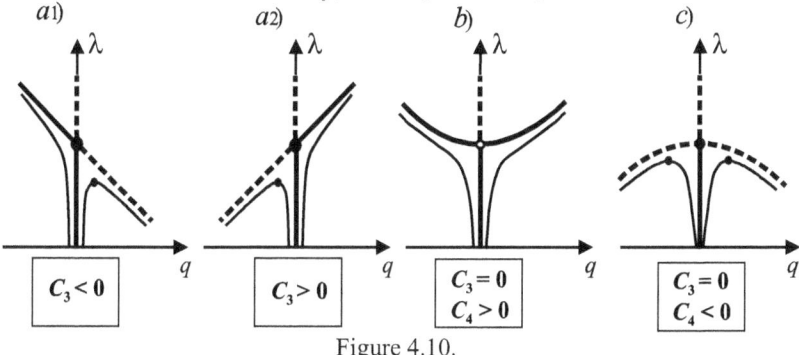

Figure 4.10.

If we now consider the equilibrium state curves (Fig. 4.10), where the branches of stable states are shown in solid lines, and the branches of unstable states are shown in dashed lines, we will see that there is an exchange of stability between the branches at the critical point, and this critical point belongs to either the unstable branch (filled circle), or to the stable branch (open circle). Bold lines refer to an ideal system, while thin lines represent the behavior of a system with initial imperfections.

Here are some simple examples of mechanical systems, (Fig. 4.11) the behavior of which corresponds to the curves given in Figure 4.10.

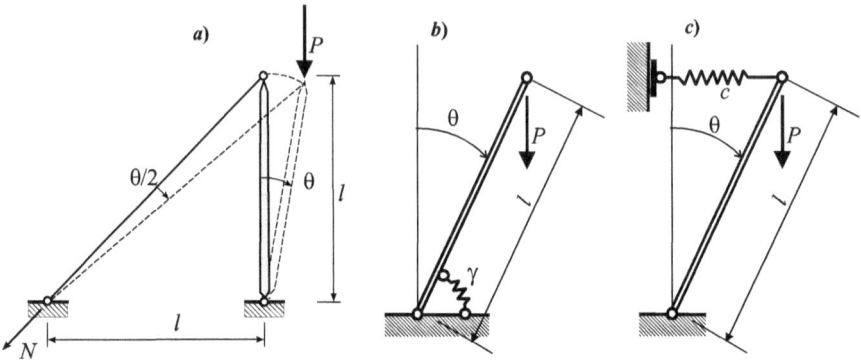

Figure 4.11.

a) If we consider a rigid column supported by an elastic oblique constraint with a stiffness parameter k (Fig. 4.11,*a*), and consider the deviation angle of the column θ as a generalized coordinate of this system, then it is easy to write an equilibrium equation in moments with respect to the column base point

$$Pl\sin\theta = Nl\sin\left(\frac{\pi}{4}-\frac{\theta}{2}\right),$$

where N is a guy tensile force.

The guy strain ε is defined by the following value

$$\varepsilon = \cos(\theta/2)+\sin(\theta/2)-1.$$

Therefore

$$N = k\left[\cos(\theta/2)+\sin(\theta/2)-1\right].$$

After substitutions into the above equilibrium equation and some transformations we obtain

$$P = \frac{k}{\sqrt{2}}\frac{\left[\cos(\theta/2)+\sin(\theta/2)-1\right]\left[\cos(\theta/2)-\sin(\theta/2)\right]}{\sin\theta}..$$

The graph of the function $P = P(\theta)$ is shown in Fig. 4.12

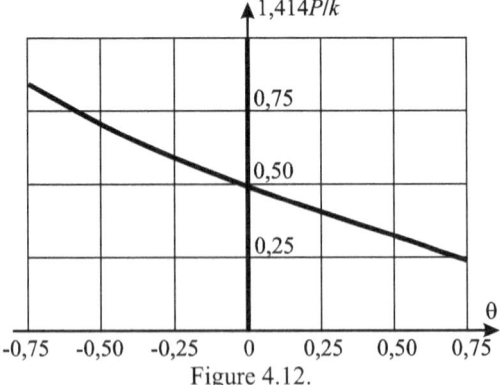

Figure 4.12.

The expression for the potential energy is obviously as follows

$$U = \frac{1}{2}kl\sqrt{2}\left[\cos(\theta/2) + \sin(\theta/2) - 1\right]^2 - Pl(1-\cos\theta).$$

Taylor expansion keeping terms up to the fourth order gives

$$U = \frac{l}{2}\left(\frac{k}{2\sqrt{2}} - P\right)\theta^2 - \frac{kl}{8\sqrt{2}}\theta^3 + \frac{l}{24}\left(P - \frac{kl}{8\sqrt{2}}\right)\theta^4 + \ldots.$$

This shows that in this case $C_3 < 0$, and

$$P_{cr} = \frac{k}{2\sqrt{2}}.$$

It is also clear that when $\theta = 0$, the equilibrium is maintained at any load value P – vertical line in Fig. 4.12. As we see from this figure, the qualitative picture of the structural behavior really coincides with that shown in Fig. 4.10,*a* (*asymmetric bifurcation*).

b) The following expression can be written for a rigid column elastically restrained from rotating about a support hinge by a spring with the stiffness γ

$$U = \frac{\gamma}{2}\theta^2 - Pl(1-\cos\theta) = (\gamma - Pl)\frac{\theta^2}{2} + Pl\frac{\theta^4}{24}\ldots.$$

The expansion of the total energy function of the system in powers θ when $P = \gamma/l = P_{cr}$ has the form $U = (P_{cr}l/24)\theta^4 > 0$, therefore, the branching curve is symmetric as in Fig. 4.10,*b* (*symmetric stable bifurcation*).

c) If a rigid column is restrained from rotating by a spring that maintains its horizontal position, as shown in Fig. 4.11,*c*, the total potential energy of the system is

$$U = \frac{cl^2}{2}\sin^2\theta - Pl(1-\cos\theta) = (cl^2 - Pl)\frac{\theta^2}{2} + \left(\frac{Pl}{24} - \frac{cl^2}{6}\right)\theta^4 + \ldots.$$

The critical load value corresponding to the bifurcation point is equal to $P_{cr} = cl$, and in the bifurcation point

$$U = -\frac{cl^2}{8}\theta^4 < 0,$$

we have a case corresponding to Fig. 4.10,*c* (*symmetric unstable bifurcation*).

The ratio between the critical loads of ideal systems and the limit loads of the system with imperfections depend on the type of a critical point, i.e. an idea of risk of reaching the critical state can be formed here.

Let us illustrate it by analyzing a system shown in Fig. 4.11,*c*.

Let us introduce a dimensionless parameter x, which defines the value of the initial imperfection of the system. More precisely, let the value of the initial deviation of the column from the vertical position be equal to xl. yl denotes the total deviation of the top of the column from the vertical position, where y can be considered as a dimensionless parameter characterizing this deviation (Fig. 4.13).

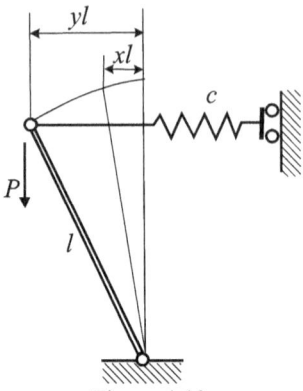

Figure 4.13.

The condition that moments about the support are equal to zero can be written as follows

$$Pyl = c(yl - xl)\left[l\sqrt{1-y^2}\right],$$

or

$$Py = cl(y-x)\sqrt{1-y^2} \qquad (4.19)$$

The critical force P_{cr} is determined from the condition $dP/dy = 0$, which leads to the equation

$$\frac{dP}{dy} = cl\left(\frac{x}{y^2}\sqrt{1-y^2} - \frac{y-x}{\sqrt{1-y^2}}\right) = 0.$$

It follows from this equation that

$$\frac{x}{y^3}(1-y^2) - \left(1 - \frac{x}{y}\right) = 0; \qquad y = x^{1/3}.. \qquad (4.20)$$

Substituting (4.20) into (4.19) allows to determine the relationship between the critical load and the dimensionless parameter of the imperfection of the system

$$P_{cr} = cl\left(1 - x^{2/3}\right)^{3/2}..$$

Since in this problem $P_{cr,id} = cl$, when there are no initial imperfections, the sensitivity of the critical load to the imperfections of the system is defined by the following ratio $\eta = P_{cr}/P_{cr,id} = (1 - x^{2/3})^{3/2}$.

The classic Koiter result lies in the fact that the reduction of the critical load due to the initial imperfections is a power function with the exponent 1/2 for asymmetric bifurcation and the exponent 1/3 for symmetric unstable bifurcation.

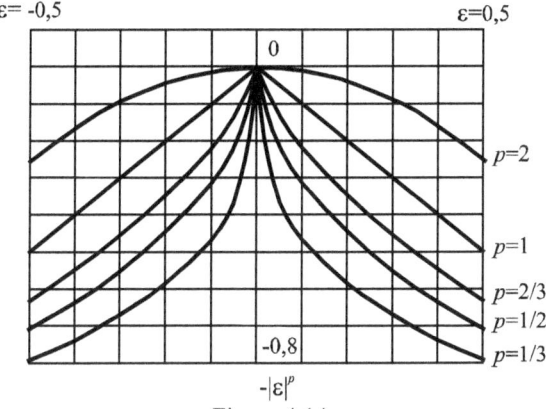

$-|\varepsilon|^p$

Figure 4.14

Thus, the limit load of a real system has a correction for the imperfection of type $k|\varepsilon|^p$, where k is a positive constant defined by the specific features of the problem, and the exponent p depending on the type of bifurcation is a positive rational fraction. The smaller the value p, the more responsive is the system to imperfections (Fig. 4.14).

It should be noted that systems with a stable bifurcation point are not very sensitive to imperfections. On the contrary, systems with an unstable bifurcation point show significant sensitivity to imperfections. Even small differences between a real structure and an idealized design model can lead to a noticeable decrease in the value of the critical force.

In the conclusion of this section, we would like to note the following: we have described the transition from an ideal system to an imperfect one above, introducing the initial perturbation parameter, but in reality the research logic is the reverse: we create a model of an idealized system dropping its initial imperfections. Consequently, in the "general case" (i.e., for all cases except some exceptional ones), the real structure behaves differently than the ideal one, and the analysis, which is limited only to finding bifurcation points, may turn out to be insufficient. In particular, in the case of an unstable bifurcation point, the transition from an ideal system to an imperfect one leads to a noticeable decrease in the value of the critical load, i.e. there is high sensitivity to the effect of imperfections, which is not the case for stable bifurcation points.

It should be noted here that the study of an idealized (and therefore, in some sense, degenerate) system provides important information about a wider class of non-degenerate systems, since it allows to predict their properties, provided that the "imperfection" of the real structure is sufficiently small, which is often the case.

Detection of an unstable bifurcation point serves as a warning about the strong sensitivity of the system to initial imperfections, which at least raises the question of increasing the commonly used value of the stability factor of safety.

Conversation 4.4. Global Stability. Upper and Lower Critical Load

It is useful to consider an example of a structure which buckles not at the bifurcation point, but at the limit point. A von Mises truss is one of the simplest examples (Fig. 4.15,*a*).

It is assumed here that the diagonals are incompressible, and the entire elastic part of the system is concentrated in the tie, which is modeled by a spring of stiffness c inserted into it. The strain state itself is described by the angle θ.

The expression for the potential energy of this system is

$$U = \frac{1}{2}c\Delta_1^2 - P\Delta_2 = 2cL^2\left(\cos\theta - \cos\alpha\right)^2 - PL\left(\sin\alpha - \sin\theta\right)$$

Hence it follows that the equilibrium state curve is determined by the equation

$$\frac{\partial L}{\partial \theta} = -4cL^2\left(\cos\theta - \cos\alpha\right)\sin\theta + PL\cos\theta = 0$$

or

$$P = 4cL\left(1 - \frac{\cos\alpha}{\cos\theta}\right)\sin\theta \qquad (4.21)$$

a)

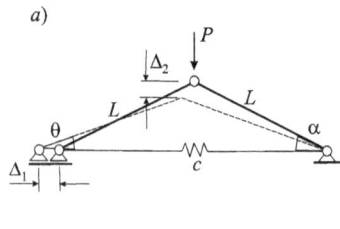

b)

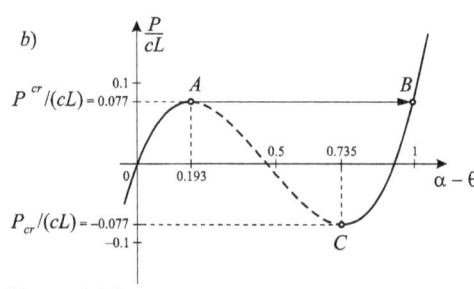

Figure 4.15.

The graph of this relationship for the value tgα = 0,5 is shown in Fig. 4.15,*b*. The following condition is satisfied in the limit point

$$\frac{dP}{d\theta} = 4cL\left(\cos\theta - \frac{\cos\alpha}{\cos^2\theta}\right) = 0 \qquad (4.22)$$

This example also shows a jump effect, when the system subjected to an increasing load reaches the limit point A and then jumps to the point B on a new stable branch of equilibrium states. This buckling is caused by large displacements.

It is obvious that the point A of the equilibrium trajectory shown in Fig. 4.15,*b*, corresponds to the unstable equilibrium state of the system. At the same time any point on the segment of an equilibrium trajectory from the point 0 to the point A (except for the point A itself) must be classified as points with a stable equilibrium state.

We see that the jump to the branch C-B of the equilibrium trajectory can take place not only from the point A, but from any point on the segment 0-A. You just have to apply a finite perturbation to the system (not an infinitesimal one, which is implied by the very definition of the classic concept of the loss of stability).

In the theory of the stability of equilibrium, such effects are defined by the concept of global buckling. Unlike the classic concept of local buckling, the global buckling, i.e. a jump to a different equilibrium trajectory of the system, occurs when a finite energy barrier is overcome. If a certain external perturbation is enough to overcome this barrier, the engineer cannot remain indifferent to this possibility. However, much more extensive information about the expected external perturbations is required to assess the risk of the jump.

Such concepts as the upper critical load and the lower critical load are closely related to the concept of global stability. The load *P* corresponding to the point A of the equilibrium trajectory in the Fig. 4.15, *b* is called the *upper critical load*. While the load *P* corresponding to the point C o f the equilibrium trajectory is called the *lower critical load*.

In the case when it is necessary to distinguish the upper and lower critical loads, we will use separate designations:

P^{cr} – upper critical load;
P_{cr} – lower critical load.

The concepts of upper and lower critical loads are introduced because the global buckling can occur only when the loads *P* are within the following limits

$$P_{cr} \leq P \leq P^{cr}.$$

Let us consider another example of a simple mechanical model (Fig. 4.16,*a*), which enables to explain the behavior of a cylindrical panel compressed along the generatrices.

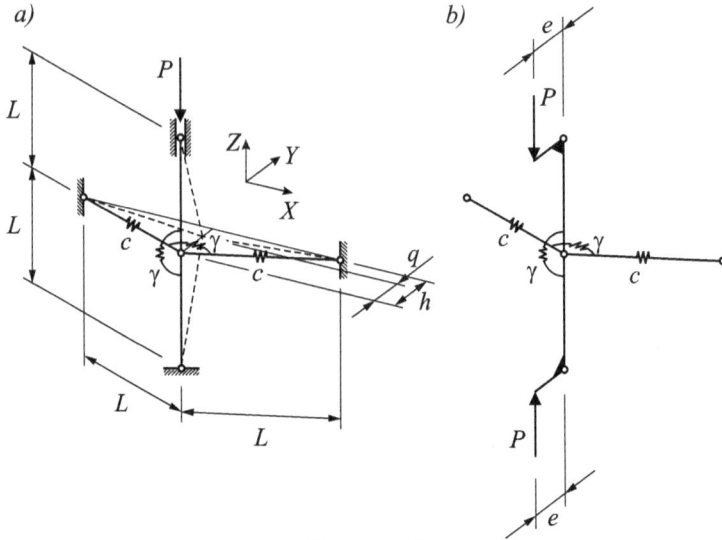

Figure 4.16.
The model consists of four bars which are rigid in bending and simply supported at the ends. Two horizontal bars can change their length due to the telescopic springs with the stiffness c inserted into these bars. There are two rotary springs with the stiffness γ in the central node of the model. One of these springs resists the change in the angle between the vertical bars, while the other resists this change between the horizontal ones. In the initial (undeformed) state the horizontal springs have a turning point in the central node. The value of this turn is characterized by the rise h, as shown in Fig. 4.16,a.

It should be noted that the displacements in different directions are treated differently in this problem – we will assume that the system has only one degree of freedom (the displacement q of the central node along the Y axis), while the displacements of this node along the X axis breaking the symmetry of the system are excluded.

It is assumed that the buckling causes a nodal displacement q and when the rise h is small, the turn angles θ of vertical and horizontal bar elements of the model are: $\theta = 2q/L$. The vertical displacement of the application point of the force P at small strains can be determined as follows

$$u = 2L\left(1 - \cos\frac{\theta}{2}\right) \approx 2L\left[1 - 1 + \frac{1}{2}\left(\frac{\theta}{2}\right)^2\right] = \frac{q^2}{L}$$

The potential energy is given by the following expression

$$U = 4\gamma q^2/L^2 + c\Delta^2 - Pq^2/L, \qquad (4.23)$$

where Δ is the axial shortening of transverse bars. Assuming that the rotation angles θ are small, the value Δ can be expressed in terms of the displacement q as

$$\Delta = (q/L)(h - q/2). \qquad (4.24)$$

If we substitute (4.23) into (4.24) and use a dimensionless displacement
$$\delta = q/h,$$
and replace the arbitrary ratio between the rotational stiffness of the springs γ, preventing the mutual rotation of the elements, and the axial stiffness c with a fixed ratio, which can be written as follows $\gamma = ch^2/8$, we will obtain

$$U = c\frac{\delta^2 h^4}{2L^2} + c\frac{\delta^2 h^4}{L^2}\left(1 - \frac{\delta}{2}\right)^2 - \frac{Ph^2\delta^2}{L}. \qquad (4.25)$$

Differentiating (4.25) by δ, we obtain the following equilibrium condition

$$\frac{dU}{d\delta} = \frac{2\delta h^2}{L}\left[\frac{ch^2}{2L}\left(3 - 3\delta + \delta^2\right) - P\right] = 0,$$

and when $\delta \neq 0$, we have

$$P = \frac{3ch^2}{2L}\left(1 - \delta + \delta^2/3\right). \qquad (4.26)$$

In the linear analysis, the terms containing δ and δ^2 are omitted in the brackets of this formula, i.e. the behavior of the horizontal springs, which do not work in the initial undeformed (subcritical) state, is neglected. This leads to a linear criterion for the loss of equilibrium stability

$$P^{cr} = \frac{3ch^2}{2L}. \qquad (4.27)$$

The superscript cr is used in the designation of the critical load to show that the formula (4.27) determines the upper critical load. In the linearized model the behavior of the considered system for the case when $P = P^{cr}$ is described by a horizontal line 1 – 2, shown in Fig. 4.17.

If we take into account the longitudinal stresses caused by large deformations, the post-buckling behavior is described by the equation (4.26) and the curve 1 – 3 – 5 in Fig. 4.17. We have a nonlinear model once the load reaches its maximum allowable value P^{cr}. However, according to (4.26), the load required to maintain equilibrium should decrease with increasing strain, and this decrease prevails when the values δ are not too large and the quadratic term is still small. Ultimately, since the strains continue to increase, the equilibrium load becomes increasing starting from the minimum point 3 and moving to the point 5. Moreover, for all values of P from the level of the point 1 (upper critical load P^{cr}) to the level of the point 3 (lower critical load P_{cr}), the system has two shifted equilibrium positions in addition to the initial one.

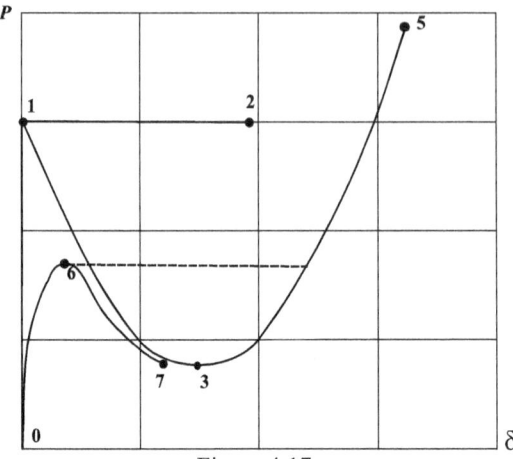

Figure 4.17.

If we consider an imperfect model in the analyzed problem, for example, take into account the eccentricity of the applied load as shown in Fig. 4.16,b, then the following term $-2Peq/L$ is added to the expression for the total potential energy, where e is the eccentricity of the load application. In this case the relationship between the displacement and the load is as follows

$$P = \left[\frac{3ch^2}{2L}(1-\delta+\delta^2/3)\right]\frac{1}{1+e/(h\delta)}. \quad (4.28)$$

The graph (4.28) for the case when $e/h = 0{,}1$ is shown as a curve $0 - 6 - 7$ in Fig. 4.17. According to this curve, the equilibrium stability is exhausted at the point 6 when the load is approximately equal to 55% of the upper critical load according from (4.27) given by the linear theory.

Question:

You have mentioned that it is necessary to overcome a finite energy barrier. However, a small (even infinitesimal) trial perturbation is usually used to check the stability of the system. And what can you say about testing the stability of equilibrium by applying a larger perturbation?

Answer:

In order to analyze this case, it is necessary to consider the nonlinear behavior of the system. The part of the potential function curve that lies between its two minima is called the energy barrier. The peak of the energy barrier is an unstable equilibrium state where the potential function has a maximum.

The energy barrier can be overcome by applying an artificial perturbation to the system, i.e. a deformation that takes the system over the energy barrier. The energy equal to the height of the barrier must be expended before passing the barrier and returned afterwards. The disturbance at which the system reaches the peak of the energy barrier is called the critical disturbance.

However, the energy barrier can turn out to be very insignificant, and then a stable equilibrium state is almost equivalent to an unstable one due to the high probability of the occurrence of perturbations exceeding the critical one.

As an example, let us consider a very high rigid parallelepiped supported on a rigid horizontal plane and subjected to an axial vertical force P applied to its upper base (Fig. 4.18,a). This parallelepiped is theoretically stable for any value of P. However, even a very small inclination of the parallelepiped axis can move the force P to the edge of the lower base and cause overturning.

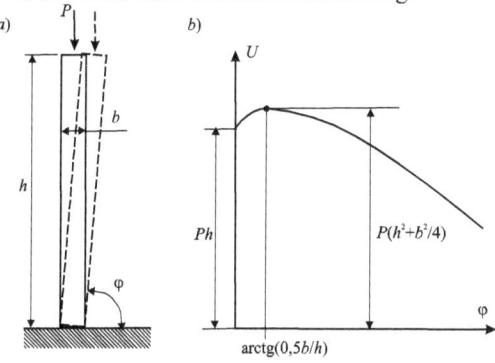

Figure 4.18

The potential energy of the system here is equal to

$$U = P(h\cos\varphi + 0,5a\sin\varphi),$$

where φ is the angle of the inclined parallelepiped axis, h is the height, and b is the width of the base.

The graph of this function is shown in Fig. 4.18,b. When $\tg\varphi = b/2h$, the maximum takes place, i.e. the peak of the energy barrier. Therefore, the critical perturbation will be the deviation of the parallelepiped axis from the vertical by an angle equal to $\arctg(b/2h)$. Since the height of the energy barrier and the value of the critical perturbation are insignificant in this example, the system is actually unstable when the ratios h/b are large.

Conversation 4.5. Stability of Multiple Degree of Freedom Systems

We will start this conversation with an example of the simplest system with two degrees of freedom, which enables to consider almost all the features of problems with a finite number of degrees of freedom greater than one.

The design model of the considered system is shown in Fig. 4.19. It consists of three hinged rigid bars with elastic supports. A compressive force P is applied to the free ends of the bars. It is assumed that the bars have the same lengths and the elastic supports have the same stiffness factors. The settlements of supports u_1 and u_2 will be taken as independent parameters defining the strain state of the system.

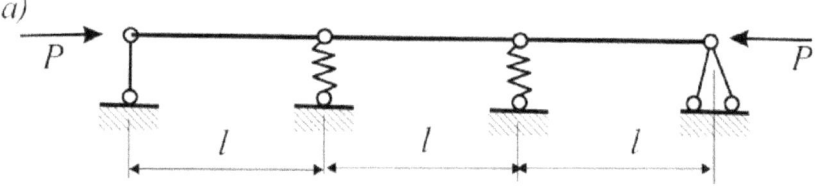

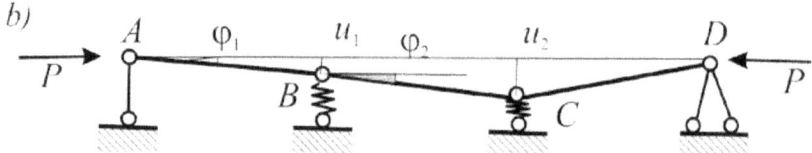

Figure 4.19

Let us solve the problem of stability of this system assuming that the deformations u_1 and u_2 are small in comparison with the lengths of the bars. We can write the equilibrium equations leaving only the terms with u_1 and u_2. in the first degree, and the expression for the potential energy — the terms not higher than the second degree u_1 and u_2.

Let us take the condition that the projections on the vertical axis of all forces in the node B_y are zero as the first equilibrium equation, and the condition that the projections on the vertical axis of all forces in the node C are zero as the second one (Fig. 4.19, b).

The following forces are acting in the node B: the reaction of the support B, equal to βu_1, where β is the stiffness factor of the support, and two forces acting along the first and second bars equal to $P\cos\varphi_1$ and $P\cos\varphi_2$ at the angles φ_1 and φ_2 to the initial direction of the bar axis. Assuming that the sines of the angles φ_1 and φ_2 are equal to their tangents u_1/l and $(u_2-u_1)/l$, and the cosines are equal to one with an accuracy up to the terms of the first order of smallness, we write the equilibrium equations as follows

$$\left.\begin{array}{l}-\beta u_1 + Pu_1/l + P(u_1-u_2)/l = 0 \\ -\beta u_2 + Pu_2/l + P(u_2-u_1)/l = 0\end{array}\right\}. \quad (4.29)$$

After simplifications we get

$$\left.\begin{array}{l}(2P-\beta l)u_1 - Pu_2 = 0 \\ -Pu_1 + (2P-\beta l)u_2 = 0\end{array}\right\}. \quad (4.30)$$

One of the solutions of the resulting system of equations $u_1 = u_2 = 0$ means that the undeformed state of the system will be an equilibrium form at any P. In addition to this trivial solution, there are also undefined solutions obtained from the condition that the determinant of the coefficients of system (4.30) is equal to zero:

$$\begin{vmatrix} 2P-\beta l & -P \\ -P & 2P-\beta l \end{vmatrix} = 0. \quad (4.31)$$

The equation (4.31) gives:

$$(2P-\beta l)^2 = P^2; \quad P_1 = \beta l/3, \; P_2 = \beta l. \quad (4.32)$$

Thus, the critical states of the system will occur when $P = P_1$ and when $P = P_2$. Of the two obtained critical forces only the smaller one is of practical importance $P_1 = \beta l/3$.

Let us now write an expression for the potential energy of the system:

$$U = 0,5\beta u_1^2 + 0,5\beta u_2^2 - Pl\left\{0,5(u_1/l)^2 + 0,5\left[(u_2-u_1)/l\right]^2 + 0,5(u_2/l)^2\right\}. \quad (4.33)$$

The first two terms here represent the elastic energy of the supports, and the expression in braces describes the shortening of the broken bar axis projection after the deformation.

The surface given by this formula in rectangular coordinates u_1, u_2 is a second order surface. When $P = 0$, it is a paraboloid of revolution with its vertex at the origin (Fig. 4.20, a). When $0 < P < \beta l/3$, the surface (4.33) will be an elliptic paraboloid (Fig. 4.20,b), which has one extreme point $u_1 = 0$, $u_2 = 0$, where U is minimal. Therefore, when $u_1 = u_2 = 0$, the system will be in a stable equilibrium state.

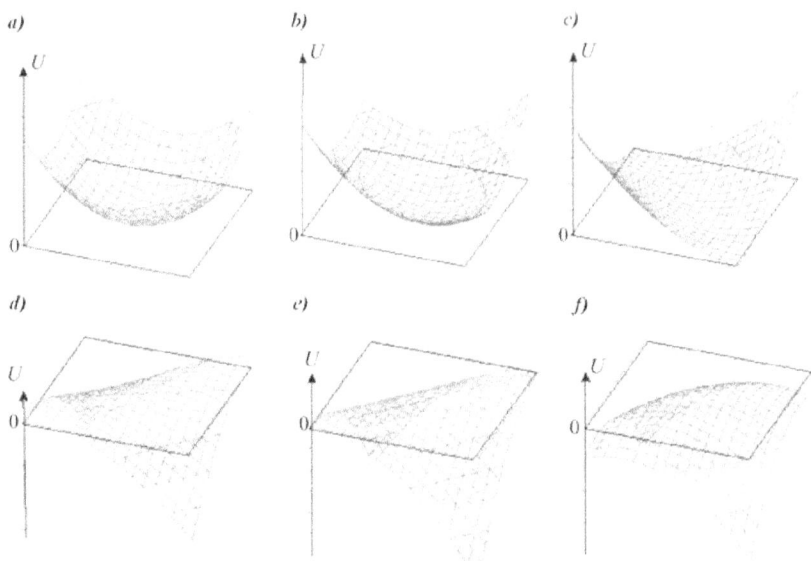

Figure 4.20

When $P = \beta/3$, the function (4.33) becomes

$$U = (\beta/6)u_1^2 + (\beta/3)u_1 u_2 + (\beta/6)u_2^2 - (\beta/6)(u_2 + u_1)^2$$

The surface described by this function is a parabolic cylinder with generatrices parallel to the line $u_1 + u_2 = 0$, lying in the plane $U=0$ (Fig. 4.20,c). In this case we have a whole line where the function reaches its minimum value equal to zero. It corresponds to an indifferent equilibrium state typical of the critical states of the system within its small strains.

When $P_1/3 < P < P_1$, the surface (4.33) turns into a saddle-shaped hyperbolic paraboloid (4.20,d). There is an equilibrium position at the origin, but it will be unstable in the direction of one of the principal curvatures of the surface.

When $P = P_1 = \beta l$, the formula (4.33) turns into

$$U = (\beta/2)(u_2 - u_1)^2.$$

The surface U turns into a parabolic cylinder opening downward (Fig. 4.20,e). In this case there are an infinite number of equilibrium positions defined by the line $u_1 = u_2$, but all of them will be unstable.

Finally, when $P > \beta l$, the surface U turns into an elliptic paraboloid opening downward (Fig. 4.20,f). In this case, there is one equilibrium position, which is unstable in any direction, and the system will have two degrees of instability.

The equations of equilibrium can be easily obtained from the formula (4.33), as the conditions of zero derivatives $\partial U/\partial u_1$, $\partial U/\partial u_2$, which must be satisfied at the extreme points of the surface U.

The equilibrium conditions in the critical states $P = P_1$ and $P = P_2$ can be written as follows:

$$u_1 + u_2 = 0 \quad (\text{when } P = \beta l / 3);$$
$$u_1 - u_2 = 0 \quad (\text{when } P = \beta l).$$

There is an uncertainty of the solution here, which is expressed in the uncertainty of the numerical values of the deflections u_1 and u_2. The relations between them, however, are quite certain and define the buckling modes corresponding to a certain critical load. An inversely symmetrical buckling mode shown in Fig. 4.21,a, where $u_1 = -u_2$ corresponds to the first critical force. A symmetrical buckling mode shown in Fig. 4.21,b corresponds to the second critical force. In this mode $u_1 = u_2$. The actual buckling mode will be a mode corresponding to a smaller critical force, i.e. inversely symmetrical.

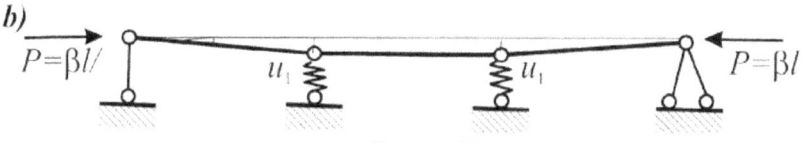

Figure 4.21

It is not difficult to generalize the approach demonstrated in this example to a system with n degrees of freedom. If the strain state of the system is defined by several parameters $u_1, u_2, ..., u_n$, then the potential energy will be a function of these parameters

$$U = U(u_1, u_2, ..., u_n). \qquad (4.34)$$

The following equations must be satisfied in the equilibrium state

$$\partial U / \partial u_1 = 0; \quad \partial U / \partial u_2 = 0; \ldots \partial U / \partial u_n = 0. \qquad (4.35)$$

However, not all equilibrium states $u_1^0, u_2^0, ..., u_n^0$, satisfying the conditions (4.35) are stable. In order to establish this, we will try to determine whether there can be an adjacent equilibrium state

$$u_1^0 + u_1, u_2^0 + u_2, ..., u_n^0 + u_n. \qquad (4.36)$$

To simplify the calculations, we take such an origin of displacements so that $u_1^0 = 0, u_2^0 = 0, ..., u_n^0 = 0$, then the expansion of the function U in a series of the considered equilibrium state will be as follows

$$U = A_1 u_1 + A_2 u_2 + \ldots + A_n u_n +$$
$$+ \frac{1}{2} \Big(B_{11} u_1^2 + B_{12} u_1 u_2 + \ldots + B_{1n} u_1 u_n +$$
$$+ B_{21} u_2 u_1 + B_{22} u_2^2 + \ldots + B_{2n} u_2 u_n + \quad (4.37)$$
$$\ldots\ldots\ldots\ldots\ldots\ldots\ldots\ldots\ldots\ldots\ldots\ldots\ldots\ldots$$
$$+ B_{n1} u_n u_1 + B_{n2} u_n u_2 + \ldots + B_{nn} u_n^2 \Big) + R.$$

Here A_i and B_{ij} are the values of the derivatives $A_i = \partial U / \partial u_i$ and $B_{ij} = \partial^2 U / \partial u_i \partial u_j$ taken at the point $u_1 = u_2 =, \ldots, u_n = 0$, and R is a remainder term representing higher degrees of expansion

It follows from the equilibrium conditions that $A_1 = A_2 = \ldots = A_n = 0$, and since we assume that the deviations $u_1, u_2, \ldots, u_n$ are small, we can neglect the remainder term. Then we will have

$$U = \frac{1}{2} \sum_{i=1}^{n} \sum_{j=1}^{n} B_{ij} u_i u_j ,$$

and the equilibrium equations (4.27) will be written as follows

$$\left.\begin{array}{l} \partial U / \partial u_1 = B_{11} u_1 + B_{12} u_2 + \ldots + B_{1n} u_n = 0 \\ \partial U / \partial u_2 = B_{21} u_1 + B_{22} u_2 + \ldots + B_{2n} u_n = 0 \\ \ldots\ldots\ldots\ldots\ldots\ldots\ldots\ldots\ldots\ldots\ldots\ldots \\ \partial U / \partial u_n = B_{n1} u_1 + B_{n2} u_2 + \ldots + B_{nn} u_n = 0 \end{array}\right\}. \quad (4.38)$$

It is easy to see that these equations have a solution $u_1 = u_2 =, \ldots, u_n = 0$, but we need to know whether they have other non-zero solutions. This can only happen when the determinant is zero

$$D = \begin{vmatrix} B_{11} & B_{12} & \cdots & B_{1n} \\ B_{21} & B_{22} & \cdots & B_{2n} \\ \cdots & \cdots & \cdots & \cdots \\ B_{n1} & B_{n2} & \cdots & B_{nn} \end{vmatrix} = 0. \quad (4.39)$$

This condition corresponds to the critical state of the system.

It is useful to relate the coefficients of the equation (4.38) to the expressions for the energy of the system. To do this, we will consider the case of loading the system with "dead" external forces $P_1, P_2, \ldots, P_n$, which do not change their direction during the deformation of the system. Let these forces vary synchronously in proportion to the load intensity parameter λ preserving the ratios between their components. Then there is the potential of external forces $\Pi_s (u_1, \ldots, u_n)$ and the following equality is satisfied for the respective components

$$P_i = \lambda \frac{\partial \Pi_s(u_1,...,u_n)}{\partial u_i} \quad (i=1,2,...,n). \tag{4.40}$$

If we denote the potential energy of deformations as $E(u_1,...,u_n)$, then in the equilibrium position of the system its total potential energy U

$$U = E(u_1,...,u_n) - \lambda \Pi_s(u_1,...,u_n) \tag{4.41}$$

considered as a function of generalized coordinates, takes a stationary value. In other words, in the equilibrium state

$$\frac{\partial U}{\partial u_i} = \frac{\partial E}{\partial u_i} - \lambda \frac{\partial \Pi_s}{\partial u_i} \quad (i=1,2,...,n) \tag{4.42}$$

Let us expand the expression for the potential energy of deformation and the expression for the force potential in series in the vicinity of the considered equilibrium state

$$E = \sum_{i=1}^{n} \frac{\partial E}{\partial u_i} u_i + \frac{1}{2} \sum_{i=1}^{n} \sum_{j=1}^{n} \frac{\partial^2 E}{\partial u_i \partial u_j} u_i u_j + \frac{1}{6} \sum_{i=1}^{n} \sum_{j=1}^{n} \sum_{k=1}^{n} \frac{\partial^3 E}{\partial u_i \partial u_j \partial u_k} u_i u_j u_k + ...,$$

$$\Pi_s = \lambda \sum_{i=1}^{n} \frac{\partial \overline{\Pi}_s}{\partial u_i} u_i + \frac{\lambda}{2} \sum_{i=1}^{n} \sum_{j=1}^{n} \frac{\partial^2 \overline{\Pi}_s}{\partial u_i \partial u_j} u_i u_j + ... \quad . \tag{4.43}$$

The fact that the undeformed state of the system is self-balanced means that when there are no external actions

$$\frac{\partial U}{\partial u_i} = \frac{\partial E}{\partial u_i} - \lambda \frac{\partial \Pi_{bl}}{\partial u_i} = 0 \quad (i=1,...,n).$$

Moreover, since the displacements are small u_i $(i=1,2,...,n)$, it is enough to consider only the quadratic terms of the series. Then

$$U = \frac{1}{2} \sum_{i=1}^{n} \sum_{j=1}^{n} \frac{\partial^2 E}{\partial u_i \partial u_j} u_i u_j - \frac{\lambda}{2} \sum_{i=1}^{n} \sum_{j=1}^{n} \frac{\partial^2 \overline{\Pi}_s}{\partial u_i \partial u_j} u_i u_j \quad .$$

and the equilibrium equations

$$\frac{\partial U}{\partial u_i} = \sum_{j=1}^{n} \frac{\partial^2 E}{\partial u_i \partial u_j} u_j - \lambda \sum_{i=1}^{n} \frac{\partial^2 \overline{\Pi}_s}{\partial u_i \partial u_j} u_i = 0 \quad (i=1,2,...,n).$$

The matrix of the coefficients of this system of equations which are linear with respect to u_i $(i=1,2,...,n)$

$$R_\lambda = \left[\left[\frac{\partial^2 E}{\partial u_i \partial u_j} - \lambda \frac{\partial^2 \overline{\Pi}_s}{\partial u_i \partial u_j} \right] \right] \tag{4.44}$$

is called *the full tangent stiffness matrix of the system*. The meaning of this name follows from the fact that this matrix is actually a generalized characteristic of the instantaneous stiffness of a system at a certain point of its equilibrium state.

The concept of a full tangent stiffness matrix of a system is one of the key ones in the theory of stability of the equilibrium state of a mechanical system. Therefore, we will consider this concept in more detail and illustrate its application using the example of a simple mechanical system (Fig. 4.22). In this case it is possible to demonstrate the technique of obtaining components of a tangent stiffness matrix without using the expressions for the energy of deformation and the work of external forces, i.e., by a method based on the equilibrium equations alone.

However, these equations must be written for the strain state of the system taking into account the internal forces which appear in the elements of the system in its equilibrium state studied for stability.

We will assume that the bars with the length l shown in the Fig. 4.22 are rigid, so that all deformations are concentrated in three springs with the stiffnesses c_1, c_2, c_3, respectively.

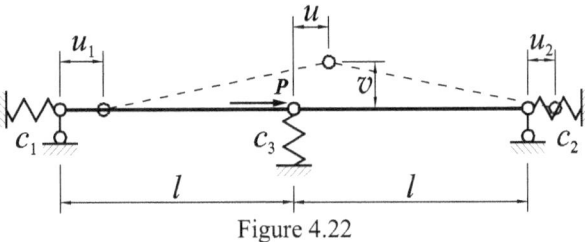

Figure 4.22

We will take the horizontal u and vertical v displacements of the application point of the force P as the generalized coordinates of the system. Indeed, these two parameters completely define the position of the mechanical system in space, since it is assumed that the lengths of the bars do not change. Let us denote the values of horizontal displacements of the end points of the first and second springs as u_1 and u_2, respectively (the expected deformed state of the system is shown in a dashed line in Fig. 4.22) and find them from the condition of non-deformed bars

$$u_1 = l + u - l\sqrt{1-(v/l)^2}, \quad u_2 = -l + u + l\sqrt{1-(v/l)^2}.$$

Let us denote the longitudinal force in the bar 1 as N_1, and the longitudinal force in the bar 2 as N_2. These forces are assumed to be calculated for the considered equilibrium state. It is obvious that

$$N_1 = c_1 u_0 = P\frac{c_1}{c_1+c_2}, \quad N_2 = c_2 u_0 = P\frac{c_2}{c_1+c_2}.$$

In this case the force N_1 is positive when the bar 1 is in tension, and the force N_2 is positive when the bar 2 is in compression.

The equilibrium equation for the longitudinal displacement u of the central node:

$$(c_1 + c_2)u = P.$$

In order to write the second equilibrium equation, let us consider the strain state of the system, taking into account the deviations from the considered equilibrium state, which may occur at buckling.

If we analyze the equilibrium of each element of the system, we will find (Fig. 4.23), that a shear force $Q_1 = N_1 v/l$ develops in the left bar, and a shear force $Q_2 = N_2 v/l$ develops in the right bar.

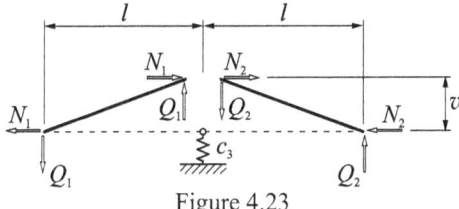

Figure 4.23

Therefore, in the case of transverse deviation of the central node by a unit value $v = 1$, the total reactive force r_{22} acting on this node will be the sum of two values

$$r_{22} = c_3 + \left(\frac{N_1}{l} - \frac{N_2}{l}\right) = c_3 - P\frac{c_2 - c_1}{(c_1 + c_2)l}.$$

Thus, the full tangent stiffness matrix is as follows

$$R_\lambda = \begin{bmatrix} c_1 + c_2 & 0 \\ 0 & c_3 - \lambda\dfrac{c_2 - c_1}{l(c_1 + c_2)} \end{bmatrix}$$

or

$$R_\lambda = R_0 - \lambda G = \begin{bmatrix} c_1 + c_2 & 0 \\ 0 & c_3 \end{bmatrix} - \lambda \begin{bmatrix} 0 & 0 \\ 0 & \dfrac{c_2 - c_1}{l(c_1 + c_2)} \end{bmatrix},$$

where the first row and the first column of these matrices refer to the longitudinal displacement u of the central node, and the second row and the second column refer to the transverse displacement v of this node. The structure and composition of the matrix R_0 are quite straightforward. Its components correspond to the usual linear formulation of the problem. And the matrix G which is called the geometric stiffness matrix characterizes the stability problem.

Question:

It was said in the first conversation of this cycle that the stability check is performed in order to understand how the system reacts to a small deviation from the equilibrium position. However, can't we apply such a perturbation or take into account that the load causes deviations from the initial configuration of the system (therefore, it receives a perturbation) and perform the calculation taking this circumstance into account?

Answer:
This issue has already been considered in the conversation 4.2, but for a single degree of freedom system. It was shown there that a p arametric load of a cer tain intensity can cause large displacements of the system leading to its buckling.

However, if the system has many (sometimes even an infinitely large number of) degrees of freedom, it is clearly not enough to perform a check for only one type of perturbation. In order to make sure that the system is stable, we would have to go through all possible variants of this perturbation. If we consider only a few variants, we might find ourselves in a situation where we are sure that in the case of the considered disturbances the system stays within the stability boundaries, but we do not know the distance to this boundary. Moreover, this distance can turn out to be very small or we might even cross the boundary in the case of other perturbations that we did not consider.

So as you can see, the check you are talking about (it is usually called the "P-Δ analysis") can be useful, but it cannot replace the stability check.

Conversation 4.6. Multiparameter Loading. Papkovich Theorem

The case when a structure is subjected to only one fixed type of external actions is the exception rather than the rule. The engineer usually has to deal with a set of independent loads, and these loads can act in various combinations.

Thus, there is a problem of choosing the worst combination of external actions, both in terms of the structural strength, and in relation to the stability margin in the equilibrium states corresponding to different combinations of the external actions.

We will start with a simple example. Suppose that two independent forces P_1 and P_2 are applied to an elastic system shown in Fig. 4.24, the values of these forces can vary in a wide range and they can act in two opposite directions. Three bars in this system are assumed to be rigid. If we fix the ratio between the forces P_1/P_2, then we will be able to find the equilibrium state of the system following the standard procedure, and determine the stability boundaries of this equilibrium state.

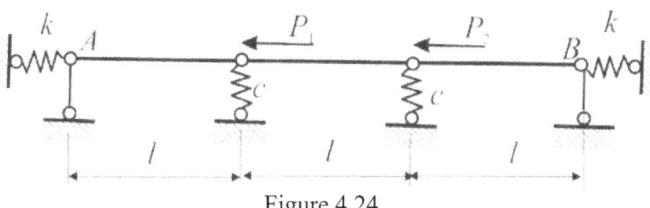

Figure 4.24.

Let us write the equilibrium equations for the expected deformed state of the system at the moment of buckling. The hypothetical buckling mode of the system is shown in Fig. 4.25.

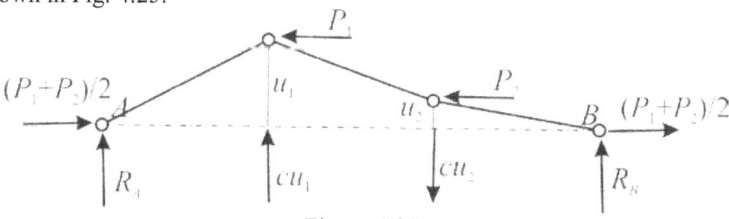

Figure 4.25.

In the linear formulation of the stability problem of the considered equilibrium state, the reactions in the horizontal springs with the stiffness c, will be the same and equal to $(P_1 + P_2)/2$, as shown in Fig. 4.25.

The reactions R_A and R_B of vertically fixed supports can be easily determined by writing the equilibrium equations in moments with respect to the points A and B. We have

$$R_A = \frac{1}{3}\left(2c + \frac{P_1}{l}\right)u_1 + \frac{1}{3}\left(c + \frac{P_2}{l}\right)u_2, \quad R_B = \frac{1}{3}\left(c - \frac{P_1}{l}\right)u_1 + \frac{1}{3}\left(2c - \frac{P_2}{l}\right)u_2.$$

Let us now use the condition of zero moments in hinge nodes. It gives

$$R_A l - \frac{P_1 + P_2}{2}u_1 = 0, \quad R_B l + \frac{P_1 + P_2}{2}u_2 = 0.$$

Substituting the above expressions for the reactions R_A and R_B, we obtain a system of two linear homogeneous equations for u_1 and u_2

$$(4cl - P_1 - 3P_2)u_1 + (2cl + 2P_2)u_2 = 0,$$
$$(2cl - 2P_1)u_1 + (4cl + 3P_1 + P_2)u_2 = 0.$$

Equating the determinant of this system of equations to zero, we obtain that the following equality is satisfied in the critical state of the system

$$4c^2 l^2 + 4cl(P_1 - P_2) - (P_1 + P_2)^2 = 0. \tag{4.45}$$

It is convenient to use dimensionless force variables p_1 and p_2, assuming that

$$p_1 = P_1/(cl), \quad p_2 = P_2/(cl).$$

Then the equation (4.45) can be written as

$$4 + 4(p_1 - p_2) - (p_1 + p_2)^2 = 0. \tag{4.46}$$

This equation defines a certain curve in the plane of the parameters p_1 and p_2, as shown in Fig. 4.26.

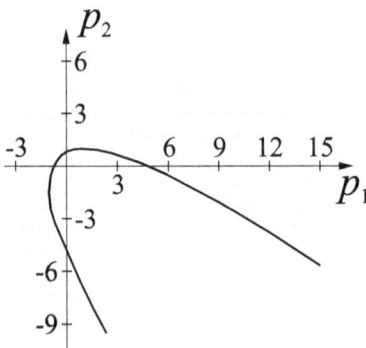

Figure 4.26.

It is clear that the two-dimensional area Ω, bounded by this curve, is the area of the equilibrium stability of the system. The equilibrium is unstable outside this boundary. The stability area Ω (not darkened) is shown in Fig. 4.26, the boundary of which satisfies the equation (4.46). As we can see, the point $(p_1 = 0, p_2 = 0)$ belongs to the stability area Ω, which is understandable, since this point corresponds to an unloaded system. However, the most important thing is that the area Ω is a convex area.

It should be noted that the critical loads in this problem do not depend on the stiffness of the horizontal springs k[11].

It is not accidental that the area Ω in this problem is convex. It turns out that the following important theorem by P.F. Papkovich is true

> *In the case of the combined loading of an elastic mechanical system, the equilibrium stability area Ω, plotted in the space of loadings within the linearized formulation of the equilibrium stability problem is a convex area containing the origin.*

The most important practical significance of the Papkovich theorem lies in the fact that the calculations of the stability of equilibrium states of a structure can be performed on the basis of the conclusions of this theorem not for any possible combination of loadings, but only for certain fixed variants of loadings. Then, with a guaranteed sign of error, it is possible to estimate the region of stability, replacing its true boundary with a set of hyperplanes. The stability area can then be assessed with a guaranteed error sign, replacing its true boundary with a set of hyperplanes. Let us consider this in more detail.

The classic theory of the stability of equilibrium considered in most courses of structural mechanics and usually used in the structural analysis assumes that all internal forces increase in proportion to one parameter, and the ratio between them remains constant. This behavior of internal forces is typical not for all systems; for many of them (especially nonlinear ones), it is necessary to take into account the fact that the ratios between internal forces in the system change with increasing loads. Therefore, if a critical (in terms of stability) load intensity is found and the concept of the stability factor of safety is related to it, the calculation has to be performed simulating the increase of the load, and not the increase of internal forces.

However, even for linear systems the stability factor of safety obtained by the classic method might not have a clear physical meaning. Indeed, imagine a structure with elements highly compressed by the constant load G_0 from the self-weight, and in addition loaded by the temporary load P_0 (Fig. 4.27).

---

[11] It is only important here that both horizontal springs (on the left and on the right end of the system) have the same stiffness. If they have other stiffness ratios, the critical forces will be different.

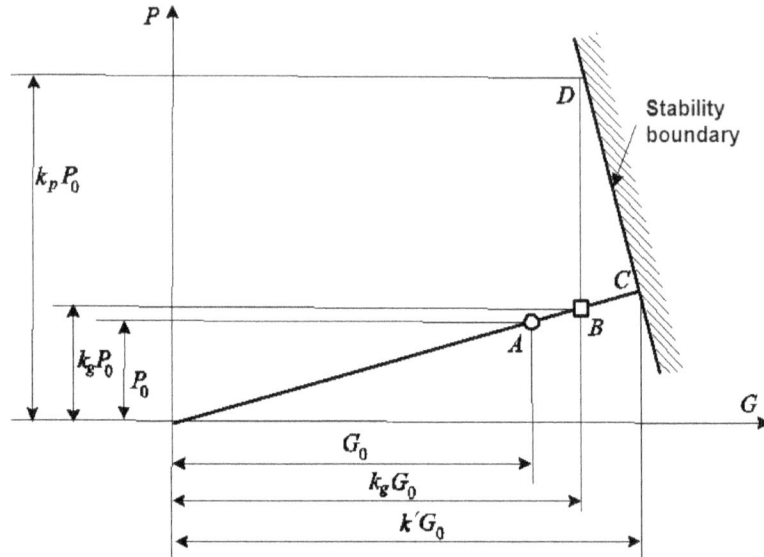

Figure 4.27.

The factor of safety $k' = 1{,}25$ for the total load corresponds to the clearly unrealistic growth of the self-weight by 25%. If we consider the growth of the self-weight, for example, by 10% (i.e. take $k_g = 1{,}1$), the temporary load has to increase much more to achieve the critical state. Naturally, under such reasoning, a graphical illustration of which is given in Fig. 4.27, a rather modest factor of safety of 1,25 appears in a completely different light ($k_p > 1{,}25$).

The result will obviously greatly depend on the type of the stability boundary, and if it has another configuration, all the factors of safety can turn out to be such that the value $k_p P_0$ will be much lower. It is important to note the insufficient accuracy of the analysis of the system with the usual interpretation of the stability factor of safety.

If the analyzed structure is important, the values of the critical load parameter should be calculated separately for each load case. If these results are obtained, and the critical loads $P_{i,cr}$ ($i = 1,\ldots, m$) are determined for each of the m load cases, the Papkovich theorem about a convex stability area can then be used for the linear system.

In particular, it follows from this theorem that the plane

$$\sum_{i=1}^{m} \frac{P_i}{P_{i,cr}} = 1 \qquad (4.47)$$

is located not further from the origin than the true stability boundary, which is shown in Fig. 4.28 for a two-dimensional case.

The straight line (4.47) is designated as AB in the figure, and it replaces the true stability boundary with a large margin. The solution can be refined by determining the critical value of the system for a certain combination of loads (point C on the OC ray) and approximating the AB curve by the ACB broken line.

CONVERSATIONS ABOUT THE STRUCTURAL MECHANICS

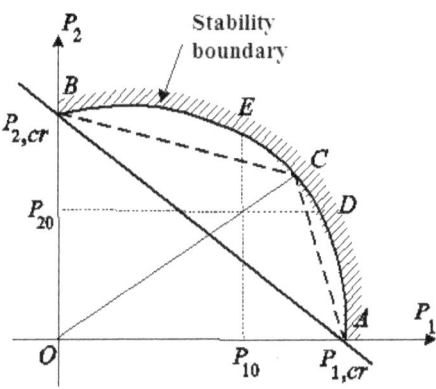

Figure 4.28

Question:
The design codes propose to check the stability of each bar, but almost nothing is said about checking the stability of the system as a whole. Does it mean that if all elements of the system are stable, the system is stable as well?

Answer:
No, it does not. In order to prove it, let us consider an example of the simplest structure consisting of two hinged bars, shown in Fig. 4.29 (a high von Mises truss). Unlike a flat von Mises truss, where the snap-through buckling occurs at the central node, the lateral displacement is the buckling mode in our case (Fig. 4.29,a), and the critical load is P=24235 tons.

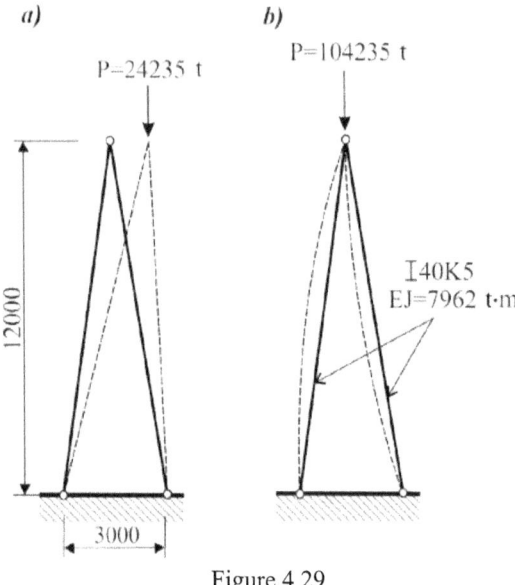

Figure 4.29

The local buckling of bars (Fig. 4.29,*b*) occurs at a m uch larger load of *P*=104235 tons and is less dangerous, and when the load is *P*=24235 tons, both bars of the system are stable.

Conversation 4.7. Effective Length

Standards for the stability analysis of bars have always been created on the basis of the experiments which were usually performed on simply supported bars. The results were applied to more complex boundary conditions of bars according to the theory of the so-called "equivalent" bar and its effective length.

The concept of effective (free, equivalent) length was introduced by F.S. Yasinsky [13] in order to generalize Euler's formula to the case of axial compression of a linearly elastic flat bar with arbitrary boundary conditions. According to F.S. Yasinsky the effective length is a conditional length of a simply supported single-span bar which has the same critical force as the given bar. This approach was widely accepted and was included in the design codes of almost all countries.

Unfortunately, it must be admitted that this approach to solving the problem of stability of bar structures does not have a clear theoretical justification. In fact, one difficult problem (checking the stability of an arbitrary bar) was replaced by an equally difficult one — determination of equivalent (effective) lengths of bars.

According to the established tradition and F.S. Yasinsky's definition, in order to determine the effective length, it is necessary to apply the method of the stability analysis of systems with straight bars and nodal loads, assuming elastic deformations (see for example [13]). Longitudinal forces in bars should be taken into account, while transverse loads and eccentricities causing the bending of bars should usually be excluded from consideration.

In design practice the effective length of the bar l_0 is usually determined according to the following formula

$$l_0 = \mu l, \tag{4.48}$$

where μ is the effective length factor which depends on the boundary conditions of the bar and the type of load; l is the geometric length of the considered bar.

If we consider the results of the study of the stability of single-span bars with different boundary conditions and select the lengths l of each of these bars so that they have the same critical force, it can be observed (see for example [6]), that the buckling modes of these bars are different parts of the same sinusoid

$$y = \sin\frac{\pi x}{l_0}. \tag{4.49}$$

This fact is illustrated graphically in Fig. 4.30. It should be noted here that the effective length l_0 is equal to the distance between adjacent inflection points, i.e. a half sine wave (4.49).

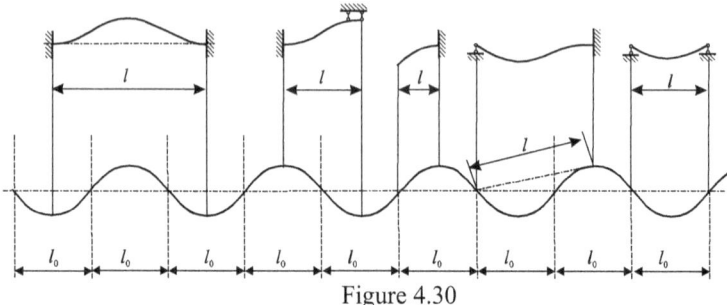

Figure 4.30

However, all of the above was essentially related to the consideration of plane design models and plane strain states. Only for them does it make sense to consider the distance between the inflection points of the bending line taken as the effective length.

The buckling mode of a spatial model can turn out to be such that the bending line of the bar does not belong to one of the principal planes of inertia even if it remains a plane curve. Then the question arises: in which plane is the effective length equal to the distance between the inflection points?

Since even in the case of plane bar systems the effective length of compressed bars has to be determined both in the plane and out of the plane of the system, there is an inconsistency with the F.S. Yasinsky's definition here as well. Indeed, let us consider a spatial bar which is simply supported in both principal planes of inertia and has the cross-sectional moments of inertia I_x and $I_y = 4I_x$. In the case of axial compression this bar buckles under the load

$$P_{cr,x} = \frac{\pi^2 E I_x}{l^2} \quad (l_{0,x} = l). \tag{4.50}$$

If we now technically determine the effective length $l_{0,y}$ such so that the buckling in this plane occurs at the same load value, then it follows from the equality

$$\frac{\pi^2 E (4I_x)}{l_{0,y}^2} = P_{cr,x} = \frac{\pi^2 E I_x}{l^2} \tag{4.51}$$

that $l_{0,y} = 2l$, although since this bar is simply supported we should have $l_{0,y} = l$.

The codes require checking the stability of the bar independently in its two principal planes. But this recommendation can be implemented only when the stability analysis is performed for each plane independently, assuming that the deformation out of the considered plane is impossible. In order to do this, practicing engineers should proceed as follows: perform two stability analyses alternately prohibiting the deformation in one or the other principal plane of inertia (for example, assuming either $I_x = \infty$, or $I_y = \infty$) and determine the effective length factors μ_x and μ_y.

Other problems arise in those cases when the principal axes of inertia of the elements of a spatial system are not parallel to each other, and the buckling mode, as well as the effective lengths, turns out to be dependent on the orientation of these axes in the system.

A useful example is shown in Fig. 4.31. It considers a spatial frame with four columns connected by non-deformable hinged bars at the top.

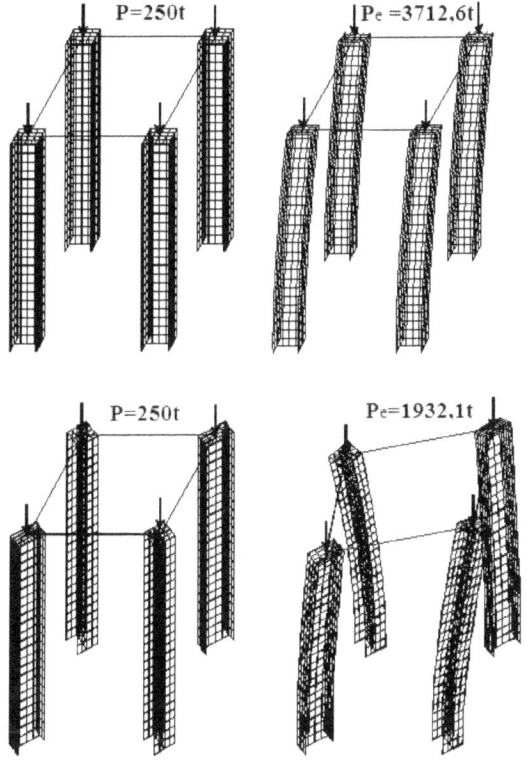

Figure 4.31

In the first case 6 meter I-section columns (web 800×30, flanges 600×30) fixed at the base are oriented in such a way that their webs are parallel, and in the second example they are turned by 45° and form a cyclically symmetric system. A compressive force of 250 t is applied to the top of each column.

In the first case the stability factor of safety turned out to be equal to 14,851, and it corresponds to the synchronous flexural buckling mode. The buckling mode in the second case is such that the columns experience torsion in addition to bending, which results in a factor of safety of 8,728.

The end fixation of the bar, its cross-section and the applied force have not changed, while the critical force of the system P_e (and hence the free lengths) have almost doubled. It means that the effective length can be reliably predicted only for a stand-alone bar (not included in the spatial structure), but we can not consider buckling of a bar belonging to a certain structure, because the structure buckles as a whole.

Finally, we can mention another problem that does not arise in the case of plane design models: even if the ends are simply supported, the hinges can be oriented not in the direction of the principal axes of inertia of the cross-section. For example, if the cylindrical hinges are rotated with respect to the principal axes of inertia by an angle φ (Fig. 4.32,*a*). The critical load in this case varies within a rather wide range which depends on the ratio of principal moments of inertia and the value of the angle φ. The corresponding results are graphically presented in Fig. 4.32,*b* [10].

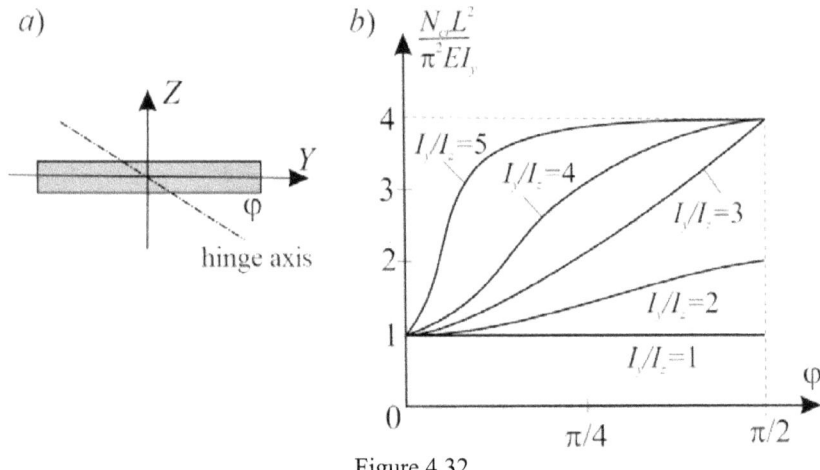

Figure 4.32.

The effective length method is used so often apparently because it enables to thoroughly study the behavior of only one standard structure — a simply supported bar. The effect of the inaccuracies of manufacturing and erection, the role of the inelastic behavior etc. are estimated for it, and all the results of this study form design graphs and tables intended for the practical use of the designer. Thus, the effective length method serves as a bridge between the general stability analysis of the system and the standard checks. However, the above examples show that this bridge is too narrow in some respects.

It should also be noted that the effective length of bars of the same system is different for different combinations of loads, although a simplified approach is usually used in the design practice (it is allowed, for example, in Sec.6.11* of SNiP II-23-81*), which allows to determine the effective lengths only for combinations of loads resulting in the greatest values of longitudinal forces and to use the obtained values for other load combinations. It is implicitly assumed that there is such a combination, where the compressive forces in all elements get maximum values. However, we can easily imagine a structure where this assumption is not fulfilled and, therefore, the problem of selecting a combination of loads to check the stability of the system cannot be considered solved.

At the same time, it should be recognized that the effective length method enables to obtain a satisfactory solution for many problems, and its common presence in the codes has not led to the failures of the structures constructed according to these codes. This suggests that we can hope for improvement of this method, and therefore it is important to understand its advantages and disadvantages.

References

1. *Alfutov N.A.* Fundamentals of S tability Analysis of Elastic Systems. — M.: Mashinostroenie, 1978. (Second edition. — M.: Mashinostroenie, 1991.)
2. *Bezukhov N.I., Luzhin O.V.* Stability and Dynamics of Structures in Examples and Problems. — M.: Stroyizdat, 1963.
3. *Volmir A.S.* Stability of Elastic Systems. — M.: Fizmatgiz, 1963.
4. *Geronimus J.L.* Theoretical Mechanics. — M.: Fizmatgiz, 1973.
5. *Kornoukhov N.V.* Selected Works on Structural Mechanics. — Kiev: Academy of Science of Ukraine, 1963.
6. *Leites S.D.* Stability of Bar Systems // Designer's Handbook. Analysis and Theory. Volume 2.— M.: Stroyizdat, 1973.— p. 186-269.
7. *Panovko Ya.G., Gubanova I.I.* Stability and Oscillations of Elastic Systems. Modern Concepts, Paradoxes and Mistakes. *Third Edition.*— M.: Fizmatgiz, 1979.
8. *Papkovich P.F.* Works in Structural Mechanics of S hips. V.4 Stability of Ba rs, Floors and Plates — L.: Sudostroyeniye, 1963.
9. *Perelmuter A.V., Slivker V.I.* Design Models of Structures and a Possibility of Their Analysis. *Second edition.* — Kiev: Steel, 2002; *Third edition.* — M.: DMK, 2007.
10. *Perelmuter A.V., Slivker V.I.* Stability of Equilibrium of Structures and Related Problems. Volume 1. General Theorems. Stability of Ind ividual Elements of Mechanical Systems.— M.: SCAD SOFT, 2010
11. *Rzhanitsyn A.R.* Stability of Equilibrium of Elastic Systems. — M .: Gostekhteorizdat, 1955.
12. *Feodosyev V.I.* Selected Problems and Questions in Strength of Materials. — M.: Nauka, 1967.
13. *Yasinsky F.S.* Selected Works on S tability of Bars in Compression. - M.-L .: Gostekhizdat, 1952.
14. *Koiter W.T.* Over de stabilities van het elastisch evetwicht. PhD Thesis. Delft University of Technology, Amsterdam - Paris — 1945.

Cycle 5

Fundamentals of Dynamic Analysis

 *It is probably no exaggeration to say that oscillations, in the broadest sense of the word, have a prominent and even primary place in many respects among both the free natural processes and those used in engineering*

I.D. Papaleksi

Conversation 5.1. Static and Dynamic Structural Analysis

Unfortunately, the traditional engineering education pays little attention to the dynamic problems. Through numerous exercises, students develop a certain intuition for the problems of static structural analysis, but "a feel for dynamics" remains completely undeveloped. Moreover, they are practically incapable of describing dynamic actions and selecting the criteria when it is necessary to perform the dynamic analysis (perhaps with the exception of a few cases covered by the codes).

In the static calculations considered in the previous sections the time factor was ignored, i.e. all parameters did not depend on time. It would seem that the calculations involving the time factor should be considered dynamic. However, in practice, there is a rather large group of problems where, on the one hand, the actions and/or properties of the system vary in time, but, on the other hand, this happens so slowly that the response of the system at each moment in time can be obtained by a static analysis using the action and system parameters related to this moment in time. This type of analysis is called *quasi-static*. It is also said that the actions, parameters of the system and responses vary *in slow time* [9].

If a problem can not be considered in slow time, then we have to deal with variations *in fast time*. Additional forces depending on time derivatives usually appear in calculations in this case. These are first derivatives – velocities (resistance to motion is usually related to them), and second derivatives – accelerations (forces of inertia are related to them).

It should be noted that the boundary between "slow" and "fast" time is rather vague and individual for each system. A certain action variation rate can allow to perform calculations "in slow time" for one system, while for another one they will have to be performed "in fast time".

The need to perform calculations "in fast time" is usually related to the relative values of the inertial terms of the equations of motion. If the product of mass and acceleration reaches significant proportions of the forces generated by stiffness, the calculations have to be performed "in fast time". This consideration is entirely true, but there is one more possibility to take into account: not only the inertial forces related to accelerations can take rather large values, but the forces related to velocities as well.

Quasi-static calculations are usually distinguished as a separate class, and dynamic calculations are defined as calculations in fast time. And unlike static problems, which are usually solved with the help of ordinary algebraic or transcendental equations, it is necessary to solve differential equations with time derivatives in this case.

The number of *dynamic degrees of freedom* is an important characteristic of the system. It is equal to the number of independent parameters that define the position of all masses for any possible displacement of the system at any time. If masses are concentrated at certain points in a system, this system is said to have a finite number of degrees of freedom (it is called discrete). If the masses are distributed along the elements of the system, then this system has an infinitely large number of degrees of freedom and is called a system with distributed parameters.

It is easy to see that in the case of a discrete system the number of dynamic degrees of freedom may be not equal to the number of static degrees of freedom. Let us, for example, consider the system shown in Fig. 5.1. The elongation, bending and torsion of the bar can result in the displacements Δ_x, Δ_y and Δ_z in the direction of the coordinate axes, and the rotations φ_x, φ_y and φ_z about these axes of the mass at the end of the bar, i.e. the system has six dynamic degrees of freedom (the number of static degrees of freedom, which define the bar configuration, is infinite).

However, some simplifications can be made when solving the problems. We can, for example, neglect the elongations of the bar Δ_x as compared with the displacements Δ_y and Δ_z, moreover, the angles of rotation of the mass are often neglected, and then we are left with a system with two dynamic degrees of freedom.

This shows that the number of dynamic degrees of freedom depends not only on the geometry of the system and its masses, but also on the required accuracy of the solution.

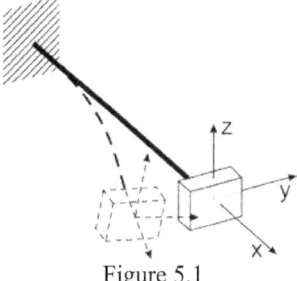

Figure 5.1

Systems with distributed parameters whose motion is described by partial differential equations are usually discretized in some way. The simplest method is the concentration of point masses at individual points of the structure or the introduction of rigid bodies with the moment of inertia of these masses in addition to the actual mass. Another discretization method is to use generalized displacements described by certain functions, in the same way as it is done in the finite element method.

Conversation 5.2. Oscillations of a Single Degree of Freedom System.

The mechanics courses consider the main types of forces that can act on a particle: time dependent, position dependent, and velocity dependent forces. In most cases, the generalized forces that act during oscillations of mechanical systems are reduced to these types. Let us consider them in more detail dealing here only with single degree of freedom systems.

Generalized *driving forces* are external forces of type $P(t)$, which are the given time functions; these forces cause forced oscillations. The sources of driving forces, as well as their time variation laws are very diverse, although the periodic driving forces are the most common ones.

In some cases the excitation of oscillations is given kinematically, when a certain motion is "prescribed" to some points of the system. In particular, the seismic motion of the base of the structure or the excitation of vehicle oscillations when moving along an uneven path are considered as kinematic. As will be shown below, any kinematic excitation can be given as a certain equivalent force excitation, i.e., replaced by the action of corresponding forces.

Generalized *position forces* are forces that depend on the configuration of the system, i.e. on the generalized coordinates. The restoring forces that arise when the system deviates from the equilibrium position and are directed so as to return the system to this position are of particular importance. These are the forces that contribute to free oscillations.

Restoring forces arise in mechanical systems with elastic elements due to the deformation of these elements during oscillations (elastic forces). In other cases gravity (pendulum) or buoyancy (ship) can act as a restoring force.

The relationships between the restoring forces and the generalized coordinates are usually nonlinear; however, when small oscillations are studied (which is sufficient in many cases), the linearization of these relationships is often acceptable.

The generalized *friction forces* depend on the generalized velocities (at least on their sign) and are directed opposite to the motion. Friction forces arise in the joints and supports of the mechanical system (*structural friction*), as well as in the material of its elements (*internal friction of the material*). This category also includes the *resistance forces of the medium* (liquid, gas) where oscillations occur. These and similar forces are also called friction forces. Friction forces usually impede the development of oscillations, for example, cause the damping of free oscillations. These forces act in mechanical systems called dissipative.

When creating a design model it is very important to neglect the insignificant force components reasonably and to simulate the properties of those taken into account in the analysis correctly. Thus, when determining the natural frequencies of mechanical systems, the action of friction forces can be neglected in most cases; they can be neglected, but such simplifications should be done carefully, bearing in mind that seemingly small effects can sometimes be the cause of important consequences. Thus, even very small friction forces must be taken into account when analyzing damping of free oscillations, as well as when determining the resonant or near-resonant amplitudes of forced oscillations.

One of the peculiarities of the problems of dynamics is the consideration of the *forces of inertia I*, which create inertial resistance to the velocity variation. According to Newton's second law, these forces are defined as the product of mass and acceleration. We should keep in mind that the inertial property called mass is not the same as the weight of the body. Weight G is the force that the body exerts on its support, and it is determined by the following formula $G = mg$ (m is the mass, g=9,81 m/sec^2 is the gravitational acceleration) and if the body weighs 10 kgf (kilogram-force), then its mass is equal to 1,0191 kg or 1,019 kgf/m.

If the body rotates with an angular velocity $\dot{\varphi}$ (rad/sec) and an angular acceleration $\ddot{\varphi}$ (rad/sec^2), then the mass moment of inertia J_ω (kg·m^2= kgf·m·sec^2) is the measure of its inertia instead of the mass. And the inertial resistance to rotation is $M = J_\omega \ddot{\varphi}$.

If the deformation of the system is defined by the displacement of one point where the entire mass of the structure is concentrated, this system has one dynamic degree of freedom. For the sake of simplicity we will assume that the elastic resistance R is modeled by a spring, and the viscous resistance to motion Q is modeled by a certain damping device (Fig. 5.2.*a*).

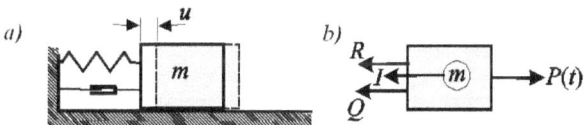

Figure 5.2

The equation of motion can be written on the basis of d'Alembert principle, which states that if forces of inertia are added to the given (active) forces acting on a point of the mechanical system, we will obtain a balanced system of forces. The D'Alembert principle enables to apply simpler static methods to the solution of the problems of dynamics, therefore it is widely used in engineering practice, in the form of a kinetostatic method.

Take into account that the mass is subjected to (Fig. 5.2,*b*):
- the exciting force *P(t)*;
- the force of inertia $I(t) = m\ddot{u}(t)$;

- the elastic resistance force $R(t) = k u(t)$, where k is the stiffness of the spring;
- the inelastic resistance force, which will be considered proportional to velocity (Voigt model) $Q(t) = c\dot{u}(t)$, where c is the damping constant.

According to d'Alembert principle, these forces are in dynamic equilibrium at all times:

$$I(t) + Q(t) + R(t) = P_i(t),$$

which leads us to the differential equation of motion of a single degree of freedom system:

$$m\ddot{u} + c\dot{u} + ku = P(t). \qquad (5.1)$$

The obtained equations are written for the case when the exciting force is applied directly to the mass. Let us show how the equations of motion change when this condition is not satisfied (see Fig. 5.2). We will use here another designation of stiffness $r_{11} = k$. Then the equation of equilibrium of the mass subjected to all forces applied to the system will be

$$m\ddot{u} + c\dot{u} + r_{11}u = r_{11}\Delta(t),$$

and the displacement of the mass point

$$u = -\delta_{11}m\ddot{u} - \delta_{11}c\dot{u} + \Delta(t),$$

where $\Delta(t)$ is the time-varying displacement of the mass under a statically applied load;

$\delta_{11} = \dfrac{1}{r_{11}} = \dfrac{1}{k}$ is the compliance of the system at the mass point.

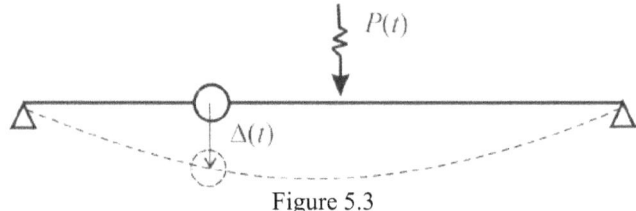

Figure 5.3

Thus, the problem of oscillations of a single degree of freedom system reduces to an ordinary second-order differential equation. An equation is called ordinary if the unknown function depends on one variable, and the highest order of the derivative included in the differential equation is called the order of this equation.

Free oscillations

As we know from calculus, the complete solution of a differential equation is the sum of two solutions: the solution of a homogeneous equation with a zero right-hand side (a general solution), and a certain solution of a nonhomogeneous equation (a particular solution). When applied to (5.1), the homogeneous equation

CONVERSATIONS ABOUT THE STRUCTURAL MECHANICS 209

can be written as
$$m\ddot{u} + c\dot{u} + ku = 0$$
$$\ddot{u} + (c/m)\dot{u} + \omega^2 u = 0, \quad (5.2)$$

where $k/m = \omega^2$.

The equation (5.2), which does not include the exciting force $P(t)$, describes the behavior of the system removed from the equilibrium state at the initial time and then left to itself. This system is said to perform *free oscillations*[12].

The parameter ω is a constant value that depends solely on the elastic and inertial properties of the system and is independent of the oscillation excitation conditions, and is therefore called the *natural frequency* of the system $\omega = \sqrt{k/m}$. The natural frequency is the number of free oscillations per 2π units of time. The *period* of free oscillations, i.e. the duration of one complete cycle of oscillations, is determined by the formula $T = 2\pi/\omega$.

The solution of the equation (5.2) has the form $u = Ge^{st}$, and after substituting it into (5.2) we obtain
$$\left[s^2 + (c/m)s + \omega^2\right]Ge^{st} = 0.$$

Since Ge^{st} is not equal to zero, we obtain the quadratic equation after the reduction. It has the following solution
$$s = -\frac{c}{2m} \pm \sqrt{\left(\frac{c}{2m}\right)^2 - \omega^2}. \quad (5.3)$$

The character of the solution depends on the ratio of values $\alpha = c/(2m)$ and ω.

When there is no friction, when $c=0$ and, therefore $\alpha = 0$, the solution of the equation (5.2) becomes:
$$u(t) = u_0 \cdot \cos\omega t + \frac{\dot{u}_0}{\omega} \cdot \sin\omega t. \quad (5.4)$$

Thus, the free oscillations of the conservative single degree of freedom system are harmonic (Fig. 5.4) and occur with the natural frequency of the system.

---

[12] The study of free oscillations is of particular interest due to the practical problems of motion of a mechanical system after a certain disturbance of its equilibrium state. However, it is not the only thing that determines the importance of the study of free oscillations. As will be clear from the following, the free oscillation characteristics completely determine the individual dynamic properties of a mechanical system and are extremely important in the analysis of its forced oscillations.

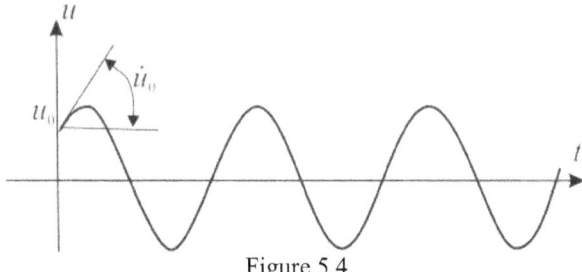

Figure 5.4

In the general case when damping is small and $\alpha^2 < \omega^2$, the solution (5.3) gives a pair of complex conjugate roots $s_{1,2} = \alpha \mp i\omega$, and the general solution of the homogeneous equation is

$$u = C_1 e^{(\alpha + i\omega)t} + C_2 e^{(\alpha - i\omega)t}.$$

Conversion of the exponential function of the imaginary argument into trigonometric form gives the final expression for the general solution

$$u = e^{\alpha t}\left(A\cos\tilde{\omega}t + B\sin\tilde{\omega}t\right).$$

Here A, B are arbitrary constants defined by the initial conditions, i.e. displacement $u_0 = u(0)$ and velocity $\dot{u}_0 = \dot{u}(0)$ at the initial time, and $\tilde{\omega} = \sqrt{\omega^2 - \alpha^2}$ denotes the angular (circular) frequency of a system with viscous friction. The following values are often used $n = \tilde{\omega}/(2\pi)$ – technical frequency and $T = 1/n$ – period.

Let us find the constants of integration from the initial conditions. Suppose that at the initial time the mass had a coordinate u_0 and velocity $\dot{u}_0$. Then

$$u_0 = A,$$

$$\dot{u}_0 = -\alpha e^{-\alpha t}(A\cos\tilde{\omega}t + B\sin\tilde{\omega}t) + \tilde{\omega}e^{-\alpha t}(-A\sin\tilde{\omega}t + B\cos\tilde{\omega}t) =$$
$$= -\alpha A + \tilde{\omega}B.$$

Hence $B = (\dot{u}_0 + \alpha u_0)/\tilde{\omega}$, and

$$u(t) = e^{-\alpha t}(u_0 \cos\tilde{\omega}t + \frac{\dot{u}_0 + \alpha u_0}{\tilde{\omega}}\sin\tilde{\omega}t). \tag{5.5}$$

The behavior of $u(t)$ is shown in Fig. 5.5.

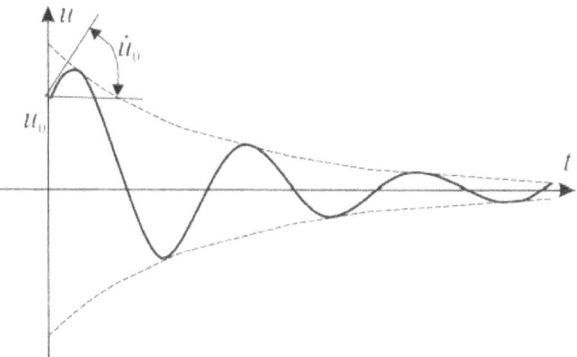

Figure 5.5

Note that the ratio of two successive maximum deviations remains constant:

$$\frac{u(t)}{u(t+T)} = \frac{Ae^{-\alpha t}}{Ae^{-\alpha(t+T)}} = e^{\alpha T}.$$

Consequently, maximum deviations decrease exponentially.

The natural logarithm of the ratio of two successive maximum deviations is called the *logarithmic decrement*

$$\delta = \ln\frac{A \cdot e^{-\alpha t}}{A \cdot e^{-\alpha(t+T)}} = \alpha T. \qquad (5.6)$$

The dimensionless quantity δ characterizes the damping rate. Here are some values:

steel bridges: $\delta=0,085$,
RC roof beams $\delta=0,28$;
RC bridges $\delta=0,315$.

Note that the factor $e^{-\alpha t}$ in (5.5) becomes equal to 0,01 when $\alpha t = \delta(t/T) = 4,53$. It means that the initial amplitude decreases 100 times (i.e. oscillations practically stop), for example, for steel bridges in 4,53/0,085=53 oscillations, and for reinforced concrete bridges — in 15 oscillations.

If the damping is so great that $\alpha^2 > \omega^2$, then the roots $s_{1,2}$ are real, negative.

The general solution: $u = C_1 e^{s_1 t} + C_2 e^{s_2 t}$ is a decreasing function. Oscillations do not occur after the deflection, and the system returns to its equilibrium position (Fig. 5.6).

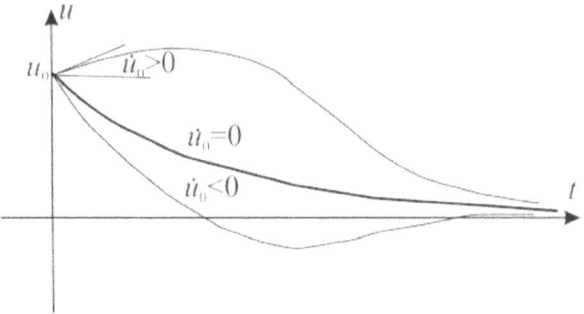

Figure 5.6

Note that the viscous dissipative force exponentially reduces the amplitude of free oscillations, but its effect on the frequency (and hence period) of free oscillations is insignificant.

Indeed, let us consider small oscillations with noticeable dissipation, for example, when each amplitude is twice as small as the previous one, i. e. $A_n/A_{n+1} = 2$. Then the logarithmic damping decrement $\delta = \ln 2 = 0,693 = \alpha T$, and the parameter is $\alpha = 0,693/(2\pi)$ $\tilde{\omega} = 0,11\tilde{\omega}$. Therefore, $\tilde{\omega} = \sqrt{\omega^2 - \alpha^2} = 0,994\omega$.

Forced oscillations with harmonic excitation

Let us return to the equation (5.1). Assuming that the exciting force varies in time according to the expression $P = P_0 \sin\theta t$, and there is no resistance, we will have

$$m\ddot{u} + ku = P_0 \sin\theta t, \quad (5.7)$$

or

$$\ddot{u} + \omega^2 u = \frac{P_0}{m}\sin\theta t. \quad (5.8)$$

The particular solution of the equation (5.8) is

$$u(t) = C\sin\theta t, \quad (5.9)$$

and, substituting (5.9) into (5.8), we get

$$\left(-\theta^2 + \omega^2\right)C\sin\theta t = \frac{P_0}{m}\sin\theta t. \quad (5.10)$$

The equality (5.10) must hold for all values of time t, and this is only true when $\left(-\theta^2 + \omega^2\right)C = P_0/m$, hence

$$C = \frac{P_0}{m\omega^2\left(1 - \theta^2/\omega^2\right)}. \quad (5.11)$$

Given that $m\omega^2 = k$, and introducing the parameter of the relative excitation frequency $\beta = \theta/\omega$, we will write

$$u(t) = \frac{P_0}{k(1-\beta^2)}\sin\theta t. \quad (5.12)$$

Adding the general solution of the homogeneous equation, which is the reaction of the system with free oscillations, to (5.12), we obtain

$$u(t) = A\sin\theta t + B\cos\theta t + \frac{P_0}{k(1-\beta^2)}\sin\theta t. \quad (5.13)$$

The constants A and B are chosen so as to satisfy the initial conditions. Assuming zero initial conditions ($u(0) = \dot{u}(0) = 0$) we will have

$$u(t) = \frac{P_0}{m(\theta^2 - \omega^2)}\left(\sin\theta t - \frac{\theta}{\omega}\sin\omega t\right). \quad (5.14)$$

The obtained solution is the difference between two harmonic components with different frequencies. In reality, this process can be observed only at the very beginning, since the resistance forces not taken into account when writing the equation cause a gradual damping of oscillations with the natural frequency ω. Therefore, after some time, the oscillations become almost monoharmonic with frequency θ.

Thus, the most significant, stationary part of the process (*steady* forced oscillations) is described by the expression (5.12).

The amplitude of these oscillations, occurring with a frequency θ, is determined by the expression

$$A = \frac{P_0}{k|\theta^2 - \beta^2|}, \quad (5.15)$$

where the denominator (*dynamic stiffness*) characterizes the effective stiffness of the system under harmonic excitation. The expression (5.15) can be written as

$$A = u_{st}\mu, \quad (5.16)$$

where $\mu = 1/|1 - \theta^2/\omega^2|$ is the dynamic amplification factor. It shows how many times the amplitude of the steady forced oscillations A is greater than the displacement $u_{st} = P_0/k$ caused by the statically applied force P_0.

It is not difficult to see that when $\theta \to \omega$ (*resonant mode*) the dynamic amplification factor tends to infinity. In reality, the solution is finite, as can be seen if we consider a system with friction.

Question:
It was said that in the case of the rotational degrees of freedom the mass moment of inertia J_ω rather than the mass is the measure of inertia. Can you give any examples?

Answer:
Mass moments of inertia for three elementary bodies:

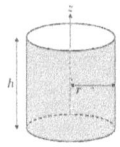 

$J_z = mr^2 / 2$ (solid cylinder of radius r, height h and mass m);

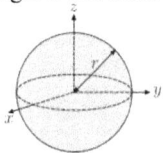

$J_z = 2mr^2 / 5$ (solid ball of radius r and mass m);

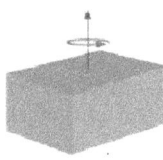

$J_h = m(w^2 + d^2)/12$ (solid cuboid of height h, width w, depth d and mass m)

Question:
The inertial force is proportional to the acceleration according to Newton's law, the elastic force is proportional to the displacement according to the Hooke's law, and why is the damping proportional to the velocity? What is the physical nature of the inelastic resistance forces?

Answer:
The nature of dissipative forces, which inevitably accompany any oscillation, is diverse and complex. If we suppose that the motion is resisted by the medium (liquid or gaseous, friction in the supports) or by the internal friction forces (this term is collective and conditional, since the internal processes might not be related to friction), then the value of the dissipative forces is in some way related to the value of the velocity, which has been proved by experiments.

In order to simplify the analysis, the viscosity properties which are linearly dependent on the velocity are attributed to the dissipative forces.

Fig. 5.7 shows the relationships between the forces of the so-called viscous resistance (Fig. 5.7,*a*) / dry friction (Fig. 5.7,*b* and 5.7,*c*) and the velocity.

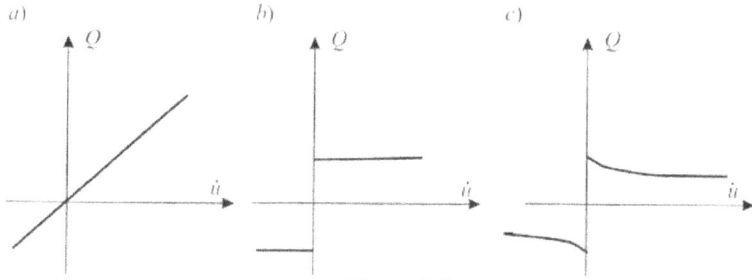

Figure 5.7

The dissipative force of *viscous friction* is proportional to velocity $Q = c\dot{u}$. Factor c = const.

The *dry friction* force depends on the sign of the velocity and is therefore described by a discontinuous function, which in the simplest case of the so-called Coulomb friction is piecewise constant and is described by the following mathematical expression

$$Q = c \cdot \text{sign}\,\dot{u}.$$

If we introduce this term into the oscillation equation, it will become nonlinear.

Whatever the nature of the dissipative forces, their direction at any time is opposite to that of the velocity.

Conversation 5.3. Resonance

Most engineers are familiar with the resonant oscillation mode, when the frequency of the external action coincides with the natural frequency and the amplitudes increase rapidly as a result. In the case of an idealized system with no energy loss the resonance causes the amplitudes to increase unlimitedly, but this increase can be very large in a real system as well.

The effect of friction on forced oscillations occurring far from resonant modes is usually small, and is often neglected in practical calculations. However, friction must be taken into account near the resonance, otherwise the errors in the amplitudes of forced oscillations become unacceptably large. Taking into account the viscous friction the equation of motion can be written as

$$m\ddot{u} + c\dot{u} + ku = P_0 \sin \theta t, \quad (5.17)$$

or

$$\ddot{u} + 2\omega\zeta\dot{u} + \omega^2 u = (P_0/m)\sin \theta t, \quad (5.18)$$

where ω is the natural frequency of the undamped system; $\zeta = C/C_{cr}$ is the damping ratio; $C_{cr} = 2\sqrt{km}$ is the critical damping coefficient, i.e. the value of the coefficient C, starting from which the deviated system returns to its equilibrium state without oscillations.

We will write the final solution of the equation (5.18) at once without considering the actual solution procedure which can be found in any book on structural dynamics:

$$u(t) = e^{-\omega\zeta t}(u_0 \cos \tilde{\omega}t + \frac{\dot{u}_0 + \omega\zeta u_0}{\omega}\sin \tilde{\omega}t) -$$

$$-e^{-\omega\zeta t}(B_1 \cos \tilde{\omega}t + \frac{\beta B_1 + \theta B_2}{\omega}\sin \tilde{\omega}t) + \quad (5.19)$$

$$+B_1 \cos \theta t + B_2 \sin \theta t.$$

where

$$B_1 = -\frac{P_0}{m} \cdot \frac{2\omega\zeta\theta}{(\omega^2 - \theta^2) + (2\omega\zeta\theta)^2}; \quad B_2 = \frac{P_0}{m} \cdot \frac{\omega^2 - \theta^2}{(\omega^2 - \theta^2) + (2\omega\zeta\theta)^2}.$$

Thus, the displacement caused by the harmonic excitation consists of three components:
- free damped oscillations with frequency $\tilde{\omega}$ which depend on the initial conditions;

- free damped oscillations with frequency $\tilde{\omega}$ which depend on the parameters of the exciting force rather than the initial conditions;
- forced oscillations with frequency θ.

Fig. 5.8,*a* shows a motion diagram for the case $\theta > \tilde{\omega}$, when high frequencies of free damped oscillations are superimposed on low frequencies of forced oscillations (relatively high-frequency natural oscillations are quickly damped if time is measured in periods of forced oscillations), and Fig. 5.8,*b* shows the opposite picture of "slow" damping of transient oscillations for the case $\theta < \tilde{\omega}$.

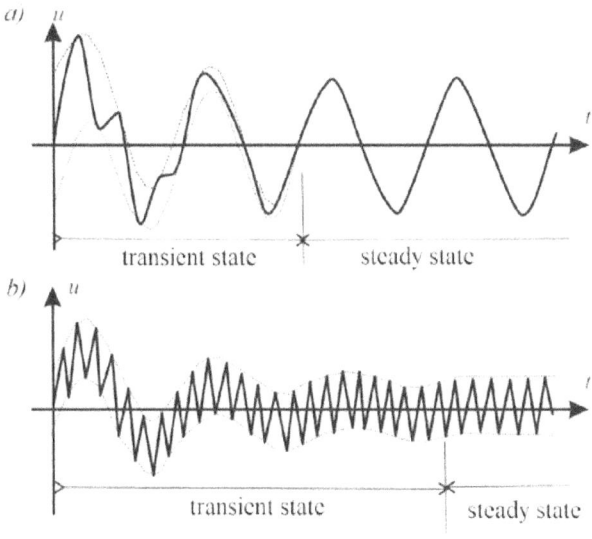

Figure 5.8

Once the transient process is completed and steady forced oscillations take place, the motion caused by the vibration load is harmonic and can be described by the following expression

$$u(t) = B_1 \cos\theta t + B_2 \sin\theta t, \qquad (5.20)$$

or (given that $B_1 < 0$)

$$q(t) = B\sin(\theta t - \psi), \qquad (5.21)$$

where $B = \sqrt{B_1^2 + B_2^2} = \dfrac{P_0}{m\sqrt{(\omega^2 - \theta^2)^2 + (2\omega\zeta\theta)^2}}$ is the amplitude of steady forced oscillations;

ψ is the phase difference between the mass motion and the exciting force.

The obtained formulas lead to the following conclusions:
- displacements of the system occur with the frequency of the exciting force, but lag in phase;

- when the excitation frequencies θ are small compared to the natural frequency ω, the lag is small;
- when the excitation frequency and the natural frequency are equal $\omega = \theta$, the phase is $\psi = \pi/2$, i.e. when the force is maximum, the displacement is zero.

The dynamic amplification factor μ, i.e. the ratio of the forced oscillation amplitude $|u(t)|_{max}$ to the displacement of the mass due to a statically applied force, is defined by the following formula:

$$\mu = \frac{|u(t)|_{max}}{u_{cr}} = \frac{\omega^2}{\sqrt{(\omega^2 - \theta^2)^2 + (2\omega\zeta\theta)^2}} = \frac{1}{\sqrt{(1-\xi^2)^2 + (2\omega\zeta\xi)^2}},$$

where $\xi = \theta/\omega$.

This amplitude has a maximum value when $\theta/\omega = \sqrt{1-2\zeta^2}$, and when $\mu = 1/\left[2\zeta\sqrt{1-\zeta^2}\right]$, the graph of its variation in the function of the ratio θ/ω is shown in the Figure 5.9.

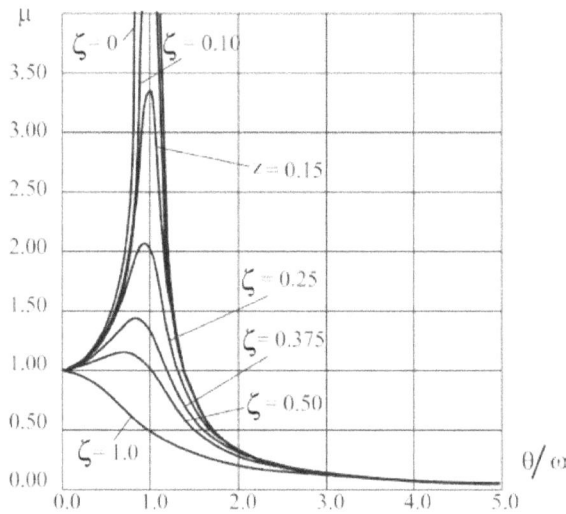

Figure 5.9

It should be noted that oscillation amplitudes decrease when natural frequencies increase compared to the excitation frequency, since the region $\theta/\omega > 1$ is characterized by lower values of the dynamic amplification factor.

Moreover, the dynamic amplification factor is little different from one at small values of $\xi = \theta/\omega$. If, for example, we neglect the dynamic effects with the values of order of 5%, we can easily calculate that when there is no damping $\mu<1,05$, when $\xi<0{,}218$ or $T_B/T_0>4{,}59$ which is the same (T_B is the period of the driving force, T_0 is the natural period).

It can be concluded from this example and a series of similar problems [7] that a time-varying driving force can be considered as static when its period is 5÷7 times greater than the natural period.

A special case of excitation is shown in Fig. 5.10, where oscillations are caused by an unbalanced mass m_e, which has an eccentricity e and rotates with an angular velocity θ. The exciting force in this case is determined as $P = m_e e \theta^2 \sin\theta t$, and the dimensionless amplitude has the maximum value $\mu_{max} = (1-2\zeta^2)/\left(2\zeta\sqrt{1-\zeta^2}\right)$.

$$\mu = \frac{u_{max} m}{em_e} = (\theta/\omega)^2\left[\left(1-\frac{\theta^2}{\omega^2}\right)^2 + \left(2\zeta\frac{\theta}{\omega}\right)^2\right]^{-1/2} \quad (5.22)$$

The graph of this function is given in Fig. 5.10. It shows that in this case the recommendation for preventing the resonance has an adverse effect.

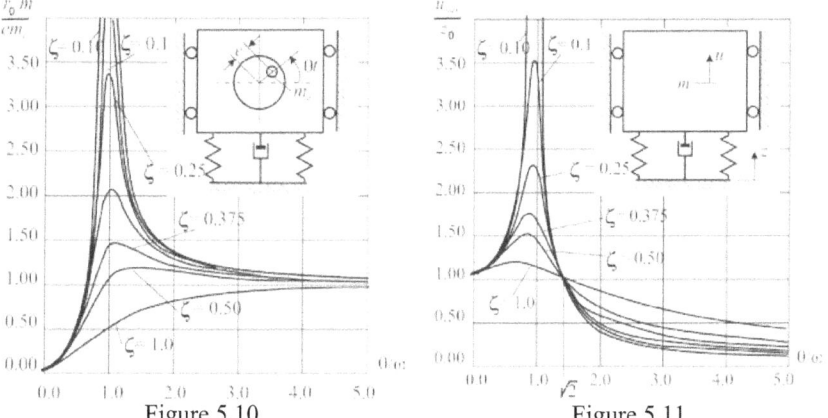

Figure 5.10   Figure 5.11

Finally, we can consider another case of harmonic excitation, when the equation $z = z_0\sin\theta t$ describes the ground motion. The dimensionless displacement amplitude is defined by the following expression

$$\frac{y_0}{z_0} = \sqrt{\frac{1+(2\zeta\theta/\omega)^2}{\left(1-\theta^2/\omega^2\right)^2 + (2\zeta\theta/\omega)^2}} \quad (5.23)$$

The graph of this function is shown in Fig. 5.11. It resembles the graph in Fig. 5.9, but here all the curves pass through the point with abscissa $\theta/\omega = 1{,}414$. In this case, it is also advisable to reduce the natural frequency. Almost all seismic isolation systems are created in this way. Their natural frequencies are reduced with the help of all sorts of compliant supports.

The design shown in Fig. 5.11 is used in vibration isolation systems and the ratio u_{max}/z_0 in some sense characterizes the quality of vibration isolation, which, as can be seen from the graph, is effective only at frequencies $\theta/\omega > 1,414$, while the presence of damping in it is generally undesirable.

Conversation 5.4. Equations of Motion of a Multiple Degree of Freedom System

Any real structure has a mass distributed over its entire volume. However, fairly accurate results of its analysis can be obtained, assuming that the mass of the structure is concentrated in some of its characteristic points. Therefore, for simplicity, we will consider a system that consists of weightless elastic elements carrying point masses (Fig. 5.12,*a*), i.e. a system with a finite number of degrees of freedom.

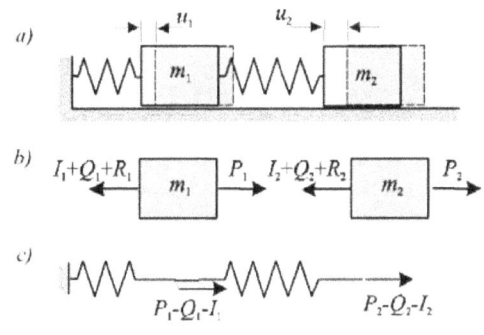

Figure 5.12

The equations of motion of this type of systems can be obtained by the direct or inverse method.

According to the *direct method*, concentrated masses are distinguished from the system, and each of them is considered as a free particle subjected to forces which are expressed in terms of the selected generalized coordinates (Fig. 5.12,*b*).

The *inverse method* is opposite to the direct one: once the concentrated masses are separated, the remaining "massless skeleton" of the system is considered, and the displacements caused by the external forces and forces of inertia are determined for the mass points (Fig. 5.12,*c*), i.e., a real force of inertia acts on the elastic skeleton of the structure rather than being applied to the mass[13].

---

[13] Y.G.Panovko notes [6]: "... the expression "inertial forces act on a beam during oscillation" contains ambiguity, since it is not clear what is implied by a "beam". If we are talking about a real beam, i.e. an elastic system that has a mass, then the above expression is essentially wrong; if its elastic skeleton is called a "beam", the expression becomes true, but then it should have been better formulated".

Let us use the *direct method*, taking into account that each (for example, i–th) mass is subjected to:
- the exciting force $P_i(t)$;
- the force of inertia $I_i(t)$;
- the elastic resistance force $R_i(t)$;
- the inelastic resistance force $Q_i(t)$.

According to d'Alembert principle, these forces are in dynamic equilibrium at all times:

$$I_i(t) + Q_i(t) + R_i(t) = P_i(t) \quad (i = 1,...,n). \tag{5.24}$$

The elastic resistance force can be expressed through the displacements using the components of the stiffness matrix $\boldsymbol{K}$

$$R_i(t) = \sum_{j=1}^{n} K_{ij} u_j(t) \quad (i = 1,...,n). \tag{5.25}$$

Further, we assume that the inelastic resistance force is proportional to the velocity (viscous friction condition) and, using the dissipation coefficient matrix $\boldsymbol{C}$ we obtain:

$$Q_i(t) = \sum_{j=1}^{n} C_{ij} \dot{u}_j(t) \quad (i = 1,...,n). \tag{5.26}$$

The forces of inertia are equal to the product of mass and acceleration; therefore, the equations of dynamic equilibrium can be written as follows:

$$m_i \ddot{u}_i(t) + \sum_{j=1}^{n} C_{ij} \dot{u}_j(t) + \sum_{j=1}^{n} K_{ij} u_j(t) = P_i(t) \quad (i = 1,...,n) \tag{5.27}$$

Inertial Properties

If the rotational inertia has to be taken into account for a certain mass, then it is convenient to relate its displacements to the center of mass C (Fig. 5.13). Forces of inertia I_i and I_j are applied at the point C. The moment of inertia I_k corresponds to the angular displacement u_k.

The simplest method of creating a design model of a real structure with concentrated masses is based on the fact that the total mass of each bar is concentrated at its ends, i.e. at the points where the displacements of the system are determined.

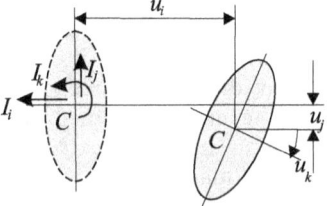

Figure 5.13

For example, a frame (Fig. 5.14,*a*) with distributed masses $\tilde{m}_1$, $\tilde{m}_2$, $\tilde{m}_3$ on bars is divided into three segments, and the mass of each of them is equally distributed between the ends of the segment (Fig.5.14,*b*) as point masses m_1, m_2, m_3, so that

$$m_1 = \tilde{m}_1 a/2,$$
$$m_2 = \tilde{m}_2 b/2,$$
$$m_3 = \tilde{m}_3 c/2.$$

As a result it is replaced by a weightless frame (Fig. 5.14,*c*) with two point masses, each one equal to the sum of point masses that were located at the ends of the bars adjacent to the node.

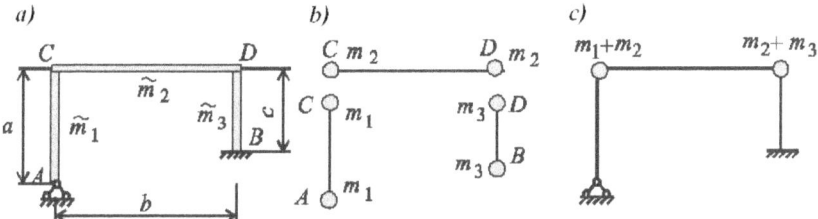

Figure 5.14

When another approach is used, it is taken into account that during the oscillations the forces of inertia in the bars are proportional to the accelerations of the points, i.e. they are defined by the shape functions according to the finite element method, since the spatial distribution of accelerations coincides with the spatial distribution of displacements. These forces define the end reactions, and conditional masses and mass moments of inertia are assigned to the nodal points creating nodal inertial forces and moments that cause the same reactions as the inertial forces of real distributed masses.

For example, the elements of the mass matrix of the bar element considered in the conversation 2.1 are calculated by the following formulas:

$$m_{ij} = \int_0^L \psi_i(x) \cdot \tilde{m} \cdot \psi_j(x) \cdot dx,$$

where $\psi(x)$ are functions that interpolate the displacements of points within a finite element. If we express these functions as Hermite polynomials, we will obtain the mass matrix:

$$\left[\!\left[m_{ij}\right]\!\right] = \frac{\tilde{m}L}{420} \begin{bmatrix} 156 & 22L & 54 & 13L \\ 22L & 4L^2 & 13L & -3L^2 \\ 54 & 13L & 156 & -22L \\ -13L & -3L^2 & -22L & 4L^2 \end{bmatrix}.$$

This mass matrix is called consistent. Unlike the point mass method, it does not have a diagonal form, which causes certain difficulties in calculations. Therefore, the point mass method is preferred or other approximate methods for the diagonalization of the mass matrix are used.

One of such methods is to consider the distributed mass as the load on the element (i.e., it is assumed that the inertial forces are constant along the length), and it is reduced to the nodal loads by the formula

$$m_i = \int_0^L \tilde{m} \cdot \psi_i(x) \cdot dx .$$

Then the mass matrix of a simple bar will be

$$\left[\left[m_{ij}\right]\right] = \frac{\tilde{m}L}{12} \begin{bmatrix} 6 & 0 & 0 & 0 \\ 0 & L & 0 & 0 \\ 0 & 0 & 6 & 0 \\ 0 & 0 & 0 & L \end{bmatrix},$$

i.e. half the mass of the bar transferred to the end node acquires also the moment of inertia equal to $\tilde{m}L^2 / 12$.

Natural Oscillations

If the system is given initial displacements (for example, by applying a force P_0), the displacement configuration will change with the development of free oscillations, because the forces of inertia $I(t)$ which were not involved in the initial deformation of the system will come into play (Fig. 5.15).

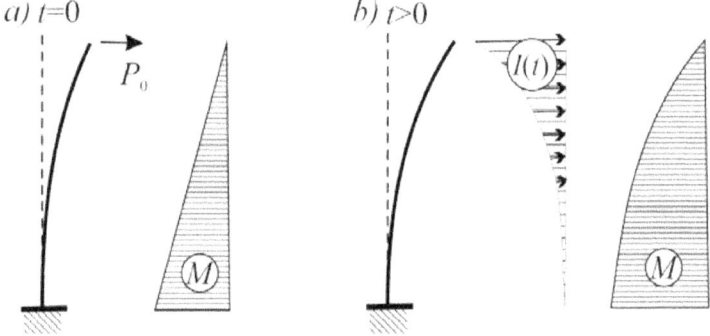

Figure 5.15

But there are such excitation modes, (natural modes), when the configuration does not change.

In order to demonstrate the validity of this statement, let us consider the equation (5.27), assuming that there are no external exciting forces and resistance forces. Then we will have

$$m_i \ddot{u}_i(t) + \sum_{j=1}^n K_{ij} u_j(t) = 0 \quad (i = 1,...,n). \tag{5.28}$$

Suppose that free oscillations are harmonic with an unknown frequency ω:

$$u_i(t) = X_i \sin \omega t. \qquad (5.29)$$

Substituting (5.20) into (5.28) leads to a system of equations

$$-m_i X_i \omega^2 \sin \omega t + \sum_{j=1}^{n} K_{ij} X_j \sin \omega t = 0 \quad (i = 1, \ldots, n), \qquad (5.30)$$

Since these equations must always be satisfied, they can be reduced by $\sin \omega t$ and we can obtain the equations for the amplitudes X_i:

$$\left(\sum_{j=1}^{n} K_{ij} - m_i \omega^2 \right) X_i = 0 \quad (i = 1, \ldots, n). \qquad (5.31)$$

Equations (5.31) have a trivial solution $X_i = 0$ $(i-1,\ldots,n)$, which corresponds to a fixed system, but they can also have a nonzero solution if the determinant of this system of equations is zero. This can happen under certain frequency values (*natural frequency*), for which the following equality is satisfied

$$\det \begin{bmatrix} K_{11} - \omega_0^2 m_1 & K_{12} & \cdots & K_{1n} \\ K_{21} & K_{22} - \omega_0^2 m_2 & \cdots & K_{2n} \\ \cdots & \cdots & \cdots & \cdots \\ K_{n1} & K_{n2} & \cdots & K_{nn} - \omega_0^2 m_n \end{bmatrix} = 0. \qquad (5.32)$$

The last expression is called the characteristic equation of the problem, and when the determinant is expanded, it turns into an *n*-th degree equation with respect to ω_0^2. As we know from algebra, a polynomial equation of the *n*-th degree has *n* roots

$$\omega_{0,k}^2 \ (i = 1, \ldots, n).$$

The numbered set of positive values $\omega_{0,k}$ arranged in ascending order forms the so-called *spectrum of natural frequencies*

$$\omega_{0,1} \leq \omega_{0,2} \leq \cdots \leq \omega_{0,n}.$$

Each eigenvalue and each natural frequency has a corresponding set of amplitudes of generalized coordinates satisfying the equation (5.32).

If we substitute one of the natural frequency values (for example, ω_s) into the equations (5.31), we can try to solve the resulting system with respect to the values $X_i^{(s)}$ $(i = 1, \ldots, n)$ which make up the eigenvector (*natural mode*) corresponding to this frequency. Since the substitution of ω_s leads to equations with a degenerate matrix of coefficients, it is not possible to find all the values $X_i^{(s)}$ $(i = 1, \ldots, n)$. We can assign a random value to one of the components of the eigenvector, then the remaining (*n*-1) components of the eigenvector can be found from the system of equations truncated in this way.

> Since we have assigned a random value to one of the components of the eigenvector, we have found not the actual values $X_i^{(s)}$ $(i = 1, \ldots, n)$, but only their ratio.

Let us consider an example of a simple system with two degrees of freedom (Fig. 5.16).

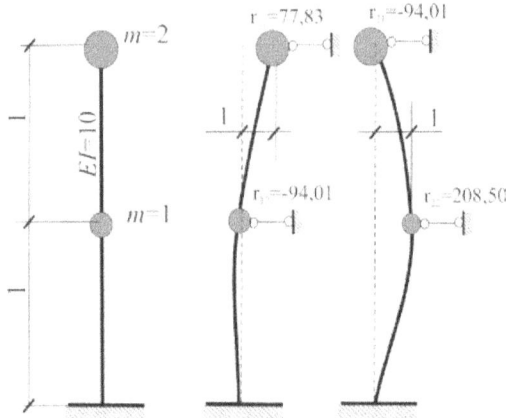

Figure 5.16

The equations of type (5.31) can be written for this system as follows

$$\left.\begin{array}{l}\left(77{,}83-2\omega^2\right)X_1 - 94{,}01 X_2 = 0 \\ -94{,}01 X_1 + \left(208{,}50 - \omega^2\right)X_2 = 0\end{array}\right\}$$

Equating the determinant of the system of equations to zero, we obtain a biquadratic equation

$$\left(77{,}83 X_1 - 2\omega^2\right)\left(208{,}50 - \omega^2\right) - 94{,}01^2 = 0,$$

or

$$2\omega^4 - 494{,}83\omega^2 + 7389{,}675 = 0,$$

the solution of which gives two values of the natural frequency

$$\omega_{0,1} = 3{,}995; \quad \omega_{0,2} = 15{,}213.$$

Let us determine the corresponding natural modes (Fig. 5.17) from the first equation, assuming $X_1=1$.

$$X_2^{(1)} = 1; \quad X_1^{(1)} = (208{,}5 - 15{,}964)/94{,}01 = 2{,}048;$$
$$X_2^{(2)} = 1; \quad X_1^{(2)} = (208{,}5 - 231{,}451)/94{,}01 = -0{,}244.$$

CONVERSATIONS ABOUT THE STRUCTURAL MECHANICS 227

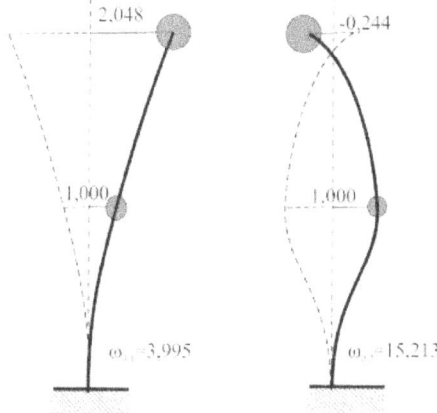

Figure 5.17

The process of obtaining natural modes is called *modal analysis*.

Question:
If the initial deviation follows the natural mode, then free oscillations retain this mode, and what are the free oscillations like in the case of an arbitrary mode of the initial deviation of the system?

Answer:
If a system with n degrees of freedom is arbitrarily deviated from the equilibrium position and then released, then the free oscillations excited in this way can be represented as a sum of n terms, each one being a natural mode varying with the respective natural frequency and damping rate.

The following situation is often observed: the deviation of the system has the given mode at the initial time, but then the free oscillations are performed according to a natural mode with the respective frequency. This is due to the fact that natural oscillations according to other modes (components of the total motion) are quickly damped.

Conversation 5.5. Properties of Natural Modes

Natural modes are the characteristics of a dynamic system (their passport), since they are not related to any external actions. They play a large role in the dynamic analysis, therefore the main properties of natural modes should be considered in more detail.

As mentioned above, a system with n degrees of freedom has exactly n natural frequencies with corresponding natural modes.

> *Only linear systems have natural modes, nonlinear systems do not have any natural modes.*

It follows from this statement among other things that natural modes characterize small elastic oscillations, i.e. the modal analysis of a nonlinear elastic system can relate only to its linearized analog (*small oscillations around the shifted equilibrium state*).

If a system has two or more close natural frequencies, it becomes difficult to determine the corresponding natural modes correctly. The closer the natural frequencies, the more difficult it is to distinguish the natural modes. A pendulum suspended on a spherical hinge can perform free oscillations in one plane (for example, X0Z), as well as in the Y0Z plane perpendicular to it, and the oscillation frequency will be the same. Thus, the modes of the oscillations in both of these planes can be considered as natural. It is also clear that the pendulum can oscillate in any other plane, and this motion can be represented as a sum of oscillations in the X0Z and Y0Z planes.

> *In the considered case of a multiple eigenvalue, any linear combination of two natural modes is a natural mode as well.*

In the general case this statement can be proved by the following reasoning: if the natural modes $X_i^{(k)}$ and $X_i^{(s)}$ $(i=1,...,n)$ correspond to one value of the natural frequency ω_0, let us consider the equations satisfied by these modes

$$\left(\sum_{j=1}^{n} K_{ij} - m_i \omega_0^2 \right) X_i^{(s)} = 0;$$

$$\left(\sum_{j=1}^{n} K_{ij} - m_i \omega_0^2 \right) X_i^{(k)} = 0 \quad (i=1,...,n).$$

Let us multiply the first system of equations by a, the second one — by b, add them and we will obtain the following system of equations

CONVERSATIONS ABOUT THE STRUCTURAL MECHANICS 229

$$\left(\sum_{j=1}^{n} K_{ij} - m_i \omega_0^2\right)\left(aX_i^{(k)} + bX_i^{(s)}\right) = 0 \quad (i = 1,...,n),$$

which is satisfied by a linear combination of modes at random a and b

$$X_i = aX_i^{(k)} + bX_i^{(s)} \quad (i = 1,...,n).$$

It would seem that the possibility of creating any number of linear combinations of natural modes which takes place in the case of multiple frequencies contradicts the statement that the system has exactly n natural modes (according to the number of natural frequencies), but the system does have exactly n *independent* natural modes.

> Each natural mode is determined only up to a factor, its frequency does not depend on the amplitude.

This statement can be proved by the fact that if $X_i^{(s)}$ $(i=1,...,n)$ is the solution of the system of equations (5.31), then $aX_i^{(s)}$ $(i=1,...,n)$ satisfies these equations as well.

It can be noted here that if a piano string is tuned to a particular note (natural mode), this tune is not affected by the key striking force, although the volume changes.

> *Natural modes are orthogonal.*

There is a relationship between the amplitudes $X_j^{(s)}$ and $X_j^{(k)}$ defining two natural modes (s and k) that expresses an important property of *orthogonality* of natural modes. Let us establish this relationship using the general equations (5.31) for amplitudes. When $\omega^2 = \omega_{0,s}^2$, any i-th line of the system written for the s-th frequency, can be represented as

$$\sum_{j=1}^{n} K_{ij} X_j^{(s)} = m_i \omega_{0,s}^2 X_i^{(s)} \quad (i = 1,...,n). \quad (5.33)$$

Let us multiply each of the equalities (5.33) by the corresponding components of the natural mode $X_i^{(k)}$, sum all the obtained expressions, and we will get the following equality:

$$\sum_{i=1}^{n}\sum_{j=1}^{n} K_{ij} X_j^{(s)} X_i^{(k)} = m_i \omega_{0,s}^2 \sum_{i=1}^{n} X_i^{(s)} X_i^{(k)}. \quad (5.34)$$

However, according to (5.31)

$$\sum_{j=1}^{n} K_{ij} X_j^{(k)} = m_i \omega_{0,k}^2 X_i^{(k)}, \quad (5.33)$$

Substituting this expression into (5.34), we obtain

$$m_i \omega_{0,k}^2 \sum_{i=1}^{n} X_i^{(s)} X_i^{(k)} = m_i \omega_{0,s}^2 \sum_{i=1}^{n} X_i^{(s)} X_i^{(k)}. \quad (5.35)$$

Since $\omega_{0,s}^2 \neq \omega_{0,k}^2$, then the equality (5.35) can be satisfied only in the case when the first orthogonality condition is satisfied

$$\sum_{j}^{n} X_j^{(k)} m_j X_j^{(s)} = 0 .\qquad(5.36)$$

The second orthogonality condition is obtained in exactly the same way

$$\sum_{i=1}^{n}\sum_{j=1}^{n} X_i^{(k)} K_{ii} X_j^{(s)} = 0 .\qquad(5.37)$$

Conditions (5.36) and (5.37) show that natural modes are orthogonal with respect to both masses and rigidity. They are called the *kinetic energy orthogonality* conditions and the *potential energy orthogonality* conditions, respectively.

> *Natural modes and the respective natural frequencies are completely determined by the stiffness and inertial properties of the system. You should keep in mind that the orthogonality of the natural modes is not necessarily related to the orthogonality of a custom Cartesian coordinate system in which the design model is described.*

A question "What is the value of the longitudinal natural frequency of the building?" makes no sense if the natural mode is not longitudinal. These questions are usually echoes of some instructions related to buildings of a certain type (for example, single-story industrial buildings with a system of parallel load-bearing frames) not critically transferred to an inappropriate situation.

Question:
Some guides recommend to avoid designs where the torsional natural mode is among the first ones.
What is the reason? Is there anything wrong with the structures having a torsional natural mode?

Answer:
There is nothing wrong with this design. These recommendations most likely come from the tradition of using 2D design models, when a 3D bearing frame was represented by a set of 2D frames or trusses.

However, an example of a simple structure, the model of which is shown in Fig. 5.18, gives an idea that quite a decent structure the first (multiple) natural frequency of which is torsional, has first three equal natural frequencies with the following value $\omega_0 = \sqrt{2c/(\mu a)}$, where c is the stiffness of an elastic support (column), μ is the mass of a unit floor slab area. This structure can hardly be considered as durable.

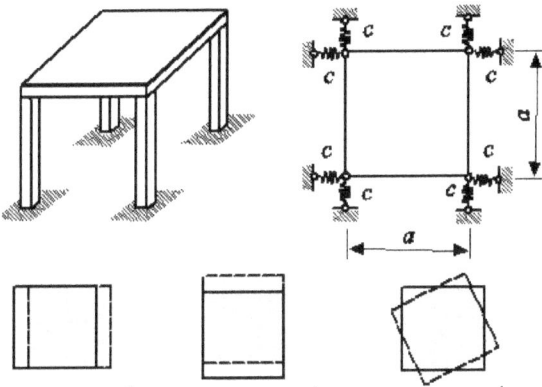

Figure 5.18

There is one more reason for the origin of this recommendation, which is related to the seismic analysis. The thing is that translational ground oscillations are the most studied ones, and they are usually the ones considered in the analysis. However, an earthquake can cause rotational ground excitations as well, which have a considerable effect on the structures whose torsional natural modes are among the first ones. And if the standard calculation method does not allow to consider this situation adequately, let us avoid it then by declaring that it is not recommended to use the respective structures The tail is truly wagging the dog here.

Question:
How to select a reasonable scale factor for a natural mode? Are there any recommendations?

Answer:
The simplest method is to take the maximum natural mode component as one and to give all other components as fractions of one. This process is one of the methods of *normalizing* the natural modes.

The natural modes shown in Fig. 5.17 were normalized in this way.
Some design software perform the normalization of natural modes using the concept of a generalized mass

$$M^{(s)} = \sum_{i=1}^{n} X_i^{(s)} m_i X_i^{(s)} \quad (s = 1,...,n),$$

and the following values $Z_i^{(s)} = Z_i^{(s)}/\sqrt{M^{(s)}}$ (*orthonormal* modes), which leads to the relationships

$$\sum_{i=1}^{n} Z_i^{(s)} m_i Z_j = \begin{cases} 1, \textit{if } i = j; \\ 0, \textit{if } i \neq j. \end{cases}$$

In the above example

$$M^{(1)} = 2,0 \cdot 2,048^2 + 1,0 \cdot 1,0^2 = 9,389,$$

$$M^{(1)} = 2,0 \cdot 0,244^2 + 1,0 \cdot 1,0^2 = 1,119.$$

Orthonormal natural modes can be given as vectors

$$\mathbf{Z}^{(1)} = \frac{1}{\sqrt{9,389}} \begin{bmatrix} 2,048 \\ 1,000 \end{bmatrix} = \begin{bmatrix} 0,668 \\ 0,326 \end{bmatrix}, \quad \mathbf{Z}^{(2)} = \frac{1}{\sqrt{1,118}} \begin{bmatrix} -0,244 \\ 1,000 \end{bmatrix} = \begin{bmatrix} -0,231 \\ 0,945 \end{bmatrix}.$$

Modes normalized in this way with respect to the stiffness matrix satisfy the conditions

$$\sum_{i=1}^{n}\sum_{j=1}^{n} X_i^{(s)} K_{ij} X_j^{(s)} = \begin{cases} \omega_{0,s}^2, \textit{if } i = j; \\ 0, \textit{if } i \neq j. \end{cases}$$

Conversation 5.6. Forced Oscillations of a System with a Finite Number of Degrees of Freedom

Dynamic actions are very diverse in their nature. These can be force actions, when an external load is applied to a structure, or kinematic, in the case of a forced deformation of individual elements of the system. However, the intensity and/or the application point of the action vary with time in both cases.

Forced oscillations of a linear discrete system are described by a system of ordinary differential equations (5.27). We will begin the analysis of these equations with an important special case, when the system of equations has a sinusoidal right-hand side, and when there is no viscous resistance, the equations can be written as

$$m_i \ddot{u}_i(t) + \sum_{j=1}^{n} K_{ij} u_j(t) = P_i \sin \theta t \quad (i=1,...,n), \qquad (5.38)$$

where P_i is the amplitude value of the load acting in the direction of the displacement u_i; θ is the frequency of the excitation.

The particular solution of the inhomogeneous differential equation:

$$u_i = X_i \sin \theta t \quad (i=1,...,n), \qquad (5.39)$$

where X_i is the amplitude value of the displacement $u_i(t)$.

Then $\ddot{u}_i = -\theta^2 X_i \sin \theta t$, and after substituting it into the equations (5.38), we obtain

$$-\theta^2 m_i X_i \sin \theta t + \sum_{j=1}^{n} K_{ij} X_j \sin \theta t = P_i \sin \theta t \quad (i=1,...,n). \qquad (5.40)$$

Since t is a random time, there is an equivalent system of inhomogeneous algebraic equations

$$\sum_{j=1}^{n} \left(K_{ij} - \theta^2 m_i\right) X_j = P_i \quad (i=1,...,n). \qquad (5.41)$$

If the matrix $\mathbf{K}_\theta = \left[\!\left[K_{ij} - \theta^2 m_i \right]\!\right]$ has the inverse $K_\theta^{-1} = \left[\!\left[d_{ij} \right]\!\right]$, then

$$X_i = \sum_{j=1}^{n} d_{ij} P_j \quad (i=1,...,n). \qquad (5.42)$$

Thus, the amplitude values of displacements depend on the load, mass, and frequency of the exciting force (since they determine the values of the coefficients

d_{ij}), but do not depend on time. The particular solution describes steady forced oscillations.

You should keep in mind that the fact that the inertial forces $\theta^2 m_i$ are involved in the formation of the coefficients of equations (5.41) leads to some unusual effects. Thus, there are cases when the maximum oscillation amplitude of a structure subjected to a harmonic concentrated force $P \cdot \sin(\omega t)$, is observed not in the force application point, but in a completely different place. Dynamic vibration absorbers (anti-vibrators) are based on this very principle, and an example of this design is shown in Fig. 5.19,a.

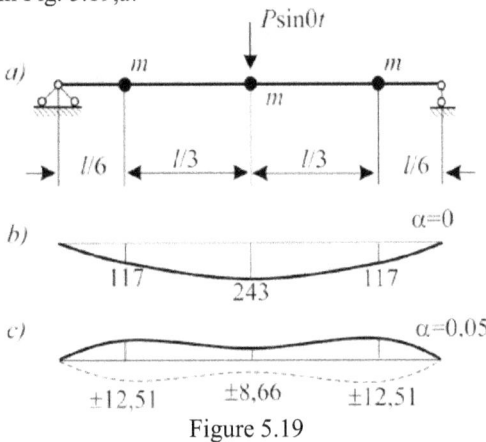

Figure 5.19

We will write the solution of this problem at once, leaving its derivation to you. The oscillation amplitudes of the masses near the supports are

$$X_1 = X_3 = \frac{P}{\beta} \cdot \frac{117}{1 - 369 m\theta^2/\beta + 3240 \left(m\theta^2/\beta\right)^2},$$

and that of the mass in the center of the beam is

$$X_2 = \frac{P}{\beta} \cdot \frac{243 - 3240 m\theta^2/\beta}{1 - 369 + 3240 \left(m\theta^2/\beta\right)^2}.$$

where $\beta = 9 \cdot 1296 EJ/l^3$.

Fig. 5.19,b shows a static deflection mode calculated for the value $\alpha = m\theta^2/\beta = 0$, assuming that $P/\beta = 1$. And if we assume that $\alpha \neq 0$, we will obtain a buckling mode shown in Fig. 5.19,c, where the oscillation amplitudes of the end masses exceed the amplitude in the center of the beam where the load is applied.

Why does it all seem like an unbelievable trick to a "statically trained" reader then? The reason is apparently that looking at the design model we see only the elastic system and the force applied to it, and the forces of inertia are invisible to us.

> *Independence and invariability in time of the configuration enable to use the natural modes as a measure of oscillations of a linear system, just as the independence and stability of the weight of a set of weights enable to weigh any body.*

In particular, one of the main methods for solving differential equations of motion is the decomposition of this motion into natural modes. The property of orthogonality of the natural modes plays an important role here.

As in the free oscillation problem, we will start with the equations which do not contain terms describing dissipative forces:

$$m_i \ddot{u}_i(t) + \sum_{j=1}^{n} K_{ij} u_j(t) = P_i(t) \quad (i=1,...,n). \quad (5.43)$$

Assuming that the natural modes of a dynamic system $X_i^{(s)}$ $(i,s=1,...,n)$ are predefined, we will seek a solution in the form of a sum

$$u_i(t) = \sum_{s=1}^{n} X_i^{(s)} \Psi_s(t) \quad (i=1,...,n), \quad (5.44)$$

where $\Psi_s(t)$ $(s=1,...,n)$ are certain time functions.

It should be noted that the solution can be represented as a superposition of natural modes only for the linear problems.

Then the equation of motion becomes

$$m_i \sum_{s=1}^{n} X_i^{(s)} \ddot{\Psi}_s(t) + \sum_{j=1}^{n} K_{ij} \sum_{s=1}^{n} X_j^{(s)} \Psi_s(t) = P_i(t) \quad (i=1,...,n). \quad (5.45)$$

Multiply each equation by $X_i^{(k)}$ and sum them, then after changing the order of summation we get

$$\sum_{s=1}^{n} \left(\sum_{i=1}^{n} X_i^{(k)} m_i X_i^{(s)} \right) \ddot{\Psi}_s(t) +$$
$$+ \sum_{s=1}^{n} \left(\sum_{i=1}^{n} \sum_{j=1}^{n} K_{ij} X_i^{(k)} X_j^{(s)} \right) \Psi_s(t) = \sum_{i=1}^{n} X_i^{(k)} P_i(t). \quad (5.46)$$

Due to the property of orthogonality of the natural modes only the terms with $k=s$ will remain in the left-hand side of the equality, all the rest are zero. Therefore, the equation becomes

$$\sum_{k=1}^{n} \left(\sum_{i=1}^{n} X_i^{(k)} m_i X_i^{(k)} \right) \ddot{\Psi}_k(t) +$$
$$+ \sum_{k=1}^{n} \left(\sum_{i=1}^{n} \sum_{j=1}^{n} K_{ij} X_i^{(k)} X_j^{(k)} \right) \Psi_k(t) = \sum_{i=1}^{n} X_i^{(k)} P_i(t),$$

and taking into account that

$$\sum_{i=1}^{n} K_{ij} X_j^{(k)} = \theta^2 m_i X_i^{(k)},$$

After performing some elementary transformations, we obtain the following system

$$\left[\ddot{\Psi}_k(t) + \theta^2 \Psi_k(t)\right]\left\{\sum_{i=1}^{n} X_i^{(k)} m_i X_i^{(k)}\right\} = \left\{\sum_{i=1}^{n} X_i^{(k)} P_i(t)\right\}. \quad (5.47)$$

The expressions in braces represent numbers. The one in the left-hand side is called the reduced mass $M_k = \left\{\sum_{i=1}^{n} X_i^{(k)} m_i X_i^{(k)}\right\}$, and the one in the right-hand side is called the reduced generalized force $Q_k = \left\{\sum_{i=1}^{n} X_i^{(k)} P_i(t)\right\}$ during the oscillations according to the *k*-th natural mode.

After introducing these designations, the equation turns into the equation of forced oscillations of a single degree of freedom system:

$$M_k \ddot{\Psi}_k(t) + \theta^2 M_k \Psi_k(t) = Q_k(t). \quad (5.48)$$

Since the index k takes values from 1 to n, we have n equations of type (5.48). Thus, by selecting natural modes as the generalized coordinates, we obtain n separate differential equations, each of which defines one unknown function $\Psi(t)$ instead of a system of n differential equations for n unknown functions. The solution of the system of equations is the sum of the solutions of each of the equations, as follows from (5.44).

Since there is no reliable initial information on the distribution of forces of inelastic resistance to motion, it is usually sufficient to consider damping of a transformed system introducing a term proportional to velocity into each of the obtained separate equations, and the following equations are used instead of (5.48)

$$M_k \ddot{\Psi}_k(t) + C_k \dot{\Psi}_k(t) + \theta^2 M_k \Psi_k(t) = Q_k(t). \quad (5.48)$$

The above method used when solving a problem of forced oscillations of a system without dissipation, is called the *principal (or normal) coordinate method*.

Most of the dynamic structural analysis methods recommended by the codes operate with the decomposition (5.44) into natural modes. The calculation is performed using a split system of equations, each of which determines a displacement for a certain natural mode

$$u_i^{(s)}(t) = X_i^{(s)} \Psi_s(t) \quad (i = 1,...,n). \quad (5.49)$$

The responses of the system (for example, moments or stresses) are also determined by the formulas of the type (5.49) for each natural mode separately, with the only difference that the values $X_i^{(s)}$ are replaced by the values $M^{(s)}$ or $\sigma^{(s)}$ related to the respective natural mode (the generalized symbol $A^{(s)}$ will be used hereinafter instead of $X^{(s)}$, $M^{(s)}$, $\sigma^{(s)}$ etc.).

These responses are time functions, and their summation must be performed for the same moments of motion. But this implies solving an unsteady-state dynamic problem and taking into account all the transient processes in the system, which requires much more detailed information than that available to us. Only the so-called modal response $A_{\max}^{(s)} = \max_t \left| A^{(s)} \Psi_s(t) \right|$, which is the maximum value of the response of the system for the *i*-th mode, can usually be determined for each natural mode. There is a problem of summation of modal responses, which in the general case are not achieved simultaneously, and it is rather difficult to determine the extreme value

$$A_{\max} = \max_t \left| \sum_{s=1}^{n} A^{(s)} \Psi_s(t) \right| \qquad (5.50)$$

and we can only obtain more or less correct estimates of this value.

There are several methods of summing modal responses. The upper bound estimate, which does not take into account the fact that modal responses reach their extreme values at different time, is the easiest one to obtain

$$A_U = \sum_{s=1}^{n} \left| A_{i\max}^{(s)} \right|. \qquad (5.51)$$

The difference between A_U and $A_{\max}$ can be quite large, therefore other estimates have been proposed. The inertial force estimation

$$I_R = \sqrt{\sum_{s=1}^{n} \left(I_{\max}^{(s)} \right)^2}. \qquad (5.52)$$

which is usually called "the most probable response value", is very popular in the seismic resistance theory.

This approach is based on the hypothesis that the time to reach an extremum is a uniformly distributed random variable in all modal responses, which is consistent with many observations, although it is not a well-established fact.

The summed inertial forces are considered normally distributed and centered in the case of a uniform time sampling. Then the summation rule for dispersions of normally distributed variables is implemented, which leads to the formula (5.52). Statistical independence of the summed values plays the main role here – the "Square Root of the Sum of the Squares (SRSS)" rule for summing the dispersions is valid only in this case. The cases of natural frequencies which are close, or not close but high (compared to the carrier frequencies) are examples of the fact that statistical independence is sometimes violated. Therefore, the SRSS rule is incorrect in these cases, and the error usually leads to non-conservative results.

It should be noted that the use of formula (5.52) leads to the loss of signs of the modal components of the seismic response, which can cause confusion in some cases. For example, sections under compression and bending disappear, all of them turn out to be under tension and bending.

A rather typical example of this situation is the case of multiple frequencies, when the natural modes corresponding to this frequency are determined up to a certain random value. Thus, for example, a vertical cantilever bar with equal principal cross-sectional stiffness values has multiple natural modes, which are determined up to a random rotation about the Z axis, as shown in the plan in Fig. 5.20, where in the case a) natural modes are directed along the coordinate axes, and in the case b) they are rotated by 45°. If the seismic impulse acts along the X axis, then in the case a) there will be no response for the second mode, and all the displacements will lie in the (X,Z) plane.

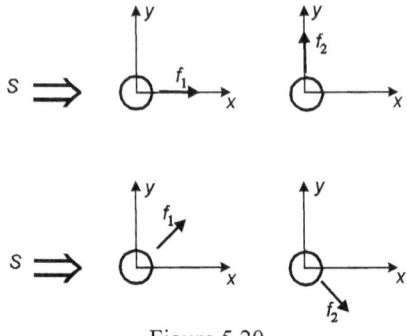

Figure 5.20

Both natural modes will be excited in the case b), but the fact that components along the Y axis have opposite signs and cancel each other will be lost when the "Square Root of the Sum of the Squares" rule is used. As a result, it will turn out that the displacements are excited not only in the direction of the seismic shock, but in the perpendicular direction as well. As you can see, the conclusion depends on the random value when selecting a pair of natural modes corresponding to a multiple frequency.

Question:
A technique was shown above where damping was taken into account in the normal coordinate method after the decomposition into natural modes. How versatile is this technique?

Answer:
The modal method of dynamic analysis, as a method of decomposition into natural modes, is the most widely used in problems of dynamics of linear systems. The decomposition into natural modes of an undamped system is usually used.

However, unlike mass and stiffness matrices, the damping matrix is not diagonalized in generalized modal coordinates. It is often "diagonalized" by simply removing non-diagonal terms, especially since it happens automatically when Rayleigh damping is used (*proportional damping*), i.e. the damping matrix C from the equation (5.61) is formed as a weighted sum of the stiffness matrix and the mass matrix

$$C_{ij} = \alpha m_{ij} + \beta K_{ij},$$

where α and β are arbitrary proportionality factors [4, p. 163].

But even if the Rayleigh technique is applied to systems where different parts have different damping, the non-diagonal terms do not vanish. It is especially common for the structure-soil interaction models. For a structure the relative level of damping, i.e. the conversion of mechanical energy into heat, comprises 3-7% of the critical damping. The dominant damping mechanism for subsoil is related to wave energy dissipation, and it can reach 30-70%. In this case, the use of the modal method turns out to be questionable, and it can lead to non-conservative solutions.

Moreover, the use of natural modes, which, as mentioned above, are considered as constant, implicitly assumes that any disturbance will immediately spread over the entire structure, i.e. the speed of wave propagation is assumed to be infinite. In reality, this speed is finite and the kinematic excitation of oscillations (for example, from the seismic motion) reaches distant points of the structure after some time. If this time is negligible compared to the primary natural period, then the hypothesis about the instantaneous propagation of disturbances is acceptable. However, the wave propagation time can turn out to be rather significant for high-rise structures, and in this case it is necessary to refine the modal analysis. Neglecting wave effects can cause an error of about 30% in buildings with a height of 100 meters and more [5].

Question:
How to determine the dynamic effect of equipment? Where can I find the relevant initial data?

Answer:
This information should actually be given in the documentation for the installed equipment. If there is no such documentation, some data can be found in the literature (see, for example, [2]), and some things can be calculated.

A load from the machinery with unbalanced rotating masses can serve as an example. Suppose, for example, that a machine with a total mass M, which is applied to the shaft axis, is mounted on a structure (Figure 5.21). An unbalanced mass m rotates at a distance r from the axis of rotation on a shaft with an angular velocity ω.

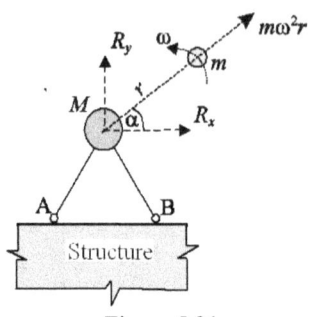

Figure 5.21

The resulting centrifugal force $m\omega^2 r$ acts at an angle $\alpha = \omega t$ at a certain time t. Thus, the forces $R_x = m\omega^2 r \cos(\omega t)$ and $R_y = m\omega^2 r \sin(\omega t)$ act on the shaft (the fact that both these forces should be applied is often overlooked).

When transferring these forces to the structure, it should be taken into account that the machine is attached to the structure at the points A and B, located at some distance from the axis of rotation.

Question:
In this lecture you said that using the formula (5.52) to sum modal responses leads to a loss of signs. Can it cause any other troubles?

Answer:
When (5.52) is used, not only a re the signs of individual components of the internal structural response lost, but the correspondence between displacements, internal forces, moments, shear forces, etc. is violated as well. In particular, the Zhuravsky theorem is not satisfied. This is clearly illustrated in Fig. 5.22.

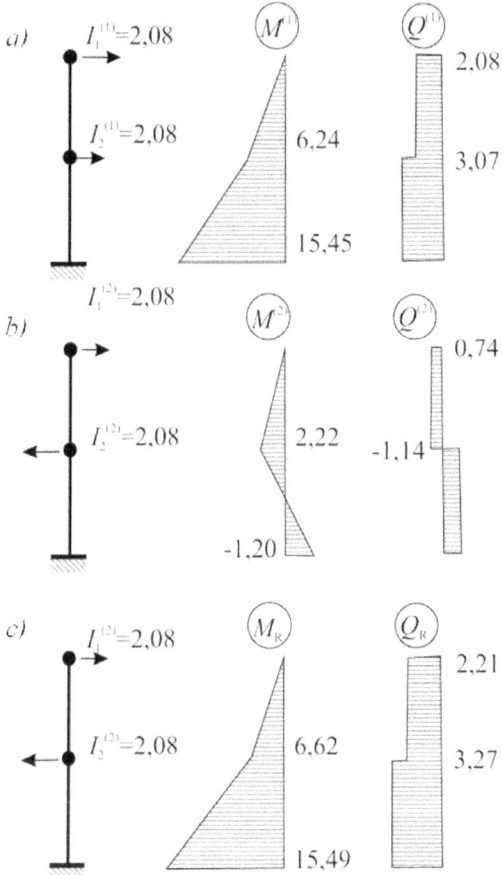

Figure 5.22

Moreover, if we check the equilibrium of the nodes, it turns out that it is satisfied in each natural mode, but there is no equilibrium in the resultant mode.

Question:
What if the number of dynamic degrees of freedom is not equal to the number of static degrees of freedom? Are there any special difficulties?

Answer:
In the dynamic analysis n, which is the number of components of the vector **u** where the forces of inertia are involved (the number of dynamic degrees of freedom), can often be much less than that of the static components. The nodal rotations can serve as a typical example. They usually have a much smaller dynamic effect than the linear displacements and are therefore not taken into account in the number of dynamic degrees of freedom (their moments of inertia are neglected).

If some inertial components of the load are not taken into consideration, it creates a problem of the dynamic analysis of a *system with an incomplete number of masses*.

In order to solve this problem, we have to divide the components of the displacement vector into two parts, so that the first one $\mathbf{X}_0$ contains the displacements corresponding to zero forces of inertia, and the second one $\mathbf{X}_1$ contains the displacements related to the inertial forces, then we can write the system (5.31) in the following form

$$\begin{bmatrix} \mathbf{K}_{00} & \mathbf{K}_{01} \\ \mathbf{K}_{10} & \mathbf{K}_{11} \end{bmatrix} \begin{bmatrix} \mathbf{X}_0 \\ \mathbf{X}_1 \end{bmatrix} = \omega^2 \begin{bmatrix} 0 & 0 \\ 0 & \mathbf{m}_{11} \end{bmatrix} \begin{bmatrix} \mathbf{X}_0 \\ \mathbf{X}_1 \end{bmatrix}. \tag{5.53}$$

The sub-vector $\mathbf{X}_0$ is excluded from this system, and the dimension of the modal analysis problem decreases dramatically in the result of the given *static condensation procedure*. The problem is reduced to the following one

$$(\mathbf{K}_{11} - \mathbf{K}_{10}\mathbf{K}_{00}^{-1}\mathbf{K}_{01} - \omega^2 \mathbf{M}_{11})\mathbf{X}_1 = 0. \tag{5.54}$$

Let us illustrate this idea with the following example. We will consider a beam with two point masses $m_1 = m$ and $m_2 = 2m$ (Fig. 5.23,a). The span length is $l=3$m. The beam has a constant bending stiffness EI=const and an infinitely large stiffness with respect to longitudinal strains: $EA = \infty$.

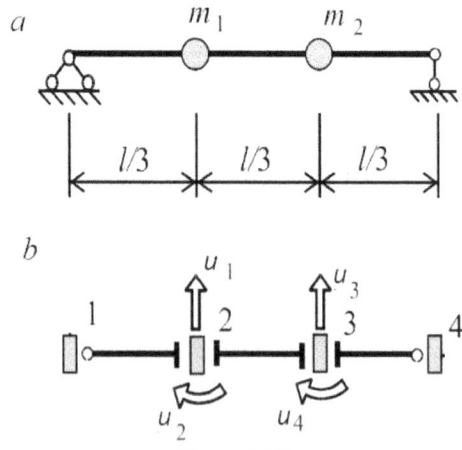

Figure 5.23

A design model of a beam with four degrees of freedom u_1, u_2, u_3, u_4 is shown in Fig. 5.22,b.

The stiffness matrix is compiled in the traditional manner and looks as follows

$$\|[K]\| = EI \begin{vmatrix} 0,555 & -0,333 & -0,444 & -0,666 \\ -0,333 & 2,333 & 0,666 & 0,666 \\ -0,444 & 0,666 & 0,555 & 0,333 \\ -0,666 & 0,666 & 0,333 & 2,333 \end{vmatrix}, \quad (5.55)$$

and the system of equations describing free oscillations:

$$\left.\begin{array}{l} \left[0,555 - m\omega^2/(EI)\right]X_1 - 0,333X_2 - 0,444X_3 - 0,666X_4 = 0 \\ -0,333X_1 + 2,333X_2 + 0,666X_3 + 0,666X_4 = 0 \\ -0,444X_1 + 0,666X_2 + \left[0,555 - 2m\omega^2/(EI)\right]X_3 + 0,333X_4 = 0 \\ -0,666X_1 + 0,666X_2 + 0,333X_3 + 2,333X_4 = 0. \end{array}\right\} \quad (5.56)$$

The second and fourth equations from (5.56) do not contain inertial forces. The displacement amplitudes X_2 and X_4 should be expressed from them, and then substituted into the first and third equations.

Solving the second and fourth equations together, we obtain

$$\begin{array}{l} X_2 = 0,0667X_1 - 0,2667X_3; \\ X_4 = 0,2667X_1 - 0,0667X_3. \end{array} \quad (5.57)$$

Substituting the obtained values into the first and third equations of the system (5.56) we get:

$$\left.\begin{array}{l} (0,355 - \lambda)X_1 - 0,311X_2 = 0 \\ -0,156X_1 + (0,178 - \lambda)X_2 = 0 \end{array}\right\}, \quad (5.58)$$

where

$$\lambda = m\omega^2/(EI). \quad (5.59)$$

Equating the determinant of the system (5.58) to zero, we can write the condition for the existence of natural oscillations:

$$\begin{vmatrix} (0,355 - \lambda) & -0,311 \\ -0,156 & (0,178 - \lambda) \end{vmatrix} = 0, \quad (5.60)$$

or

$$(0,3555 - \lambda) \cdot (0,1778 - \lambda) - 0,3111 \cdot 0,1556 = 0.$$

The solution of this quadratic equation

$$\lambda = 0,2667 \pm 0,2373 = \begin{cases} 0,0294, \\ 0,5040, \end{cases}$$

and the natural frequencies:

$$\omega_{0,1} = \sqrt{0,0294EI/m} = 0,1715\sqrt{EI/m},$$
$$\omega_{0,2} = \sqrt{0,5040EI/m} = 0,7099\sqrt{EI/m}.$$

In order to determine the natural modes, we drop one of the equations in the system (5.60), for example, the second one. Substitute the value of the first natural frequency into the remaining equation:

$$(0,3555 - 0,0294)X_1 - 0,3111X_3 = 0,$$

and assuming that $X_1^{(1)} = 1,0$, we obtain $X_3^{(1)} = 1,0482$. And the following values can be obtained from the relationships (5.57): $X_2^{(1)} = -0,2128$, $X_4^{(1)} = 0,1968$.

The displacement amplitudes of the second natural mode are calculated in the same way.

When solving dynamic problems, it is not necessary to take into account all the obtained natural modes; many of them are not actually excited by a certain external action. The problem of selecting a reasonable number of natural modes is usually solved by a trial method, since it is rather difficult to obtain an a priori estimate. However, some design codes regulating the analysis for certain dynamic actions recommend to take into account a particular number of natural modes. SNiP 2.01.07–85, for example, limits the range of frequencies that should be taken into account when calculating structures for wind pulsations, and SNiP II–7–81 states that not less than 10 modes should be used in the seismic analysis of concrete dams and not less than 15 modes for soil dams. U.S. codes and the latest editions of the national codes are more consistent. They require that the sum of generalized masses for the considered natural modes is not less than a certain percentage of the total mass of the system.

The determination of the percentage of the retained mass is especially important when there are local low frequency modes in the lower part of the spectrum. Buildings and structures with subsystems having significantly different stiffness or inertial properties (Fig. 5.24) can serve as an obvious example.

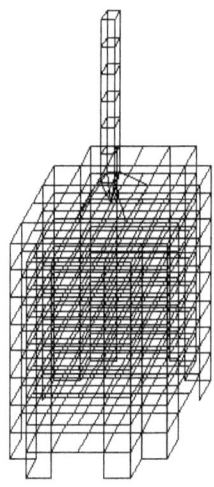
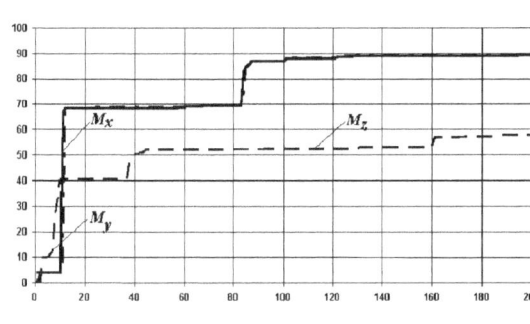

Figure 5.24.   Figure 5.24
                   5.

Fig. 5.25 shows the relationship between the percentage of the retained masses in the X, Y and Z directions and the number of considered natural modes for this structure. Where M_x, M_y, M_z are the sums of modal masses in the case of an action along the X, Y and Z axes respectively. It can be seen from this figure that the first 6-7 natural modes simply do not affect the solution, since they are related to the local movement of the lightweight superstructure (the chimney) and create the so-called "whip effect".

> *Fulfilling the requirement of retaining a certain percentage of the total modal mass of the structure reduces the risk that a certain very flexible part of the structure ("whip"), whose natural oscillations define the first natural modes, will be taken into account, while the oscillations of the rest of the structure will be neglected.*

Question:

We have considered cases when oscillations were caused by time-varying forces applied to the structure. However, seismic oscillations are related to the ground motion. How is the problem formulated in this case?

Answer:

We will proceed from the equation (5.27), which can be written in the matrix form

$$M\frac{d^2(u+Z_0)}{dt^2} + C\frac{du}{dt} + Ku(t) = 0. \quad (5.61)$$

It is taken into account here that the inertial forces (the first term) are defined by absolute accelerations of masses, the displacements of which are equal to the sum of earthquake-induced ground displacements Z_0, and relative displacements **u** (structural deformations are related to them) (Fig. 5.26).

Transferring the given ground acceleration to the right-hand side, we obtain

$$M\frac{d^2u}{dt^2} + B\frac{du}{dt} + Ku(t) = -M\frac{d^2Z_0}{dt^2}. \quad (5.62)$$

If the ground displacements Z_0 do not coincide in direction with the degree of freedom displacements **u**, then (5.62) should be replaced by the following relationship

$$M\frac{d^2u}{dt^2} + B\frac{du}{dt} + Ku(t) = -M\frac{d^2Z_0}{dt^2}J_x, \quad (5.63)$$

where J_x is the vector the components of which are the cosines of the angles between the direction of the ground displacement and the degree of freedom displacements of the system.

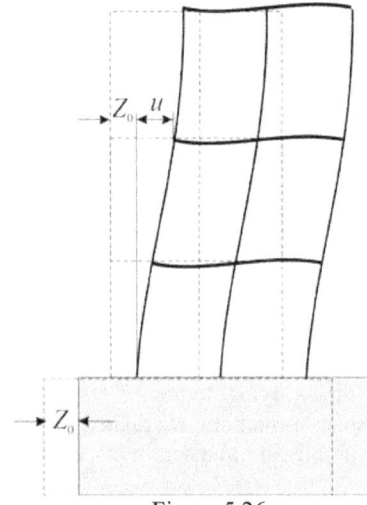

Figure 5.26

In the case of a *linear* system, it is possible to solve the system of equations (5.63) by the method of decomposition into natural modes and obtain the solution in the following form

$$\mathbf{u}(t) = \mathbf{\Psi}\mathbf{X}(t),\qquad(5.64)$$

where $\mathbf{X}(t)$ is the vector of unknown normal coordinates, which are the time functions, and do not depend on the position of a point in space. Their variation in space is entirely defined by the natural modes, which are represented by the columns of the matrix $\mathbf{\Psi}$. Matrix $\mathbf{\Psi}$ satisfies the orthogonality conditions

$$\mathbf{\Psi}^T\mathbf{M}\mathbf{\Psi} = \begin{cases} 0 & (j\neq k) \\ \mu_j & (j=k) \end{cases};\quad \mathbf{\Psi}^T\mathbf{K}\mathbf{\Psi} = \begin{cases} 0 & (j\neq k) \\ \omega_j^2\mu_j & (j=k) \end{cases},\qquad(5.65)$$

where ω_j is j-th natural frequency, and μ_j is the *modal mass* corresponding to the j-th mode.

After substituting (5.64) in (5.63) and multiplying by the matrix $\mathbf{\Psi}^T$ we obtain the following equation

$$\mathbf{\Psi}^T\mathbf{\Psi}\ddot{\mathbf{X}}(t) + \mathbf{\Psi}^T\mathbf{M}^{-1}\mathbf{C}\mathbf{\Psi}\dot{\mathbf{X}}(t) + \mathbf{\Psi}^T\mathbf{M}^{-1}\mathbf{K}\mathbf{\Psi}\mathbf{X}(t) = -\mathbf{\Psi}^T Z_0 \mathbf{J}_x.$$

If we assume (the case of proportional damping), that orthogonality conditions similar to (5.65) are satisfied for the dissipation matrix $\mathbf{C}$, the system of equations splits into separate equations of the form

$$\mu_j \ddot{X}(t) + 2\zeta_j \omega_j \mu_j \dot{X}(t) + \omega_j^2 \mu_j X(t) = -\mathbf{\Phi}^T \mathbf{MJ}_x \ddot{Z}_0(t) \quad (j=1,\ldots,n),$$

or, after dividing by μ_j,

$$\ddot{X}(t) + 2\zeta_j \omega_j \dot{X}(t) + \omega_j^2 X(t) = -\Gamma_j \ddot{Z}_0(t) \quad (j=1,\ldots,n),\qquad(5.66)$$

where

$$\Gamma_j = \frac{\mathbf{\Psi}^T \mathbf{MJ}_x}{\mu_j}.$$

The value Γ_j is called a *modal participation factor*. It is a measure of how strongly the j-th mode contributes to the response of the structure when subjected to force/displacement excitation in a specific direction.

The equation (5.66) is the oscillation equation of a single-mass system with a natural frequency ω_j and a coefficient of inelastic resistance ζ_j. Its solution can be easily obtained for any given action for the fixed value of resistance ξ_j and the given value of natural frequency ω_j (natural period $T_j = 2\pi/\omega_j$).

Thus, due to the participation factor the kinematic excitation $\ddot{Z}_0$ is included in the right-hand side of the equations of dynamic equilibrium, i.e. takes the form of forces acting on the masses of the system.

Question:
A danger of resonance when the frequency of the disturbing force coincides with the natural frequency has been demonstrated for a system with one degree of freedom. And how does resonance arise in systems with many degrees of freedom? Are

there any peculiarities here?

Answer:
If all disturbing forces vary according to the same law
$$P_i = P_i^0 \sin\theta t \quad (i=1,...,n),$$
then the solution of the equations of motion (5.38) can be obtained in the following form:
$$u_i = X_i \sin\theta t \quad (i=1,...,n),$$
where X_i is the amplitude value of the displacement $u_i(t)$,
which can be found by solving a system of algebraic equations:

$$\left.\begin{aligned}
K_{11}X_1 + K_{12}X_2 + ... + K_{1n}X_n - m_1\theta^2 X_1 &= P_1^0 \\
K_{21}X_1 + K_{22}X_2 + ... + K_{2n}X_n - m_2\theta^2 X_2 &= P_2^0 \\
&\cdots\cdots\cdots\cdots\cdots\cdots\cdots\cdots\cdots\cdots \\
K_{n1}X_n + K_{n2}X_n + ... + K_{nn}X_n - m_n\theta^2 X_n &= P_n^0
\end{aligned}\right\}.$$

and according to the Kramer formula
$$X_i = D_i/D \quad (i=1,2,...,n),$$
where D is the determinant of this system of equations, and D_i is the cofactor which is obtained from the determinant by replacing the i-th column with a free term column.

When the frequency θ coincides with one of the natural frequencies, the determinant D vanishes and the amplitudes X_i become infinite.

In other words, the system gets into resonance every time the excitation frequency is equal to one of the natural frequencies.

A phenomenon in a sense opposite to resonance, which can be called *antiresonance*, can be observed in systems with several degrees of freedom in addition to the actual resonance [7].

In static problems, the force P applied to an elastically fixed body (Fig. 5.27.*a*), always causes its displacement u. The situation may be different in dynamic problems, and we will illustrate this with an example of a system with two degrees of freedom (Fig. 5.27.*b*), subjected to a harmonic load
$$P = P_0 \sin\omega t.$$

a)
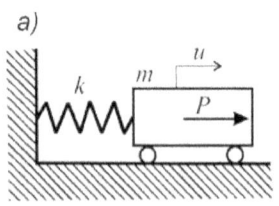
b)
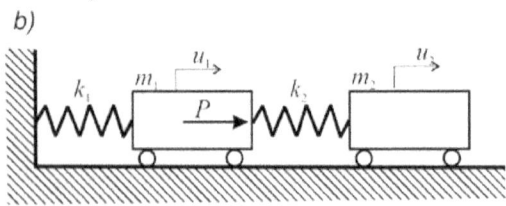

Figure 5.27

The equations of motion of this system are:

$$-k_1u_1 + k_2(u_2 - u_1) + P_0 \sin \omega t = m_1\ddot{u}_1$$
$$-k_2(u_2 - u_1) = m_2\ddot{u}_2$$

Suppose the frequencies of the oscillations are equal to the frequency of the disturbing force, i.e. the displacements are expressed as:

$$u_1 = A_1 \sin \omega t, \quad u_2 = A_2 \sin \omega t.$$

Then the following conditions must be satisfied for amplitudes

$$-A_1 m_1 \omega^2 + k_1 A_1 - k_2(A_2 - A_1) = P_0$$
$$A_2 m_2 \omega^2 + k_2(A_2 - A_1) = 0$$

which give the following solutions:

$$A_1 = \frac{P_0(k_2 - m_2\omega^2)}{(k_1 + k_2 - m_1\omega^2)(k_2 - m_2\omega^2) - c_2^2},$$

$$A_2 = \frac{P_0 k_2}{(k_1 + k_2 - m_1\omega^2)(k_2 - m_2\omega^2) - c_2^2}$$

It is seen that the amplitudes depend on the frequency of excitation. They become infinite, when the denominator in their expressions becomes zero

$$(k_1 + k_2 - m_1\omega^2)(k_2 - m_2\omega^2) - c_2^2 = 0,$$

which indicates the occurrence of resonances. Since this condition is a quadratic equation with respect to the square of the frequency, such resonances (roots of the equation) occur at two frequencies. These resonant frequencies are exactly equal to the natural frequencies of the considered system.

However, it should be noted that the amplitude A_1 can vanish as well, which happens at the frequency of excitation

$$\omega^* = \sqrt{k_2/m_2} .$$

At this frequency we will have

$$A_1 = 0, \quad A_2 = -P_0/k_2.$$

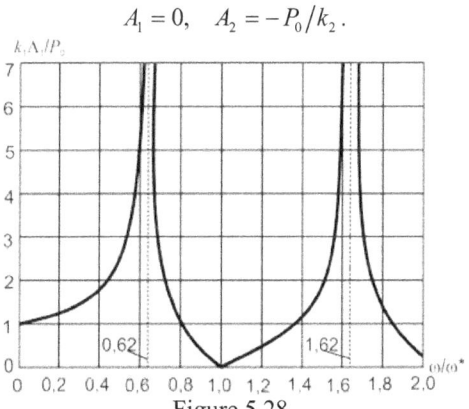

Figure 5.28.

Equality $A_1=0$ deserves special attention: the first mass remains motionless, although the disturbing force is applied to it. This amazing effect is impossible in static problems. It arises in dynamic problems due to the inertial force acting at the application point of the disturbing force. These forces are equal in magnitude and opposite in direction. Numerous *dynamic vibration absorbers* are based on the antiresonance phenomenon.

Figure 5.28 shows the variation of amplitude A_1 with the frequency of excitation ω*, in the case when $P_0=1$, $k_1=k_2=1$ and $m_1=m_2=1$. Antiresonance at ω=ω* is clearly visible here, as well as two resonances at ω=0,62 and ω=1,62.

Conversation 5.7: Quasi-Static Analysis and the Dynamic Amplification Factor

One of the most common ways to approximate the dynamic effects of a load with a time-varying value or position is to multiply this load, which is considered as static, by the *dynamic amplification factor*. This type of simplified analysis is called *quasi-static*.

In the conversation 5.3 the dynamic amplification factor was determined as the ratio of the amplitude of forced oscillations $|u(t)|_{max}$ to the displacement of a mass due to a statically applied force. Such a ratio can actually be considered for any reaction of the system (internal force, stress etc.) to the respective static reaction. It should be noted that in all of these cases we are talking about a single degree of freedom system, therefore it is necessary to transform the structure to an equivalent single degree of freedom system ("equivalent linear oscillator").

Indeed, these ratios, for example for the displacements of different masses in a multiple degree of freedom system are not necessarily equal. The system shown in Fig. 5.13 can serve as an example. The dynamic amplification factor of its middle mass is equal to μ_1=8,66/24,3=0,36, and that of its end masses is μ_2=12,51/11,7=1,17.

At the same time, many design codes provide recommended dynamic amplification factor values for certain loads not even mentioning that we are dealing only with single degree of freedom systems. Moreover, many guides on these codes claim that the dynamic amplification factor was determined from a series of experiments. Isn't there a contradiction?

First of all, it should be noted that what is commonly referred to as a dynamic load is often technically not a load. The structure is subjected to a time-varying action, and the inertial forces arising during the motion of the structure caused by this excitation are commonly called the dynamic loads. Moreover, the concept of the load variation rate is not absolute. This rate must always be measured in time units which are natural for the considered structure and are determined by the natural period.

Thus:

> In the general case, the dynamic load is inseparable from the dynamic properties of the structure and is often not an **action**, but a result of the load-structure **interaction**.

Since the results of the dynamic analysis depend both on the properties of the applied load and on the properties of the structure this load is applied to, the value of the dynamic amplification factor makes sense only when both of these components of the design model are determined and the load this factor is applied to is indicated.

The above applies to those situations where the frequency characteristics of the load are in the near-reasonant area. If the oscillations are far from resonance, we can consider a dynamic factor of a certain load, determining it as the ratio of the dynamic action on the structure to its static component. Quite typical here is the case of a mobile load, where the effects of wheel impacts at rail joints or other dynamic effects of a mobile train create a load on the supporting structure, which exceeds the mobile dead load.

This is the case, for example, for the dynamic amplification factor $k_d=1,1$ or $k_d=1,2$ for the crane load (depending on the crane operation mode). The design codes provide different values of the dynamic amplification factor $(1+\mu)$ for bridges, depending on the span (length of the influence line segment), mobile load type (train or car load) and the design (beam or arch bridges, steel or reinforced concrete etc.). These factors summarize the numerous experimental data regularly acquired by the bridge testing stations during the acceptance tests, as well as the data from special studies. They also refer to the values of the maximum components of internal forces, and are used only in the ultimate limit state analysis.

Note, for example, that the values $1+\mu$ for railway bridges changed during the transition from the codes of 1931-56 to the codes of 1962 and later. This is due to the fact that the loads from steam locomotives, which have significant unbalanced masses, had been previously considered, and then diesel and electric locomotives with much smaller unbalanced masses were considered as the main load.

If the design is not known in advance, modal dynamic amplification factors are sometimes used. They are applied to the results of the calculation for each natural mode, i.e., to a set of individual single degree of freedom systems.

Here we use the fact that the exact solutions of the dynamic problem and, hence, the expressions for the dynamic amplification factor are known for a single degree of freedom system subjected to certain types of "standard" loads. Such loads include all kinds of pulse actions. Plots of the dynamic amplification factor for different short-term actions are shown in Fig. 5.29 depending on their relative duration $\tilde{\tau} = \omega \tau / (2\pi)$.

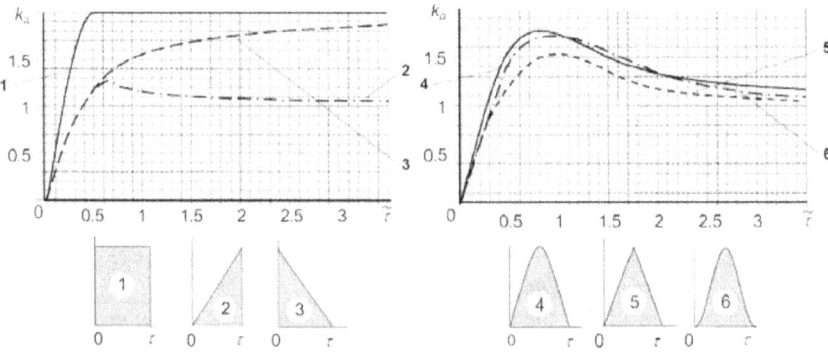

Figure 5.29

There are also other known values of the dynamic amplification factor, for example, for the aircraft crash impact [2], and a body freely falling from a height h, $k_d = 1 + \sqrt{1 + 2h/z_{st}}$ (z_{st} is the deflection due to a statically applied force equal to the weight of the falling body) etc.

Question:
Seismic codes provide the values of the "spectral dynamic amplification factor β". What is it?

Answer:
It is an unsuitable term used only in the national codes. This factor is called a response spectrum in all other codes, which describes the physical nature of this parameter in the seismic analysis much better.

Indeed, the dynamic amplification factor is usually a ratio between the reaction to a dynamic action and the reaction to a static action. However, in the case of a seismic action there is no such static action that has to be multiplied by the dynamic amplification factor. And the physical nature of the "spectral dynamic amplification factor" is not clear from its name.

In fact, this standard seismic analysis is based on the so-called linear spectral theory of M. Biot. This theory uses earthquake induced accelerations of pendulums with different natural periods. The maximum values of the accelerations of these pendulums caused by the ground motion during real earthquakes are represented in a function of the natural period of the pendulum (test oscillator) and form the response spectrum which serves as the basis for determining the seismic load (Fig. 5.30).

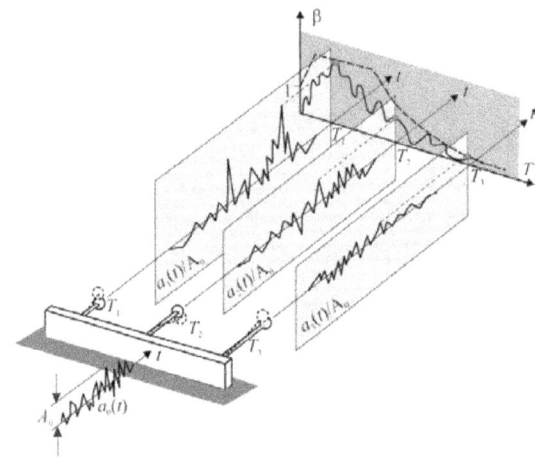

Figure 5.30
The response spectrum is used to determine the contribution of each natural mode to the seismic reaction of the structure, namely, the inertial forces (the seismic load) arising during the natural mode motion are determined.

References

1. *Aleksandrov A.V., Potapov V.D., Zylev V.B.* Structural Mechanics. Book 2. Dynamics and Stability of Elastic Systems. — M.: High School, 2008.
2. *Birbraer A.N., Roleder A.J.* Extreme Actions on Structures.— Saint Petersburgh Polytechnic University Publishing House, 2000.
3. Dynamic structural analysis. (Designer's manual) — M.: Stroyizdat, 1984.
4. *Ray W. Clough, Joseph Pensien.* Dynamics of Structures — M.: Stroyizdat, 1979.
5. *Napetvaridze Sh.G., Khachatryan S.O.* Wave Processes in Structures of Buildings under Seismic Influences — M.: Nauka, 1987.
6. *Panovko Ya.G.* Introduction to the Theory of Mechanical Oscillations. — M.:Nauka, 1980.
7. *Panovko Ya.G, Gubanova I.I.* Stability and Oscillations of Elastic Systems — M.: Nauka, 1987.
8. *Perelmuter A.V., Slivker V.I.* Design Models of Structures and a Possibility of Their Analysis.— M.:DMK Press, 2007.
9. *Tyapin A.G.* Consideration of interaction with the base in calculations for seismic actions — M.: ASV, 2014.
10. *Holopov I.S.* Structural Analysis of Buildings under Dynamic Actions (a course of lectures). — M.: ASV, 2012.

Cycle 6

Now Let's Try to Fly

 *Boarding of a new experimental airliner has ended. Stewardess: "On board of our aircraft you will find a swimming pool on the first floor and a tennis court on the top floor. There is also a cinema in the middle part, a bar on the left, and a library on the right... And now let's try to take off and fly with all this crap."*

An old joke

A true engineer should trust his eyes more than any formula; he must remember the words of the naturalist and philosopher Thomas Huxley: "Mathematics may be compared to a mill of exquisite workmanship, which grinds your stuff to any degree of fineness; but, nevertheless, what you get out depends on what you put in; and as the grandest mill in the world will not extract wheat flour from peas cods, so pages of formulae will not get a definite result out of loose data", so the engineer should pay the greatest attention to the stuff he puts in.

A.N. Krylov

Structural Mechanics is the theoretical basis for a number of more specific subjects, such as the Design of (Steel, Concrete, Timber etc.) Structures, or some special courses like the Design of Bridges. However, the transition from general theoretical problems to specific realistic problems of structural strength, rigidity and stability often implies not only selecting structural mechanics tools, but also using some additional hypotheses or methods.

The latter can often be found in the design codes, although due to the long-standing and essentially incorrect tradition, they are not explicitly described. Unfortunately, the course books follow this tradition as well. Their design recommendations resemble recipes in a cookbook. In other words, as the epigraph says, we yet have to take off and fly with all that baggage of structural mechanics on board.

If we follow the common belief that the goal of structural mechanics is to develop methods for structural strength and stability analysis, then the content of this cycle could be defined as "Near-Structural Mechanics" or "Post-Structural Mechanics".

Conversation 6.1. Limit State Method

As centuries-old experience of building shows, the problem of structural durability and safety has always existed and is still important nowadays. The development of philosophy of providing safety of the designed buildings and structures passed several stages and in its main direction it has always developed under the slogan of ever more detailed prediction of the structural performance, study of nature of the loads acting upon these structures, more distinct description of requirements to the structural form and terms of implementation of such requirements.

The history of construction shows that gross errors can be found even in the most perfect ancient structures revealing the ignorance of the basics of strength of materials and the theory of structures. Superstitious fear of the unknowable secret of material compelled builders even to turn to supernatural powers for help using prayers (which can still be found nowadays), spells and even sacrifices. The profession of builder has been considered very responsible since ancient times, and possible construction errors had very serious consequences for those, who made them.

However, the structural safety codes were usually very vague. The earliest known written building code is included in the Code of Hammurabi, dating back to about 1772 B.C. It says:

- If a builder build a house for some one, and does not construct it properly, and the house which he built fall in and kill its owner, then that builder shall be put to death.
- If it kill the son of the owner the son of that builder shall be put to death.
- If it kill a slave of the owner, then he shall pay slave for slave to the owner of the house.
- If it ruin goods, he shall make compensation for all that has been ruined, and inasmuch as he did not construct properly this house which he built and it fell, he shall re-erect the house from his own means.
- If a builder build a house for some one, even though he has not yet completed it; if then the walls seem toppling, the builder must make the walls solid from his own means.
- If any one be too lazy to keep his dam in proper condition, and does not so keep it; if then the dam break and all the fields be flooded, then shall he in whose dam the break occurred be sold for money, and the money shall replace the corn which he has caused to be ruined.

Building codes can even be found in the Bible (Deuteronomy, Chapter 22, Verse 8): "When you build a new house, make a parapet around your roof so that you may not bring the guilt of bloodshed on your house if someone falls from the roof".

Builders determined strength intuitively, by the trial-and-error method; they learnt from accidents and failures of structures. Every accident added new knowledge to the builders, posed new problems. When there was not enough knowledge, a *factor of safety* and allowable stresses were introduced (and are still introduced now) into engineering calculations. Since nobody knew, what unpredictable unexplored phenomena are taken into account by this factor and whether its value is correct, and it should not be any less, it was in fact the *coefficient of ignorance*.

Theoretical foundations of the structural analysis were formulated in the methods of structural mechanics which had formed as an independent scientific discipline by the mid-19th century. Its appearance enabled to set the rules of structural design. The factor of safety was introduced for the first time into the building science by the famous French engineer and scientist L.M.A. Navier. In 20th of the XIX century he suggested to set the design allowable stresses which must be much less than the ultimate ones and at which the structure must work reliably.

W.J.M. Rankine, a famous Scottish mechanical engineer and physicist, defined the factor of safety as the ratio in which the breaking load exceeds the working load. W.J.M. Rankine also pointed out the difference between a steady load and a moving load. The latter produces much greater stresses and strains than the steady load, and therefore the factor of safety for a moving load must be considerably greater than for a steady load. He took the minimum factor of safety for the moving load as $k=4,0$.

This permissible working stress had been included into the codes and building regulations for different materials and structures by the end of 19th and the beginning of 20th century.

Allowable stresses adopted in different countries had considerably different values. Thus, the allowable stresses for the structural steel in England were based on a factor of safety of 4 applied to the average ultimate strength of about 432-494 N/mm². The London County Council 1909 Act specified a permissible working bending stress of 116 N/mm² for both tension and compression. In Russia the Teaching Manual [24] recommended allowable stresses for wrought iron structures of 80 N/mm² in tension and 65 N/mm² in compression. And in Germany these values were 115 and 95 N/mm², respectively.

The allowable stresses had subsequently seen many changes, and since the 1940s the allowable stresses for steel structures were based on the factor of safety of about 2 but applied to the *minimum yield point* σ_y instead of the average ultimate strength.

In the Soviet Union, for example, the yield strength σ_y for St3 steel was taken as 240 N/mm². The factor of safety took into account many adverse factors affecting the structural behavior and, in particular, depended on the number and type of loads applied to the structure. Till 1942 the maximum factor of safety of $k=1,7$ and the minimum allowable stress of $[\sigma] =140$ N/mm² had been used in the calculations for loads which were permanent or often coincided, for example, dead loads and snow. When a greater number of loads and rare loads were considered (hurricane, thermal action), the allowable stress was taken as $[\sigma] =170$ N/mm², and $k=1,4$. In 1942 the values of allowable stresses were increased to 160 and 180 N/mm². The factors of safety were taken as 1,5 and 1,33 respectively.

At first, i.e. at the end of the 19th century the design of reinforced concrete was based on elastic theory using the allowable stresses. However, in 1904 A.F. Lolleit showed in his paper "On the Strength Factor of Reinforced Concrete Structures" [17] that the analysis of flexural reinforced concrete elements based on the elastic stage of their behavior is completely unacceptable. He wrote: "the critical load corresponding to the instantaneous equilibrium immediately preceding the failure ... enables to determine the safety margin with an accuracy satisfying the most rigorous requirements".

His ideas (as well as the similar ideas of the American engineer Charles S. Whitney) were implemented in 1930s [18, 42]. However, the transition from the allowable stress to the allowable force did not change the basic paradigm of the allowable stress design. Just the ultimate load of the reinforced concrete element instead of its ultimate stress was divided by the factor of safety.

Thus, starting from the 19th century, the allowable stress design method based on the factor of safety, which was established on the basis of engineering intuition and design and operation experience, was used in the structural analysis until the 1950s.

Meanwhile, a number of papers suggested the development of other structural analysis methods. In 1926 M. Maier proposed to use probabilistic methods for selecting the values of the parameters included in the analysis instead of the allowable stress design method [38]. In 1929 N.F. Khotsialov, taking into account the variability of the main parameters, proposed a design method based on a certain regulated probability of structural failure [28]. However, N.F. Khotsialov's formulation "Design allowing for a possible accident" was met with strong resistance and his ideas were rejected for a long time. The ideas of M. Maier and N.F. Khotsialov were significantly developed in the works by N.S. Streletsky, M. Plot and W. Wierzbicki, A.M. Freudenthal [26, 35, 42, 44], where not only strength characteristics of the material were used as random variables but the parameters of the loads as well. And in this case the probability of failure in the form of violation of some regulated requirements was considered instead of the probability of an accident.

However, the allowable stress design method has a number of other disadvantages. The main ones are: all structures were calculated with the same factor of safety regardless of the types of loads and performance conditions of the structural elements; the safety factor did not take into account operational requirements.

Therefore, the semi-probabilistic limit state method was a significant step in the development of structural analysis. It does not have these disadvantages and is essentially a practical implementation of some ideas of the probabilistic approach. Being deterministic in form, it uses the statistical analysis methods for determining the safety factors. The conventional system of safety factors was proposed in 1945 by I.I. Goldenblat, M.G. Kostyukovsky and A.N. Popov and formed the basis of the calculation procedure for the development of the codes.

The limit state method was introduced in the USSR as the guiding principle for structural analysis on January 1, 1955 with the approval of the first edition of the Building Code. This method has subsequently gained global acceptance and is currently the basis of most international and national design standards, in particular, of the Eurocode system, where it is called "the partial safety factor method" [34].

> *Two names, "the limit state method" and "the partial safety factor method", reflect the most significant aspects of this method, and each of these aspects has a certain independence.*

If this method is considered in the context of using the limit states, then you should keep in mind that the method is based on the idea of performing a detailed analysis only for the limit states of the structure and the design requirements are developed for them. Besides the known advantages, this approach has a serious disadvantage. If, for example, we consider the strength condition as one of the limit states and design the structure ensuring that this condition is not violated during the entire service life with a certain degree of confidence, we know almost nothing about the level of actual stresses corresponding to the normal (non-limit) state under the most frequent operating conditions.

For example, the reinforced concrete design codes are based on the idea of considering the limit state of a section when the compressive stresses in concrete reach the ultimate value due to the plastic deformation of the reinforcement. However, this Lolleit's hypothesis does not hold under normal conditions and there is completely different stress state, which should, for example, form the basis for the study of rheological processes like creep.

The states of the structure most frequently occurring under the operating conditions usually define its durability. However, the following structures can turn out to be almost equivalent according to the limit state analysis: a dam with a normal loading not far from the allowable value (for example, 80% of the design value), and a chimney with a very rare design load and a normal loading equal to, for example, 15% of the design value.

> *If we fix our attention on the system of partial safety factors, we will see that one general factor of safety has been replaced by the product of several (partial) factors each one related to a certain aspect of the safety problem (load type, material properties, importance of the structure, etc.)*

This component of the limit state method provoked intensive research of these factors and the development of the codes. The refinement in the application of a combination of partial safety factors provides (or rather should provide) the equal probability of the limit states of the above structures with drastically different normal states in terms of the proximity to the limit one.

However, there is a certain inconsistency here as well, since we can rely on the equal safety only in the case of the factors (for example, external actions), which were considered in the design and the statistical characteristics of which were used when specifying the design factors of the method. And in the case of a certain beyond the design basis random excitation the probability of exhaustion of 20% of the reserve in the first case is much higher than the exhaustion of 85% of the reserve in the second case.

In the second half of the 20th century numerous works were performed on the formation and improvement of probabilistic methods, i.e. preparation for the transition to the next stage of the development of the structural analysis – direct design assessment of the structural safety. However, a tradition has been established to identify safety only with the absence of failures, and this has become almost a standard in the work of both domestic and foreign researchers.

Two groups of limit states are introduced in the fundamental standards: ultimate limit states which lead to complete unserviceability, and serviceability limit states which obstruct the normal use or reduce its durability compared to the design service life. The previous editions of codes considered a 3-rd group of limit states on the formation and excessive development of cracks, but the idea of distinguishing it as a separate group was later abandoned.

> *In accordance with the current codes for limit state design it is assumed that the operation of a building or structure will stop before its actual load-bearing capacity is exhausted, and this fact is declared as one of the **postulates** of the limit state method.*

This is the way GOST 27751-88, which was valid for many years, formulates the condition of the ultimate limit state, defining them as the states "..., that lead to complete unserviceability of structures, subgrade (of buildings or structures) or to a complete (partial) loss of bearing capacity of buildings and structures". This formulation implies that besides the loss of bearing capacity, such events as the termination of operation due to the unprofitability of further maintenance can serve as a criterion of the ultimate limit state. Thus, for example, the Kiev TV tower which had been built on the Khreshchatyk street in the early 50-s was demolished, because the transition to new types of antennas required unreasonably expensive upgrading. In other words, the formulation of GOST 27751-88 considers the obsolescence in addition to the wear as one of the reasons for the transition to the ultimate limit state.

By the way, the term "complete unserviceability" requires definition in each specific case. If an old building has a faulty piping system, we have to decide whether to install new pipes or demolish the building. If the building is of historical interest, it can be converted into a non-residential museum, in which case we establish its unsuitability as a residential building.

> *Many famous old buildings and monuments have actually been out of order for a long time in this sense. For example, the pyramids at Giza (Fig. 6.1) are often considered as examples of durability, but in the strict sense of the word they have long been out of order. They no longer serve and can not serve their intended purpose, their surfaces are badly damaged.*

Figure 6.1. The pyramid of Khafre in Giza (26th century BC) – present-day look

When justifying the above postulate (the termination of operation precedes the exhaustion of the bearing capacity), it is usually indicated that the material diagram is not ideal (Fig.6.2.*a*), and has an ascending branch (Fig.6.2.*b*) or that gradual loss of consistency of statically indeterminate systems occurs while maintaining the bearing capacity. These arguments, however, apply not to all types of structures and not to all forms of bearing capacity exhaustion (for example, to sudden failures such as buckling or brittle fracture). This is apparently the reason for the dual nature of the formulation of GOST 27751-88.

Technically, it turns out that accidental collapses are, in a sense, nonstandard events, and accident statistics cannot be used to estimate the actual level of safety, because this statistics does not include many cases when a structure is put out of service without any accidents.

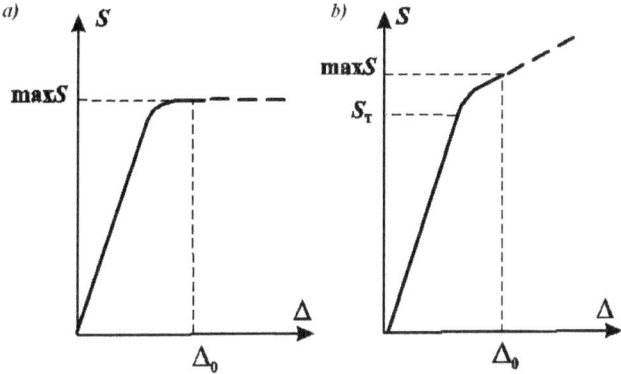

Figure 6.2.

More reasonable definitions are given in the international standard ISO 2394 [37]:

«3.1.1. ... ultimate limit states concerning the maximum load-bearing capacity (are related to safety)»

and in the Eurocode [34]

«3.3. (1) Ultimate limit states are states associated with collapse or with other similar forms of structural failure.

(2) States prior to structural collapse, which, for simplicity, are considered in place of the collapse itself, may be treated as ultimate limit states.

(3) The ultimate limit states concern:
the safety of the structure;
the safety of people".

A similar position was taken by the new standard GOST R 54257-2010 [9], where the following limit states are introduced:

- ultimate limit states are the states of structures the excess of which leads to the loss of their bearing capacity;
- serviceability limit states — if they are exceeded, normal structural operation and comfort conditions are violated, and the durability resource is exhausted;
- special limit states are states caused by abnormal conditions or abnormal loadings, the excess of which leads to a structural failure with catastrophic consequences.

The relationship between safety requirements and the limit state design is usually considered obvious and is indicated by identifying failure (the main concept of the safety theory) with reaching the limit state. And although the concept of failure is generally broader than the list of situations related to the limit states, it can be acceptable as a first approximation.

It should be noted that both regulatory and scientific literature related to the structural safety traditionally consider almost exclusively the principles of ensuring reliability based on providing a "safety margin". The way of ensuring reliability related to performing control, verification, repair and replacement of structural parts and other actions during operation has been studied much less and is practically not regulated.

However, if we take a broader look at reliability, it is necessary to consider the whole complex of problems leading to possible failures (Fig.6.3). Then the place and role of design codes in ensuring reliability will become obvious, as well as their relationship to the problems of control and its insufficient accuracy.

The failure flowchart shown in Fig. 6.3 contains all the main stages of the life cycle (design, prefabrication, on-site works, and technical maintenance), which are depicted in bold rectangles. Light rectangles show documents regulating the above stages, and dark rectangles show processes performed when creating a structure. Using recommendations and regulatory guidelines only partially prevents errors at the respective stages. And the life cycle processes themselves can generate errors, which, in theory, should be counteracted by the respective control procedures, but no control can guarantee the absolute absence of errors and some of them get into the next stages of the structural life cycle.

Objective and subjective hazards are depicted as two flows, the configuration of which characterizes the degree of assumption of objective hazards and the possibility of error accumulation.

It should be noted that hazards can not only accumulate during the transition from one stage to another, but also interact with each other and errors made at one stage of the life cycle stimulate errors at another stage.

The simplest example is an error in space planning (design stage), which results in a hindered access to the structure. This in turn leads to poor maintenance and initiates an error at the technical maintenance stage.

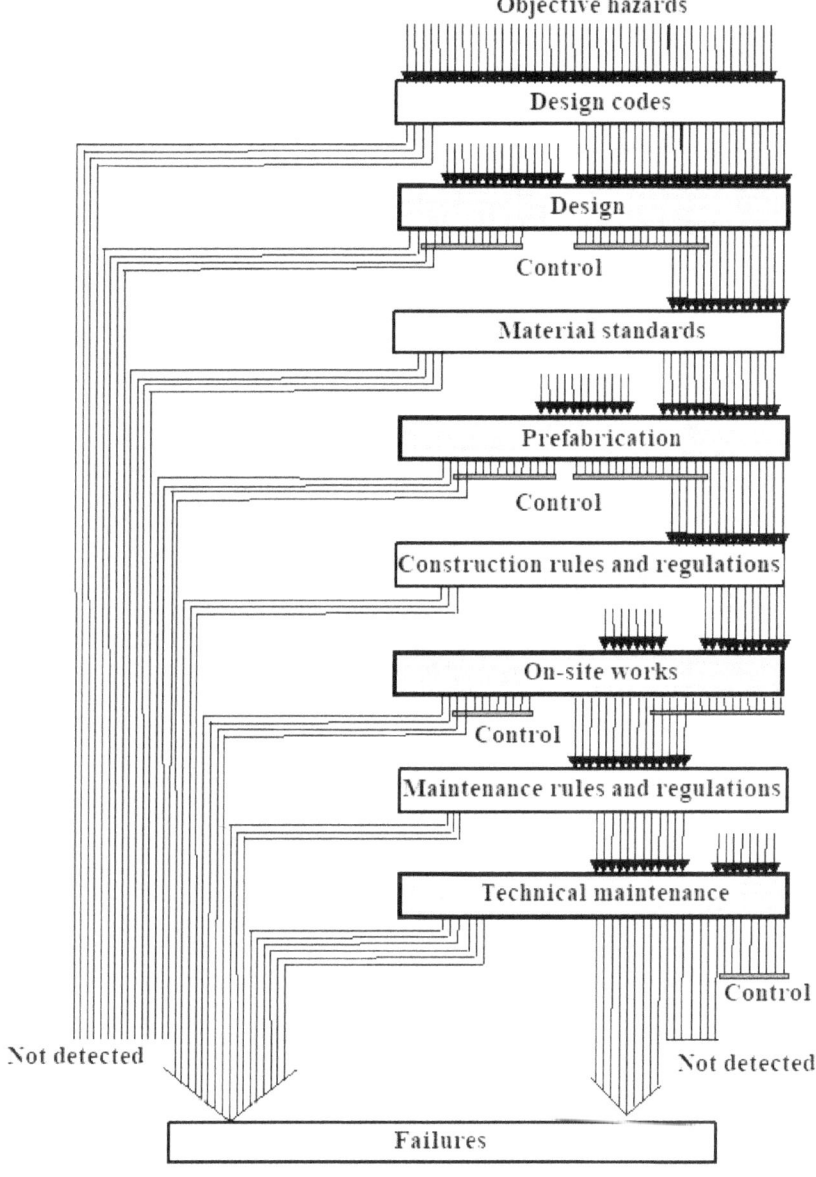

Figure 6.3.

Question:
It took decades to implement the limit state method abroad. Can it be explained by simple ignorance of Soviet works or were there other considerations?

Answer:
I believe that the main role here was played by the lack of statistical data in the mid-50s to substantiate the values of partial safety factors (the authors of the method admitted it and relied on future studies, making the results fit the experience based solutions).

Since the command system of introducing innovations is not common for Western countries, there were no opportunities to convince the engineering community of the urgent need to change the design approach, especially since fitting to previous experience did not give a noticeable economic effect. In particular, some economy was achived for structures primarily subjected to dead loads with minimum overload factors, namely the economy of 3...10% for trussed rafters, while the crane beams remained practically unchanged, and the columns of industrial buildings either remained unchanged, or even became slightly heavier.

It should be noted that the idea of succession/continuity is present in Western standards as well. Thus, the 'Foreword' to CP110 [31] states that "...insufficient relevant statistical data are available to enable a design method in complete accord with probability theory to be developed". However, it was claimed that the partial factor system had the advantage that "Subsequently it will simplify the incorporation of amendments to the Code as new knowledge becomes available with regard to variations in loads and strengths".

When writing the Eurocodes, the European Committee for Standardization (CEN) faced the fact that some countries that used the limit state method feared that some calculations based on the allowable stress method would indicate a formal violation of the requirements of the limit state method. Other countries, where the allowable stress method was used, indicated that the existing structures turned out to be less economical when recalculated using the limit state method. Thus, modern Eurocodes are the result of a compromise, and only in their next editions can we expect full probabilistic validity/justification of all standard requirements.

Question:
What is the role of structural mechanics in the beyond design stages of the life cycle shown in Fig. 6.2?

Answer:
Design problems usually arise at all stages of the life cycle of a structure, and therefore using the methods of structural mechanics is inevitable.
As an example, let us consider only the problems that are hardly even mentioned in university courses.

One of such problems arises when testing the structures. These can be, for example, acceptance tests, or regular control tests of mass-produced structures in factory conditions. It is necessary to solve at least two design problems here — to select a control loading (or their set) with the highest efficiency in terms of checking the strength of all structural elements, and to develop a convincing measure assessing the compliance of the test results with the required quality level.

The second problem is related to the organization of monitoring of the used structure, when it is necessary to find the most informative set of monitored parameters, and to develop a methodology for assessing the state of the structure based on their measurement. A typical problem here is the problem of vibration analysis of the existing structure, when they try to estimate the level of damage by measuring the trend of the natural frequency values.

The latter has become quite popular and therefore it is worth making the following remark. Some authors propose to determine the dynamic structural characteristics by analyzing the results of low-intensity effects (for example, natural microseisms). However, the dynamic characteristics of the building, obtained by applying a low-intensity excitation, correspond to a dynamic system, including not only the bearing structures, but also a complex of secondary non-bearing elements, which do not take the design loads. Thus, the result may not refer to the system we are interested in.

Question:
The ultimate limit state is usually related to an ultimate value of a certain structural parameter (ultimate strength, loss of equilibrium stability etc.). And what can you say in this regard about the serviceability limit state?

Answer:
There is usually a noticeable uncertainty here, and the considered limits are conditional in many respects. However, the Eurocodes [34], for example, differentiate between reversible and irreversible serviceability limit states.

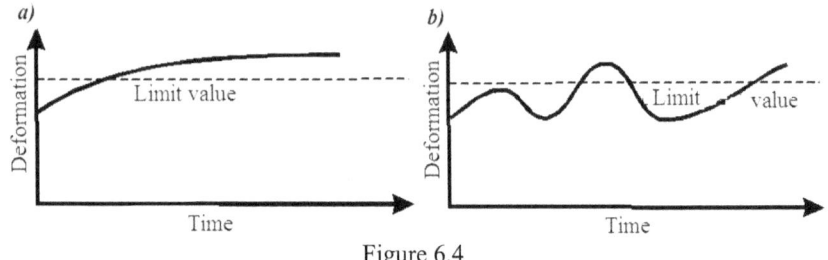

Figure 6.4

Irreversible limit states (Fig. 6.4.*a*) occur where some of the consequences remain after the actions that exceed the limit have been removed (for example, local damage or concrete creep deformations). And reversible limit states (Fig. 6.4.*b*) do not develop and sometimes even disappear after the actions that exceed the limit have been removed after the actions that exceed the limit have been removed (for example, displacements caused by wind loads or excessive vibration).

The limit values of the irreversible limit states are usually based on the serviceability considerations. Although quite reasoble values can be determined in some cases, they are usually conditional in a certain sense. For example, it is difficult to prove that a deflection of 1/250 of the span is acceptable, while a deflection of 1/245 of the span is unacceptable.

A time interval is usually set for reversible limit states, during which this state can be violated. For example, in the case of beam radio, when noticeable rotation angles of antennas reduce the reception quality, it can be conditionally assumed that such quality decrease is acceptable for 5% of the time. This approach is used in the Ukrainian codes [11].

Question:
Structural strength and stability analysis is performed using design combinations of internal forces. However, the codes do not provide any rules for selecting these combinations. Moreover, different methods are used in practice and they give different results. Can you comment on this?

Answer:
There are practically no structures designed to take only one load case. The real design of load-bearing structures is the design of systems subjected to many independent load cases, each one creating a cer tain pattern of internal forces in the elements of the system. The problem of selecting design combinations of forces (DCF) is one of the main ones in the design of load-bearing structures.

This selection is usually based on the superposition principle, which means that the calculations are performed as for a linear system. Linearity also implies that a loading will either be entirely included in the DCF, or it will be dropped (if it creates an unloading effect), and thus you will have only $2n$ combinations (where n is the number of loadings) to select from. It is easy to see that in the case of the real values of the parameter n the number of possible combinations becomes so large, that the problem can not be solved by the straightforward enumeration method.

It should be noted here, that the geometrically or physically nonlinear analysis will in fact require certain guessing of the design combination, because a corresponding algorithm for selecting DCF has not yet been elaborated.

As for the linear systems, the following algorithm is still used for selecting DCF:
- determine the combination causing the maximum moment and find the corresponding longitudinal and shear forces;
- determine the combination causing the minimum moment and find the corresponding longitudinal and shear forces;
- determine the combination causing the maximum longitudinal force and find the corresponding moment and shear force;

and so on.

This rule is traditional and is given in many textbooks (see, for example, [16, p. 366], [8, p. 95]). However, there is a certain danger of missing dangerous situations. The idea of a counterexample is clear from Fig. 6.5, where the points in M-N coordinates show values for certain loadings and their combinations. Extreme values define a dotted rectangle passing through points 1, 3, 6, 8 and it is these combinations that form the basis of the selection of sections, when a traditional rule for selecting unfavorable combinations is used. The load-bearing capacity of the selected section related to the extreme stresses $-R_t \leq N/A \pm M/W \leq R_c$, is such that it defines the darkened rectangle which has covered the design points 1, 3, 6, 8.

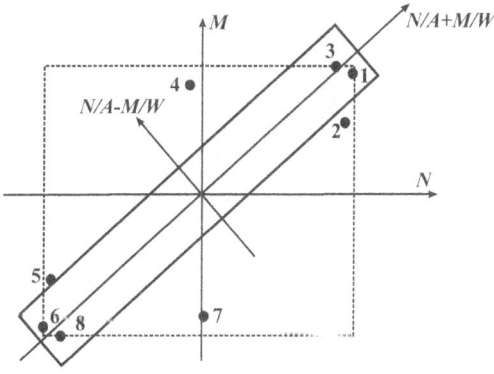

Figure 6.5.

However, other points, for example 4 and 7, are left outside the load-bearing capacity area, and since they did not define the design combinations of forces, they will not be considered in the analysis. The rule "extreme force and its corresponding forces" is obviously not very reliable.

Therefore, other algorithms have been proposed, which take into account the logical relationships between loadings reflecting the physical meaning of loadings and requirements of various design codes [1, 7]. But, unfortunately, the traditional rule which was proved unreliable almost half a century ago, is still commonly used by engineers. In truth, there is nothing more difficult than refuting myths.

Conversation 6.2. Conditional and Real Factor of Safety

It has already been noted in the previous section that the limit state method is based on the idea of performing a detailed analysis only for the limit states of the structure, without considering its normal states. Focusing only on the failure states, with a practical focus on the ultimate limit state, as the one determining the structural form, is not only an advantage of the considered method.

Since the structure is in the normal operating state during its design life and the destructive changes in the material of the structure occur for these states (for example, corrosive processes or the fatigue damage accumulation), then the analysis of a structure which has normal behavior and is far from exhausting its strength and stability becomes defining in terms of ensuring operational reliability and durability. Calculations in the operational stage can play a decisive role for many structural parameters. In this regard, L.I. Iosilevsky [11] notes: "The engineer's loss of design control over the structure during its transition from a "healthy" (normal, operational) state to the limit one is nothing else but a failure in the methodology for the design prediction of the behavior of a bearing structure under loads... The resulting logical vacuum between the operational and limit state is unacceptable".

It would seem that the serviceability limit state checks could eliminate this methodological failure, but the thing is that this group of states is the limit one as well, i.e. corresponds to quite rare extreme structural and environmental parameters. For example, snow or wind loads acting on a structure reach their characteristic values once in five to seven years, and are quite far from the normal operating conditions.

In most cases the main inequality of the limit state method is as follows

$$\psi \cdot \gamma_n \cdot \gamma_f F_n \leq \gamma_c \cdot \gamma_m \cdot R_n \tag{6.1}$$

where ψ, γ_c, γ_f, γ_m, γ_n are the load combination factor, service factor, safety factors for load and material, and the importance factor of a structure, respectively; F_n and R_n are the characteristic values of the generalized action and resistance, which are used to estimate the limit states.

The value

$$K = \left(\psi \cdot \gamma_n \cdot \gamma_f\right) / \left(\gamma_c \cdot \gamma_m\right) \tag{6.2}$$

is sometimes identified with the standard factors of safety of the system.

It is easy to see that the factor K is not very different from one, which implies a coincidence of the design limit state with the true structural performance limit, although it is not even nearly the case in reality. The true factors of safety are significantly greater than one, since the actual structural performance limit differs from that assumed as the design limit state. The estimate (6.2) does not correspond to the true safety margin of the system, mainly because the actual exhaustion of the bearing capacity is usually related to a number of nonlinear effects, which noticeably redistribute the forces in the system as it approaches the failure. Due to this redistribution, the estimate obtained using (6.2), and calculated using an entirely different design model (usually linear) may turn out to be either too high or too low.

> *Thus, we see that not only does the use of the limit state method not determine the difference between the behavior of the system at the operational stage, which was discussed above, but also estimates the margin separating the transition from the design (usually conditional) limit state to the true bearing capacity limit of the system quite approximately.*

In order to obtain more reliable judgements, it is necessary to perform experiments and/or special calculations by methods other than those given in the codes.

In the case when we are dealing with a structure subjected to a single load, the determination of the factor of safety based on a physical experiment or numerical modelling is obvious. It is necessary to achieve the "failure" of the structure or of its mathematical model by increasing the design load F_d to the maximum possible value F^*, and to determine the real factor of safety k as the ratio:

$$k = F^*/F_d .\qquad(6.3)$$

The use of this method in the case when the structure is subjected to several loads is related to the assumption that all loads vary in proportion to one parameter, while the ratio between them remains constant. This pattern of load behavior is not typical for all cases, and it is often necessary to take into account the fact that the ratios between loads vary with increasing load intensity.

Even in the simplest cases, the factor of safety k obtained by the above method may not have a clear physical meaning. Indeed, let us consider a structure subjected to a dead load G_0 and a live load P_0 (Fig. 6.6). The factor of safety $k' = 1,25$ for the total load is equal to the ratio of the lengths of the OC and OA segments and corresponds to a clearly unrealistic increase in its dead weight by 25%. If we consider the possible increase of loads as for the self-weight, for example, by 10% (i.e., assume $k_g = 1,1$), which corresponds to the transition to the point B, then the live load must increase much more in order to achieve the critical state (point D). Naturally, with such reasoning, a graphic illustration of which is given in Fig. 6.6, a rather modest factor of safety of 1.25 appears in a completely different light, since k_p is much greater than 1,25.

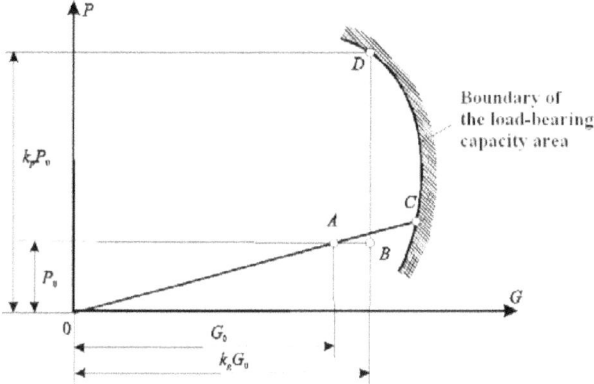

Figure 6.6.

The result will obviously greatly depend on the boundary of the load-bearing capacity area, and in the case of its different configuration all the factors of safety can turn out to be such that the value $k_p P_0$ will be much smaller. However, it is important to note the very fact that the accuracy of the system analysis with the usual interpretation of the factor of safety is insufficient.

If we add to this that the transition to the actual failure state is related to a change in the nature of the structural behavior and the generalized parameters of structural resistance determined in most cases by a simple linear calculation are not just multiplied by a certain coefficient such as the safety factor for material or for load, the conditionality of the very concept of the factor of saefty of type (6.2) becomes obvious. In reality, the redistribution of stresses in the case of nonlinear behavior of the material near the ultimate strength values can drastically change the estimate (6.2).

Thus, it should be stated that there is a certain barrier between the ultimate limit state and the actual failure state, and its value is usually unknown.

Question:
We obviously can not know the value of the real factor of safety for each specific case. However, there are some experimental data and it would be interesting to know at least the order of this value.

Answer:
For most types of modern structures the value of the real factor of safety ranges from 1,3 to 1,8. However, these values vary not only depending on the design, but they have also changed considerably over the past hundred and fifty years.

Engineers immediately understood that the strength properties of materials can have noticeable variability and, in order to ensure the structural safety, they took the value of the allowable stress much (three to four times) less than that determined by material strength tests. This strength, however, usually varies between a few percent, and higher variability is extremely rare. In practive, large differences between calculated and actual strength values are always caused by other reasons.

Modern steel structures designed according to Eurocode-3 have a factor of safety of 1.3-1.45, and reinforced concrete structures designed according to Eurocode-2 have a factor of safety of about 1.5-1.57.

Question:
It was said above that Rankine had defined the factor of safety as the ratio in which the breaking load exceeded the working load. However, this factor is determined in a different way in the formula (6.3). Are these definitions equivalent?

Answer:
They are equivalent for a l inearly deformed system, when the ratio between loads and the ratio between stresses caused by these loads are equal. In reality the breaking load appears only in the inelastic stage, when the structural behavior is nonlinear.

This circumstance is one of the factors that underlie the difference between the conditional and real factors of safety.

It should be noted that there are other definitions of the factor of safety used in the design practice as well. Thus, for example, the Mohr-Coulomb strength theory is often used in soil mechanics. It states that the failure does not occur on a certain plane if the following inequality holds

$$\tau < \sigma \cdot tg\varphi + c, \qquad (6.4)$$

where τ is the shear stress, σ is the normal stress on the considered plane, φ is the angle of internal friction, c is the cohesion. The factor of safety is sometimes defined as a v alue, dividing the soil resistance parameters $tg\varphi$ and c by which would turn (6.4) into an equality. This approach is based on the fact that unlike most structures, where the load variability is much higher than the resistance variability, the most variable factors of soils are their design characteristics. Therefore, when assessing the factor of safety, it is more logical to vary the resistance rather than the load.

Question:
Literature describes numerous cases when the design load value was exceeded significantly, but it did not lead to a failure. What can you say about this?

Answer:
Strength requirements are formulated as a comparison of the loading effect F and the load-bearing capacity R (naturally, expressed in the same units). When analyzing the reliability and finding the probability of inequality $F \le R$, the probabilistic characteristics of the loading effect are usually identified with the probabilistic characteristics of the load. This is fundamentally wrong, although for some reason this error is usually ignored.

A design combination of loads and a design combination of internal reactions of the system (forces, stresses, displacements) are entirely different things, and their probabilities may differ by several orders of magnitude. For example, for the crane load:
- the local pressure in the wall of the crane beam is caused by one crane – the probability is equal to the probability of the maximum wheel pressure;
- the design load for the cross-section of a large-span crane beam is caused by two cranes, and its probability is equal to the probability of simultaneous occurrence of maximum pressures on a wheel of different cranes in combination with the probability of placing the crane wheels in an unfavorable position on the influence line;
- the design vertical load on the column – the same, but it is necessary to consider the case of simultaneous coincidence of the maximum pressure on the wheel from four cranes;
- the design horizontal load on the column – its probability is equal to the probability of placement of two cranes on the influence line, plus the probability of simultaneous braking in one direction of trolleys with the maximum possible load or simultaneous occurrence of lateral forces with the same directions for all four cranes.

Another example is a wind load acting on a tower. The appearance of a design force in a structural element is related here to the random wind direction. Moreover, the wind pressure distribution along the height given in the codes is a certain envelope of the real wind speed and its probability is far from one. It is no wonder that the entire world history of high-rise construction does not know any cases of tower collapse due to the wind load (with the exception of tornado and the combination of wind and ice, and even then it mainly applies to guyed masts).

The combination factors, which are calculated for the "load in general" as well, take into account the mentioned features of the real structural loading only to a very small extent. Neglecting a number of real uncertainties is an additional safety factor for the designed structures, of course.

> The above examples show that if the design load values are exceeded, it does not necessarily mean that the strength conditions are violated.

Another reason for the "beyond design" strength can be the fact that the material strength of a structure has much higher values than the minimum ones given in the codes.

> However, the fact of violation of the limit inequality suggests of the structural conditions which were not anticipated by the designer, and hence not calculated and not analyzed. There are no guarantees of safety is this case.

This is undesirable, even if the accident did not occur. Especially, if we take into account that the value of the above margin is only an estimate, but not a guaranteed fact. Many structures may not even have these margins, especially nowadays with a general decline in the quality of manufacturing, installation and the thoroughness of control of the material properties.

Question:
Is the factor of safety a stable design characteristic?

Answer:
You should keep in mind that the safety factor can vary in time (for example, due to structural wear), and today we usually have to provide a certain given value of the safety factor during the design life T_{ef} which is not related to the variation of this factor in time in any way

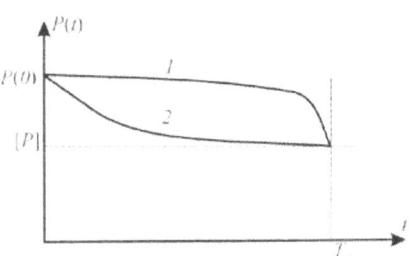

Figure 6.7.

In this case it will turn out that the structures with an actual safety factor $k(t) = P(t)/[P]$ defined by the graph 1 or graph 2 (Fig. 6.7) and satisfying the requirement $k(t) \geq [k]$ over the entire design interval have equal safety, although the structure 1 is more reliable "in general". This fact is not yet taken into account in the modern codes.

Question:
Design codes are including requirements for the nonlinear analysis of the structural behavior. On the other hand, we can limit ourselves to the linear analysis,

but the results can be very different. And which one should be considered correct is not known. Can you comment on this contradiction?

Answer:
The introduction of nonlinear calculations into design practice became possible, on the one hand, due to the intense development of computer technology, and on the other, as a result of the development of software products implementing nonlinear calculation procedures.

The designer encounters a number of contradictions here. The first one (which is not always noticed) is the rule of using safety factors, the values of which are justified today by the linear probabilistic analysis. The criteria for limit state analysis, formulated in terms of limit forces, may not be applicable when there is no proportionality between the actions (loads) on the system and the effects of these actions.

Such problems occur, for example, in a calculation of a geometrically nonlinear system, where internal forces can increase more slowly than the load, or faster. In the first case (it refers to the majority of suspended structures), we are dealing with geometrically strengthening systems, and in the second case these systems are called geometrically degrading.

Let us first consider the case of a geometrically strengthening system (Fig. 6.8,a). Let the external load be a random variable with a unimodal distribution and we are interested in the load variation range $[F_1, F_2]$. The internal force variation range $[S_1, S_2]$ corresponds to it.

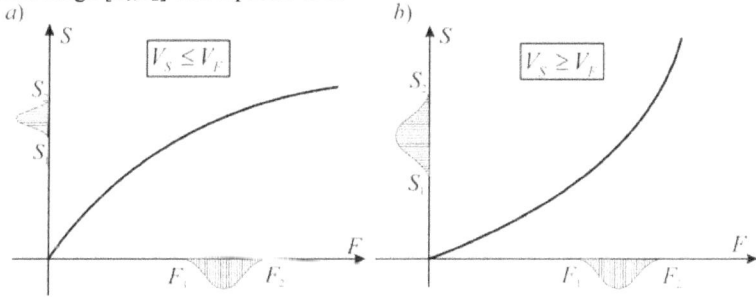

Figure 6.8.

The $[F_1, F_2]$ range is greater than $[S_1, S_2]$, therefore there is the following relationship between the standards of random variables $\tilde{F}$ and $\tilde{S}$: $\sigma_S \leq \sigma_F$. However, the distribution density curves must have equal areas $\tilde{F}$ and $\tilde{S}$, because they correspond to limit values with equal probability. So the mathematical expectations $\overline{S} \geq \overline{F}$. Hence, the chain of inequalities

$$V_S = \frac{\hat{S}}{\overline{S}} \leq \frac{\hat{F}}{\overline{S}} \leq \frac{\hat{F}}{\overline{F}} = V_F$$

Similar reasonings lead to the following inequality for geometrically degrading systems $V_S \geq V_F$.

Therefore, safety factors for load should be reduced for geometrically strengthening systems, and increased for geometrically degrading systems. An alternative recommendation would be to use different values of the special service factor. Unfortunately, design codes do not provide these data.

Does it all mean that we should never use nonlinear analysis? Of course not. Modern practice sometimes demonstrates the application of nonlinear analysis, not to mention the fact that there are a number of structures which simply can not be designed without performing the geometrically nonlinear analysis (cable-stayed roofs, mast structures, etc.).

But in a broader context, nonlinear analysis acts as an auxiliary tool that complements and refines the results of linear calculations. A typical example is presented in [14]. This work describes the techniques of nonlinear behavior analysis of the foundation slab and floor slab elements of the "Federation" tower in the MIBC "Moskva-City" (Fig. 6.9).

Figure 6.9.

The authors indicate that preliminary calculations based on the linear approach were performed first. They helped to determine the peculiarities of the structural behavior and adjust the finite element model. And only then was the behavior of the considered fragments refined to take into account the nonlinear behavior of reinforced concrete. It concerned the verification of deflections and the crack opening width.

Conversation 6.3. Robustness

No protective measures and safety factors can guarantee the *absolute* reliability of all elements of the system. We have to allow for the possibility that some local defects and damages will appear in the structure, the nature of which may be unknown to us. They can be caused by human errors, poor workmanship, rare effects not taken into account in the design etc. in short, all sorts of surprises that lead to significant consequences. These effects are very rare. American economist
Nicolas Nassim Taleb [40] named similar events "black swans"[13]. From the point of view of these surprise events vulnerability of the design object is an important characteristic.

Vulnerability is a parameter characterizing a possibility of causing damages of any nature to the considered system by some external means or factors. Vulnerability is closely related to a well-known characteristic of "robustness" and to an additional characteristic — "mobilization" suggested in [22].

An explicit robustness requirement was first proposed for the draft Ukrainian codes [20] back in 1998, but it was implemented only in 2009 [11] after long debates and bureaucratic red tape.

If the robustness is considered as usual as in a manner spatial characteristic which shows how a local perturbation spreads throughout the space of the system and whether this local destruction can get a disproportionately large development "in breadth", then we will consider a time characteristic as mobilization showing the readiness and ability of the system to react to a local in time (pulse) unexpected perturbation.

Noticeable absence of the structural mobilization, as well as insufficient robustness, should serve as a reason for the increased attention and use of some protective measures described below.

The concept of robustness began to develop in construction much later than in other areas of technology, primarily in earthquake engineering, although the term "robustness" was not always used. In particular, there was an idea of distinguishing the so-called *main load-bearing structures*. Their reliability prevents the building or structure from complete failure under accidental actions, even if it can no longer be used for its intended purpose without major repairs.

In the general case there can be different types of requirements to the state of a structure that has undergone an accidental action:

---

[13] Juvenal said: "rara avis in terris nigroque simillima cygno"(lat.) - a "good man is as rare, as a black swan", since there was a hypothesis that all swans were white. It had been correct until a black Australian swan was discovered in 1700...

- the structure is fully or partially functional after the damage;
- new requirements are imposed on a structure during the response to damage (the structure must not collapse for a certain time, for example, necessary to evacuate people and/or valuable equipment, etc.);
- the repair of the structure is possible and reasonable after the damage.

The robustness condition is formulated depending on the selected requirements. If, for example, the last option is selected, we can assume that the robustness of the structure is provided if the primary failure leads to a destruction only within a limited area with an allowable size regulated by the codes or agreed with the customer in advance.

These requirements are selected depending on the considered accidental situation, when two different strategies are used for specified and unspecified causes of this situation. Both options have to be considered in the general case — the case of an identified accidental action, for example, explosion or impact from a vehicle, or localized failure arising from an unspecified cause such as a human error or poor workmanship (Fig. 6.10).

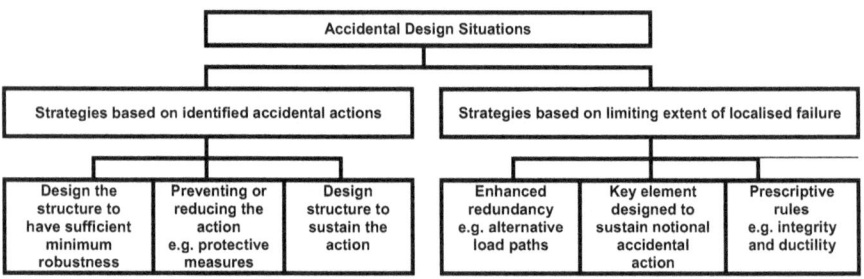

Figure 6.10.

Measures for mitigating the risk of accidental actions are considered and these measures include, as appropriate, one or more of the following strategies:

a) preventing the action from occurring, or reducing the probability and/or magnitude of the action;

b) protecting the structure against the effects of an accidental action by reducing the effects of the action on the structure;

c) ensuring that the structure has sufficient robustness.

The following approaches for limiting the extent of localised failure arising from an unspecified cause are considered:

a) designing key elements to sustain the effects of a model of accidental action;

b) designing the structure so that in the event of a localised failure the stability of the whole structure or of a significant part of it would not be endangered;

c) applying prescriptive design/detailing rules that provide acceptable robustness.

The reaction of a structure to the failure of a certain element in the frame has to be determined in both cases. There are the following possible types of failure of an element in the design model:
- installation defect, when the element is simply not installed or attached so carelessly that it can not be considered as a part of the system from the very beginning;
- relatively slow failure of a stressed element of the model;
- fast failure of a stressed element, which is accompanied by a corresponding dynamic effect caused an outburst of forces at the release of the accumulated elastic potential energy.

The design analysis will be different for each of these cases. In the first case we simply consider a design model without the "failed" element, which was never actually included in the system in the first place.

In the second case it should be taken into account that since the transformed system must not experience any influence of its removed part, the considered operation of removing an element (constraint) essentially consists of two steps:
- making the interaction forces between the removed and remaining parts of the system equal to zero;
- modifying the design model.

Finally, in the third case it is usually assumed that the constraint is removed instantly, then the system reacts to it as to a suddenly-applied load equal to the reaction of the constraint at the moment of its removal and opposite in direction. In accordance with the 2nd Newton's law an acceleration jump occurs, while the velocities and displacements remain continuous, and the system begins to oscillate freely.

The difference in the response of a system to gradual or sudden removal of an element (constraint) can be quite significant and the dynamic effects must be taken into account. It was shown in a number of studies that danger comes not only from the instant removal of an element (node, section), but from the resulting dynamic effect on the remaining elements.

A dynamic analysis is actually required here, but an approximate quasi-static analysis based on energy considerations is often used, the essence of which lies in the following reasoning [5].

Suppose that stresses and strains in the failing element of the initial n times statically indeterminate system were equal to $\sigma_n^s, \varepsilon_n^s$ respectively, and in the case of a modified n-1 times statically indeterminate system they became $\sigma_{n-1}^s, \varepsilon_{n-1}^s$. These values can be found by the usual static analysis, but we are interested in the dynamic values $\sigma_{n-1}^d, \varepsilon_{n-1}^d$. The level of potential strain energy at the point of static equilibrium is determined by the following expression

$$U(\varepsilon_n^s) = \int_0^{\varepsilon_n^s} \sigma(\varepsilon) d\varepsilon,$$

and the specific work of external forces is determined by the product of σ_{n-1}^{s} and the corresponding strain increment.

The condition of constant total specific energy of the system leads to the following expression

$$U\left(\varepsilon_{n-1}^{d}\right) - U\left(\varepsilon_{n}^{s}\right) = \sigma_{n-1}^{s} \cdot \left(\varepsilon_{n-1}^{d} - \varepsilon_{n}^{s}\right),$$

that means the equality of the areas of the curvilinear trapezoid $AacC$ and the rectangle $AkdC$ in Fig. 6.11. Hence the strain ε_{n-1}^{d} can be found from the equality condition of areas of the darkened triangles akb and bdc. The following relationships are obtained for the linear elastic system

$$\varepsilon_{n-1}^{d} - \varepsilon_{n-1}^{s} = \varepsilon_{n-1}^{s} - \varepsilon_{n}^{s}; \quad \sigma_{n-1}^{d} = 2\sigma_{n-1}^{s} - \sigma_{n}^{s}.$$

Thus, it turned out that the reaction of the removed constraint is applied to the transformed system with a dynamic factor of 2,0. This factor is somewhat reduced for the linear elastic system.

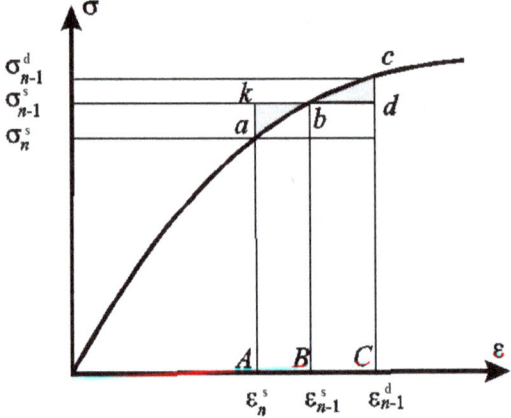

Figure 6.11.

It was essentially assumed that the strain of the system at its maximum displacement coincides with the static form of equilibrium once the constraint is disabled. This assumption is valid only for a system with one degree of freedom, but is not true in the general case. The correct solution can be obtained only by the dynamic analysis of the system with a removed constraint.

Removing a constraint excites free oscillations in it which are determined by the initial conditions, i.e. the elastic displacements of the intact system and zero velocities.

Question:
Recently, the issue of progressive structural collapse has been widely discussed. How is this problem related to the robustness?

Answer:
The term "progressive collapse" appeared as a result of the literal translation of the unsuccessful English term. Indeed, any failure from brittle to fatigue and corrosive is a time-evolving process, i.e. progressive, which means that there is no such thing as "non-progressive" collapse.

The progressive (avalanche-like) collapse is usually defined as the sequential (chain) failure of the bearing structures and bases, leading to the collapse of the entire structure or its parts due to its initial local damage.

We are basically dealing with the analysis of the structural behavior after the local damage, and this is the problem of structural robustness. Thus, the problem of the so-called progressive collapse is in fact nothing else but a particular criterion of the particular formulation of the robustness problem.

> *You should, however, keep in mind that the robustness is a property of the system, and the progressive collapse is a characteristic of the process. But you should not equalize a process characteristic which is dangerous in the case of failure (for example, the "domino" effect) with undesirable consequences of an accident (for example, significant economic damage from the final collapse value).*

The following mistake is often made in the formulation of the problem: a relationship between the damage and the characteristics of the structural response to the damage is considered instead of the relationship between the damage and the ability of the damaged structure to perform its intended function. A typical example is a local damage of a tank wall, resulting in a complete failure of the tank (it can not be used to store liquid), although there was no avalanche-like collapse.

> *Hence, the progressive collapse is only one type of undesirable structural response to local failure.*

Question:
It was mentioned that in the general case the effect of the constraint removal should not be analyzed by the quasi-static method using the dynamic factor. Is there a big difference between such a quasi-static approach and the results of dynamic analysis?

Answer:
This difference can be quite significant and it is related to the reasoning used for a system with one degree of freedom

when justifying the quasi-static method.
It was assumed that the dynamic displacements are always proportional to the static ones during the oscillations. But even if it is true at the initial time, it will not necessarily be true later.

In particular, it concerns the elements with strains drastically different from the static form of equilibrium after the constraint is disabled; the error can reach tens of percents. For example, Table 6.1 provides the comparison of the forces appearing after the sudden removal of the element 6-12 of the truss, the model of which is shown in Fig. 6.12.

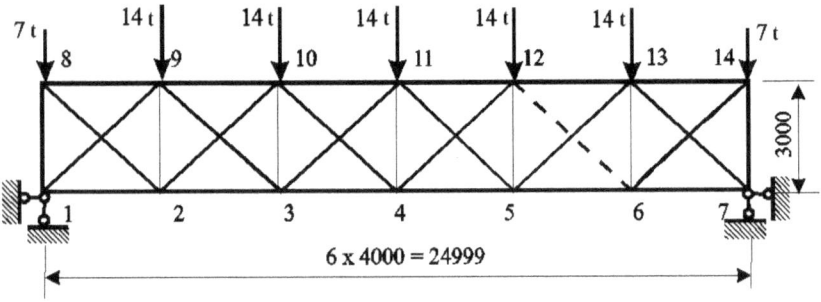

Figure 6.12.

Table 6.1

Element be-tween nodes	Forces (t), obtained by:		Difference, %
	a quasi-static analysis	a dynamic analysis	
1-2	-20,13	-36,21	78
2-3	13,50	11,18	-17
3-4	31,74	34,86	10
4-5	39,30	35,03	-11
5-6	-50,65	-20,29	-60
6-7	-13,56	-30,66	126
4-10	-2,14	-7,88	269
3-10	2,88	7,39	156
7-13	-50,51	-58,02	15
12-13	-118,00	-94,54	-20

Conversation 6.4. Bearing Capacity Analysis According to Design Codes

It has already been mentioned that in addition to clear rules of structural mechanics design codes provide additional recommendations and requirements which are often not explicitly formulated and in some cases contradictory. This leads to a number of unexpected results, in particular, to the appearance of a non-convex load-bearing capacity area.

> *It should be noted that it is the convexity of the load-bearing capacity area that allows us to limit ourselves only to checks of extreme combinations of loads, because the positive result of such checks automatically means that all other conceivable combinations of loads are acceptable.*

The absence of the convexity property of the considered area can lead to many undesirable consequences related to the fact that, traditionally, evaluating unfavorable combinations of internal forces, engineers either do not consider some actions at all, or take them fully into account. For a nonconvex area, however, a combination with intermediate (not extreme) values of internal forces can turn out to be an unfavorable one.

It is easy to see that the following situation can occur (Fig. 6.13): the standard requirements are met when two independent loads P and Q are considered separately, or their total sum $(P+Q)$ is considered, and they are violated if you consider an "incomplete" combination $(P+\lambda Q)$ where $\lambda < 1$.

There is a firm belief that the load-bearing capacity area is convex, which is based on the following theories:
- according to Drucker's postulate, the boundary yield surface is convex in the space of internal forces for an ideal elastic-plastic system [13, p. 366];
- according to the Papkovich theorem, the stability area is convex in the space of loads acting on the system [19, p. 85].

Although these theories are obviously true, they, unfortunately, do not correspond to the properties of the above-mentioned load-bearing capacity area, which is entirely defined by the codes. Neither the classic theory of plasticity, for which Drucker's postulate is valid, nor the bifurcation (Euler's) theory of equilibrium stability, for which the Papkovich theorem is proved, is used in the codes.

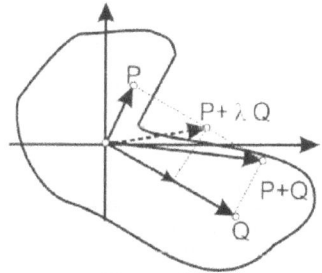

Figure 6.13

Moreover, when generating the load-bearing capacity area, it is also necessary to consider other code requirements (strength, stability, limit slenderness, crack resistance), which leads us far beyond the validity of the above-mentioned theories. Therefore, the area in the space of internal forces, the points of which correspond to a combination of these forces which satisfies all the code requirements is somewhat narrower than the area defined only by the strength and stability conditions. But we will still call it a load-bearing capacity area.

ARBAT, KRISTALL and DÉCOR programs of the SCAD Office package enable to generate load-bearing capacity areas for sections of bar elements of reinforced concrete, steel and timber structures, respectively.

Let us demonstrate by examples that in the case of a standard approach there can be nonconvex load-bearing capacity areas.

SP 63.13330.2012-Reinforced Concrete Structures

The load-bearing capacity area is shown in Fig. 6.14. Two types of crack resistance requirements of the codes have been considered. In this case there are two reasons for nonconvexity.

The jump AB, which is typical for all cases, is defined by the postulate of the theory of reinforced concrete, which provides for the immediate exclusion from the operation of the tension area of concrete when tensile stresses appear in it.

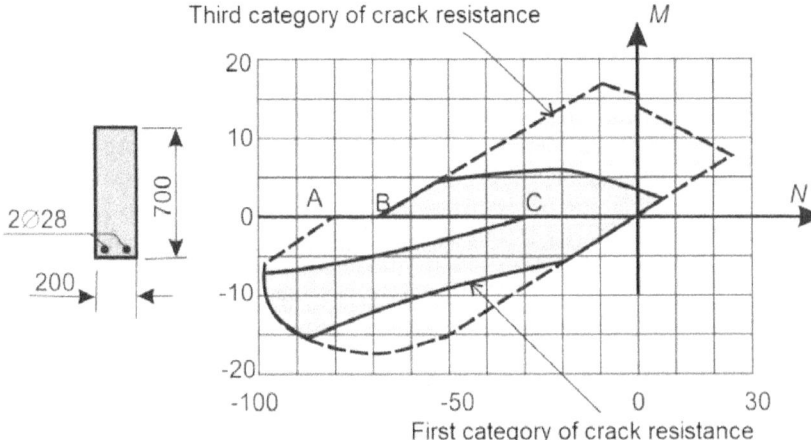

Figure 6.14.

The BC jump at the transition from the third category of crack resistance to the first one is more complicated. In this case, the load-bearing capacity area sharply narrows, which is quite expected and, moreover, it acquires a very sophisticated shape, due to a new method of checking reinforced concrete elements for crack resistance, which appeared in the 2003 edition of SNiP.

Old SNiP 2.03.01-84 did not lead to such effects, the BC jump did not occur there.

Steel Structures (SP 16.13330.2011)

Let us consider a cross-section in the form of a symmetric welded I-beam with a 400×10 mm web and 200×10 mm flanges made of steel with the design strength $R_y = 2050$ kg/cm². The effective length of the bar in both principal planes is 600 cm, the service factor and the importance factor are taken as $\gamma_c = 1,0$ and $\gamma_n = 1,0$.

The boundary of the load-bearing capacity area on the DEFGH section is defined by the strength condition under the combined action of tension and bending, on the CD and IH sections – by the condition of stability of in-plane bending, and on the IKABC section – by the condition of stability out of the bending moment plane (Fig. 6.15).

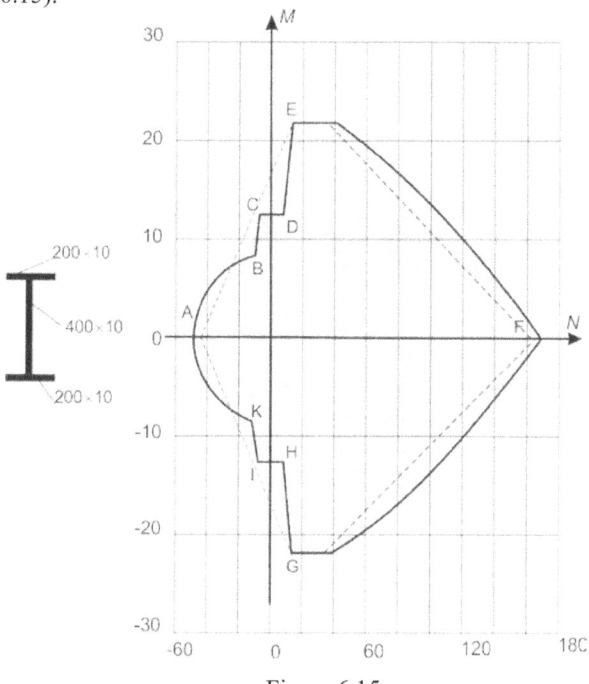

Figure 6.15

The non-convexity of the boundary on the IKABC section is related to the change in the type of the relationship between the coefficient c and the value of the relative eccentricity m. This coefficient is included in the condition for checking the stability out of the plane of bending of a bar under bending and compression, and is calculated according to the formulas (112) - (114) of SP 16.13330.2011.

The graphs $c = c(m)$ for three values of the length of the considered bar is given in Fig. 6.16. A characteristic break at the value $m = 10$, where the function $c = c(m)$ changes from a linear to a hyperbolic one corresponds to the points K and B in Fig. 6.15.

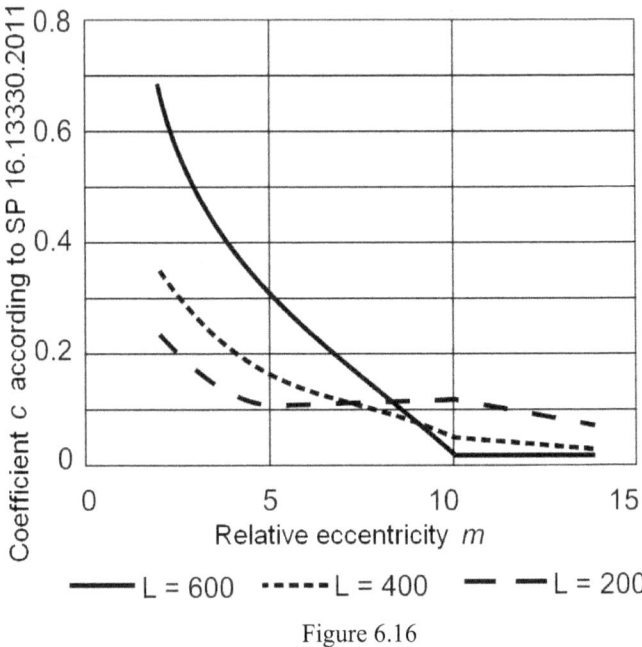

Figure 6.16

The nonconvexity of this section does not appear when the element has small out-of-plane slenderness, in spite of the fact that the break in the curve $c = c(m)$ does not disappear, but for such design cases the condition of stability out of the bending moment plane is not determinative.

The configuration of the CDE and IHG sections is determined by the codes specifying that the stability of in-plane bending should be checked only at the values of the relative eccentricity $m > 20$. DC and JK rays in Fig. 6.15 correspond to this value of m, the fatality of which is difficult to understand.

The dashed line in Fig. 6.15 shows the load-bearing capacity area calculated according to the requirements of EUROCODE-3. This is not the place to discuss the methods adopted in EUROCODE, but the fact that the allowable area is convex speaks for itself.

SP 64.13330.2011 - Timber Structures

Let us consider a 3 m long pine bar with a rectangular cross-section 500×80 mm. The load-bearing capacity area is shown in Fig. 6.17.

The jump at the transition from the area $N > 0$ to the area $N \leq 0$ is defined by the formulations of Sec. 6.14 and 6.20 of the codes, which provide the stability check requirements only for elements under bending or under bending and compression. The codes do not consider this check for bar elements under tension and bending.

However, it is obvious that if the tensile force values are very small, this check must be performed. In this case, the boundary of the load-bearing capacity area of the section would pass along the dotted curve in Fig. 6.16.

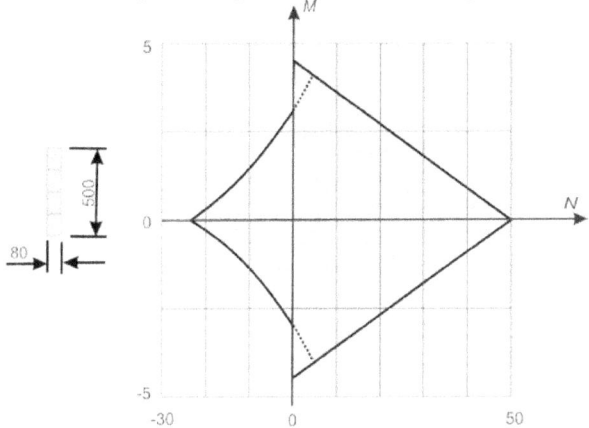

Figure 6.17.

Much of the above is related to the insufficient adjustment of standard requirements, which were often developed on the principle of precedent, when detected particular effects were turned into general standard requirements without proper verification.

The traditional approach based on the manual calculation generated all sorts of "simplifications", which allowed to skip some checks in the case of a certain qualitative attribute (as for timber elements under bending and compression) or a limit value of a parameter (as at $m < 20$ for steel elements under bending and compression). This led to inconsistencies in different checks. Modern technologies enable to detect such inaccuracies.

You should, however, take into account the following differences from the manual calculation:
- many intermediate results allowing to notice the existing inconsistencies are not available to the engineer;
- the computer program cannot respond to considerations like "this case is not typical"; it works in the entire physically acceptable range of calculation parameters.

These are the reasons for increased requirements for the recommendations of the codes that should avoid unreasonable "simplifications".

Question:

Codes mention only the checks of bar structural elements. And we know how to determine the stress-strain state of 2D and 3D structures as well, but the codes do not provide any means for verifying the allowability of the obtained structural behavior. Can you comment on this?

Answer:

The problem is that the analysis should concern the load-bearing capacity of the entire structure rather than the stress-strain state in its particular points. There are established criteria for analyzing cross-sections of bar systems, and the violation of strength conditions is interpreted as a failure of a bar.

It indicates a loss of load-bearing capacity for a statically determinate system. But for statically indeterminate systems, which do not even fail when an element is removed, this condition is also interpreted as a limit one: in any case, it indicates a serious violation of the assumptions used in the calculation.

And what happens, for example, in the analysis of plates? Here, knowing the bending moments and torques in the plate, we can easily determine the normal and tangential stresses in the outermost layer and compare them with the strength conditions of the material. But then we can only say that the fracture of the plate will not start until the strength conditions are violated at least at one point. This may serve as an estimate, but the quality of this super-careful estimate may turn out to be very low. Indeed, the beginning of fracture does not always mean the exhaustion of the load-bearing capacity of the plate, since the failure of its part does not usually lead to the collapse of the entire plate.

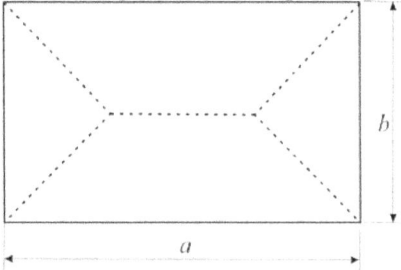

Figure 6.18.

At the same time, you should keep in mind the following peculiarity of brittle fracture: the first cracks, which appear at the most stressed points, quickly propagate in random directions to the underloaded areas and lead to the collapse of the entire sample or plate. Therefore, it is advisable to verify the strength condition at least at one point of a brittle elastic plate.

In the case of materials with plastic properties, it is necessary to consider the limit equilibrium state, when sufficient plastic hinges are formed to turn the structure into a mechanism. Thus, the calculation of rectangular slabs with supports on all four sides and the ratio of the larger span to the smaller one $a/b<3$ is based on a limit state characterized by the formation of linear plastic hinges shown in Fig. 6.18 [3]. For a slab with a ratio $a/b=1,6$ and thickness h the limit value of the uniformly distributed load which causes this state is

$$q_{\lim} = 4,056 \frac{\sigma_T h^2}{b^2},$$

where σ_T is the yield strength of the slab material. The stresses reach the yield point in the surface layers of an elastic slab of the same size under the following load

$$q_{\lim} = 1,938 \frac{\sigma_T h^2}{b^2}.$$

An almost double margin of safety is rather typical, although there are examples where this margin is significantly smaller.

Due to a psychological misunderstanding some designers try to alleviate the detected local overstresses by increasing the load-bearing capacity of the respective parts of the structure. Forgetting that the finite element analysis is performed for a continual system, they begin to treat the finite-dimensional design model as a certain structure consisting of structural members corresponding to the finite elements. And then, by analogy with the bar system, they begin to strengthen the members of this non-existent structure.

Conversation 6.5. Design Calculations and Optimal Design

The real purpose of designing is to select such a design, which is the most efficient (optimal) in terms of a certain accepted criterion used to evaluate the quality indicators of the structure. This means that in the general case the task is to minimize the objective function $f(\mathbf{X})$ throughout the set of allowable values of the unknown vector of variables $\mathbf{X}$, the components of which are the sought-for parameters of the system.

The allowable value itself is determined by a certain set of equations and inequalities that should be satisfied by the components of the vector $\mathbf{X}$. In other words, we are dealing with a constrained extremum problem (a problem of mathematical programming):

$$f(\mathbf{X}) \to \min$$
$$g_i(\mathbf{X}) = 0 \quad (i = 1,...,n);$$
$$g_i(\mathbf{X}) \leq 0 \quad (i = n+1,...,m).$$

The origin of constrained and unconstrained extremum problems in construction design is related to three sources:
- laws of nature, which are often formulated as extreme (variational) principles;
- caution that forces to consider the worst (extreme) possible conditions of the designed structure;
- the desire to obtain the best possible result.

The implementation of the latter aspiration is the essence of the optimal design problems.

The optimal structural design problems have long attracted the attention of researchers. Their active study began in the second half of the 20th century due to the achievements in the theory of decision-making and the theory of operations research, and also due to the widespread use of computer technology. This allowed to develop the appropriate methods, to calculate numerous options and solve complex mathematical problems in the foreseeable time. At present, the optimal design theory is an important and developing branch of solid mechanics. There are many hundreds of publications in this field, and this number is constantly growing. As stated in [39] "The ethics of our profession today does not allow any design for a structure without optimization".

> *It would seem that everything is fine, but a natural question arises: why is it that in over fifty years the optimal design method has not become an ordinary design tool, like, for example, the finite element method that appeared even a little later?*

It should be noted that such questions have been asked before. This problem, for example, is considered in [33] in the chapter titled "Why Were Practical Engineers Reluctant to Adopt Structural Optimization?". Answering this question, the authors present four groups of arguments:

- Why should we look for the best design if an acceptable, hence, a good one can be found?
- There are very few applications and the optimal solutions are not sufficiently realistic.
- The thesis that a process of optimization against buckling leads almost inevitably to designs which are very sensitive to initial imperfections.
- Optimum structures obtained through deterministic optimization do not necessarily have high reliability.

These arguments were made for aircraft engineering. If we consider building structures, the emphasis may shift, but the arguments will not disappear.

We will at once reject arguments claiming that the optimization problems are too difficult to solve. Modern computer technologies allow to eliminate these difficulties and to obtain the solutions of reasonably formulated problems of optimal design.

Due to the analysis of the current situation with the introduction of the optimization method it is useful to consider the question of whether the optimization is effective. Comparison of optimal designs with the experience based ones rarely shows savings greater than a few percent. If the author of a certain publication indicates a more significant result, then most likely the "common" designs that have been selected for comparison are not the best ones.

However, there are some exceptions. Thus, it is almost obvious that there are three main areas for the effective application of the optimal structural design:

a) Designing fundamentally new types of structures or structures intended for operation in unusual conditions, when you can not rely on the previous experience and obtaining an optimal design even if some conditions are not taken completely into account can serve as a good start for a real design. The design of an offshore ice-resistant oil platform can serve as an example here (Fig. 6.19).

Figure 6.19.

b) Improvement of serial structures when even insignificant savings have a great effect due to multiple repetitions.

c) Designing structures of very high unit cost, where a small weight reduction covers all the costs of finding the optimal design even when the optimization effect is relatively small.

It is easy to see that the mentioned directions of application of optimization approaches do not apply to mass construction, and it is difficult to count on the transformation of rigorous optimization methods into the common design tools. The "down to earth" building structures are commonly designed with the help of the approach based on the iterative recalculation of a structure which sets goals of providing faultlessness, technological and operational efficiency, sometimes accompanied by the idea of finding a structure of uniform strength or creating a structure which is rational in some other way.

It should be noted that all sorts of target refinement does not always significantly affect the result, therefore we will consider a very interesting remark made in the book by E. Haug and J. Arora [27] regarding the reaction of an engineer and a mathematician to the result of optimization. As an illustration, consider the well-known problem of the optimum height of a steel I-beam. It is shown that a change in the optimum height h_{opt} by 20% in a certain direction leads to an increase in the mass of its running meter by only 3...4%. That is, from the point of view of mathematics, the residual is measured on the h axis and, therefore, points $0.8h_{opt}$ and $1.2h_{opt}$ are considered as a very rough approximation because of their considerable distance from the global minimum of the objective function (Fig. 6.20)

And from the engineering point of view the deviation from the global minimum of the objective function can be considered a good approximation to the optimal design and, since the obtained result is quite acceptable, "the designer should not miss this opportunity when selecting a design" [27, p. 99].

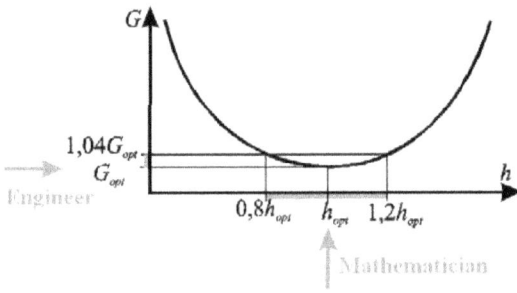

Figure 6.20.

This idea was apparently first expressed and considered by V.N. Gordeev, who suggested to seek for the entire set of solutions adjacent to the point of extremum and to analyze it in more detail, instead of finding only this point [10, 29]. Since the majority of real optimization problems have a "smooth extremum", i.e. even a noticeable deviation from the ideal solution does not significantly change the value of the objective function, this makes it possible to take into account additional conditions that are difficult to formalize (for example, the discreteness of certain parameters) staying within the set of solutions which are close to optimal.

The concept of uniform strength was introduced in 1638 by Galileo Galilei who determined the form of a beam of uniform strength. He considered the bending of a cantilever beam (with a rectangular cross-section of constant width and variable height) loaded with a point load at the end of the cantilever. Galileo proved that the ultimate limit state is reached at every cross-section when this beam has a longitudinal form of a quadratic parabola. As it turned out later the problem of the form of a minimum weight beam is reduced to the problem solved by Galileo Galilei, provided that the normal stresses do not exceed a given value of σ_0. Thus, a cantilever beam of uniform strength is also a beam of minimum weight. Other examples have been found as well when the condition of uniform strength provides the minimum weight of the structure.

This circumstance has largely determined the interest in finding structures of uniform strength, a problem that makes sense in the case of a single loading. If we are dealing with a structure designed to withstand several different load cases, the problem of uniform strength was generalized and formulated as a problem of a fully stressed structure all the elements of which work at the ultimate stress level at least under one of the possible load combinations.

However, further studies have shown that the concepts of uniform strength (as well as full stress) and optimal weight do not always coincide.

It is obviously not a problem to find a design of uniform strength for a statically determinate system, because changing the sections does not affect the distribution of forces in the structural elements. And is it possible to select such sections for a statically indeterminate system, so that the stresses in all its elements are equal to the given value? It turns out that this problem can not be solved in the general case.

For example, it was established by Maurice Levy back in 1873 that an optimal truss degenerates into a statically determinate one, and his theorem states:

> *In the case of one loading, among all possible trusses the configuration of which is defined by a certain set of bars connecting specified nodes and having given supports there is a statically determinate truss with minimum weight.*

Indeed, if we consider a statically determinate main system obtained from the given one by removing the redundant constraints and select the sections for the main system, we will thus determine the end displacements for the removed "redundant" constraints, and hence their strains. Consequently, no selection of sections in these bars can result in the desired predetermined values of stresses (and hence strains). This sets the search limit in this direction.

> *The maximum that can be achieved when seeking for a system with predetermined stresses is to select the desired sections in a statically determinate main system and to ensure that the stresses in the redundant bars are less than the given value* [24].

A statically indeterminate truss of minimum weight can be created only in exceptional cases, unlike the structures the elements of which experience a non-uniform stress. Such structures can always be designed to have uniform strength if we vary the cross-sectional shape of the elements [6]. However, these structures can turn out to be quite peculiar.

An example of designing a portal frame with unknown cross-sectional dimensions and the orientation of its principal axes is shown in Fig. 6.21 (a – the frame, b – the cross-section, c – the solution). If we decide not to determine the cross-sectional rotation angle, assuming that the direction of the principal axes is fixed, we can find the design of uniform strength which turns out to be 23,4% heavier. The fixation of certain structural parameters generally makes the system heavier, and there is a vast field for compromises between the desire to minimize the material consumption and to simplify the design.

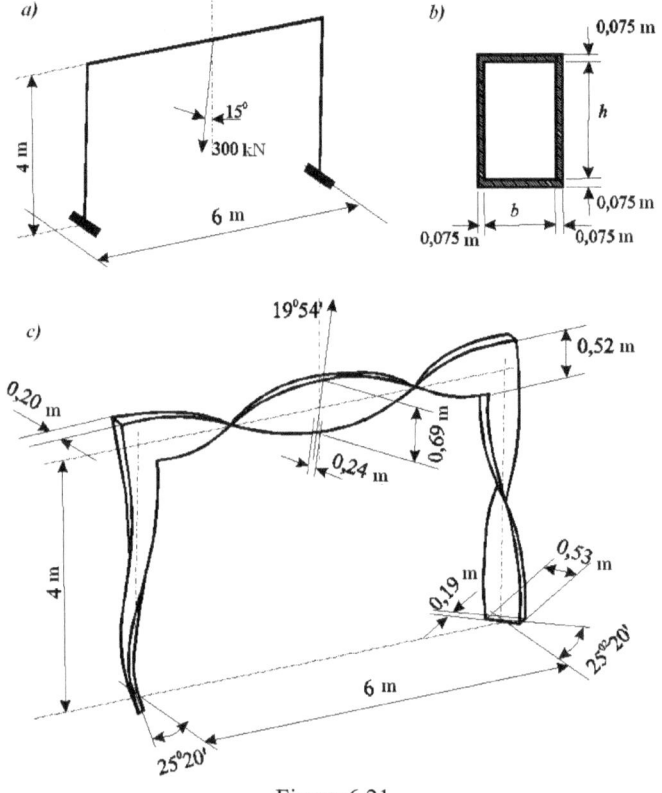

Figure 6.21.

The transition to a design estimation based on economic indicators sometimes leads to the resolution of the above compromise, but there may be a problem of comparing expenses for different time periods here. For example, when evaluating the effectiveness of an investment project, the comparison of different indicators of the initial cost and current expenses is carried out by discounting them to one point in time. The discount rate (E), equal to the acceptable rate of return on equity, is used to reduce the expenses for different time periods, results and effects . The latter are multiplied by the discount factor $\alpha_t=1/(1+E)^t$ for discounting. But if the investor has transferred the structure to another economic entity that will bear operating costs, then an acceptable value of E may be different for them.

For example, how can an owner of the purchased apartment come to terms with the fact that he has to pay a lot for heating, because the investor did not provide the effective thermal insulation and thus saved on construction costs. The investor can use the savings as capital and receive income from them, but the actual user and the owner has no relation to these incomes. It is obviously necessary to formulate the terms of a certain compromise, but as far as we know this problem does not yet have an exact formulation.

It should also be noted that the discount rates for individual periods remain practically the same or change insignificantly in a stable market economy. However, we have a completely different situation in the case of inflation, stagnation, financial crisis, etc. Then the banks change the bank interest rate on the invested capital, and the discount rates follow, i.e. they are subject to change.

However, the studies in the field of optimal design are not limited to pragmatic considerations. An optimal design can be useful, because in real life designing it can serve:
- as a benchmark for evaluating a real design;
- as a guideline, when real-life designing is considered as a step-by-step process of moving away from an ideal design in order to fulfill the requirements not taken into account in the optimal design.

It should be noted that in the works on the optimization of building structures the main parameters defining the design purpose and utilization are assumed to be given and, as a rule, are not subject to revision.

However, it is sometimes useful to break this tradition and consider a broader formulation of the optimal design problem, when the problem of optimizing the parameters of the technological process is considered together with the problem of optimizing the design of a building or structure, where this process takes place. [41] is one of the few examples of this approach. It considers the problem of optimal design of a wind energy converter (Fig. 6.22), when the design variables included not only the tower design parameters (geometry D, d and wall thickness t), but also the main performance characteristics (its design capacity W, hub height H and the wind wheel radius R).

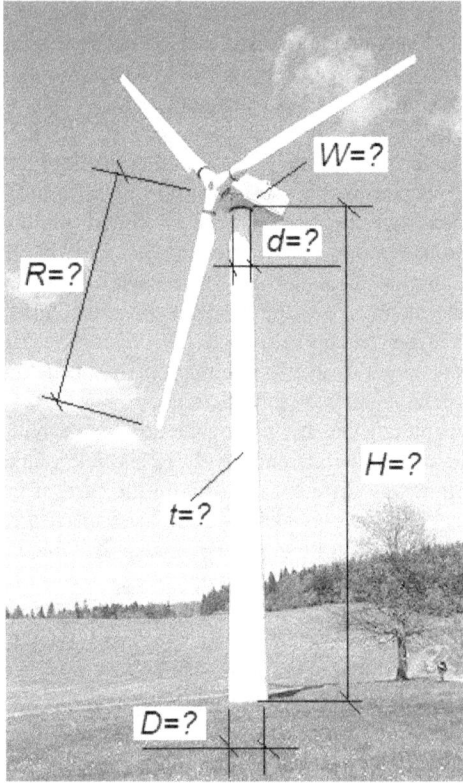

Figure 6.22.

We can easily extend the classic Shukhov problem on the optimal tank for petroleum products, assuming that the tank volume is variable and taking into account the loss of petroleum products from small and large breaths, the accident possible damage and other technical and economic indicators depending on the tank volume.

The studies aimed at the analysis of certain rules and methods for selecting designs, which are believed to lead to optimal (or more accurately, rational) designs seem to be quite important. Thus, for example, a study of a well-known concept indicating the economic feasibility of the continuous growth of the unit capacity of industrial facilities (for structures, the principle of material concentration in the main structures) was performed in [22]. It turned out that if we take into account the restrictions defined by the safety conditions, then this concept has a limited applicability, which is of fundamental importance.

The thing is that the growth of unit capacity of machines, equipment, structures and facilities is usually not accompanied by the same increase in their reliability, and this can lead to large-scale losses, such as, for example, in the case of the Chernobyl disaster.

We would also like to point out that there is a certain connection between the principle of material concentration in the structure and the robustness problem. Indeed, it follows from the principle of concentration that there are strong structural elements the failure of which is most likely related to the general collapse of a building or structure. However, no increase in the factor of safety of such key elements can provide zero probability of their failure, for example, due to gross errors or other human factors, which are the most common causes of accidents and disasters. But it means that the problem of ensuring robustness for the structures of this type can be aggravated.

Question:

The design of statically indeterminate structures is usually performed as an iterative process where sections of the elements are first specified, then the structural analysis is performed and the stresses are checked. If the latter turn out to be too high or too low, new sections are selected and the analysis is performed again. And what can you say about the iteration convergence?

Answer:

There is no proof of the convergence of this iterative process, but there are no examples of divergent iterations or their looping in the design practice as well, although there were cases when the number of iterations was not small. But we are more interested in the solution obtained by these iterations.

First of all, it should be noted that at each stage of the iterative process we operate with a certain distribution of internal forces, found as a result of the calculation of the considered system, and, therefore, satisfying equilibrium conditions. In other words, the solution is found within a set of equilibrium (statically allowable) systems. While the conditions of compatibility of deformations which are left unobserved during the iterations turn out to be violated, because the deformations of the elements of the system with sections selected based on the strength condition are different.

When it comes to the result of the iterative process, three characteristic examples are given in [4], indicating the possible outcome of the iterations, where fully stressed sections are selected at each stage (Fig. 6.23).

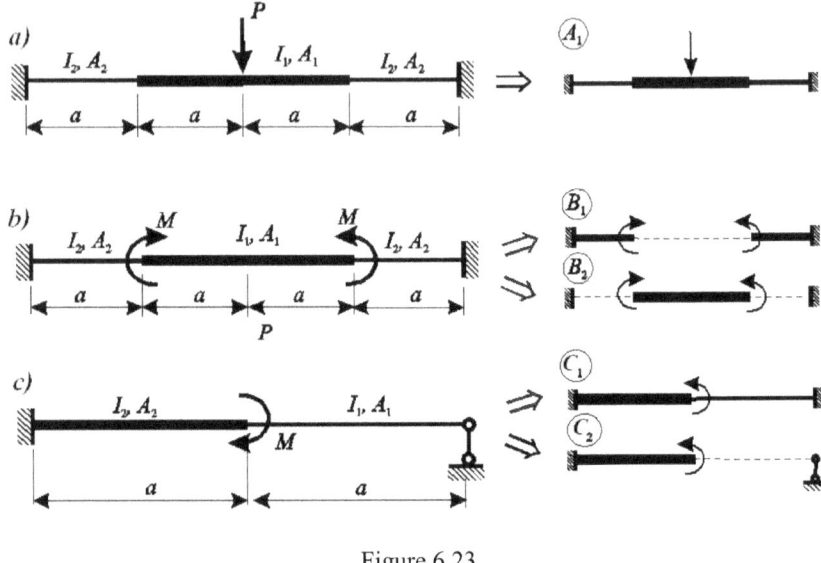

Figure 6.23

In the case of the problem shown in the Figure 6.23.a the iterative process converges to a uniform strength design A_1, which is also a minimum weight design.

The result of the iterative process for the problem shown in Fig. 6.23.b depends on the initial state. If at the beginning we have $I_2 > I_1$, then we obtain the design B_1 with two cantilevers and a degenerate middle segment, otherwise the iterations converge to a degenerate design B_2, where a middle beam is subjected to balanced moments. One of these designs corresponds to a minimum weight system.

Finally in the case of the problem 6.23.c iterations also converge to various uniform strength designs depending on the initial distribution of rigidities, but only the design C_2 is also a minimum weight system.

It should be noted that the iterative process can be completed when the change in cross sections no longer has a significant effect on the change in internal forces in the system. The estimate obtained in [20] for the increment ΔS_k of internal forces S_k $(k=1,...,m)$ can be useful here, which can be written as an inequality for trusses

$$\max_r |\Delta S_r| \le \sqrt{\sum_{k=1}^{m} S_k^2 \left(\frac{\Delta A_k}{A_k} - \alpha \right)}, \text{ where } \alpha = \sum_{i=1}^{m} \left(S_i^2 \frac{\Delta A_i}{A_i} \right) \Bigg/ \sum_{j=1}^{m} S_j^2 .$$

Here A_k and ΔA_k $(k=1,...,m)$ are cross-sectional areas of truss bars and their increments.

It should also be noted that if the selection of sections affects the load, the divergence of iterations can take place. A similar remark applies to problems where the load is formed by the oncoming flow of liquid or gas, when the selected structural shape can affect the distribution of external actions and their intensity. Thus, when external forces that define the parameters of the design, in turn, depend on this design, feedback takes place, and effects similar to the loss of equilibrium stability can be observed in the problems with feedback.

There is, for example, a formal analogy between the problem of the dead weight effect on the theoretical volume of a bar with given stresses and the problem of the stability of an elastic system, which can be easily demonstrated with the simplest example of a constant-section beam.

If A is the cross-sectional area, and $W = \rho A$ is the moment of inertia (the factor ρ is defined by the shape of the cross-section), then the following condition can be written for the given value of the allowable stress σ

$$A = \frac{W}{\rho} = \frac{(q+\gamma A)L^2}{8\sigma\rho}; \quad A = \frac{q}{8\sigma\rho - \gamma L^2}.$$

Here q is the load acting on a beam, γ is the specific weight of the material of the beam, L is its span. It is easy to see that when $L = \sqrt{8\sigma\rho/\gamma}$ the cross-sectional area becomes infinitely large and the "self-buckling" occurs.

We can also consider a more general problem, where we will proceed from the system of equations of the displacement method (see Conversation 1.6)

$$\mathbf{QFQ^T u = p + q},$$

where $\mathbf{Q}$ is the rectangular matrix of equilibrium equations; $\mathbf{F}$ is the internal stiffness matrix; $\mathbf{u}$ is the nodal displacement vector; $\mathbf{p}$ is the external nodal load vector; $\mathbf{q}$ is the dead weight nodal load vector.

Let us express the vector $\mathbf{q}$ in terms of the parameters of the system

$$\mathbf{q} = \frac{\rho\gamma}{2}\mathbf{CL}a,$$

where $\mathbf{C}$ is the cosine matrix relating the orientation of the bar and direction of the dead weight load; $\mathbf{L}$ is the diagonal bar length matrix; a is the cross-sectional area vector; γ is the specific weight of the structural material; ρ is the scale factor which enables to proportionally change the length of all the bars (adjust structural dimensions).

If we assume that all the bars have the same stress σ, then the cross-sectional areas must be equal to

$$a = \sigma^{-1}\mathbf{N},$$

where $\mathbf{N}$ is the vector of longitudinal forces in bars. These forces can be expressed in terms of the deformations $\Delta = \mathbf{Q^T u}$ and if E is the elastic modulus, they will be determined by the formula

$$\mathbf{N} = E \cdot \mathbf{CL^{-1}C^T u}.$$

Then the dead load vector can be given as

$$\mathbf{q} = \rho\frac{E\gamma}{2\sigma}\mathbf{CLQL^{-1}C^T u}.$$

The stiffness matrix of the system:

$$QFQ^T = EQL^{-1}aQ^T$$

And after substituting the expressions for the stiffness matrix and the vector **q** into the equations of the displacement method, we obtain

$$QL^{-1}aQ^T u = \rho \frac{\gamma}{2\sigma} CLaL^{-1}Q^T u + p.$$

If the system is loaded only with its own weight, i.e. $\{P\}=0$, then we have an eigenvalue problem with respect to the scale factor ρ

$$\left(QL^{-1}aQ^T - \rho \frac{\gamma}{2\sigma} CLaL^{-1}Q^T\right) u = 0.$$

If the structural dimensions exceed the critical value ρ, the "self-buckling" can occur.

Question:

The term "inverse problem of structural mechanics" is sometimes used in the literature. Is this formulation just another name for the optimization problem?

Answer:

It is not so in the general case, because it even might not be a goal to achieve the best design or to obtain an extreme property for the considered system when solving the inverse problems of structural mechanics.

Let us consider this in more detail.

The stress-strain state of a system (for the sake of simplicity, we will consider only bar structures), the determination of which is the direct problem of structural mechanics, can be found if we know:
- the topology and geometric dimensions of the structure;
- the support constraints and other boundary conditions;
- the types of sections and their dimensions;
- the physical model of the material;
- the external actions.

All these data are defined by a certain set of parameters and if not all of them are specified, then you can specify some elements of the stress-strain state, and select its other elements and unknown parameters of the structure so that the problem is completely solved. This problem of structural mechanics is called inverse.

Thus, an inverse problem is not always based on the optimal design conditions. The conditions of uniform strength, constant distribution of the elastic specific values over the system, the requirement that the natural oscillations belong to a certain range etc. are often used to find the unknown parameters. However, there are inverse problems, where unknown parameters are found for a system with extreme properties, and these are not necessarily the properties of the minimum weight (cost).

A problem of finding a system with the given material consumption that can take the maximum load can serve as a typical example. Another example is the problem of finding installation spots for additional supports (from the allowed positions) that maximize the critical buckling load. Another inverse problem of structural mechanics, which is not related to extremality conditions, is the problem of selecting the parameters of a dynamic vibration damper tuned to a predetermined frequency.

Conversation 6.6. Comparison of Calculated and Experimental Data

Numerous papers have been published claiming that it is necessary to provide experimental validation of the used design models. Nevertheless, such works are not very common, and their methodology leaves much to be desired.

Albert Einstein said: "A theory is something nobody believes, except the person who made it. An experiment is something everybody believes, except the person who made it." And this is true as long as the interpretation of experimental results is reduced to a fragmentary comparison of some measurements with the calculated data and conclusions like "*...there is good agreement*", "*... data are qualitatively identical*" or, at best, "*... the discrepancy does not exceed so many percent*".

Fig. 6.24.*a*, which is borrowed from a scientific publication, makes this comparison in a graphic form and can serve as a typical illustration.

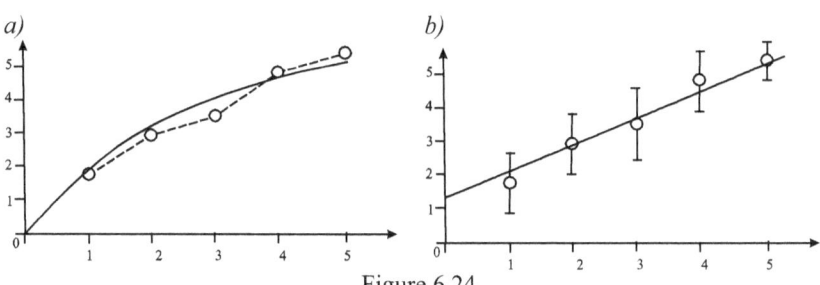

Figure 6.24

If we consider the diagram of experimental results given in Fig. 6.24.*b*, which provides both the mean values and the scatter characteristics (unfortunately, the latter are usually absent), it is easy to see that other theoretical relationships do not contradict the experimental data, for example, a linear dependence shown as a dashed line.

At the same time, applied science uses sufficiently justified and approved methods for processing observation data. In particular, there are numerous proposals for using the least-squares method. Its ideology has become dominant and has created a tradition of using a sum of squares of differences between the components of the vector of experimental data y_i^e and their calculated values y_i as a measure of proximity

$$S_0 = \sum_{k=1}^{n}(y_k^e - y_k)^2$$

If heterogeneous quantities are measured in an experiment (for example, displacements, rotation angles, strains etc.), weighting factors ω_k are used which not only determine the degree of confidence in various measurements, as is usually done when weighted sums are used, but also normalize them to a homogeneous data array.

On the other hand, absolute differences of type $(y_k^e - y_k)$ are rarely used in practice to assess the accuracy of measurements. A relative error which is called a "correction factor" [14]

$$\delta_k = (y_k^e - y_k) / y_k^e,$$

is used more often. It can be used to write an expression for the sum of squares of relative errors

$$S_\delta = \sum_{k=1}^{n}(y_k^e - y_k)^2 / (y_k^e)^2,$$

which uses values $1/(y_k^e)^2$ as weighting factors, and is homogeneous because values δ_k are dimensionless. The difference between experimental and calculated values is shown better by the maximum relative deviations

$$\Delta_k = \frac{y_k^e - y_k}{\min(|y_k^e|,|y_k|)}.$$

If d measurements of each studies value have been performed, and experimental averages have been found

$$\overline{y}_k^e = \frac{1}{d}\sum_{j=1}^{d} y_{kj}^e,$$

then the following value will be the measure of discrepancy between these averages and the calculated data

$$S_{ad}^2 = \frac{d}{n-1}\sum_{k=1}^{n}\left[\frac{\overline{y}_k^e - y_k}{\min(|\overline{y}_k^e|,|y_k|)}\right]^2,$$

called an *adequacy dispersion*.

In order to make reasonable judgments about the adequacy dispersion value, it is necessary to have a certain scale of comparison for the considered structure. A measure of the results scatter of repeated measurements is often used as such a scale.

Indeed, if this scatter is large, then the physical model itself is rather unstable with respect to the random conditions that arise during each repetition of the ex-

---

[14] Experimenters usually assume that the difference between the unit and the average value of correction factors defines the systematic error, and the scatter of their values defines the random one. But it is true only for "well-designed structures" and is not always confirmed in practice, especially when the checks are performed for drastically different loadings.

periment. In this case the requirement of good agreement between the calculated and experimental data is no longer valid. In other words, the more stochastic the behavior of the structure, the more difficult it is to predict.

The so-called *repeatability dispersion* is a measure of experimental data scatter

$$S_{cp}^2 = \frac{1}{n(d-1)} \sum_{k=1}^{n} \sum_{j=1}^{d} \left[\frac{y_{kj}^e - \overline{y}_k^e}{\overline{y}_k^e} \right]^2.$$

Under the assumptions of the error distribution commonly used in mathematical statistics, the adequacy check can be performed according to the criterion

$$F_e = \frac{S_{ad}^2}{S_{cp}^2} \leq F(v_1, v_2, \alpha),$$

where $F(v_1, v_2, \alpha)$ is the table value of the Fisher criterion that depends on the number of degrees of freedom in the numerator $v_1 = n - 1$ and that in the denominator $v_2 = n(d - 1)$ at the significance level α.

As an example, let us consider the results of testing a frame structure (Fig. 6.25) given in Table 6.2. The structure was made of extended I-beams and tested in Kiev National University of Civil Engineering and Architecture

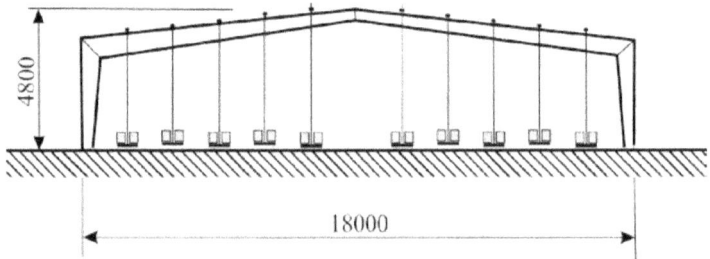

Figure 6.25

Calculations give the values of the adequacy dispersion $S_{ad}^2 = 0,60667$ and the repeatability dispersion $S_{cp}^2 = 0,48021$. The ratio $F_e = 1,253$, while the Fisher criterion for $v_1 = 20$ and $v_2 = 21 \times 3 = 63$ at the significance level $\alpha = 0,95$ is equal to 1,65. Since $F_e < 1,65$, the agreement between the calculation and the experiment can be considered satisfactory with a confidence level of 95%.

Table 6.2

CONVERSATIONS ABOUT THE STRUCTURAL MECHANICS 307

Calculat-ed	Stress values at different points of the system, kg/cm^2			
	Experimental			
	Experiment 1	Experiment 2	Experiment 3	Experiment 4
−170	−241	−273	−315	−389
−170	−147	−241	−115	−186
−170	−357	−144	42	−170
−170	−116	−205	−220	−99
−822	−777	−756	−633	−435
379	405	158	505	321
−469	−807	−722	−920	−247
2208	2121	2247	1459	1365
−166	168	189	−431	−483
−166	−142	−142	−326	−410
−157	−462	−283	−168	−142
−157	−120	−241	−126	−168
1474	1045	1303	1292	1382
−871	−344	−323	−071	−040
1477	1580	920	1208	929
−871	−323	−981	−428	−386
1477	1525	1378	1219	1819
−939	−984	−784	−462	−941
−833	−462	−662	−568	−357
−155	−225	−101	−251	−272
−155	−168	−126	−378	−347

Question:
If the results of the experimental verification strongly differ from the calculated prediction, where should you first look for the error of the design model?

Answer:
First of all, make sure that the experimental setup and its loading conditions correspond to the parameters used in the calculation.

Unfortunately, experience shows that the errors in the initial data are very common, especially in the case of complex and multi-element design models.

A.A. Kosmodemyansky writes in his informative book [15]: "*...when designing and constructing new structures (bridges, dams, airplanes, rockets, buildings) based on the vast previous experience, the engineers are so sure that the laws of mechanics are valid, that all the conclusions drawn from calculations are considered to be **absolutely true**. If there are discrepancies between theory and practice,*

a rigorous and thorough analysis is performed which usually reveals either inaccuracy of the initial data or arithmetic errors.

This mainly refers to the "precomputer" era. Now that the computer analysis is so widespread, the main sources of discrepancies are incorrect design models сейчас, incorrect use of software and (much less often) errors in software code.

Experienced designers are well aware of it, and they use all the available methods to verify the design model and the agreement between the calculation results and the structural behavior.

The control methods include the checks of:
- dimensions of the used values;
- the character of the dependence of the result on changes in the initial data, including the check of such properties as the expected symmetry (antisymmetry) or insensitivity to certain parameters;
- low sensitivity of the design model to small changes in its structure or the parameter values;
- compliance with the conclusions, following from the reciprocal theorems (displacements, forces, works).

This applies primarily to the results of static and dynamic calculations. If the calculated values are based on recommendations of the codes, you should be especially careful. Simplified approaches given in the codes are often based on additional hypotheses, which, unfortunately, are not explicitly provided and their possible application area is not always theoretically or experimentally established.

In some cases it is necessary to perform additional design checks in order to analyze the validity of these simplifications. Such checks are usually related to the analysis of the stress-strain state and require quite a thoughtful approach.

As an example, let us consider the following recommendation of the codes stating that forces in the bolts N_i of a bolted connection (Fig. 6.26) subjected to a bending moment are distributed in proportion to the distance from the bolt r_i to the center of gravity of the bolt group, i.e.

$$M = \sum_{i=1}^{n} N_i r_i,$$

and the maximum bolt force is equal to

$$N_{\max} = M \cdot \max_i r_i \bigg/ \sum_{j=1}^{n} r_j^2,$$

where n is the number of bolts on one side of the joint.

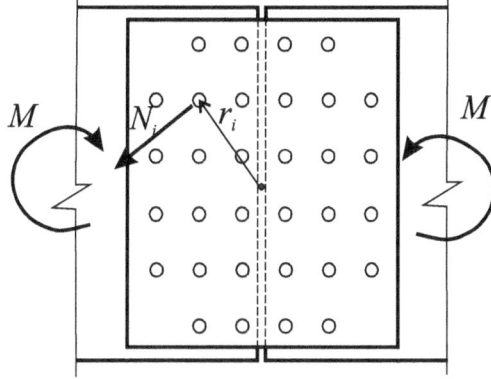

Figure 6.26.

However, this recommendation is accurate only if the gusset plate has infinite stiffness. Otherwise, you should treat it as an approximate statement and perform design checks in doubtful cases. For example, a bolted steel plate with dimensions of 0,9 m×2,4 m and a thickness of 0,02 m (Fig. 6.27) is calculated by the finite element method.

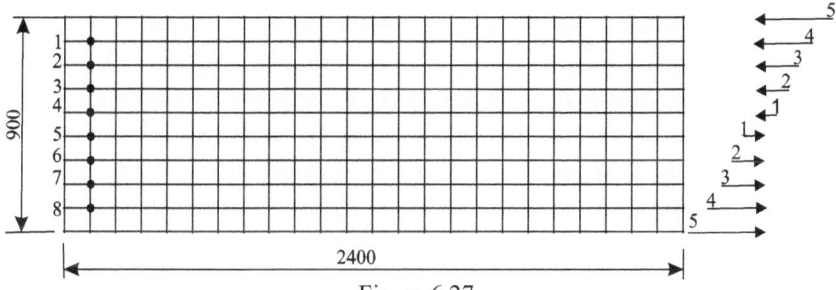

Figure 6.27

The results of the calculation and the assessment according to the recommendations of the codes are compared in the table 6.3. However, it is necessary to take into account that the calculation was performed under the assumption of elastic behavior of the system, and the recommendations of the codes are based on the idea of stress equalization for the case of the inelastic behavior of the joint. Hence, another conclusion can be made.

> *Make sure that both the experiment and the calculation are performed under the same assumptions about the structural behavior (for example, the elastic state, smallness of displacements etc.).*
> *If this is not the case, and if the experiment accurately reflects the operating conditions of the structure, then it is necessary to refine the design model.*

Table 6.3

Bolt number	FEM calculation			Standardized calculation		Δ, %
	N_x	N_z	N_Σ	N_x	N_z	
1	-9,093	-0,628	9,115	-7,917	0	13,139
2	-4,614	0,082	4,615	-5,655	0	-22,542
3	-2,490	0,262	2,504	-3,393	0	-35,517
4	-0,810	0,283	0,858	-1,131	0	-31,816
5	0,810	0,283	0,858	1,131	0	-31,816
6	2,490	0,262	2,504	3,393	0	-35,517
7	4,614	0,082	4,615	5,655	0	-22,542
8	9,093	-0,628	9,115	7,917	0	13,139

References

1. *Artemenko V.V., Gordeev V.N.* A program for calculating design stress combinations in the case of a complex logical relationship between loads. In: Computers and mechanization facilities in structural design, 1967, № 2.— p. 10–14.
2. *Baldin V.A., Goldenblat I.I., Kochenov V.I., Pildish M.Ya., Tal K.E.* Calculation of Building Structures According to the Limit States. — M.: Stroyizdat. 1951. — 272 p.
3. *Varvak P.M., Ryabov A.F. et al.* Elasticity theory handbook Kiev: Budivelnik, 1971.
4. *Vinogradov A.I.* The Problem of Optimal Design in Structural Mechanics. – Kharkiv: High School, 1973. 168 p.
5. *Geniev G.A., Kolchunov V.I., Klyueva N.I., Nikulin A.I., Pyatikrestovskiy P.K.* Durability and Deformability of Reinforced Concrete Structures at Beyond Design — M.: ASV, 2004. — 216 p.
6. *Goldstein Yu.B., Solomeshch M.A.* Variational Problems of Statics of Optimal Bar Systems — L.: Izd-vo LGU, 1980. — 316 p.
7. *Gordeev V.N., Artemenko V.V., Minkovich E.I.* Choosing the most disadvantageous combination of loads as a solution of the problem of multi-criterial optimization. — In the book: Numerical methods for analysis and optimization of structural constructions. Proceedings of Kucherenko Central Research Institute of Structural Constructions (CRISC). — Moscow: CRISC, 26-32 (1989)
8. *Gorev V.V., Uvarov B.Yu., Filippov V.V., Belyi G.I. et al.*; Steel Structures. In 3 v. — V. 2. Building structures. — M.: High school, 1999 — 528 p.
9. *GOST R 54257-2010*. Reliability of Constructions and Foundations. Basic Principles and Requirements. — M.: Standardinform, 2011.— 18 p
10. *Gordeev V.N.* Study of a Set of Similar Structures with Parameters Close to Optimal // Series VII, "Design of Metal Structures", issue 8(55).- M.: TsNIPIASS, 1974. — pp. 12-15.
11. *DBN V.1.2-14-2009*. General Principles of Reliability and Structural Safety of Buildings, Structures and Foundations. — Kiev: Ukrarhbudinform, 2009. — 37 p.
12. *Iosilevsky L.I.* Practical Methods for Managing the Reliability of Reinforced Concrete Bridges — M.: SPC "Engineer", 1999.— 295 p.

13. *Kachanov L.M.* Fundamentals of the Theory of Plasticity — M.: Nauka, 1969 — 420 p.
14. *Karpenko N.I., Karpenko S.N., Travush V.I.* Method of analysis of high-rise buildings and structures made of cast-in-place reinforced concrete based on layer refining. In: Modern industrial and civil construction, 2011, Vol. 7, №3 p. 147-163.
15. *Kosmodemyansky A.A.* Theoretical Mechanics and Modern Technology.— M.: Prosveshenie, 1969.— 255 p.
16. *Kudishin Y.I., Belenya E.I., Ignatieva V.S. et al.* Steel Structures — 10-th ed. — M.: Academy, 2007 — 688 p.
17. *Lolleit A.F.* On the Strength Factor of Reinforced Concrete Structures // Notes of the Moscow Architectural Society, Issue 1, 1904. — pp. 1-16.
18. *Lolleit A.F.* New Draft Regulations // 1 st All-Union Conference on Concrete and Reinforced Concrete. 20-25 April in Moscow. Conference proceedings — M.: 1930.
19. *Papkovich P.F.* Structural Mechanics of Ships. V.2. Combined Bending and Stability of Bars, Bending and Stability of Plates — L.: Sudostroyeniye, 1941 — 960 p.
20. *Perelmuter A.V.* The Effect of Stiffness Variation on Force Redistribution in a Statically Indeterminate System // Structural Mechanics and Structural Analysis, 1974, № 5. — pp. 64–67.
21. *Perelmuter A.V.* Selected Problems of Reliability and Safety of Building Structures. 3-rd ed., revised and updated. — M.: ASV, 2007.— 256 p.
22. *Perelmuter A.V.* About One Concept in the Theory of Constructions. // Metal Constructions. 2010. №4. — pp. 233-238.
23. *Perelmuter A.V., Pichugin S.F.* Issues on Estimation of Building Structure Vulnerability // Magazine of Civil Engineering, 2014, №5. — pp. 5-14.
24. *Rabinovich I.M.* On the Theory of Statically Indeterminate Trusses. Laws of Distribution of Forces; the Method of Allowable Stresses; Initial Forces in Statically Indeterminate Trusses. — M.:Transzheldorizdat, 1933. 136 p.
25. *De Roshefor N.I.* Illustrated Teaching Manual Divided into Lessons. Manual for Creation and Controlling the Estimates, Designing and Implementing Works. 5-th edition.— Saint-Petersburg, 1910. — 694 p.
26. *Streletsky N.S.* Statistical Basis of the Safety Factor of Structures. — M.: Stroyizdat, 1947.— 92 p.
27. *Edward J. Haug, Jasbir S. Arora.* Applied Optimal Design: Mechanical and Structural Systems. – M.: Mir, 1983. – 478 p.
28. *Khotsialov N.F.* Safety Factors // Construction Industry. 1929, № 10. — pp. 840-844.
29. *Shimanovsky V.N., Gordeev V.N., Grinberg M.L.* Optimal Design of Space Grid Roofing. — Kiev: Budivelnik, 1987.— 224 p.
30. *Adams H.* The Practical Designing of Structural Ironwork. — London: E. & F.N. Spon, 1894.
31. *Alasdair N. Beal, Thomasons Leeds.* A history of the safety factors // The Structural Engineer, 2011, Vol. 89, № 20.
32. *CP110 Part 1:1972* The Structural Use of Concrete: Part 1 Design, Materials & Workmanship. — London: British Standards Institution, 1972.
33. *Elishakoff I., Ohsaki M.* Optimization and Anti-Optimization of Structures under uncertainty. — London: Imperial College Press. 2010. — 402 p.
34. *EN 1990:2001.* Eurocode. Basis of structural design. Brussels: CEN. 2002. — 89 p.

35. *Freudenthal A.M.* The Safety of Structures // Proc. ASCE, 1947. vol.112, №1. — P. 125-180.
36. *Garstecki A., Ścigałło J.* Alternative method of finding load combinations for design reinforced concrete structures // Proceedings of the 7th International Conference "Modern Building Materials, Structures and Techniques"— Vilnius: 2001 (Full text on CD-ROM).
37. *ISO ST 2394.* General Principles on Reliability for Structures. — 1994, 50 p.
38. *Maier M.* Die Sicherheit der Bauwerke und ihre Berechnung nach Grenzkaften anstatt nach zulassigen Spannungen. — Berlin: Springer Verlag, 1926. — 73 p.
39. *Mungan I.* Structural engineering and structures from antiquity to the present // Proc. IASS Symposium 2001, Nagoya, Japan. — P. 1-3.
40. *Nassim Nicolas Taleb.* The Black Swan: The Impact of the Highly Improbable. — New York: Random House, 2007. –.394 p.
41. *Perelmuter A., Yurchenko V.* Parametric Optimization of Steel Shell Towers of High-Power Wind Turbines // Procedia Engineering, 2013. Vol.57. — P. 895 – 905.
42. *Plot M.* Nor sur la nation de coefficient de securite // Annals des points et chausses. — Paris: 1936. Vol. II. Fase 7.
43. *Whitney Charles S.* Bridges; a study in their art, science and evolution. — New York: W.E. Rudge, 1929. — 400 p.
44. *Wierzbicki W.* Safety of Structures as a Probability Problem. — Warsaw: Przeglad Techniczny. 1936. — 690 p.

Contents

Preface	3
References	8

Cycle 1. Fundamentals of Statics and Kinematics 9
Conversation 1.1. A Few Words about the Design Model: Hypothesis Analysis 11
Conversation 1.2. Basic Concepts. Principle of Virtual Displacements 18
Conversation 1.3: Static and Kinematic Equations 23
Conversation 1.4: Properties of Solutions 27
Conversation 1.5. Comparison of Properties of Statically Determinate and Indeterminate Systems 36
Conversation 1.6. Force and Displacement Methods 42
Conversation 1.7. Prestressing 52
Conversation 1.8. Variational Principles 60
References 64

Cycle 2. Finite Element Method 66
Conversation 2.1. Idea of the Finite Element Method 68
Conversation 2.2: Boundary Conditions 78
Conversation 2.3: Meshing Parameters. FEM Convergence 82
Conversation 2.4. Finite Elements are Different 89
Conversation 2.5. Division into Finite Elements 94
Conversation 2.6. FEM Design Models 97
Conversation 2.7. Analysis of the Calculation Results 103
References 107

Cycle 3. Nonlinear Static Problems 108
Conversation 3.1. Preliminaries about Nonlinear Problems 110
Conversation 3.2. Physically Nonlinear Problems 116
Conversation 3.3. Behavior of Elastic-Plastic System under Increasing Load 122
Conversation 3.4. Extreme Properties of the Yield Limit State 125
Conversation 3.5. Geometric Nonlinearity 131
Conversation 3.6. Structural Nonlinearity 141
Conversation 3.7. Genetic Nonlinearity 148
References 107

Cycle 4. Stability of Equilibrium 156
Conversation 4.1. Basic Concepts of Stability Theory 158
Conversation 4.2. Stability of a Single Degree of Freedom System 163
Conversation 4.3. On the Role of Initial Imperfections 170
Conversation 4.4. Global Stability. Upper and Lower Critical Load 176
Conversation 4.5. Stability of Multiple Degree of Freedom Systems 182
Conversation 4.6. Multiparameter Loading. Papkovich Theorem 191
Conversation 4.7. Effective Length 197
References 201

Cycle 5. Fundamentals of Dynamic Analysis 202
Conversation 5.1. Static and Dynamic Structural Analysis 204
Conversation 5.2. Oscillations of a Single Degree of Freedom System... 206
Conversation 5.3. Resonance 216
Conversation 5.4. Equations of Motion of a Multiple Degree of Freedom System 221
Conversation 5.5. Properties of Natural Modes 228
Conversation 5.6. Forced Oscillations of a System with a Finite Number of Degrees of Freedom 233
Conversation 5.7: Quasi-Static Analysis and the Dynamic Amplification Factor.. 251
References 254

Cycle 6. Now Let's Try to Fly 255
Conversation 6.1. Limit State Method 257
Conversation 6.2. Conditional and Real Factor of Safety 271
Conversation 6.3. Robustness 279
Conversation 6.4. Bearing Capacity Analysis According to Design Codes... 285
Conversation 6.5. Design Calculations and Optimal Design 292
Conversation 6.6. Comparison of Calculated and Experimental Data......... 304
References 310

Contents... 313

Anatoly V. Perelmuter

CONVERSATIONS ABOUT THE STRUCTURAL MECHANICS

Short Course of Lectures

Translation from Russian by Tatyana Veryuzhkaya

Signed for printing 25.06.2019. Format 60×90/16 Offset paper.
Times type. Conventional 19,75 printed sheets.

ASV Construction, Sweden, Mardvagen 16 131 50 Saltsjo-Duvnas

www.ingramcontent.com/pod-product-compliance
Lightning Source LLC
Chambersburg PA
CBHW070809300426
44111CB00014B/2461